RENEGADE LAWYER

THE LIFE OF J.L. COHEN

PATRONS OF THE SOCIETY

Aird & Berlis

Blake, Cassels & Graydon LLP

Davies Ward Phillips & Vineberg LLP

Gowling, Strathy & Henderson

McCarthy Tétrault

Osler, Hoskin & Harcourt LLP

Torkin Manes Cohen & Arbus LLP

Torys

Weir & Foulds

The Osgoode Society is supported by a grant from
The Law Foundation of Ontario.

THE LAW
FOUNDATION
OF ONTARIO

The Society also thanks The Law Society of Upper Canada
for its continuing support.

RENEGADE LAWYER
The Life of J.L. Cohen

LAUREL SEFTON MACDOWELL

Published for The Osgoode Society for Canadian Legal History by

University of Toronto Press

Toronto Buffalo London

Printed in Canada

ISBN 0-8020-3513-2

∞

Printed on acid-free paper

Canadian Cataloguing in Publication Data

MacDowell, Laurel Sefton, 1947–
Renegade lawyer : the life of J.L. Cohen

Includes bibliographical references and index.
ISBN 0-8020-3513-2

1. Cohen, J.L. (Jacob L.). 2. Labor lawyers – Canada – Biography.
I. Osgoode Society for Canadian Legal History. II. Title.

KE416.C63M32 2001   340'.092   C2001-930745-4
KF345.Z9C63 2001

University of Toronto Press acknowledges the financial assistance to its
publishing program of the Canada Council for the Arts and
the Ontario Arts Council.

This book has been published with the help of a grant from the Humanities
and Social Sciences Federation of Canada, using funds provided by the Social
Sciences and Humanities Research Council of Canada.

University of Toronto Press acknowledges the financial support for its
publishing activities of the Government of Canada through the Book Publishing
Industry Development Program (BPIDP).

For my children

The real personality of the individual, and his view of life are my theme, rather than the ways of the race in general, as viewed by a casual and hostile human eye.

Ernest Thompson Seton

Life was given to us to enjoy the good we derive from it. But it is through suffering that we become grateful for life, and only then do we begin to know it.

Esther Cohen

Contents

Ontario & To. centric

Part Three: War and Aftermath, 1939–1946

Part Four: Relations with the Law Society, 1945–1950

Foreword

THE OSGOODE SOCIETY
FOR CANADIAN LEGAL HISTORY

It is only a slight exaggeration to suggest that J.L. Cohen invented labour law in Canada. For many years, principally the 1920s to the 1940s, he excited strong emotions in many quarters, from friend and foe alike. Extremely bright and incredibly hard working, he took up the cases of unions and, very often, of Communist politicians and was regarded in establishment circles as an unrepentant radical and fellow traveller. Pugnacious and determined in his advocacy, he did not suffer fools gladly and sometimes he paid a price for his unorthodoxy. But he was too dominant in his field to ignore, and Liberal politicians such as Premier Hepburn in Ontario and Prime Minister Mackenzie King were pleased to use his services, at least so long as it suited them.

In this biography, Laurel Sefton MacDowell is warmly sympathetic but never uncritical. Here we learn to admire if not to like this gritty and determined advocate, and it is difficult not to be deeply moved by the tragic conclusion to the career and life of a man who contributed so much to the causes in which he believed. This book adds considerably to our understanding of several important and dramatic themes in our recent past and will be read with much pleasure and profit.

The purpose of The Osgoode Society for Canadian Legal History is to encourage research and writing in the history of Canadian law. The Society, which was incorporated in 1979 and is registered as a charity, was founded at the initiative of the Honourable R. Roy McMurtry, a former attorney general for Ontario, now chief justice of Ontario, and officials of the Law Society of Upper Canada. Its efforts to stimulate the study of legal history in Canada include a research-support program, a graduate student research-assistance program, and work in the fields of oral history and legal archives. The Society publishes volumes of interest to the Society's members that contribute to legal-historical scholarship in Canada, including studies of the courts, the judiciary and the legal profession, biographies, collections of documents, studies in criminology and penology, accounts of significant trials, and work in the social and economic history of the law.

Current directors of The Osgoode Society for Canadian Legal History are Robert Armstrong, Jane Banfield, Kenneth Binks, Brian Bucknall, Archie Campbell, Kirby Chown, J. Douglas Ewart, Martin Friedland, Elizabeth Goldberg, John Honsberger, Vern Krishna, Virginia MacLean, Wendy Matheson, Roy McMurtry, Brendan O'Brien, Peter Oliver, Paul Reinhardt, Joel Richler, James Spence, Richard Tinsley, and David Young.

The annual report and information about membership may be obtained by writing: The Osgoode Society for Canadian Legal History, Osgoode Hall, 130 Queen Street West, Toronto, Ontario. M5H 2N6. Telephone: 416-947-3321. E-Mail: mmacfarl@lsuc.on.ca.

R. Roy McMurtry
President

Peter N. Oliver
Editor-in-Chief

Acknowledgments

As with all large projects, thanks are owing to many people: to William Kaplan, who told me to stop talking about writing a biography of Cohen and to do it; to Christopher Moore, who, inadvertently, made a casual remark which suggested the book's title to me. I thank the librarians at the National Library who found *Esther's Story*, and the staff at the Industrial Relations Centre library, University of Toronto, especially Elizabeth Perry and Bruce Pearce, for their assistance.

I wish to thank Laura Legge QC, who assisted me in gaining the Law Society of Upper Canada's permission to read Cohen's file, the Law Society itself for granting me access, its past archivist, Susan Binnie, for her consultation and advice, and its present staff person, Susan Lewthwaite, for her quick answer to my persistent questions. I am grateful to Michael Levine, who encouraged me and provided access to some family members and private papers, and to Professor John Scott Cowan and Nick De Munnik for permission to use some family photographs. My research assistants at the University of Toronto – Richard White and Michelle Leung from the department of history, Amy Sproule-Jones and Dan Reid from the Centre for Industrial Relations – were most helpful and their efforts saved me a great deal of time.

I want to thank Alison Dias at the University of Toronto in Mississauga for her assistance with the photographs. I am grateful to William Magee of the department of sociology, University of Toronto, who suggested background reading to assist me in understanding Cohen's personality complexities. I thank colleagues who read and commented on several chapters, particularly Rick MacDowell, chair of the Ontario Labour Relations Board, and Professor Mary Jane Mossman at Osgoode Hall Law School. Sylvia Bashevkin of the department of political science, University of Toronto, has been a friend who has given me encouragement and helpful professional advice.

I want to thank Gerald Hallowell, Jill McConkey, and Anne Laughlin at the University of Toronto Press, Peter Oliver and Marilyn MacFarlane at the Osgoode Society for their advice and patience, John Parry for copy editing an early version of the manuscript, and Curtis Fahey for copy editing the completed work. I am grateful to the SSHRC for essential research funding. This book has been published with the help of a grant from the Humanities and Social Sciences Federation of Canada, using funds provided by the Social Sciences and Humanities Research Council of Canada.

I particularly want to thank my husband, Carl Berger, who has been a supportive companion for many years, a good listener, a tactful critic, and who prodded me to 'finish the book.' Some factors in my early life contributed to my interest in Cohen and to my understanding of him, including my own early loss of a parent, my experience through friends of Jewish culture, my family's involvement in events described here, and my own work in the labour movement where I knew many trade unionists. I have admired a number of labour lawyers. David Lewis, Andrew Brewin, and Ted Jolliffe were shadowy figures in my childhood who turned up in Cohen's papers. Arthur Goldberg, for many years the general counsel of the United Steelworkers of America (USWA), who served briefly in the 1960s as American secretary of labor and on the U.S. Supreme Court, and Bernard Kleiman, his sucessor with the USWA, were lawyers my parents discussed as I listened. As a young adult, I knew Martin L. Levinson and Jeffrey Sack, and these associations informed my study of Cohen. Lastly, it seems appropriate, since their grandfather was a trade unionist and their father is a labour lawyer, to dedicate this biography to my children – Lawrence, Stephen, and Jennifer – with love.

LAUREL SEFTON MACDOWELL

Abbreviations

ACCL	All-Canadian Congress of Labour
ACW	Amalgamated Clothing Workers
CBRE	Canadian Brotherhood of Railway Employees
CCCL/CTCC	Canadian and Catholic Confederation of Labour/ Confédération des Travailleurs Catholiques du Canada
CCF	Co-operative Commonwealth Federation
CCL	Canadian Congress of Labour
CHWU	Canadian Hosiery Workers Union
CLDL	Canadian Labour Defence League
CMA	Canadian Manufacturers' Association
CPC	Communist Party of Canada
CSU	Canadian Seamen's Union
CCL	Congress of Canadian Labour
CIO	Congress of Industrial Organizations
DOCR	Defence of Canada Regulations
IDIC	Industrial Disputes Inquiry Commission
ILGWU	International Ladies Garment Workers Union
IUMMSW	International Union of Mine Mill and Smelter Workers (Mine Mill)
IUNTW	Industrial Union of Needle Trades Workers
IWA	International Woodworkers of America
IWW	Industrial Workers of the World
LPP	Labour Progressive Party

LWIU	Lumber Workers Industrial Union
NASCO	National Steel Car Corporation
NCDR	National Council of Democratic Rights
NWLB	National War Labour Board
OBU	One Big Union
ORWLB	Ontario Regional War Labour Board
SWOC	Steelworkers' Organizing Committee
TLC	Trades and Labour Congress of Canada
UAW	United Auto Workers
UEW	United Electrical Workers
UGWA	United Garment Workers of America
ULFTA	Ukrainian Labour Farmer Temple Association
UMWA	United Mineworkers of America
UPWA	United Packinghouse Workers of America
USWA	United Steelworkers of America
WPTB	Wartimes Prices and Trade Board
WUL	Workers' Unity League

RENEGADE LAWYER

THE LIFE OF J.L. COHEN

Introduction

J.L. Cohen was an architect of the Canadian industrial-relations system which emerged during the Second World War. He was one of the first specialists in labour law representing unions and he served as a member of the National War Labour Board (NWLB) in 1943, when it held a public inquiry into the causes of industrial unrest. It called for the introduction of collective-bargaining legislation, a recommendation that the government accepted. Cohen contributed substantially to the form of the new law, to the conciliation process that was an integral part of 'the system,' and to the administrative procedures and jurisprudence developed by early labour bodies charged with managing it. His legal work included the areas of minimum-work standards and civil liberties. In his book *Collective Bargaining in Canada* (1941), Cohen critiqued wartime labour policy and expressed his own, definite ideas on the subject, which were influenced partly by contact with American trade unionists on his frequent trips to New York where he learned about the labour-policy notions being discussed there. Thus, he was a 'labour intellectual' in Canada, similar to those supporting Roosevelt's New Deal, and, like them, he was influenced by the catastrophe of the Great Depression, which stimulated a legal framework for labour relations in the United States. In a more general sense, Cohen is among a small minority of 'radical lawyers,' such as the great American counsel Clarence Darrow or the contemporary Canadian advocate Thomas Berger, who represent the less powerful and seek to use the law to reform society and to protect civil liberties.

Canada had no New Deal recovery measures like the National Industrial Relations Act (Wagner Act, 1935). Nevertheless, Canadians listened to President Roosevelt's messages of hope in his 'fireside chats' on the radio, and fragments of the New Deal crossed the border. Those fragments – industrial-standards legislation, the industrial (CIO) union movement, and later collective-bargaining legislation – were embraced by Cohen, who worked actively to achieve Canadian legislation embodying such ideas. In the United States the state supported reform, but in Canada the governments' response to the Depression was ad hoc, limited, and fiscally conservative.[1] When the new industrial unions, often represented by Cohen, pressed employers for recognition and governments for the passage of a Canadian Wagner Act, they faced opposition from both groups. Thus, the environment in the two countries was different enough that innovative legislation and union growth in the United States preceded comparable developments in Canada. After much pressure, by the end of the Second World War, Canada had minimum labour standards and collective-bargaining legislation similar but not identical to that in the United States, as well as a rudimentary social-welfare state.[2]

Though many progressive lawyers working for the government in Washington were caught up in the ferment of the New Deal, in Canada the absence of an activist, reformist response to the Depression or bold leadership like Roosevelt's meant that Cohen stood out as a lawyer, working in relative isolation with trade unionists and civil libertarians. Unlike the American New Deal lawyers, whom Peter Irons describes as emerging from law school 'with a veneer of progressive liberalism over a foundation of doctrinal orthodoxy and apolitical professionalism,'[3] Cohen was a genuine radical who believed in 'industrial democracy.' He was influenced by his working-class, immigrant background, his early exposure to trade unionism, the cases he took in the 1920s involving radicals, and the seering experience of the 1930s Depression; these factors mingled with progressive New Deal ideas about using the state to reform capitalism. As new legislation was slowly adopted in Canada, Cohen remained an outsider and was aggressively left wing compared to most Canadians. His views were reflected in his sympathy for but not membership in the Communist Party of Canada (CPC), cooperation at times with the Co-operative Commonwealth Federation (CCF), and a firm commitment to a strong, independent labour movement and to civil liberties. Such views did not prevent him from working for governments when they called on his expertise, but his role on such occasions represented a pragmatic attempt to achieve his legislative goals while continuing to represent his personal constituency of workers, immigrants, and trade unionists.

It is timely to review Cohen's professional life as an active lawyer and policy maker because today both the collective-bargaining system and the social-welfare state are under attack by neo-conservative politicians, and many scholars from different perspectives are re-examining the state's role. In this new political climate and global economy, it is important to understand the origins of the North American labour-relations systems in the 1930s and 1940s (including Cohen's work in Canada). More needs to written about the birth of the industrial-relations system – how it began, why it took the form it did, what ideas, issues and interests were involved in the introduction of collective-bargaining legislation, and what political compromises were made. This study provides some answers by examining J.L. Cohen's ideas and actions in the political context in which they were formulated.

The emergence after the war of greater state involvement in the economy contributed to the permanence of these labour-relations developments. It may be that such state involvement will diminish in the twenty-first century and that the labour and social legislation which resulted from the Depression and war experiences was unique, but all that remains to be seen.[4] What is evident is that, since the legislative innovations of the 1940s have influenced Canadian society for over fifty years, 'the origins of Canada's highly managed system of collective bargaining' are of contemporary interest.[5]

The industrial-relations system that Cohen and the labour movement worked to bring about has thus far been portrayed very differently from the way the participants viewed it. I seek to place its emergence in its own historical context and explain why Cohen felt so strongly that such developments were necessary. J.L. Cohen would not have agreed that the achievement of collective-bargaining legislation was, as historian Alvin Finkel termed it, a 'hollow' victory.[6] Like trade unionists of his time and today, he viewed collective bargaining as a right and a legal framework for labour relations as essential for workers to achieve improved conditions of work, some representation in industry's decision-making process, and a new status in society. This study attempts to convey the creation of the system by examining the work of one key player at the time. Cohen was not as influential in this sphere as the prime minister or senior civil servants, but as a professional and an expert he made a substantial contribution to the policy-making process.

Government regulation did lead to a more legalistic labour-relations system. In Cohen's day this process was just beginning with the passage of industrial-standards legislation in the mid-1930s, but it would accelerate after the war when he no longer practised law. Though some contemporary critics have deplored the creeping legalization of industrial relations, it was not a development that concerned Cohen since he viewed the law as a vehicle to assist the less powerful. Collective agreements, which began as simple documents, became longer, more complex, and developed guarded and technical language. The early contracts, often drafted by Cohen, 'were a means of codifying informal protective practices and creating new ones.'[7] It is important to understand the positive aspect of written collective agreements – contracts as an expression of working-class self-organization.

Although Cohen was a Marxist, his belief in collective bargaining coincided with the views of trade unionists of the day. His commitment to the labour movement resulted partly from his background, and his was an unusual perspective for a middle-class professional. But it was deepened by his experience of the Depression and by his exposure to New Deal thinking, and in the war years it resulted in a commitment to industrial democracy and workers' inclusion in the political process so that they could improve their economic and social status. Cohen was distinctly an outsider in the power structure because of his political views and class politics and because he was a Jew. Though respected professionally, he made enemies and was resented by some who were jealous of his ability, who disliked or feared his radicalism, or who were anti-Semitic. Cohen's response to such pressures was to keep busy and maintain a confident, even arrogant attitude in public while remaining isolated both personally and professionally.

A recent category of historical inquiry may help to illuminate Cohen's personality, his behaviour, and his relations with the Law Society of Upper Canada. Partly as a new direction in feminist scholarship and partly as independent inquiry,[8] new work has examined the meaning of masculinity. Historians are analysing men's private lives, their role in families, their sexuality, their social and working lives, their associations and culture, their race and ethnicity, and their relationship to the state and to the military. In the 1930s and 1940s society expected men to fulfil the role of 'the good provider.'[9] They supported their families, were protective (and paternal) towards women, and carried enormous public and private responsibilities in exchange for which they had power and preference in the labour force, in their professions, and in their families. Men were seen to be rational beings while women, in contrast, were characterized as being more emotional, a trait suited to their role as caregivers.

I have not laced this biography with these theories but I invite the reader to keep them in mind as they read about Cohen's life. To an unusual degree, he reflected the notions of manliness current in the period. He worked very hard, made a good living, and supported his family from an early age. In his public life, he worked almost exclusively with groups of men because the workplace was segregated by gender. As a lawyer, he was the epitome of the rational, educated professional, a position from which he derived status, respect, and income. It was a status that he had worked hard to attain as a person from a working-class background.

Because of his left-wing political views, intellectually his ideas about the position of women in society were progressive and enlightened compared to those of more conservative men. Cohen believed in equal pay for equal work for women, mothers' allowances, and the same minimum standards for both genders. He was not always able to implement such ideas but, where possible, he pressed them in policy-making sessions. At the same time, Cohen was part of and felt comfortable with the male culture of the day. As a lawyer, he shared the prevailing notions of what it meant to be a professional and enjoyed the elaborate rituals of the bench and the court.[10]

Like many men, Cohen separated his personal and working lives, but in his case this division was extreme. Cohen built a wall around himself and was not the same person in his private personal life, which was kept hidden, as he was in his public role. Notions of masculinity may help us to understand Cohen's disbarment as a result of the Guenard incident and his subsequent reinstatement. This excruciating and humiliating experience was triggered when, in a period of fatigue and illness, he acted inappropriately and ruined his personal reputation. The nature of his offence (assaulting a young woman) scandalized the public and the legal profession. As a radical and a Jew, he was vulnerable in his profession, and, in the early years of the Cold War, his status as a pro-union lawyer and an alleged Communist gave his enemies more than adequate ammunition. Thus, his mistake could not be conveniently buried. His story is dramatic and even tragic in and of itself, but the pathos is greater when one considers that Cohen shared the prevailing notions of what it was to be a gentlemen and a lawyer. Winning back his accreditation to practise law was not enough, because he had violated a cultural code of manhood as well as the professional code of conduct in his profession. As I researched this book, I found people years later embarrassed and reluctant to talk about Cohen, and their response highlights the shock the scandal evoked, even among people who respected him tremendously as a labour lawyer. Finally, notions of masculinity also involve ideas about dominant and subordinate males. Cohen's case can be viewed from this perspective, of a self-made working-class Jewish male being stripped of his professional credentials by a panel of Christian, prosperous, successful men.[11] Hence there are several layers of meaning to Cohen's life.

I began with a puzzle. How could a rational, intelligent man who had reached the pinnacle of his profession in his area of specialization, and who had contributed so much to many disadvantaged people, to policy making and to his country at war, make a mistake serious enough to jeopardize his marriage and destroy his career? His progressive intellectual views about women, his marriage to a professional woman and his fathering of a daughter who cared deeply about him did not fit the image of a man convicted in an assault case. I have concluded that Cohen's exhaustion, neuroses, and medical history partially explain what happened to him. There may have been people out to 'get' him, as he believed, because he did have enemies; however, with the destruction of much of the evidence surrounding the case, I have been unable to prove it. But, even if there was a conspiracy against him, in the last analysis Cohen was convicted of a criminal offence and the Law Society was bound to act. He demonstrated recklessness, a lack of judgment, and arrogance. Though he ultimately displayed extreme vulnerability, he was not simply a victim; in fact, he did not see himself that way or conduct his professional life in such a fashion.

Cohen's papers at the National Archives are comprehensive and well organized and this facilitated my writing. Cohen kept excellent records, including detailed invoices, in the conduct of his practice, and he also was a collector. He often asked for transcripts of cases, kept copies of his own correspondence as well as letters he received, and had several scrapbooks of clippings. He may have sensed that his work was significant historically; he thought of writing his autobiography later in life. In addition, I examined other sources to check his facts, evaluate his opinions, and investigate aspects of his life that puzzled me. Because Cohen was a private person, his papers are almost entirely about his professional life, although a few intriguing files reveal something of his personality. It was only by reading his mother's autobiography and talking to contemporaries that I learned about his early life, and only after I read his file in the Law Society's archives, prepared in circumstances that forced him to reveal details of his private life, was I able to understand the stress he was under to keep his personal life private while he drove himself to achieve so much professionally. Because Cohen separated his public and private selves, and because his strong desire for privacy reflected the approach of many men of his era, I chose to concentrate mostly on his working life in the first eight chapters and then reveal the inner person in the last section (chapters 9–11), just as he kept his private life hidden until near the end. It seemed to me that, if the book reflected the pattern of his life, his professional achievements would be all the more impressive in the light of his emotional limitations.

The Guenard incident was a crucial turning point in Cohen's life, which I examine chronologically, analysing those factors that contributed to the complex personality of this not always likeable but intelligent and committed person. Today, Cohen would be criticized by colleagues and society for the action that resulted in his disbarment, but we would not be as shocked as his contemporaries were. Adultery is no longer a hidden subject and since the 1970s the issue of violence against women has been much discussed. Professionally, Cohen probably would be disliked today by many for his pro-union and Marxist views, but the labour-relations system he helped to create remains admired by some and much analysed in the academy.

Q is why would this man act as he did; perhaps q should be why wouldn't he.

PART ONE

Defending Workers, 1920s–1930s

1

The Making of a Lawyer

Jacob Lawrence Cohen, known as 'Jack' to his family and 'J.L.' to trade unionists,[1] was the first child of Philip and Esther Cohen and named Jacob after his maternal grandfather, Jacob Kreenge. Esther's father had died when she was two years old and living near Wolovisk, Lithuania. Her mother, Jane Lillian, later married David Bach, a blacksmith who ran the Kreenge's family farm near Bortnich. After a freak accident, in which David Bach was run over by his horse-drawn cart and killed, his widow left their home, sent her two eldest children to relatives, and that first winter relied on the charity of wealthy neighbours. When Esther was ten, she was sent to Wolkowisk near the German border, where she attended school and synagogue and learned some German. Though a gregarious, inquisitive young woman, she knew that without a father she had to make her own way.

Her family's movements reflected not only personal hardships but changing policies towards Jews in parts of eastern Europe. Farm families were forced off the land into city ghettoes. Jews faced restrictions on worship and assembly, on entry to higher education and the professions, and on holding land and public office. Their property was frequently vandalized and some were victimized during pogroms. Such conditions stimulated movement and emigration.[2] Esther's oldest brother, Morris, gave up his apprenticeship as a tailor and was the first in the family to leave for England, where he found work in the Manchester garment trade. Aunt Yetta and her husband, Solomon Bach (David's brother), soon joined him. In 1892 Esther, aged sixteen, left Lithuania to live with Yetta's family. Shortly afterwards she learned that her mother had died, exhausted, at forty-four. In England, Esther worked first as a buttonhole maker in the men's garment industry and then in a cap factory as a finisher. In 1895, through friends, she met a capmaker, Philip Cohen, a tall, slim man with black curly hair. He was charming, spoke several languages fluently, and was knowledgeable about international affairs. Philip's family was also Lithuanian. His parents hoped that he would become a rabbi, but when his father died suddenly, his mother took the family to England, where Philip learned his trade. Soon they were betrothed in what Esther described as 'the happiest period' of her life.[3]

Esther and Philip married on 20 July 1896, and Jacob was born on 6 June 1897 in a small house on Mary Street in an industrial slum in Manchester. The young mother was overjoyed to have a son, but she was an anxious parent for, at nine months old, he contracted diphtheria. With devoted care he survived, and Esther gained confidence as a parent. Yet Jacob was never robust as a child: he was frequently ill, and as an adult he would develop both real and imagined illnesses. His sister Jane Lillian (named after Esther's mother) was born in 1899; a second sister, Tillie, arrived in 1901. Then two sons, Maurice and Abraham, were born, and in Canada in 1908, Lewis was born. After Jacob Cohen's death, Lewis would encourage his mother to write about her early life.

Though Philip's education had been cut short by his father's death, he valued learning. He spent hours teaching young Jack, and indeed all the children became avid readers. When Jack entered school at age four, he knew his alphabet and could write his name. In higher grades, he was often the best student in his class, very bright – 'the pride of our entire family' – and his teachers predicted that he would be a scholar. It was an auspicious beginning to his later, impressive legal career.[4] Philip also emphasized appearance, and though he had little money, he made sure that Jacob was well dressed. This childhood habit became ingrained, and later, as a lawyer, Cohen would be perfectly groomed, expensively attired, and always well turned-out.

As the family grew, Philip tried to earn a better living by opening a furniture business. Worried about the future, when he heard of a relative's success in Canada, he decided to move his family to North America. In 1905 he set sail, settled in Toronto, and, with the proceeds from the sale of his home and business in England, tried to establish a new enterprise. He planned to send for his wife and children, but, without enough money, he failed. Meanwhile, Esther reluctantly moved into her sister Fanny's household and, in need of money, sold remnants and ready-made cotton clothing in the market. She later rented a small house, opened a fabric business, and made children's clothes. Philip returned temporarily to Manchester in 1906 and they set up a grocery business. Though only nine, Jack understood that they were starting over and would encounter hardships. When Philip remained unhappy, in 1907 he returned to settle in Toronto.

Though Esther was heartbroken, she and her children ran the store until Philip sent transatlantic tickets. Esther, against the advice of her brother Morris, moved because the children were missing their father. This disruptive period was one of emotional turmoil and uncertainty for the entire family and changed Philip and Esther's relationship permanently. In July 1907 the family boarded the *Majestic* bound for Quebec City and enjoyed the seven-day voyage. Ten-year-old Jack, who was good looking with light brown hair and grey eyes, made friends with his 'appealing approach to people and everyone aboard the ship liked him.'[5] Upon arrival, they travelled by train to Toronto, where Philip met them in a joyful reunion at Union Station.

The Cohens were among many eastern European Jews flooding into Toronto at the time. In 1901 about 16,000 Jews lived in Canada and every year an average of 6,000 entered so that by 1911 Canada's Jewish population had grown by 370 per cent in one decade to over 75,000.[6] In Toronto alone in 1907, an estimated 8,000 to 10,000 Jews lived, and by 1913, 32,000.[7] At that time, the centre of the cohesive eastern European Jewish ghetto in Toronto was an area formerly known as 'the Ward,' bounded by Queen, Yonge, and College streets and University Avenue. It was a slum – crowded, dirty, and poor – but the location suited these recent immigrants, who had little money, needed cheap accommodation, and had to live within walking distance of their work (commonly in the clothing industry). The community provided social and spiritual services in difficult economic times, emotional security in the face of adjustments and discrimination, and cultural and religious institutions such as synagogues, schools, mutual-benefit societies, theatre, and a Jewish press. The Lithuanian shul, Goel Tzedec, for example, opened in 1907 on University Avenue. With the influx of Jewish immigrants, stores opened to sell Jewish food and books, as did kosher restaurants and delicatessens.[8]

Philip Cohen was atypical of recent Jewish immigrants in that he was not destitute, but like many of them he immediately found a job in the needle trades as a capmaker. The family moved into their new home just south of the Jewish district on Adelaide Street near people they knew. In

Toronto, the six Cohen children attended school, skated at Varsity rink, and spent summers in the parks and at the Canadian National Exhibition (CNE).

Jacob was close to his father and bore a strong physical resemblance to him. 'Jack had the same curly hair and grey eyes' and modelled himself on his father, whom he enjoyed and understood. Philip, for his part, encouraged and loved his intelligent son.[9] For a period, family life was serene and sociable. Philip organized weekly political discussion groups in his home and with his friend Jacob Fine (whom Philip had known since his student days in Lithuania and whose family also emigrated to Manchester and then in the same year as the Cohens to Toronto) he organized a group of capmakers into a union. Such activity was usual for Jewish immigrants, who formed mutual-benefit societies to assist their adjustment to their new environment. Some groups were non-partisan and mixed ethnically, some reunited people from the same locality in Europe, and others, like the Workmen's Circle, were politically left wing. Gerald Tulchinsky has noted 'a dedicated working-class orientation to these associations,'[10] which actively sought better working and community conditions for their members.

Jacob's supportive father exposed him from an early age to high educational expectations, political discussions of a socialist and probably also a nationalist (Zionist) nature, and trade unionism. His mother ensured that the children received religious education at the synagogue. Cohen's parents carried with them the cultural baggage of many eastern European Jews in Canada, involving what Tulchinsky has described as 'a complex mix of philosophies such as Marxism, socialism, anarchism, zionism, bundism and other ideals,' but they also were pious, religious people in the conservative and orthodox traditions of Judaism.[11]

In their second summer in Toronto, the cap factory where Philip worked burned down. Unable to find other employment, he began selling combs, costume jewellery, and trinkets at the CNE. In becoming a pedlar, Philip took up an occupation pursued by other Jewish immigrants because it required little capital, provided an income, and had no competition from non-Jews who regarded it as a low-status, menial job. When unexpectedly he did well, he did not return to factory work but travelled with fairs throughout Ontario. At the suggestion of his cousin Isaac Davidson, who ran a general store in Burke's Falls, Philip began to sell supplies in northern Ontario to railway workers and hardware goods to lumber camps. His movement into a larger Ontario market perhaps resulted from competition in Toronto, where by 1916 there were six hundred Jewish rag pedlars.[12] But in 'New Ontario,' northern communities were receiving Jewish people who moved in response to economic opportunities, so Philip Cohen's shift in locale was not unusual.[13] Esther opposed the northern venture but was ignored, and when business prospered the family moved to a larger house on Portland Street near Queen and Bathurst. Their move farther west in the city occurred as the Jewish community expanded to encompass Spadina Avenue and Bathurst Street.[14]

When Jack turned thirteen in 1910, he had his bar mitzvah and was admitted as an adult to the synagogue. Philip made a special trip home to Toronto for the large celebration, but then he returned to Cochrane. Writing to Esther that he would return at the winter's end, he sent an individual message to each child and told Jack – prophetically, as it turned out – that since he had had his bar mitzvah he was, in Philip's absence, 'the man of the house.'[15] A few hours after reading this letter, Esther was informed in a telegram delivered by a policeman that her thirty-eight-year-old husband had fallen through ice and drowned. She was stunned and could not move, cry, or speak. She kept the news to herself until the next morning.

When their mother first told Jacob and Jane the news of their father's death, Jack burst into tears but said she was not to worry. Esther wrote, 'I looked at my two young children – Jack 13 years and Jane 11 – my two young champions who needed so much championing themselves.'[16] After Esther left the room, Jack turned to his sister and said, 'From now on we have to look after mother. We can't mention Daddy at all because that will only make her cry.' It took a week for Philip's body to reach Toronto for the funeral. Esther was thirty-six. Bewildered, she felt that her life was over. Gradually, she regained her strength, sustained by her faith in God, and began again. She had been on her own before when she and Philip were in different countries, and unlike her mother who also was widowed early in life, she would not die young of stress and exhaustion. This may be partly because young Jacob took on so much responsibility. Esther later recalled, 'I was unable to do anything without his advice.'[17] As the eldest child, he took his father's place as the family's principal breadwinner.

The death was a tragedy for the whole family, but for thirteen-year-old Jack the loss of his father and the parent to whom he was devoted was especially traumatic and changed his life dramatically. 'He felt all the responsibility for his mother and five brothers and sisters was thrust upon him.'[18] For the rest of his life he carried with him a 'continuing sense of tragedy' about his father's death, but when it happened he responded pragmatically to the situation, as his father had done when he lost his parent. Later, he remembered his feeling 'of utter fatigue' in this period, and his sister Jane recalled that Jack changed after his father's death, becoming more serious and authoritarian.

Left with few savings and no income, the Cohens were in a precarious position. After the funeral Jack and Maurice sought the rabbi's advice, but when he told them to pray, Jack thanked him for his impractical response and left the synagogue.[19] Religion had been part of his early life, for Esther kept a kosher home and the family attended synagogue at Rosh Hashanah and Yom Kippur. She described young Jack as 'Jewish-minded,' but later in life, with his busy career and his Marxist outlook, he began to change. Many Jewish youths, particularly of Polish, Russian, or Lithuanian background, were exposed intellectually to reformist or revolutionary ideas, and as socialists and nationalists they sought alternatives to traditional Judaism, espoused state solutions to social issues, and supported secular Jewish, often socialist groups. Cohen remained part of the Jewish community in a social and cultural sense, but he became less religious.[20]

In adolescence, Cohen did bookkeeping to earn money, and he used this skill and his talent for public speaking to participate in Jewish community groups established to collect money to help newcomers.[21] Like many recent Jewish immigrants, he and his family were sympathetic to Zionism, which by 1910 in Toronto was being discussed widely. For people who had experienced much strife, the idea of a Jewish homeland represented what Esther described as the 'dream of a new world and of peace.' Zionism became part of Canadian Jewish identity and probably influenced Jacob, but he has left no record of his views on this subject.[22]

During the crisis precipitated by Philip's death, the family was visited by social workers who, in front of Jack, discussed separating the children. He asked them to leave. In the meantime, friends of the Cohens raised five hundred dollars to convert the Portland Street house into a neighbourhood grocery store. Jacob Fine, Philip's old friend, presented the money and plan to them. At the time, Fine's third son, Frank, attended high school with Jack, and another son, Louis Fine, would become a distinguished public servant and work often with Cohen later in life.

The friends' suggestion was practical since many eastern European Jewish immigrant families in Toronto 'strove to establish small businesses – grocery stores, junkyards and clothing shops' – both to make a living and to avoid dependence on non-Jewish employers and discrimination.[23] Besides, the Cohens had experience in the business in Manchester. Aware that starting such an operation was complex and time-consuming, Jacob appeared distressed but accepted the proposition. He oversaw the enterprise in which his mother and siblings worked, and became the bookkeeper. The family bought a small carriage so the boys could make deliveries. Jane, as the oldest daughter, 'became the mistress of the house, of the kitchen and looked after the smaller children.' In this way, the family survived the first year after Philip's death with enough food and clothing.

A year later, when 'J.L.' was fourteen, he began to make some decisions for himself. He wanted to earn more money and have better clothes. He quit high school in his second year and took a six-dollar-a-week clerk's job at the law firm of J.P. White (at Adelaide and Church streets). After two months, realizing that he needed more education, he started night school; in two years, he completed high school. By age sixteen, he was making the important decisions in the family – 'there could be no dispute about it.' With his senior matriculation, Jack wanted to enrol in university but the family could not afford it. A good and motivated student, he began studying through correspondence courses at Queen's University and, after two years, he enrolled at the Law Society of Upper Canada to become a lawyer. He would need to article for two years, working for little pay, but during this time he would be eligible to attend lectures at Osgoode Hall Law School. After three years of classes while working at the law firm, he could be called to the bar.

During his legal training at White's firm, Cohen lived at an incredible pace. He was in the office all day long, attended classes or studied in the evenings, and helped his family in the store on weekends. He was a small man, not very tall or strong and weighing just 110 pounds. His diminutive build irritated him because, as his mother recalled, 'he desired to do more than his body was able to accomplish,' but he made up for it: 'his spirit was strong; he could with his thoughts and energy exceed several boys his age.'[24] He wasted little time, studied during meals, and had no hobbies, few recreational interests, or much social life. In 1916 the Cohens moved to a large three-storey house on Borden Street with a verandah and a big yard shaded by trees. The second floor was rented out to cover expenses and the family used the first and third floors. Jack and Lewis shared a spacious bright front room with a desk, a large comfortable chair, and a small table with a reading lamp. Here, Jack worked long hours reading and writing to advance himself and to support his family. When he recalled those years later he realized that his youth had slipped away.

He got along with everyone in the law office. J.P. White was an established lawyer who concentrated on his three hobbies – revolver shooting, golf, and his farm in the Rouge Hills. His frequent absences allowed Cohen to gain much experience, since the bulk of the firm's work was left to young subordinates. In addition, Cohen made acquaintances through the family grocery business, and when customers learned that he was preparing to be a lawyer, they would entrust their legal problems to him. In 1918 Cohen graduated with a bronze medal, placing third in his class at Osgoode Hall Law School.[25] He had to wait several months until he was twenty-one to be called to the bar, and during that time he visited New York. A Toronto friend who edited a Jewish journal provided him with some contacts and he made new acquaintances, including an editor of a Yiddish daily.[26]

Cohen was atypical of his peers in the legal profession in that about half of them had university degrees before entering law school and most came from professional and business families. Even among the minority of Jewish students, Cohen was different because virtually all of them had attended university before taking law, and most in the inter-war years came from families that had overcome poverty.[27] By becoming a lawyer, Cohen gradually emerged economically from what was still predominantly a working-class Jewish community, though he would continue his associations with it in his practice.

While it is difficult to know the extent of discrimination that Cohen faced because he did not refer to it, anti-Semitism in pre- and post-First World War Canada was a fact of life, fuelled by religious bigotry, stereotypes about eastern European Jews, and ignorance of Jewish cultural and community life.[28] Wealthy Jews were excluded from social organizations, such as the York Club, some boating clubs and golf courses, and the Lawyers' Club, founded in 1922, which excluded non-whites, non-Christians, and women. Jews were barred from certain resorts and hotels, and as they began to work outside factory jobs, they seldom were hired in department stores or as bank clerks. Those graduating from university could not find work teaching and so instead turned to law and medicine. Christopher Moore has found that 'disfavoured minorities' faced barriers at every level of the law profession and that in the 1920s and 1930s 'the fiercest anti-ethnic campaign' was against Jews, particularly eastern European immigrants, whose newness to Canada contributed to public intolerance.[29]

In 1918, the year Cohen graduated, the Law Society of Upper Canada initiated a requirement that law students (as well as lawyers) had to be British subjects. Unlike professional schools and many universities such as McGill, the Law Society and Osgoode Hall Law School did not have formal, limited Jewish quotas, but the society's staff did keep track of the number of Jewish students.[30] While the Law Society thereby avoided exercising formal discrimination, the profession was deeply discriminatory in practice. Stephen Speisman notes that 'even independent professionals found Toronto life rife with discrimination. Lawyers and engineers could not find employment with Gentile firms' and Jewish graduates from medical schools were refused internships in hospitals.[31] The greatest hurdle for Jewish law students, particularly in Toronto, was finding work as articling students and later as practising lawyers. Even top students were seldom hired in large, established firms in the 1920s and had to article for Jewish lawyers or obscure, marginal practitioners. Once admitted to the profession, 'virtually all Jewish lawyers had to start their own practices,' depend mostly on their own communities for clients, and often support themselves by doing other work as well as law.[32] In all of these respects, Cohen's early career was fairly typical though he had work in a law firm while he studied law and after he graduated. Senator David Croll, who was called to the bar in 1924 and was a law clerk at Davis and Healey in Windsor, was invited to Toronto to work for Hughes and Agar. He recalled, 'The invitation was a stroke of good fortune, since it was not easy for Jews to become articled to firms in Toronto, where prejudice effectively hindered their entry into some professional careers.'[33] Cohen undoubtedly experienced discrimination from peers at law school but apparently ignored it since this was his preferred defence mechanism. He remained focused on his work, on achieving his call to the bar, and on his family's needs.

Anti-Semitism in Toronto thus permeated the legal profession when Cohen started to practise law in the 1920s – not coincidentally a decade 'of intense activity in Jewish Toronto' as that community began 'to experience a growing self-assurance.'[34] During the Depression of the next decade, anti-Semitism persisted, with many people resenting all immigrants who held jobs, and violent incidents broke out. In the Christie Pits riot of 1933 in Toronto, hundreds of youths attacked a Jewish baseball team in a conflict that lasted six hours while police stood by and made only two arrests.[35]

Anti-Semitism affected individuals. For example, Bora Laskin, the future chief justice of the Supreme Court of Canada, returned to Toronto in 1937, with a BA and MA from the University of Toronto, a law degree from Osgoode Hall, and an LLM from Harvard Law School. He hoped to teach law but could find only a part-time job with the provincial Attorney General's Department and, with the help of friends, got a job writing case headnotes for fifty cents each for *Canadian Abridgment*. He was rejected by every law firm he approached, and the universities were 'rife with antisemitism.' In 1911 the University of Toronto had turned down Lewis Namier's application for a lectureship because he was a Jew, despite a glowing recommendation from his Oxford tutor and a reputation as 'a brilliant prospect.' Similarly, in 1919 Dr R. Bruce Taylor, principal of Queen's publicly expressed pride that only five Jews were at the university; Jews, in his view, lowered the tone of the university, and so its administration tried to keep them out.[36] In this atmosphere, the University of Toronto took three years to hire Laskin in 1940 to teach in its honours law program. During the process of placing Laskin, Caesar Wright, Laskin's friend and a prominent professor at Osgoode Hall, acknowledged to a colleague at Harvard that Jews had limited prospects as teachers in Canada because of prejudice. Wright wrote about Laskin to Sidney Smith, dean of the Manitoba Law School, in 1939: 'Unfortunately, he is a Jew. This may be fatal regarding his chances with you. I do not know. His race is, of course, proving a difficulty facing him in Toronto so far as obtaining a good office is concerned.'[37] What was typical about the Laskin case was his passivity about anti-Semitism. Laskin, like many young Jewish males seeking employment, including Cohen, tried to work around the prejudice rather than resist it,[38] and Toronto lawyers at that time seemed to view anti-Semitism as a fact of life, to be taken into account realistically but not challenged.[39]

Gradually, as Jewish lawyers became known, they were accepted on their merits, but it was a long, slow process. This atmosphere, tinged with xenophobia against Jews, undoubtedly affected Cohen's career and position in a profession whose corporate clients determined the size, wealth, and prestige of law firms, but it is difficult to say how exactly, because he was silent on the subject. As one scholar has written, 'the psychology of religious bigotry such as anti-Semitism is complex, and a historian is only certain that such attitudes directly affect public policy or the development of a profession like law when they are manifested in overt ways. Yet, when anti-Semitic attitudes, though never publicly expressed, underlie judgements which, for those who make and rely on them, assume the form of commonplaces or unquestionable inevitabilities, then these attitudes are all the more insidious for being covert.'[40]

Following graduation, Cohen stayed at White's for a couple of years doing criminal and commercial law. His salary rose substantially, and for the first time he was able to solve the family's financial problems. Jane also worked at various jobs from the time she was fourteen, and the two incomes, as well as money taken in at the store, supported the younger children. Like his father, who valued education, Cohen saved enough to keep all his siblings, except Jane, in school.[41] In 1920 Jack opened his own office and in the first year had trouble covering expenses. But soon he was able to establish a viable general practice which handled estates, divorce, small business matters, and civil and criminal cases. Since some of the White firm's clients had followed Cohen, his business grew swiftly. Continuing as the family breadwinner, he hired his sister Jane to work as a bookkeeper and when his brother Abraham finished high school he, too, worked in Jack's office.[42]

In 1923 his office was in the Excelsior building but by 1929 he had moved it to 465 Bay Street. Sam Gotfrid, who articled for Cohen, remembered that 'Cohen was the kind of guy you either liked or hated,' which may explain why legal partnerships did not work for him. An able practitioner, he was demanding, a perfectionist, and he drove his small staff hard. He was not helpful to articling students, preferring to have them solve their own problems; he was critical of their work and took a superior attitude towards them. At the same time, he displayed a sense of humour in his dealings with students, his firm provided them with a wide variety of legal work, and his ability elicited their respect.

In addition to being a Jew, Cohen also was perceived fairly early in his career as a radical, because of the clients he represented and because of his favouring the interests of unions and workers over those of business. Specialization was an unintended effect of discrimination, for, when Jewish lawyers focused on bankruptcy or personal injury, for example, they were able to attract both Jewish and non-Jewish clients. Cohen decided to specialize in the late 1920s, but he did not do so immediately; he worked for Jewish small businessmen in general practice, and when he began to do labour cases in the clothing industry, he represented employers and unions' interests on both sides of the table.[43] Later, when he narrowed his interests to represent workers and unions only, labour law was a very new area. But Cohen was influenced partly by contacts in the United States who were caught up in the dramatic changes in labour relations there in the New Deal era.

In 1930 Jacob Finkelman was the first Jew hired to teach law at the University of Toronto and he 'introduced a pioneering course in labour law,' by which time Cohen was already working in the field.[44] Until then, labour cases arising from strikes were handled by non-specialists, and mediation/conciliation cases often involved government officials more than lawyers.[45] Finkelman called his course industrial law but in 1939 changed its title to labour law. It covered 'the sociological study of legal relations in industry, the status of unions, the law of conspiracy,' and his early writings were on picketing and labour injunctions. By the time he retitled the course, Finkelman could add new topics, often using Cohen's cases, which involved legal issues surrounding strikes, lockouts and boycotts, conciliation and arbitration, collective bargaining and industrial standards – all themes that emerged from the first standards and labour legislation that so involved Cohen in his practice.[46] When Finkelman took a leave of absence in 1943 to become registrar of the new Ontario Labour Court, Laskin taught labour law and Finkelman got to know Cohen well as a practitioner before the court.

By inclination and partly out of necessity because of discrimination, Cohen was independent and individualistic. He became a loner, did not join groups for lack of time, and never worked in a large firm. This introversion would persist throughout his life and contribute to his professional and personal isolation, even though he had an admiring extended family. Still, despite difficulties resulting from his ethnic background, his political outlook, and his personality, Cohen's achieved economic success in the 1920s.

In his domestic life, Cohen also was getting established. During one of his frequent trips to New York, he met Dorothy Aidman, a social worker. She was a Russian Jew in origin; her mother and siblings, except for a sister, Jane, who worked as a nurse in New York, were living in the Soviet Union. Dorothy corresponded with them and sent her mother a regular monthly allowance.[47] Her father had been a teacher in St Petersburg but died when Dorothy was twelve. Her grandfather in New York went back to Russia to help his widowed daughter, and on returning to the United States he brought Dorothy and Jane with him so they could continue their studies.

In 1923, after a brief courtship, Cohen married Dorothy in New York and brought her home to meet the family. Esther's first impression of the short, blue-eyed blond was not positive – 'he could have found a more beautiful girl in Toronto' – but Dorothy was well educated and pleasant and the two women tried to get along. Shortly afterwards, the couple moved out of Esther's house into their own apartment.[48] Their next move was to a large house with a great garden on Lawrence Avenue in affluent north Toronto where they hired a maid and a gardener. The family would move several times more. By living outside the ghetto, and by developing broader contacts and new clients in his work, Cohen gained more legal experience, but he also risked greater exposure to anti-Semitism than Jews who remained within their community.[49]

Lawyers did well in the prosperous 1920s; the average salary of three thousand dollars a year was not wealth, but it was a comfortable middle-class income.[50] After years of hard struggle and penury, money and the trappings of success were important to Cohen, and in the early 1920s he was driven to work by a chauffeur. Always fashionably dressed in three-piece suits, and sometimes sporting a fur-collared great coat and a cane, he appeared a man of substance. As Cohen gained prominence, many thought that he was a wealthy man. In this early part of his career before he practised labour law, Cohen worked intensely and made a great deal of money, but his expenses in maintaining his large home, sustaining his rising standard of living, and indulging his free-spending habits were enormous and he experienced much stress as a result.

From an early date there appeared to be tensions in the marriage. Several years after marrying, Phyllis, the Cohen's only child – a beautiful girl with red hair and blue eyes – was born. Dorothy doted on her daughter and was apparently happy to be a mother, although she also hired a nursemaid. Jack was active sexually and his womanizing, about which Dorothy apparently heard rumours, became notorious. The pressures surrounding money and his marriage, and the years of hard work to achieve his legal training on top of all his other responsibilities, contributed to a nervous breakdown that Cohen suffered in the mid-1920s and recovered from very slowly. His collapse resulted in less income during his convalescence, which increased his distress. A sibling wrote to 'Donia' in 1926 from the Soviet Union, 'Hope that Jack is continuing to improve. Let me know how you are feeling, what you are doing outside of admiring your daughter.'[51]

While Jack was recovering emotionally, the economy collapsed in 1929 and so the family's economic pressures continued. To cut expenses, the Cohens moved in 1931 into an apartment. The office, which Abraham kept going while Jack was recuperating, had been moved to Madison Avenue, presumably also to save money. Then in 1932 Cohen and two other Jewish lawyers, Henry Rosenberg and Louis Singer, started a firm on Adelaide Street. Rosenberg had worked in the 1920s at the firm of Moldaver and Rosenberg in the Federal Building on Richmond Street. The threesome lasted only one year; later, when Cohen chose to work on the union side in needle-trades cases, Singer opted for the management side. The two men had extensive professional dealings throughout the 1930s. Cohen and Rosenberg moved to the Federal Building but by 1935 they, too, had gone their separate ways.[52]

In the 1930s, Dorothy accepted a job with the Jewish Federation, which Esther thought was a good idea since she did not think her daughter-in-law had enough to do. Shortly afterwards, the Cohens bought another house, by which time Phyllis was in school. Esther commented that the couple in these years 'didn't seem to be happy with each other.' They were both smart and well-educated, but they competed with each other.[53] Dorothy maintained supportive friendships in New York and California by writing and visiting frequently. A letter to Dorothy from a California friend in these years, commented, 'I do hope you are all in a more cheerful frame of mind than your last letter indicated. I don't know why Jack gets so panicky as soon as things are not so bright. No one has any security nowadays and we might as well get used to it.'[54] Dorothy kept busy, but she did not work consistently at her profession after she married, which was not unusual. She was on the National Council of Jewish Women and became active in assisting Jewish refugees trying to gain entry into Canada.[55]

During frequent visits to New York while he was recovering his health, Cohen was exposed to the labour movement's growing militancy and workers' demands for unionization. His maturing social conscience, intellectual curiosity, and working-class background motivated him to examine the American labour scene thoroughly. He interviewed American labour lawyers and became convinced that collective bargaining was necessary to create a more democratic relationship between workers and employers. Besides his familiarity with unionism, Cohen's attraction to the idea of industrial democracy may have resulted from his eastern European Jewish background, for, compared to the older Canadian Jewish families, the newer immigrants had a more democratic outlook. Their idea of a Canadian 'parliament' of Jews in 1919, for example, resulted in the founding of the Canadian Jewish Congress.[56] Some childhood friends and his brother Lewis got involved in the industrial-union movement emerging in the early 1930s, so Jack was not alone in his interest in American labour issues. Cohen's upbringing conditioned him to develop 'a relationship to people in the working class' in his legal practice.[57]

Despite his success in general practice, Cohen experienced internal emotional conflict which, as a magazine article explained later, became unbearable. 'Activities of a keen commercial counsel offered no outlet for the social consciousness that was maturing within him.'[58] His lengthy illness began to improve after he decided to do work of 'social significance.' While recovering from his breakdown, he began taking labour and civil-liberties cases some radical friends brought to him, and when he defended demonstrators arrested outside the American consulate in Toronto in 1925 in connection with the Sacco-Vanzetti affair, that case began to restore his equilibrium.[59] Thereafter his legal work increasingly reflected his social outlook, and this consistency relieved some stress. He became known for championing peoples' civil liberties and as a defender of workers and unions.

In 1927, while still recuperating from his breakdown, Cohen wrote the first of several books on legislation. His *Mothers' Allowance Act in Canada* was published in Toronto by Macmillan. Tom Moore, president of the Trades and Labour Congress of Canada (TLC), wrote its preface; for fifteen years, organized labour had sought, the enactment of such legislation, which provided allowances for widows with children. Cohen acknowledged a debt of gratitude to F.N. Stapleford, general secretary of the Neighbourhood Workers Association, and to his wife. He analysed the main features of existing legislation in five provinces, compared the Canadian legislation to similar American state acts, made recommendations, and attached a draft bill. His proposal, Cohen admitted, was not costed out, but he believed in state support for social programs, commenting that 'where anything is added to the cost of one particular item of social relief, something is saved, directly or ultimately, under another item of social cost or waste.'

Writing from a legal perspective, not that of a social worker, he was an advocate for children, and in this stance he was ahead of his time. Even when Canada developed a social-welfare state after 1945, its legislation covering childrens' needs was less advanced than in many European countries or even the United States. In 1927 Cohen recommended that existing provincial legislation be broadened to include children of divorced and unmarried women; that it extend the categories of incapacity of fathers to include those in jail or on either short or long-term disability; that it include families with any number of children; that it cover children born in Canada regardless of the nationality of their parents; that it extend the age of eligible children of both sexes to sixteen years, in cases of parental incapacity of foster parents; that it raise the amount of the payments; and that the legislation be extended to all nine provinces. Cohen advocated more research to determine appropriate living standards for

law & social policy

persons receiving payments, recommended interprovincial cooperation, and urged regular meetings of the acts' administrators.

This social legislation was not charity or welfare but, for Cohen, a means to create social justice. 'Mothers' allowance legislation is an acknowledgment of State responsibility for the economic stability of family life, whether in the form of social insurance or supervised special relief.' The act's administration, for him, was as important as its content, and this view foreshadowed his later approaches to labour law. He preferred a representative administrative board which was close to the community to a government commission which might be open to patronage appointments. But, if governments opted for the commission model, he thought that appointments should be based on consultation with labour and social-service agencies and that citizens' advice was invaluable. He also advocated a case-by-case, flexible method of administration, which took account of legislative guidelines but allowed for discretion in special circumstances. He recommended an appeal process for cases that did not involve the courts.This administrative model was identical to his later approach to labour legislation and the wage policy in 1943, when he was a member of the National War Labour Board.[60]

In 1928 Cohen's client, the Canadian Brotherhood of Railroad Employees (CBRE), which was the largest industrial union in Canada and had founded the All-Canadian Congress of Labour (ACCL) in the previous year, approached him to compile and edit J.S. Woodsworth's major speeches since his election to the House of Commons in 1921 as a labour member. The CBRE was 'interested in the workers' political representation' and indeed A.R. Mosher, head of both the CBRE and the ACCL, would be the only prominent trade union delegate to the founding convention of the CCF a few years later. In the foreword of the slim volume, Mosher described Cohen as a lawyer and a 'labour specialist,' an acknowledgment of Cohen's role that year in establishing the Canadian Labour Research Bureau, whose publications included pamphlets, legislative reports, and a monthly bulletin.[61] Cohen wrote that the book expressed Woodsworth's understanding 'of Labor's attitude toward the great social and economic problems of our time.'[62] The publication of these two books in quick succession, indicated that Cohen was on good terms with the leaders of the two rival congresses – the Trades and Labour Congress (TLC) and the ACCL – which was no mean feat. As a result of his growing expertise as a labour lawyer, he had contacts with persons on the left of different ideological persuasions – both Communists and democratic socialists.

poor
sent

As one of the first labour specialists Cohen was noticed. A colleague described him around this time as a labour lawyer of growing prominence, who was outspoken, unpredictable, and possessed of a courtroom style that was witty, dramatic, and colourful.[63] In appearance he was, according to lawyer and historian William Kaplan, 'a small dapper man with a swift tongue, a large ego and a harsh unattractive personality.'[64] His self-important manner and exaggerated self-assurance was reflected in his large downtown Toronto office with his desk at one end of the room, raised on a dais so that he towered over anyone seated in the client's chair.[65] His confidence resulted partly from his successful struggle with economic adversity. At the same time, his outwardly commanding manner hid persistent internal conflicts, which gnawed at him and resulted from feelings of personal inadequacy and insecurity.

He affected people around him differently. J.B. Salsberg (a Communist Party organizer and an Ontario MPP in the 1940s) commented that Cohen was both brilliant and disliked. But J.J. Robinette, a renowned Toronto lawyer, remembered him as a pioneer in the 1930s. 'The labour movement was blossoming then and he was on the crest of the new era of collective bargaining. They [the companies] thought it was awful and they would have blamed him because it was something new for them. And you could understand they would hate any leader in that area. And then you get a fellow like Cohen who was abrasive and good and I guess you could say he was not beloved by business.'[66] Former *Globe and Mail* reporter Ralph Hyman recalled that Cohen was autocratic, aggressive, and abrasive. 'He was very much in demand by unions and he knew his labour law but he was a nasty piece of goods otherwise.'

Despite his arrogance, he wrote 'masterful' law briefs, according to Kaplan,[67] which were clear, well-researched, and analytical, and he quickly gained a reputation for sympathizing with the underdog. Cohen worked incredibly hard to rise to the top of his profession. A workaholic and a perfectionist, he put in extremely long hours and never entered a courtroom without being well prepared and fully versed in all the details of a case. David Croll declined an offer to join Cohen's firm in the early 1930s because Cohen never 'understood why you had a night off ... It was work, work, work, and he didn't appreciate the fact that there were other people in this world who wanted time for something else.'[68] Cohen was competitive, intent on winning his cases, and displayed little sympathy for the other side. But he had a certain personal strength and integrity in dealing with his clients; he refused to be manipulated. Perhaps because the law had been his vehicle for improving his own situation, he had great faith in the legal system and sought to use it creatively to effect change. As Kaplan has written, 'if there was a wrong, Cohen believed, then the law was there to make it right. And where there was no law, Cohen made new law.'[69]

To those in the labour movement who hired him in the 1930s and 1940s, Cohen's aggressiveness was a sign of his determination to win cases and legislative protection for workers. Bob Carlin, a former officer of the Mine Mill union, who met Cohen in 1939, believed that the man's self-assurance, legal knowledge, and skill gave workers confidence: 'Cohen could explain things and he took the fear out of it. He put a spinal column where there was a wishbone in working people. He'd give you encouragement that you weren't the first people on the firing line.' Most lawyers were not neutral but on the company side, and they would not take unions as clients. Cohen did so even in the Depression years, and George Burt, former director of the United Auto Workers (UAW), remembered, 'J.L. was so smart you had to have all your marbles when you argued with him and that gave him an air of arrogance.'[70] Cohen's clients admired him and his opponents disliked him because he used his exceptional legal talent and intelligence as a partisan. He enjoyed confrontation, according to his daughter; he sought to achieve as much as possible for his clients and encouraged the labour movement not to compromise until it absolutely had to.

The confidence he gained from a supportive home environment early in life, combined with the loss of his father, which necessitated Cohen's literally 'becoming a man' at a young age, created a tough, combative professional with sympathy for the disadvantaged. The drive and determination that he developed early, both to learn his craft and to earn the money needed to enable his family to survive, was channelled in his adult years into fighting cases to give other working people a chance in life. But the strain that resulted from his early experiences and the pace he set for himself as a lawyer robbed him of his adolescence, led to a nervous breakdown as a young man, and deprived him of skills for balancing personal and professional needs. As he matured, he became a man of contradictions – arrogant but vulnerable, strong but a hypochondriac, combative with opponents but an educator of clients, authoritarian in style and in relationships but a fighter for democracy in industry and society, beloved of a few but disliked by many, and respected by peers but full of self-recrimination. In the end, the contradictions engulfed him and his short but productive career came to a humiliating and tragic end.

2

Lawyer for the Communist Party,
1927–1931

J.L. Cohen's transformation into a labour lawyer representing radicals and trade unionists did not happen overnight but was a gradual process beginning in the 1920s. During that decade, he became counsel to the Canadian Labour Defence League (CLDL), a Communist organization formed in 1925, and handled civil-liberties cases, problems of employed and unemployed workers, and even a case of suspected murder.

People on the left sought Cohen's help because in the 1920s workers faced hostility from employers and politicians when they tried to organize. Despite the dominion government's suppression of the Winnipeg General Strike in 1919, political leaders feared further strikes or anarchist plots as the recent Bolshevist revolution in Russia fuelled their imaginations. Employers wanted stable, loyal, productive workforces, and they were in a position to get them. A steady stream of immigrants before the Great War and in the 1920s, as well as the movement of youths from rural to urban areas, provided them with abundant cheap labour. A brief post-war recession was followed by the boom years of expansion and prosperity. The growing economy and business confidence, combined with an aggressive 'open shop' campaign against unions by large employers in the United States and Canada, made workers cautious. As a result, organizing was difficult and the decade was characterized by low industrial conflict and a decline in union membership.[1]

Sometimes employers introduced alternative plans for employee representation in the large factories of the bustling manufacturing sector, where thousands of relatively unskilled employees worked without unions. Such plans meant consultation with employees but management retained decision-making power over basic matters such as wages.[2] The labour movement consisted primarily of exclusive craft unions of skilled, male workers, which were ineffective structures in mass-production jobs where most workers were not craftspersons. Traditionally, skilled workers were hostile to the unskilled because employers had used the latter to undermine wages, standards, and unions. Hence, most unionists were not yet interested in organizing entire workforces into industrial unions whose basis of strength was in numbers and unity rather than in skill.

In the inter-war years, the Communist Party of Canada (CPC) frequently took the initiative in organizing industrial unions among unskilled, often immigrant, workers in factories, mines, and resource industries. Its relationship to labour changed, in that it briefly supported the nationalist congress formed in 1927, the ACCL, which broke away from the older TLC of craft unions. Then in 1930, on instructions from the international Comintern, the CPC set up the Workers' Unity League (WUL), its own radical movement, which attacked 'reformist' unions. Such tactics were controversial and not always effective in promoting the party's interests or its leadership among Canadian workers, but visible public campaigns for improved working conditions, with rallies to gain public support, provoked the authorities.[3] As a centre of Communist activities, Toronto was the site of many confrontations. Police Chief Denis Draper increased surveillance of the CPC and created a 'Red Squad.'[4] Conflicts escalated and J.L. Cohen represented clients sent to him by the CPC.

THE FREE-SPEECH CASES, 1927–31

The Canadian Labour Defence League (CLDL) was a CPC body established to provide legal defence for activists and radicals who got into trouble. Headed by ex-Methodist minister A.E. Smith, it first asked Cohen in 1925 to defend five Communists arrested for vagrancy at a Sacco-Vanzetti protest demonstration in front of the American consulate in Toronto. The execution of the two Italian-American anarchists was a cause célèbre in the 1920s for 'liberals' who believed that Sacco and Vanzetti had been treated so harshly as much because they were immigrants as because they were radicals. In Cohen's words, 'the horror and the resentment aroused by the Sacco-Vanzetti cases passionately bound together men and women in all walks of life and in all parts of the world.'[5] The night before they were executed, hundreds of people in Toronto as in many other cities, anxiously held a vigil while 'waiting for some indication that the lives of the men, and the cause of liberty which they had come to represent, would be saved.'

Thereafter, Cohen accepted other CLDL cases, though he received warnings from 'kindly' friends 'on the dire fate which awaited me if I allowed myself to get "mixed up" with the cases of "extreme radicals."'[6] While the charges in such cases were not serious, public interest in them grew because they involved the issue of free speech. Ironically, one arrested man whom Cohen defended was John Leopold, a Royal Canadian Mounted Police (RCMP) officer working as an undercover agent under an assumed name of Jack Esselwein. Later he was exposed and became the chief crown witness, in full-dress RCMP uniform, in the famous 1931 trial against eight leading Communists who were convicted of contravening the infamous section 98 of the Criminal Code, which had originated as a hastily drafted order-in-council designed to 'legalize' the arrest of leaders in the 1919 Winnipeg General strike and deal with 'subversive and seditious' activities; in 1936 Mackenzie King's government would repeal it. Cohen had not suspected Leopold's identity 'and certainly,' he wrote, 'there was nothing about his demeanour or ability which distinguished him to me. If anything ... he appeared quite drab and quite dull.' But afterwards, whenever Cohen saw him at the RCMP's national office in Ottawa, Leopold never looked him squarely in the eyes.

Despite his diligent work for the CPC and his undoubted sympathy for many of its ideas, Cohen never became a party member, even though he was accused publicly of being a Communist and was seen as a 'fellow traveller' by many. He certainly defended the right of the CPC to exist legally in Canadian society. Tim Buck, CPC general secretary for thirty-three years, remembered Cohen as 'a very good friend of our party.' Pat Sullivan, leader of the Canadian Seamen's Union (CSU) and a Communist until he dramatically rejected his party affiliation at a press conference in 1947, hired Cohen in 1940 to defend him when he was interned for two years. In his memoirs he wrote, 'I do not know whether or not Mr. Cohen was a member of the Communist party, but I do know that they could rely on him.'[7] J.J. Robinette never believed that Cohen was a Communist because he liked money too much. Senator David Croll also thought that he was not a 'socialist' but simply 'believed in labouring people getting a better deal.' Cohen's daughter,

Phyllis (herself a CPC member and candidate), confirmed that Cohen was never a party member because Communist discipline was too restrictive for such an individualist. But she also noted that he had reservations about the social-democratic policies of the CCF, which were not, in his view, 'going to lead to the sort of change in society that he wanted to see.'[8]

When the CPC first approached him, Cohen was 'one of a handful of lawyers in Canada willing to represent members of the Communist Party.'[9] David Goldstick took an occasional case, and Arthur Roebuck, later a cabinet minister in Mitchell Hepburn's Liberal government in Ontario, sometimes did free work.[10] But Cohen became the usual counsel for the CPC and the CLDL, in the late 1920s for the free-speech cases and in the early Depression years for deportation cases.[11] He represented active Communists including Tim Buck; Fred Rose, a CPC leader in Montreal; and Harvey Murphy, a future trade-union leader.[12]

Because Police Chief Draper harassed CPC demonstrators for disrupting public order, such cases increased. Draper had his supporters, but the Toronto trades and labour council condemned his actions, which were a threat to all labour meetings, and students and academics as well as the Toronto Star also protested his police-state approach. Yet, despite support from other groups, the CPC chose to act alone in seeking publicity and trying to win more members.[13] Many charges for vagrancy, obstruction, or unlawful assembly against Communists resulted in convictions and jail sentences. The Communists persisted in trying to hold public meetings, to defend the right of assembly as well as protest police behaviour, which the police raided repeatedly.

Cohen's defence strategy followed a standard pattern: he tried, usually unsuccessfully, to get charges against his client reduced to a single offence; a police officer would then testify against the accused; Cohen would call the accused or other witnesses to give opposing testimony, or he would argue that no case had been made and would offer no defence. The presiding magistrate invariably ruled in favour of the officer and sentenced the accused to the maximum penalty.[14]

Cohen won a few cases. One involved activist Harvey Murphy, 'a marked man' according to the CPC newspaper the *Worker*, who was charged with disorderly conduct 'for refusing to move on when requested to do so by a police officer.' The trial was a 'farce,' since Judge Emerson Coatsworth was a police commissioner and thus virtually a party to the prosecution.[15]

According to a Communist client, some magistrates feared Cohen because he knew more law than they did and demonstrated it with his usual arrogance. Coatsworth was not intimidated, yet Cohen turned this case into a trial of Coatsworth as much as of Murphy. When the judge assisted the prosecutor, as he did frequently, Cohen objected with phrases that dripped with sarcasm. He easily discredited detective William Nursey's testimony that Murphy had been disorderly. In cross-examination he showed that the policeman, a member of the 'Red Squad,' had pursued Murphy for some time, and this lent credibility to Murphy's testimony that Nursey told him, 'You've been looking for this.'

Cohen's defence was that Murphy had moved along the sidewalk as the police requested but nevertheless was beaten up by police. It was Murphy's word against the police; this normally 'would have amounted to no contest but Cohen had so seriously damaged Nursey's credibility that the corroborative evidence of other officers was not plausible. The prosecutor tried to discredit Murphy, an immigrant, with racial slurs, but Cohen called a strong witness, activist Annie Buller, who testified that 'Mr. Murphy had been singled out for an attack. Several policemen and plainclothesmen grabbed him ... and just beat him up ... The meeting very rapidly disbanded and everybody moved.'[16]

Cohen knew the case was futile. These free-speech cases often involved the same people in court with similar results. Inevitably, Coatsworth accepted the police witnesses' evidence unconditionally and ignored the testimony for the defence. The only surprise was a lenient fine of ten dollars and costs or ten days in jail, instead of the usual twenty-five dollars or thirty days. Because the CPC sought publicity from the cases, Murphy joined six colleagues in jail.

Cohen appealed and luckily the case was heard in the Supreme Court of Ontario by Mr. Justice W.E. Raney, the former attorney general in the United Farmers of Ontario/Independent Labour Party government of E.C. Drury (1919–23). 'His populist politics had followed upon a law career devoted to uplift causes rather than making money. No friend to "the interests" he did not regard the status quo as immutable.'[17] Raney found that magistrate Coatsworth had erred in law as Cohen outlined. He quashed the conviction and ordered the Toronto police department to pay costs. Raney remarked in delivering judgment, 'I have been referred to no authority which makes refusing to move when instructed by a police officer an offence under the Criminal Code.' Coatsworth was humiliated; Raney's unusual award of costs to the defendant indicated that the prosecution's case was questionable.

Throughout hot summer days in 1929, frequent confrontations between police and CPC members continued and climaxed with a riot at Queen's Park on 13 August, in which several hundred people were arrested. In the ensuing trials, Cohen tried to protect individuals' civil liberties and to use the law as an instrument of social justice, and he argued that police and public officials should act in an appropriate and accountable manner. His reputation grew as the trials received much press coverage. Though he lost most cases, 'he won the respect of left-wing political and trade union activists. People on the left recognized that Cohen was a clever lawyer, a determined fighter and not afraid of taking on the Establishment.'[18]

In one of these cases, in September 1929, Cohen appeared before magistrate Robert Browne to defend Myer Klig, a young immigrant furrier charged with obstructing police. Constable Parker was off duty, but on 1 August he nevertheless arrested Klig at Queen's Park. Parker testified, 'I was stopping the meeting because I believed a breach of the peace was about to be committed.' Under cross-examination, Cohen established that Parker had taken Klig into the Parliament buildings and struck him continuously on his head. Cohen asked if this behaviour fell within the sphere of his duties, and the officer replied that it did. In his summation, Cohen argued that the police were not 'exercising any reasonable, lawful or necessary duty' around Communist meetings but were rather behaving as provocateurs. They arbitrarily presumed that such gatherings were not in the public interest and decided beforehand to stop them forcibly, which Cohen argued they had no right to do. The police 'cannot by wrongfully telling a man to move from a place he has a right to occupy, make that man a criminal.'[19] The magistrate accepted the police argument that there was potential for a riot and they were legally doing their duty, and Klig, suffering from an injury to his eardrum inflicted by Parker, was convicted for obstructing police and given sixty days' hard labour.

Cohen also defended women activists, including the well-known Becky Buhay. Police arrested her for vagrancy after she defended a young girl they pushed and made a 'speech about free speech' to two hundred people. Magistrate J.E. Jones accepted police testimony that she 'unlawfully did cause a disturbance in Soho Street in Toronto by impeding and incommoding peaceable passengers and thereby was a vagrant.'[20] He sentenced her to fifty dollars or thirty days. The CPC paid the fine and instructed Cohen to appeal.

In October, for the fifth time, the police broke up a free-speech rally at

Queen's Park and arrested and charged four women in the Young Communist League (YCL) with 'willfully obstructing a peace officer in the execution of his duty.' Joseph Sedgwick, a clever, ambitious young counsel at the Attorney General's Department overlooked a vagrancy charge and pressed the more serious offence of obstruction, which carried a maximum of two years' imprisonment. Magistrate Margaret Patterson was as partisan as her male colleagues in these cases. When Cohen refused to present a defence on the ground that the prosecution had not made a case, the magistrate so abruptly convicted Jeanne Corbin that she made a judicial error, enabling Cohen to appeal the sentence of thirty days.[21] The women received jail terms, and all four chose incarceration rather than the crown's offer of fines if they would stay away from Communist meetings.

Cohen defended other persons convicted under the vagrancy section of the Criminal Code, including Fred Rose, a leading Communist who in 1943 would be elected an MP in Montreal only to be convicted of espionage in 1946. In 1929 Ontario Provincial Police Inspector Charles Greenwood testified, Rose was with a 'disorderly mob' of about four hundred persons at the intersection of University Avenue and College Street. When the police tried to clear the crowd, Rose purportedly said, 'We don't have to be pushed along by these dirty scabs.'[22]

Cohen concluded from these cases that the CPC should assume an offensive stance with the police and government. In the 1929 Ontario election, when police roughed up Communist candidates and prevented them from renting meeting halls, Cohen planned charges of interference with elections.[23] When Tim Buck, for example, ran in the Toronto riding of Bellwoods and could not rent the Standard Theatre for a meeting, he had Cohen get an injunction against the Toronto police commissioners, charging that they had no right to prohibit meetings, prevent the rental of halls, or threaten to cancel licences. Two days before the election Buck was told that he could rent a hall.[24] Cohen had lost numerous free-speech cases in the lower courts, but when he embarked on this new legal strategy, he announced to the press that in the appeal cases he would test the legality of police methods.[25]

What was at issue was Police Chief Draper's right (unsustained by statute or common law) to disrupt peaceful meetings. Convictions for obstructing police or for disorderly conduct were inevitable if it were assumed that police actions were legal. Superior court judges, unlike magistrates, were more closely bound by legal reasoning, and Cohen hoped that they would separate their prejudices from the law. In

November 1929 Cohen won a test case in York County Court before Judge J.H. Denton. Charlie Sims, CPC district organizer, and five women were charged under section 98 of the Criminal Code.[26] Police were reviving this section's use and charged Sims with publishing a leaflet that advocated a change in government by 'force, violence or terrorism' and the women for distributing it to factory workers. The test case was Emily Weir's.

Crown attorney Eric Armour based his case on the offending leaflet. He defended the police campaign to suppress Communist meetings, because the CPC was rallying Canadian workers to defend the Soviet Union and leading them into a revolutionary struggle intended to overthrow capitalism and replace it with a new social order where workers would rule. In his defence, Cohen admitted that his clients distributed the leaflet but argued that the circular was not forbidden under libel law or section 98, since the term 'revolutionary' was ambiguous. He described the allegedly brutal police actions at Queen's Park that gave rise to the leaflet, reminded the court of the legal presumption of innocence, and 'managed to imply that the pretty young defendant, a kiss-curl peeking out from under her head-tugging toque, was the personification of that innocence.'[27]

Cohen won; Judge Denton found the accused not guilty and observed that no decision had previously been rendered under section 98. Relying on an 1909 English case which defined sedition as 'language calculated to advocate or to incite others to public disorders,' he could discover nothing in the circular that advocated force, violence, or terrorism or was forbidden by the Criminal Code. He concluded, 'The circular in question contains very strong and objectionable language, but in my opinion it does not contravene the law ... However one may dislike or even abhor the views advocated by the communists, the advocacy of their cause is not unlawful unless it is done in a manner contrary to law.'[28]

After Weir's acquittal, the crown dropped charges against the others. J.L. Cohen jubilantly sent copies of the judgment to Tim Buck and A.E. Smith of the CPC and CLDL respectively, to labour MPs J.S. Woodsworth and A.A. Heaps, and to another client, the Canadian Brotherhood of Railway Employees. To Woodsworth he wrote, 'In view of your repeated emphasis on the iniquity of this complete series of enactments following the Winnipeg strike situation, I am sure you will be interested in knowing that the accused were all found not guilty.'[29] The case forestalled until 1931 the use of section 98 against Communists.

Shortly after the Weir victory, the Ontario Court of Appeal quashed the conviction against Becky Buhay for vagrancy. Hugh John Mac-Donald, who worked for Cohen, presented the successful appeal case, which was celebrated in Cohen's offices. The decision, in defining vagrancy, set a precedent that might influence police behaviour. After winning the Buhay, Murphy, and Weir cases, in which he questioned the role of the police, Cohen successfully appealed Fred Rose's conviction.

Cohen lost other appeals.[30] Mr Justice W.E. Middleton of the Ontario Court of Appeal reversed the precedent in the Buhay case, that proof of actual impeding was necessary to justify a conviction of vagrancy, and decided that if impeding could be inferred in a situation, a charge could be upheld. Once again, convictions for disorderly conduct were easier to obtain because Middleton insisted that he would not try police methods, which, even if illegal, were to be obeyed.[31] Meanwhile, despite reversals of some lower court decisions on appeal, Draper continued his attacks and magistrates convicted Cohen's clients.

As he had nearly done in the 1929 provincial election, in 1930 Cohen tested Draper's intimidation of hall operators, who often refused to rent space to Communists for fear that municipal authorities would delay or refuse to renew their licences. In 1929 Draper warned that, if meetings were conducted in a foreign language and held in 'a public hall, theatre, music hall, exhibition show or other place of public amusement,' he would cancel the licence for the hall and arrest speakers.[32] Several incidents occurred. On 22 January 1929, for example, the 'Red Squad,' armed with tear gas, dispersed a crowd at the Standard Theatre at Spadina and Dundas streets and evicted Philip Halperin and Max Schur for not speaking English. A year later, the Yiddish Freiheit Choir rented the Canadian Hygeia Council hall on Elm Street for a concert. Before the event, the Hygeia Council told the choir to seek approval from the police and returned its deposit on the hall. Cohen applied for an injunction against the Canadian Hygeia Council, the Toronto Police Commission, Chief Draper, and Inspector Nursey of the 'Red Squad' in order to get a court ruling. Mr Justice Charles Garrow of the Supreme Court in Ontario upheld the Police Commission, dismissed the injunction, and the choir had to pay costs.[33]

As this episode demonstrated, Cohen often did more for his clients than argue cases: he was an adviser whose role led him into the public sphere. In the 1930 national election, Draper's force again harassed Communist candidates, broke up their meetings, and assaulted CPC candidate Charlie Sims as he spoke at a street-corner meeting. Determined to challenge such police actions, Cohen sent a detailed memo on the police chief's alleged abuses of power to Chief Electoral Officer O.M. Biggar. Biggar wrote to Toronto's Mayor Bert Wemp, questioned Draper's interference with Communist candidates, and requested an official inquiry. His letter was published in the press, and when he did not receive a satisfactory explanation, Biggar wrote a seering indictment of Draper: 'The real question ... is whether ... the police are enforcing the law or are persecuting persons who hold opinions of which they disapprove by the confiscation of printed matter found in their possession, by physical violence, by the misuse of licensing powers and by threats of the institution of criminal proceedings for which there is no foundation.'[34] Draper responded defiantly, but his force's activities subsided for the remainder of the campaign. Cohen's persistence and memo had had an effect. Yet the *Worker* was unimpressed with this civil-liberties victory, even though, presumably, individual Communist candidates were glad to be free of harassment.

Two aspects of these cases are interesting in terms of Cohen's career – his relationship with his client, the CPC – and his relationship to the courts. Cohen's goals began to diverge from those of the CPC, whose free-speech campaigns took place in a political context. Despite public opposition to police actions against Communists, and support from groups concerned about their own civil liberties, the CPC was in a radical phase, determined to act alone and ineffective in mobilizing large numbers. Indeed, internal factionalism in the party had resulted in fewer members, partly because its decision to follow the Comintern – which by this time Joseph Stalin and the requirements of the Soviet Union's foreign policy dominated – was controversial. Party rhetoric was unintelligible to many Canadians. In the summer of 1929, the CPC called for demonstrations in a campaign with the slogan, "Transform the Imperialist War of the Exploiters into the Class War for the Workers and Farmers Government!" As Ian Angus has written, 'since there was no imperialist war in progress that summer, Canadian workers must have wondered just what the party expected them to do.'[35] This extreme, confusing sloganeering against Canadian 'subordination' to Britain had little appeal. The CPC also engaged in tirades against what it called the 'social fascism' of social democrats, which alienated many on the left, and it condemned 'reformist' trade-union bureaucrats as much as capitalists and police. Unable to win more supporters with such issues or by their strategy of acting alone, the Communists became easy targets of aggressive police action. The Communist/police conflicts stifled meetings of leftist groups and increased police and state opposition to Communists, which culminated in 1931 in the trial and imprisonment of Buck and his associates.

The CPC was interested primarily in using police actions and the trials to create martyrs and gain publicity for its political ends. In 1931 Tim Buck told the party executive that 'with every demonstration that is smashed the prestige of our Party grows.'[36] Consequently, CPC leaders displayed little faith in the legal system and were unenthusiastic about victories in the higher courts. Cohen, of course, wanted to make legal points and get his clients out of jail, but when he did so, the cases ended and were no longer a source of publicity for the party. Thus, the successful appeals in the Weir and Buhay cases, which delighted Cohen, did not elicit any substantial thanks from the party hierarchy.[37]

Overall in these Communist cases, Cohen was pleased to have won some appeals, even though the judiciary had avoided the legal issue that Cohen raised – the legality of police methods. Individuals had been assisted, but the law had not been defined more precisely to protect individual rights. As a civil libertarian, Cohen took the CPC cases partly to oppose arbitrary, and what he viewed as illegal, police actions and state repression. Except for the few appeals he won, he did not achieve his goals, but he did become better known to the courts and the public as an effective lawyer who defended 'radicals.' When his aims conflicted with the Communists' desire to exploit the conflicts for political gains, Cohen became alienated from them.

Early in his career, Cohen argued these cases in the lower courts, when there was only one Jewish magistrate in Toronto. One can only speculate about the effect that Cohen's ethnic background had on his career, but the absence of Jewish judges or benchers reflected the still-limited access and acceptance of Jews in the legal profession and the judicial system. Perhaps feeling that his religion placed him at a disadvantage, but also because his nervous system was still fragile from his breakdown, Cohen carried these cases through all the stages to their conclusion but had Hugh John MacDonald, a tall, reserved Scot, argue the appeals. Discrimination could not blunt Cohen's legal arguments, constrain his performance in court, inhibit his self-confidence, or dilute his political and legal aims, but it may have influenced his legal strategy in the 1920s. His Jewish background affected his position within a profession in which Jews remained segregated and, as in society as a whole, anti-Semitism was pervasive.[38] As he matured and his legal stature grew, Cohen would argue before courts at all levels.

MAY DAY CASES

Cohen's work as CLDL counsel included cases partly caused by worsening conditions in the Great Depression. He travelled north to defend Communists in Sudbury and the Lakehead who were arrested during annual May Day parades when they clashed with groups of veterans. When the police charged the Communists with unlawful assembly, they did not arrest their opponents, for, as Inspector C.E. Watkins later told the court, 'I did not think it policy to do so.'[39]

Cohen's agent at the Lakehead was D.R. Byers, who had little sympathy for radicals but needed the work. He acted in preliminary hearings and sent the depositions of evidence to Cohen. He provided a history of the May Day celebrations in Port Arthur and Fort William, which Cohen requested as he prepared his legal briefs. In these Lakehead cases, eight of the eighteen arrested were convicted for participating in a parade that began at the Ukrainian labour temple and meandered through the community for several miles. One banner reading 'Heroes in 1914 – Vagrants in 1930' so enraged Dr B.C. Hardiman, a returned soldier, that he charged into the parade saying, 'I am no vagrant.' Some charges were withdrawn, but most of the defendants were sentenced to one month plus a twenty-five-dollar fine. One defendant, Tom Hill, received two months.

Cohen appealed the convictions in District Court and used Hill's 'as a test hearing at Osgoode Hall on the question of interference as to parades etc.' All the appeals were lost. The judges agreed with Cohen that the crux of the matter was whether people in the neighbourhood feared a breach of the peace. But, whereas Cohen argued that there was no such evidence, the court accepted the prosecution's argument that this fear existed.[40] Afterwards, Cohen wrote to Byers about the trial, noting that 'the court was very vicious upon the opening of the appeal, Riddell, J. in particular colouring the hearing with references to questions of deportation and the like.'[41]

In these May Day cases, Cohen began an exhausting schedule of working all day in Toronto, travelling all night to northern Ontario, and then appearing all the next day in court defending his clients before returning to Toronto. This routine became fairly regular as Cohen's caseload increased in the 1930s and 1940s and his life assumed a hectic and pressured pace. As his reputation as a labour lawyer grew, he increasingly defended workers attempting to organize unions, often in the north.

Cohen lost the May Day cases but won an unlawful-assembly case against CPC organizer Charlie Sims, who was arrested at a demonstration of unemployed workers. The Great Depression increased the number of unemployed in Sudbury both as a result of lay-offs and because transients arrived seeking work in the mines and smelter. The Communists were trying to organize both the nickel miners at INCO and the unemployed in the city. To discourage these efforts, Mayor Fenton and city council passed a by-law that empowered the police to break up any gathering of three or more persons. The Communists decided to test it. In August 1930 they called a meeting of unemployed, requested a permit to hold the event (even though no permit was required), were turned down by the Police Commission, and held the demonstration anyway. Police pulled Sims off his soapbox. 'What followed was the usual jack-in-the-box act with Vaara replacing Sims.'[42] Four speakers were charged with unlawful assembly.

Local lawyer J.M. Cooper represented the accused at preliminary hearings, reporting to Cohen that the judge probably would dismiss the charges for lack of evidence. Cohen presented the case at the trial, and Judge Proulx dismissed it reluctantly but in the process made prejudicial comments. He advised police as to strategy, so that future charges would stick; he warned the defendants that the Police Commission on which he served would prevent their activities; and he told the 'foreigners' that they should return to their homelands or to the Soviet Union. The *Worker* published the judge's comments and praised Cohen, 'the CLDL lawyer,' for 'ripping the crown's case to shreds.'[43] After the trial, Cohen criticized his clients for seeking permission to hold a meeting when the by-law did not require it. Apparently he feared that Judge Proulx would be bound by the earlier Middleton judgment that even invalid police orders must be obeyed.

Cohen's interest in challenging old laws, making new jurisprudence, and defending and expanding civil rights led him to develop an overall strategy, to have expectations of his clients, and to work at times for relatively little pay. The CPC's different interests increasingly conflicted with his aims, however, and despite Cohen's excellent service in 1927–31, the party found his fees 'exorbitant.' Throughout his career, Cohen kept detailed accounts and presented clients with clear, annotated bills, but with his clientele of radicals, unions, and the disadvantaged, he frequently had to request payment repeatedly and chase clients for his fees and expenses. The payments he received were often overdue. Sometimes he was not paid, or received partial payment. Cohen became displeased with his Communist Party client, whose attitude towards both the appeal trials and to paying him he found irresponsible. In August 1930, the CLDL paid him $850 but still owed over $1,100, and the fees issue continued to cause acrimony.[44]

In 1931 R.B. Bennett's government outlawed the CPC under section 98 of the Criminal Code and arrested eight party leaders, who were charged with belonging to an 'unlawful' organization.[45] Tom McEwen, leader of the Workers' Unity League (WUL), the Communist union organization, reluctantly gave himself up as the party ordered. Tim Buck attributed his surrender to Cohen, who had advised it. A.E. Smith invited Cohen to defend 'the Kingston Eight,' as they became known. He refused, despite the uncharacteristically generous retainer the CLDL offered, the civil-liberties aspect of the case, and the opportunity to challenge the 'infamous' section 98, which he believed violated the British tradition of justice since it declared 'guilt by association often in a retroactive manner.'[46] McEwen concluded that Cohen did not want to alienate his new client – the International Ladies Garment Workers' Union (the ILGWU) – by taking the case. It had fought serious internecine battles with the Communists throughout the 1920s.[47] Cohen may have considered this, but his past experience with the CLDL probably was a stronger factor.[48] Also, Buck wanted a show trial to propagandize the CPC's aims, not a simple legal defence to gain release of the accused. As L.-R. Betcherman has surmised, 'Cohen would not lend his talents to the "spectacular sort of defence" that the communists wanted.' He certainly never allowed himself to be instructed by clients on how to conduct a trial. When he learned that Buck would defend himself, Cohen 'lost his temper and washed his hands of the whole thing.'[49]

In January 1931 Cohen withdrew from all CLDL cases. When he received a letter from the CLDL, he replied sharply that 'it is, of course, obvious that the League will secure other counsel for its affairs,' so he could not understand the need for further communication 'except as a rather unhappy attempt to bring the relationship to a dignified end.' In April he sent the League a bill for $1,323.40. Smith replied that Cohen had agreed to retire the account for $400 paid in instalments, and he enclosed $100.[50]

As a result of his work in the 1920s, the RCMP set up a file on Cohen as part of its mandate to 'aid and assist civil powers to preserve law and order.' It interpreted protecting national security as keeping informed about 'pernicious propaganda' and preventing misguided persons from subverting the government of Canada, goals it pursued by recording speeches, hiring secret agents to infiltrate unions, and targeting radicals.

In the 1920s the RCMP decided its priorities, the scope of its secret operations, and the subjects to monitor, all of which remained the same for the next seventy years.[51] The file on Cohen did not inhibit his work, for, after he ceased acting for the CLDL, he remained deeply committed to the needs of workers and 'radicals.' In the Depression, he assisted individuals and unions, and in the war years he would again defend interned Communists and work with the CLDL's successor, the National Council for Democratic Rights (NCDR).

For its show trial, the League hired Cohen's former associate, Hugh John MacDonald, who, less sophisticated politically and more malleable, accepted the case on the party's terms. Cohen, of course, followed the proceedings, which included agent Leopold's sensational testimony about party activities and members. Cohen foresaw that the men would be convicted, which they were, and that the CPC would remain banned (despite Buck's dramatic speech to the jury) on the basis that, even if Communists did not advocate violence, the party's existence was a potential danger to public order.

In November 1931 the men were sentenced to five years in Kingston Penitentiary. The CPC then went underground until 1935, when it began functioning openly as a legal party with no adverse legal consequences. This changed when the war broke out in 1939. The CPC, which opposed the war because of the Nazi-Soviet Pact, was outlawed under the Defence of Canada Regulations. Some Communists were interned between 1939 and 1941. In the latter year, however, Hitler attacked the Soviet Union, and so the CPC changed tack again to support an all-out Allied war effort. Gradually, Communist internees were released with Cohen's help, but when the government continued to ban the party, it reinvented itself in 1943 as the Labour Progressive Party.

MURDER IN PORT ARTHUR?

In 1930 a much-publicized murder case fascinated Cohen and gained him some notoriety in Ontario's Attorney General's Department. When two union organizers, Viljo Rosvall and John Voutilainen, disappeared, the Lumber Workers' Industrial Union (LWIU), a Communist-influenced body, hired Cohen. The two men had left Port Arthur on 18 November 1929 to tour some camps and were last seen alive on Onion Lake. Their bodies were found in the spring in a shallow creek entering the lake. Their 'peculiar disappearance' and the cause of their deaths have remained a mystery, but the union at once suspected foul play.

The incident occurred during a lumber strike over pay which involved firms that opposed unionization and hired strikebreakers, it increased bitter factionalism between competing radical unions – the Industrial Workers of the World (IWW) and the LWIU – and it stimulated ethnic rivalry between the conservative 'whites' and the radical 'reds' in the Finnish community. When the work stoppage was nearly lost, and the spruce forests were 'dangerous and explosive: with the OPP, the strikers and the strikebreakers carrying arms,'[52] the union decided to send the men into camps at Onion Lake (twenty miles east of Port Arthur) to try to expand the strike and force employers to negotiate. Rosvall and Voutilainen were known and well liked; neither was a professional organizer. Rosvall had been a maintenance man on the Canadian Pacific Railway (CPR) and Voutilainen was a trapper. Rosvall was tough, impetuous, and active in union-camp committees, while Voutilainen was quiet but 'knew the Onion Lake area like the back of his hand.'[53] When they disappeared, the union called off the strike to concentrate on finding them.[54]

From the beginning the union believed that they had been murdered, because they were experienced woodsmen. Earlier a lumber boss had threatened organizers, but the police and the Ontario Attorney General's Department decided that the men had drowned while crossing the ice. Local police briefly questioned the chief suspect, Leonard 'Pappi' Maki (a subcontractor with non-union employees), but they did not talk to any lumbermen.[55] The union became disturbed by the lack of effort to find the union men. As Joe Farbey on the union executive wrote the CLDL, 'without a doubt these men met with foul play here.'[56] On 27 November the union sent a report to the Port Arthur *News*; on 8 December, in Port Arthur, it held an emergency mass meeting which demanded that governments act immediately to locate the missing men and learn how they vanished.[57] The CLDL also organized support; the CPC, the YCL, and the Ukrainian Labour Farmer Temple Association passed resolutions protesting the lack of action, calling for government investigations, urging workers' support for striking lumber workers, and protesting 'this new manifestation of the bosses' terror.'[58]

The union could not retain a lawyer in Port Arthur, since local lawyers did not want the case. 'This is a company owned town and it means fighting the police and the [American] Pidgeon Timber Company,' Farbey wrote to A.E. Smith. 'If we can get J.L. Cohen here' to handle it, he said, it would 'strengthen our work' and the CLDL. When Cohen was hired, the lumbermen elected a committee to work on the case, conduct their own searches, and collect evidence.[59] They placed two men in Maki's camp to listen for any incriminating information, but, as Farbey complained to Cohen, 'we can't get the police to act.'[60]

Cohen pressed for an inquiry. He asked the minister of lands and forests to initiate a search for the missing men, since the lumber companies barred union search parties from the area. Cohen wrote to ACCL president A.R. Mosher that 'the attitude towards the disappearance of these two men shown by the authorities in and around Port Arthur is most striking and particularly as compared with the diligence and intensity of activity shown if any prospector happens to stray off the path.'[61] ACCL leaders spoke to the federal labour minister with no results. Angered by the lack of concern, Cohen wrote to the Ontario attorney general several times in December asking for a probe to obtain more information. 'There is very grave suspicion that these men have met with some violence by employers who would be opposed to their mission.' In Cohen's view, 'some disaster has undoubtedly befallen them.' His request made headlines.

Eventually, Deputy Attorney General Edward Bayly responded. Cohen and Bayly knew each other from the free-speech cases. Bayly had not been sympathetic to Chief Draper's strategy towards the Communists, and in 1931 he doubted the soundness of the government's case against the CPC and left its prosecution to others. Betcherman has described Bayly as 'an exceedingly capable veteran civil servant, [who] was the closest thing the Ontario government had to a mandarin.' He had a depth of character 'that rose above the narrow confines of Canadian parochialism, but he never let this interfere with his official responses.'[62] The Ontario police told Bayly that their investigation was continuing, but Bayly believed that 'these two persons were drowned through the ice on one of the lakes.'[63]

Cohen persisted. In December, the provincial deputy minister of lands and forests instructed his wood rangers to visit the area to look for the two men. The OPP did nothing more. Hugh MacDonald, of Cohen's firm, interviewed Police Inspector W.C. Killing, who had asked a Constable Higgins to make inquiries and received his 'exhaustive report'. Higgins had interviewed Maki, the employer most under suspicion, who had threatened to 'shoot any organizer who came around his camp.' He was among the last people to see the two men, for Maki and his party had followed them for half an hour.[64] Maki was contradictory about how far behind Rosvall and Voutilainen they were, but he never denied following them. He told Higgins that, as the lumbermen walked along the eastern side of Onion Lake, Maki's group, on the west side, called them to their fire and enquired where they were going. Replying that they were going to hold a camp meeting, they proceeded north to another small camp, where Voutilainen kept provisions. Later searchers found Voutilainen's camp untouched. Maki said that he warned them to watch the ice near the shore that was broken. Killing assured Mac-Donald that the police would conduct a proper investigation but they believed that the organizers were in the ice and would not be recovered until spring.[65] MacDonald asked Killing to report Maki's threat regarding union organizers and the lumbermen's suspicion of foul play to the local police.

Cohen compiled information. Farbey dismissed the theory of the men going through the ice and drowning as foolish, for on Onion Lake 'sleighs haul provisions with five or six men walking with the sleighs' and lumbermen had travelled along it a week earlier. Even if the ice was weak, the spot where they were last seen was shallow. The lake was small enough that one could see the entire lake, so when Maki followed the men, he would have seen them go under.

Cohen cautioned union leaders not to make direct references to Maki in public, since they could be sued for libel. He had questions about the condition of the ice, as well as Maki's actions and explanation before or after talking to the police.[66] The union responded to Cohen's questions and collected affadavits, and Farbey sent a map of Onion Lake. The local press, Farbey reported, was parroting the police 'line' about its 'thorough' investigation.[67]

The affidavits of lumbermen – Erkki Haara, Hjalmar Nummela, and Ratu Pitkanen – attested to three facts. First, the day before the men were lost, the ice on the lake had held them. Second, they saw Maki leaving his camp at 10 A.M. on 18 November without any firearm. Third, they had visited Voutilainen's camp and his provisions were untouched. In other affidavits, Oscar Maijala swore that, ten months before the incident, at Kyro's store in Port Arthur, he overheard Maki threaten that if any delegates ever came to his camp, he would turn them back or shoot them in the head.[68] Sulo Lahti and Vaino Pasaanen swore that, six days after Rosvall and Voutilainen went missing, they asked Maki where he thought the two men had gone after they left him; he replied that they went to their trapline and that Victor Kemppainen had also seen them. Kemppainen denied seeing them. Paavo Vaananen, a pulp cutter, swore that at 4 P.M. on 18 November he was walking north from Maki's camp when he met Maki, who was carrying a firearm. Maki asked, 'What kind of delegate are you?' Vaananen replied, 'I am not a delegate. I am just going to the trappers' camp.' Maki said, 'Yes, yes, I know why you are going there.You are going to meet the delegates, who were on their way there, but I turned them back and told them I did not need them at the camp.' He told Vaananen firmly, 'You need not go there,' and Vaananen swore, 'I was so scared by the mood Maki was in that I turned back and walked back with him towards his camp.' These workers' affidavits were to assist the union's investigation, but at risk to their jobs if the contents became known.[69]

On 4 January 1930 Cohen wrote to Bayly again (with a copy to the *Mail and Empire*), repeating the request for a government probe and suggesting that he offer a reward for information about the missing men.[70] Bayly replied that the union members' suspicions about foul play 'does not appear to rest upon very substantial grounds.'[71] In a second testy letter, Bayly wrote to Cohen that he had spoken to the crown attorney in Port Arthur, W.F. Langworthy, who in turn had talked to the OPP and to Maki. Bayly told Langworthy that his office was deluged with unions' resolutions calling for a full investigation and pointing at Maki as responsible for the deaths. Langworthy replied that the OPP had 'used every effort, so far as I can see, to trace those men.'[72] Langworthy, whom Bayly described to Cohen as very experienced, did not believe that Maki was involved. Bayly himself was of the view that those interested in this matter should offer a reward.[73]

Discouraged, Cohen told William Burford of the ACCL that the attorney general 'does not take up any of the suggestions made, with any degree of cordiality' and likely would not act.[74] As Bayly had anticipated, with the spring break-up the bodies were recovered.[75] On 19 April 1930 two co-workers found Voutilainen's along the north end of Onion Lake, lying face up in about two feet of water. The 'boys' brought the remains to camp.[76] Four days later, Rosvall's was found a few hundred yards away, on the bank.

The discovery of the bodies ended a minor power struggle that winter. When they could not trace the men, the union, at great expense, had set up a permanent search party at Onion Lake. 'A cramped trapper's cabin a mile-and-a-half from the Maki camps became their headquarters.' Several unionists stayed there patrolling on skis and trapping for food.[77] They faced company hostility, but Maki stopped hauling pulps in February when he found the area under surveillance 'by our comrades.'[78] He became polite to the union men and lumbering almost ceased. To prevent the bodies' removal in the spring floods, the men made sure that nothing happened 'without our knowing it.' They had Cohen urge the government to lift the dam's gates at the south end of Onion Lake so that water could flow out in spring and they could search there, and they also wanted a net placed over the dam to catch the bodies, a method adopted the previous year to recover the body of a drowned horse.[79] Before Cohen could act, the lumbermen succeeded in their grim task.

After Voutilainen's body was discovered, it took two days to get it to Port Arthur to Everest Undertaking Parlour. Doctors Greizer, Eakins, and Laurie (the coroner) did a post-mortem. An inquest was scheduled. Two lumbermen looked over Voutilainen's body at the undertaker's suggestion and found some marks around the head. Suspicion in the community deepened. The police reported 'no marks ... on the body that would indicate, that there was any foul play.'

On 23 April 1930, the day that Rosvall was found, the inquest into Voutilainen's death at the Port Arthur police station concluded that he died accidentally.[80] The union, which buried Voutilainen since he had no relatives in Canada, found the verdict 'not satisfactory.' It wanted Cohen at the second inquest, convinced that 'someone is needed here at once.'[81] The second inquest was postponed, and Cohen prepared to travel north.

As Cohen travelled in the CPR club car, he must have remembered his father's drowning in the north, and the parallels may explain his interest in the case. En route he read 'several bulky tomes on medical jurisprudence' related to symptoms of drowning. He jotted down notes in pencil. What was the depth of the water? What was the condition of the body, lungs, and stomach? What wounds were present before death and after? Why did Maki not notice the men when he passed? In Port Arthur, Cohen checked into the local hotel, where later he would spend considerable time.

Since an inquest is not a contest of conflicting interests but a public inquiry, counsel for interested parties usually do not examine witnesses or make arguments. In this case, whether because of the prevailing public interest or because the authorities were unsure of the usual procedure, Cohen made the union's interest known and was allowed to cross-examine. The witnesses eagerly confirmed death by drowning, though Cohen thought their evidence unconvincing. Cohen knew that, if foul play was the cause of death, he would have to establish it by testimony from the very doctor who had performed the autopsy and concluded that the cause of death was accidental drowning. He would likely arouse the doctor's apprehension, so that 'he would either shield himself behind technical, medical and scientific terms or marshall the facts as effectively as possible in favour of his own conclusion.'[82]

Cohen did not question witnesses about the identity or location of the bodies or about the time and circumstances when the men were last seen alive. He did establish that they were engaged in union work, and he was also able to make clear the anti-union position of Maki. The doctor (possibly Greizer) testified that the autopsy showed that the men had drowned accidentally. He confirmed that one of bodies was bruised on the head. Cohen asked, 'with curiosity but with no show of medical terms,' about the colour and amount of fluid in the lungs, and 'received answers which began to form a pattern of at least doubt, if not suspicion, as to the actual cause of death.' He probed the doctor about the age, body size, and general health of the men, and asked how long the bodies were immersed in water and how that factor affected his findings.

Such questions were critical in establishing the cause of death. The existence of water is a symptom of drowning, but in his post-mortem report, the doctor wrote that the stomach's contents were normal. Becoming flustered on the stand, he replied that there was some water. Cohen wrote later, 'I then suggested that there was evidently so little water that he had not thought of mentioning it in his report.' Suddenly the doctor, 'a strong burly figure of about 6 ft. 5ins.' exploded, jumped out of the witness box, 'his face crimson with anger and excitement,' rushed up to Cohen, 'and then just as he reached me, wheeled sharply to his right, ran across and out of the court room,' slamming the door. As the astonished audience stared after him, he opened the door and shouted, 'I still say they died from drowning,' after which he slammed it shut again.[83] His exit ended Cohen's cross-examination, since nobody tried to recall him, and many were convinced that he could not stand up to the questioning. But the coroner charged the jury emphatically that accidental drowning and nothing else had caused the deaths.

Cohen could only disclose suspicious circumstances; he could not prove actual wrongdoing. In a remarkably balanced report to the union, he wrote that the witnesses seemed anxious to explain away, rather than explain, any facts that cast doubt on the doctor's finding, and the inquest discounted any suggestion of foul play. The doctor, he reported, was unwilling to probe the basis for his conclusion, could not explain the damage around the right eye, and was not frank about the water level in the stomach. His startling, hysterical, and, to Cohen, disgraceful exit from the courtroom raised doubts about his examination of the body, particularly since the union's nominee, Dr Eakins, was present during the probe of Voutilainen's body but not of Rosvall's.

The second inquest confirmed the position of the men in the water, but its depth remained contested. Police witnesses maintained that the water level was eight feet, but under cross-examination they admitted that their estimate was based on hearsay. The lumbermen believed that Onion Lake was lower than the police report said, and, as the current was weak, bodies with light backpacks would not have moved and so Maki and his men would have passed them.[84] Cohen's experienced witnesses contradicted the police, insisting that in autumn the water was never over four feet. As Cohen reported to his client, 'it seems odd that two men would fall into four feet of water and both drown. I do not believe that the evidence can go further than asserting that it seems odd, but on the other hand the inquiry seems to have been governed by a spirit which ignored any of the doubtful elements.'[85]

The coroner's jury ignored Maki's contradictory evidence, which Cohen thought was 'naive and unbelievable.' Maki claimed that his chat with the deceased had been friendly, even though they were going to organize his workers. He said he warned them that the ice was thin, admitted following them forty minutes later, but claimed not to have noticed the ice conditions. Cohen found Maki unwilling to give evidence freely and frankly.

In conclusion, Cohen reported that the matter required further investigation – not because the evidence positively indicated foul play, but because it raised doubts. From the evidence, the jury could have concluded only that the men died and were found in the water. They should not have decided anything further or been counselled to do so, because the evidence of accidental drowning was insufficient.[86]

The second inquest ended the case for Cohen, and the men's funeral was then held. A giant procession of five thousand workers marched through Port Arthur's streets to a brass band playing Chopin's *Funeral March*. The two young men were regarded as martyrs of the bushworkers' organizing struggles, victims of class conflict, and foreign-born workers cut down in their prime by a hostile, anti-union society. The event was further dramatized by an eclipse of the sun, which Alf Hautamaki, the union's secretary and a great orator, thought symbolic. He remarked in his funeral speech, 'God himself has shown us today that he, too, is ashamed of this heinous crime, ashamed that the murderers remain free.'[87] Many Finnish-Canadians continued to believe that the men were beaten unconscious and then pushed into the creek. The local press complained that the Communists were making martyrs.[88] The deaths stimulated support for the union and united the community, and they were commemorated thereafter by the labour movement.[89]

Cohen remained fascinated by this case and in 1947 thought of writing a mystery story about it.[90] He did not totally accept the lumbermen's view, because murder had not been proven, but he always believed that the evidence warranted further investigation. He had 'exerted every effort to rouse the provincial government to a sense of its responsibilities' but had failed to do so.[91] The lumber companies may have influenced the government, or Bayly may simply have believed the police. Cohen's role probably did not win him any friends in the Attorney-General's Department. The case was typical of Cohen's practice, involving as it did union organizing, drama, politics, and much publicity. It also demonstrated that, when workers sought his help, Cohen made himself available.

3

Advocate for the Poor, 1927–1939

The Great Depression was characterized by class confrontations, bread-lines, soup kitchens, thousands of unemployed persons on relief, and the deportation of immigrant workers. The crisis made a lasting impression on J.L. Cohen, whose social conscience was deepened. Union leader George Burt recalled that Cohen lived when the plight of many 'was really something' and 'Cohen was a product of those times.'

By 1935, Cohen had dissolved his partnership with Harry Rosenberg and set up his own firm, which specialized in civil-liberties issues and labour law. Many cases resulted from Depression problems and involved both employed and unemployed workers, as the following sampling indicates. In 1933 he defended furniture strikers in Stratford, organized by the WUL, who won better wages but not union recognition. Cohen's clients were charged with intimidation and obstruction of justice when a fight broke out on the picket line. Twenty-three were convicted. Cohen managed to arrange a meeting with Ontario Attorney General Arthur Roebuck, a progressive cabinet minister who in 1937 would oppose Premier Hepburn's handling of the General Motors strike in Oshawa and would be fired as a result. He agreed that the harsh sentences were 'outrageous and disgraceful' and lobbied the Department of Justice for the early parole of the men, which was granted.[1]

Cohen became involved in the public reaction to the Regina Riot of 1935, which resulted when R.B. Bennett's government forcibly halted the On-to-Ottawa Trek of unemployed relief-camp workers in Regina.

They were travelling to Ottawa to pressure the government for improved conditions when a violent clash erupted. Cohen joined the Citizens' Defence Committee, which included Montreal law professor F.R. Scott, Labour MPP Sam Lawrence from Hamilton, and western reformer William Irvine, to assist the trekkers. He helped organize fund-raising events and provided free legal advice. After Mackenzie King returned to power in 1935, he appointed the Regina Riot Commission. Cohen prepared submissions to it, tried to expose the RCMP's provocative role, and insisted that the government assume the strikers' legal costs. When Minister of Justice Ernest Lapointe refused, Cohen had to abandon the case for lack of funds.[2] He received extensive publicity from the Stratford and the Regina Riot cases and attracted a wide range of clients.

In the 1930s, Cohen spoke out publicly before self-help community organizations such as the East York Workers' Association, formed in June 1931,[3] about the severe economic conditions of the times and workers' needs. Its members discussed solutions to unemployment, helped individuals find jobs, and acted to protect the living standards of relief recipients.[4] Aided by the intervention of socialists in its activism, it also organized lectures and debates on current affairs and social policy, with liberals and conservatives on one side and socialists on the other. Visiting speakers included Premier George Henry, who represented East York; the Reverend Salem Bland, a leading exponent of the social gospel; CCF and CPC speakers; and J.L. Cohen, billed as a lawyer who represented the CPC and unions.

In 1936, when over 400,000 people were on relief in Ontario, David Croll, the minister responsible for relief, decided to force municipalities to 'houseclean' the relief rolls. Those to be purged were 'chisellers,' in Croll's words – men who refused to work or who had hidden income or assets.[5] In this contentious environment, in March 1936 Cohen spoke at a Provincial Relief Improvement Conference about his defence of Reeve Arthur Williams of East York in a case involving an action to unseat him. Existing legislation threatened to prevent the unemployed from running for municipal office, which to Cohen was an outrageous infringement of civil rights. Like others, he emphasized that relief was not a handout, that society had an obligation to the unemployed, and advocated a permanent scheme of unemployment insurance.[6] As the Depression dragged on, governments were forced to respond to such ideas.

Throughout June and July 1936, reliefers on municipal work projects became angry when payments were reduced by 15 to 50 per cent, and strikes broke out in Guelph, Penetang, and Sarnia. The most serious confrontations occurred in York and Etobicoke townships, where strikers fought police in relief offices and held and threatened staff until town councillors restored the cuts and put single men back on the rolls. Ex-WUL staffer Ewart Humphries had led the first conflict in York, and, after reading police reports, both Hepburn and Croll blamed Communists for taking advantage of the relief workers' growing unrest. The police arrested twenty-five, who became Cohen's clients, nine of whom were charged with kidnapping and sixteen with unlawful assembly.

In September, Cohen spoke at the Ontario Federation on Unemployment conference as defence counsel for the unemployed of York and Etobicoke who were about to be tried. Organized by Communists Harvey Murphy and George Harris, both of whom later joined the industrial-union movement, the gathering was attended by sixty-four delegates from twenty-eight organizations. Greetings came from Toronto's acting mayor, a Windsor alderman, Fred Collins from Toronto's Trades and Labour Council, the Reverend Ben Spence of the Committee to Aid Spanish Democracy, Reeve Arthur Williams, Graham Spry of the CCF, and Stewart Smith of the CPC.

The convention protested the provincial government's actions towards relief recipients, urging it to drop charges. It called for Ontario unemployment insurance and the right of unemployed persons to vote or be municipal or provincial candidates.[7] Hepburn was determined to try Cohen's clients, but in December, Roebuck announced: 'These men are not criminals ... I thought it wise and in the public interest that the trial should not go on and I told them to go in peace and sin no more.'[8]

Besides participating in groups and acting for unions, Cohen sometimes helped penniless individuals in trouble, such as a young man convicted for refusing a relief job on a government farm. In *Rex v. Veerman*, Cohen successfully defended a man wrongfully accused of unemployment-relief fraud; his parents were so grateful that they wished to visit Cohen's office 'to thank you personally.'[9] Such cases demonstrated the harsh treatment governments sometimes handed out to the unemployed. When such individuals landed in court, Cohen was one of the few lawyers who would take their cases – this was before the introduction of legal aid – because he believed that the justice system favoured the wealthy. He learned that workers could achieve more fairness if they organized, and, in the Depression, he consistently urged them towards self-help and unions and also sought enactment of laws favourable to them.

UNEMPLOYMENT INSURANCE

In 1935 J.L. Cohen wrote a short, timely book, *The Canadian Unemployment Insurance Act*, which a client union, the CBRE, commissioned. He sought to appeal to the general public, for in the Depression, business, labour, churches, and political parties lobbied for unemployment insurance (UI). All of them favoured a form of compensation in which employers and employees would contribute to a fund. The CPC, through demonstrations and petitions, raised public awareness about the need for a permanent UI plan, and it wanted a non-contributory plan, subsidized by employers and the state but not employees. Before the 1935 national election, as part of his 'New Deal,' Prime Minister Bennett introduced the first such legislation – the Employment and Social Insurance Act. Cohen's book was partly a response to it and his contribution to the public debate.[10]

The Reverend Salem Bland, who reviewed the book in the Toronto *Star*, praised it.[11] Cohen saw Bland's 'nice write up' during intense negotiations and sent a copy to H. Langer of the International Ladies' Garment Workers' Union (ILGWU) with the comment: 'please note carefully that he says that I am "calm and dispassionate."'[12] Such diverse publications as the CCF's *Canadian Commonwealth*, *Saturday Night*, the CBRE's paper, and the *Jewish Standard* also reviewed Cohen's book. The Winnipeg *Free Press* wrote that Cohen's analysis revealed that the legislation stressed actuarial soundness, was viewed as unemployment *insurance* rather than as a benefit, but left out about 42 per cent of the wage-earning population; it even excluded the unemployed until they were working and contributing.

Cohen sought to publicize his book in the United States and the ILGWU reviewed it in its press. The *American Labor Legislation Review* found it to be a 'logical' discussion of the advantages of non-contributory unemployment compensation over contributory systems. Cohen, it wrote, argued that 'compulsory contribution by the workers discriminates against them as a class' and evaded responsibility for unemployment or the development of a constructive social program. Thus, Cohen's position was close to the CPC's non-contributory program, since he believed in state-administered social reforms such as mothers' allowances, UI, and later collective-bargaining legislation.

In January 1936 the *American Bar Association Journal* noted that Cohen criticized the act 'from the viewpoint of one who apparently is an uncompromising Marxist,' for he argued that since permanent unemployment was part of the capitalist system, the requirement of employee contributions was objectionable. The journal praised the book's brevity but warned that it contained many basic assumptions 'of a highly controversial nature.' In its view, Cohen's proposals, though feasible, would not be translated into American law because 'we work out methods in the framework of the existing legal order' and take account of traditional social and economic beliefs.[13]

In Canada, some reviewers were as critical of Bennett's act as Cohen. Herb Orloff, a future Toronto alderman, in the CCF paper, and William Sydney, in the *Worker,* agreed with him that the act failed to meet Canadian workers' needs. Mackenzie King's new government referred the legislation to the Privy Council, which eventually ruled it unconstitutional. Canada would not pass a UI act until 1940, after the provinces agreed to a constitutional amendment that allowed the program to be national in scope in the federal jurisdiction.

Early in 1936 a Harvard Law School student working on UI sections of the U.S. Social Security Act, asked Cohen if he had drafted a statute incorporating his ideas. Cohen had not but this was soon to change.[14] Cohen's expertise and ability had impressed Premier Mitch Hepburn during the 1937 Oshawa strike at General Motors when they were on opposite sides. Despite Cohen's public notoriety as a defender of radicals and workers, he had a reputation as a first-rate lawyer. In 1943 Hepburn would applaud Cohen's appointment to the National War Labour Board, telling the Windsor *Star* that he had 'the greatest respect' for Cohen 'both as a lawyer and a gentleman.'[15] In 1937 Hepburn's government recommended that Cohen be made a King's Counsel, and in November 1938 the premier asked him to draft provincial UI legislation.

Cohen researched the provincial bill in this, his first, opportunity to learn the inner workings of the Ontario government. He consulted senior civil servants, who were cooperative.[16] H.C. Hudson, general superintendant in Ontario of the Employment Service of Canada, supplied Cohen with his notes from internal meetings on unemployment compensation which had reached some conclusions. At Cohen's request, Hudson returned from a conference in New York with valuable information 'for our study' and a contact – the assistant director of the state's Division of Placement and Unemployment Insurance – who 'promised to co-operate with you on your study of unemployment insurance.'[17] Cohen was impressed particularly with the conference reports' emphasis on simplified administrative procedures. M.M. Hood, the attorney general's secretary, provided notes on UI laws in various countries and suggested that Cohen apply the same exclusions as Bennett's 1935 bill and use the 1931 national census to estimate the numbers of people covered in different classifications.

With enthusiasm, Cohen immersed himself in the subject and sought much information. He wrote the king's printer for actuarial reports and surveys on UI legislation, corresponded with American state officials about their statutes, borrowed pamphlets from the university, and discussed his own book with the industrial-relations department of the Canadian Manufacturers' Association (CMA). The CMA supplied him with its 1938 submission to the Royal Commission on Dominion-Provincial Relations, and the Dominion Bureau of Statistics provided recent numbers of employed and unemployed in Ontario. He examined in Hansard the 1935 parliamentary debate on Bennett's bill and studied the arguments and decision of the Privy Council on the legislation.

By mid-December, Cohen was able to formulate specific policy questions to which he required answers in order to draft the bill. Was it possible to reduce both the number of weeks of contributions to a UI fund to qualify and the length of time benefits were paid out? Could the scheme increase the amount paid to dependants so that it equalled the existing relief standards for families with several children? What was the effect of establishing uniform contributions and benefits for men and women? This, it turned out, would reduce the categories, put no extra financial burden on the fund, and be less burdensome administratively. These two issues reflected Cohen's concern to protect children and his belief in equality for women and their equal treatment in the UI system. He was ahead of his time, for the dominion Unemployment Insurance Act of 1940 would treat women as marginal workers.[18]

Cohen sent a draft to Hood, Hudson, and James Hutcheon, secretary to the minister of labour, and correspondence flew back and forth about issues such as residence requirements, which Cohen reluctantly conceded were necessary to prevent an influx of workers from other provinces, and reduced coverage (the exclusion of employers of fewer than five persons), which Cohen did not like.

In December 1938 Cohen submitted his draft bill, though it still required actuarial verification. He explained to Hepburn that economy and efficiency – words premiers want to hear – had been priorities and proposed using the auditing services of the Workmen's Compensation Board, existing employment offices, and provincial savings offices to administer payments and contributions. For control and flexibility, Cohen followed the British practice of appointing one administrator of the act rather than the three-person commission provided for in the 1935 dominion act. The bill covered persons sixteen years of age and over and retained the dominion model of forty weeks of contributions to qualify and seventy-eight days of benefits. It kept three classifications of contributors but did not separate men and women. His uniform contributions and benefits for both sexes were resisted. G.N. Sheppard's report on contributions under the contemplated bill stated, 'It is obvious that the average man's need is much greater than the average woman's, both with respect to the need of the benefit and the amount of such benefit.' Cohen refuted him, noting that a man's greater need related to the number of his dependants, a circumstance provided for in the benefit clauses.[19] Cohen's bill was reviewed in the Attorney General's Department for constitutionality.

What was suggested was a system of compulsory insurance to be included in employment contracts; the minister would establish a joint fund and designate employers as collectors. Philosophically and in his book on the subject, Cohen favoured non-contributory insurance for employees, but his draft bill had both parties contributing, which was the majority view of many groups. His ability to compromise and be pragmatic politically was evident. Later, when he drafted collective-bargaining legislation for the Ontario government, he would again compromise but only so much, and by 1943, because changes in the political environment made it possible to achieve far more, he had become intractable. As a result of this first government contract, Cohen became well known to his new contacts, provincial officials in several departments.

Subsequent internal discussions resulted in a second draft, which was considered early in 1939. Humphries told Cohen that the attorney general did not know if the bill would be introduced, because it depended on Ottawa's actions. Eventually, the provinces, at Mackenzie King's urging, agreed reluctantly to a constitutional amendment to give the national government jurisdiction over UI. In 1940, as the economy emerged from the Depression, Parliament enacted legislation.

LAWYER FOR THE NEEDLE TRADES

In addition to his work with the CLDL, for workers hurt by Depression conditions, and for the Ontario government, Cohen acted 'for many of the Jewish small business men in Toronto' who wished to hire a Jewish lawyer.[20] In this role, beginning around 1927, Cohen developed expertise and a long association with the needle-trades industry. For both sides, 'he assisted in establishing work schedules, arranging piece rates and developing policies for overtime work,' and even as he rigorously defended Communists in the free-speech cases, he 'was still splitting his legal work between labour and business interests.'[21]

Sometimes Cohen appeared before the Ontario Minimum Wage Board, representing companies that owed back wages. Established in 1920, the board fined employers who violated provincial standards, investigated working conditions, and established minimum wages for women. In May 1932, for example, the board informed the Hallman and Sable company that it paid its employees below the legal minimum wage and had 'one of the worst wage sheets that we have yet received,' adding that 'under no circumstances can we afford to tolerate a condition like that.' The board told the company how much back pay it owed, warned that it could be penalized up to two hundred dollars for each employee 'as well as the arrears in wages,' and advised it to get a lawyer. The company hired Cohen to review the situation, and eventually it agreed to restore to all the women their $12.50 weekly wage for a sixty-hour week. Cohen made sure that his client sent the board a cheque for the back wages.[22] Workers criticized the board's ineffectiveness in administering standards, but employees benefitted in cases where Cohen, who was sympathetic, was the company lawyer.

Increasingly, as Cohen defined himself as a specialist in labour law, the inherent conflict of interest in working for both management and employees created professional discomfort and internal tensions for him which eventually he had to resolve. In the early 1930s the womenswear sector of the clothing industry was in chaos, partly because the Industrial Union of Needle Trades Workers (IUNTW), affiliated to the WUL, was challenging the International Ladies Garment Workers Union, but also because employers responded to Depression conditions with massive wage cuts. In July 1933 Cohen represented the Superior Cloak Company in a strike, after securing an insurance policy for the firm against riot and malicious damage. Acting on company president J.A. Posluns's advice, Cohen asked Chief Draper, his old adversary, for police protection for this outfit and also for Hallman and Sable, which Cohen represented in its strike occurring simultaneously.[23]

In the bitter ten-week dispute at Superior Cloak, the company charged two youths with malicious damage, who were found guilty and given six months in jail. In August, the 225 strikers at Hallman and Sable protested a 30 per cent wage cut and demanded a forty-four-hour work week. Cohen told Draper that the strike was 'at the instigation of the

Workers Unity League said to be an organization composed of Communists,' which was engaging in intimidation and preventing workers from returning to work. When a subcontractor was picketed, Cohen informed the police, who assured him that his client would receive 'the necessary police protection when he endeavours to engage strikebreakers on Monday morning at his factory.'[24]

Superior Cloak was a large manufacturer, and Posluns, who was fed up with strikes and wanted to reduce costs, decided to break the union. Another strike in January 1934 became a 'watershed' in the Toronto industry. Posluns locked out two hundred workers, organized the Popular Cloak Company, a 'runaway shop' in Guelph, and hired cheap, local, non-union labour. As company counsel, Cohen prepared individual contracts for the non-union workers and acted in police-court cases. Encouraged by the ILGWU and assisted by the Fur Workers Union, angry, locked-out Toronto employees travelled to Guelph to walk on a mass-picket line. Violence erupted between workers inside and outside the plant, vehicles were destroyed, police made arrests using tear gas, and Mayor R.B. Robson declared 'martial law.'[25] Despite intimidation tactics on both sides, the union had considerable public support, and the ILGWU eventually organized and negotiated agreements with both Popular Cloak and Superior Cloak which resulted in greater stability for the rest of the decade.[26]

Not suprisingly, in 1934, after a conflict with Hallman and Sable over its policy and methods, with discord between this company and his other clients, and because of his increasingly anomalous position, Cohen brought his legal practice into line with his social outlook by resigning from the boards of directors of Hallman and Sable and several other companies and relinquishing his corporate shares and privileges.[27] Thereafter Cohen worked exclusively as a labour lawyer on the union side, and to this day the employment-law field consists of lawyers who work either for companies or for unions.

By the time J.L. Cohen associated with needle-trades workers between the late 1920s and mid 1940s, they had a lengthy history of unionism in Canada. There were three main unions in the garment industry. One was the United Garment Workers of America (UGWA), launched in 1891, in the ready-made menswear industry. Another was the Amalgamated Clothing Workers (ACW), a breakaway union formed in 1914, which came to dominate the men's sector of the trade. It organized Canadian workers in the 1920s in Montreal and Toronto and held its 1926 international convention in Montreal. The ILGWU, first organized in 1900 in the two cities, had by 1930 about 2,000 Canadian members. These and other unions in associated trades, such as the Fur Workers, comprised 'the Jewish labour movement' in which Jews predominated. Attracted to the ready-made clothing industry because Jews were restricted from other jobs, some of these Jewish workers (about 10 per cent) had tailoring experience in Europe. The garment factories would employ family members, and Jewish women in Canada worked at home under contract or in plants. In 1931, over 80 per cent of Canada's Jewish population lived in Montreal, Toronto, and Winnipeg, the three clothing centres. Ruth Frager estimates that 61 per cent of men and 30 per cent of women in the Toronto clothing industries were Jewish.[28] In the interwar period the garment workforce in Toronto was roughly half men and half women, and in Montreal over 50 per cent female, so that it employed many more women than other industries.[29] In 1932 there were 461 manufacturers of womenswear in Canada and somewhat fewer in menswear, which involved more factory production in large and small shops (though the latter predominated). Jews dominated as employers and employees,[30] but non-Jewish English-Canadians in Ontario and French-Canadians in Quebec also were hired.

The needle trades and their unions, which had been part of Cohen's world as a youngster, provided him with important clients as a young lawyer becoming established and contributed to his professional stature as a labour specialist. The industry's characteristics – small fixed-capital requirements, low overhead, and a steady supply of workers – encouraged exploitation. Frequent changes in style drove the industry and created intense competition among small companies in the ready-to-wear market. The appalling conditions in the 'rag trade' or 'shmatah' business made it as difficult for manufacturers to retain a portion of the market as for unions to organize.

By the 1930s, the industry consisted of non-Jewish firms such as Eaton's and many smaller Jewish companies working on contract, such as Tip Top Tailors, owned by the Dunkelmans, and Superior Cloak, owned by the Posluns. In a fragmented market, the labour process in the industry was in flux with some sectors more mechanized than others, but employees worked long hours for such low pay that 50 per cent of them had to be subsidized by charities. Some male workers received hourly rates but other men and virtually all women were paid piecework rates, and women in 'sweatshops,' lofts, basements, and owners' private homes did contracted-out work hidden from inspectors. Foremen sometimes coerced female employees with threats, discipline, and favouritism. Employers imposed blacklists against pro-union workers and insecure employment was endemic. These conditions remained essentially unchanged until the mid-1930s and made unions and standards legislation necessary.

The 'Jewish' labour movement combatted these terrible conditions in strikes, while employers remained intensely hostile to unions. Internal factionalism created instability. In the 1920s in the United States, a Communist body, the Trade Union Educational League, inspired oppositional groups within the ACW and ILGWU, which battled their leadership for control even as they espoused policies favouring industrial unionism, political action, and organizing. By the 1930s, the Communist opposition in Canada was focused in the IUNTW, which appropriated issues the unions were already pursuing, such as control of contractors, a standard forty-hour work week, a guaranteed minimum amount of work, and production standards. The conflicts created extensive internecine warfare, but eventually the Communists lost. In Quebec, the ILGWU and the ACW faced competition also from conservative Catholic unions.[31] Occurring when unions were not firmly established and employers opposed them, internal opposition as well as depressed conditions resulted in fewer members across Canada as a whole in the 1920s and 1930s. These unions all had 'their ups and downs;'[32] collective agreements temporarily resolved the worst problems, but often accords broke down and employers resumed slashing wages, reintroducing piecework, and evading unions with runaway shops.[33] Despite weakened unions, the clothing industry had the highest strike rate in Canada except for coal mining, as unions tried to revive standards of work even as the Depression worsened conditions.[34]

Cohen's work with the needle-trades unions was important; it covered strikes, drafting collective agreements, and improving labour-standards legislation. In 1927, for example, the ILGWU hired Cohen to draft a memo to the Minimum Wage Board of Ontario opposing proposed changes to regulations that would abolish any minimum wage during the first three months of a female employee's service. The board agreed to withdraw the proposed change.[35]

Flushed with success, Cohen suggested that the board look into the wages, hours, and seasonality of the clothing industry. With conditions deteriorating, the board had Cohen list twenty factories in the ladies' garment industry for it to investigate. Cohen then wrote to the union in New York, since he wanted 'to be close in touch with the investigation so I can influence their methods and avoid an unsatisfactory conclusion.' He asked the union for guidance. 'I seem to be in a position of having started something here which should be followed up and yet with the departure of Mr. Polakoff [an organizer] I will have practically no status' with the wage board.[36]

In his pursuit of better conditions in the needle trades, Cohen's strategy was to raise minimum standards but also to encourage trade unionism. Previously, he had urged James Watt of the Toronto Trades and Labour Council to deal seriously with the standards issue.[37] The council had long dealt with the wage board, which women complained was ineffective, but in the late 1920s it became more active and held a conference on problems in the needle trades, which Cohen attended. He assembled information on standards, an issue that would engage him for years.[38] He became an expert on Ontario's minimum-standards legislation, and he found companies and unions moderately receptive to reform since both sides wanted more orderly industrial relations.

At the same time, Cohen encouraged needle-trades workers to organize to increase their strength and political clout. In October 1929 Cohen wrote to ILGWU secretary-treasurer David Dubinsky in New York about the still largely unorganized Toronto labour market. Unions in the women's clothing industry were even weaker than in the men's garment sector. Dubinsky, like Cohen, was a secular eastern European Jewish immigrant who had played a critical role against the Communists during the 1920s in the union's civil war. In 1928 his side won, but, according to historian Irving Bernstein, 'at a stupendous cost in manpower and treasure.'[39] By 1929, Dubinsky was running the union because the new president was ailing, and in 1932, at age forty, he became president. Turning his union into one of the most powerful in North America, he supported democracy in industry, the New Deal, and industrial unionism. As a leader of an ethnically diverse union, he opposed discrimination. Though he fought communism effectively, he was flexible rather than doctrinaire and hired former Communists in the 1930s. His organization had a growing number of female members, but in 1929 it was in debt, membership was low, and industry conditions were deteriorating as work shifted to sweatshops, wages and hours were concealed, and piecework increased.

In these circumstances, Cohen told Dubinsky that Toronto conditions were 'deplorable.'[40] Because the workforce was primarily Jewish, Cohen thought that its homogeneity would facilitate organization, which he advocated. The successful reorganization of the New York district raised Toronto members' expectations. Faced with competition and its members' militancy, in 1929 the international union renewed organizing in Toronto.

Acting as the ILGWU's solicitor in 1930 in the Toronto general strike in the cloak shops, which involved 1,600 workers (400 of them women) in 66 firms, Cohen drafted clauses in negotiations before he received his first retainer of one hundred dollars. Workers responded to the union's strike call, and since larger manufacturers were interested in controlling their competitors – the small shops and contractors that kept wages and prices low – the environment was receptive. Cohen sent a memo to the dominion and Ontario departments of labour and to Toronto's mayor, with a view to 'paving the road to mediation' after the strike call. He adopted an informal tone, he told Dubinsky, for 'there is so little experience in official circles here with that sort of procedure that too formal a document would have the effect of putting them on guard.' He enclosed a draft agreement to L.M. Singer, the employers' lawyer, with an explanatory memo. Singer responded with a counter-draft agreement which the parties apparently signed.

The two-year collective agreement between sixty-eight employers in the Amalgamated Garment Manufacturers Council and the ILGWU introduced a forty-four-hour work week and a minimum wage and also increased wages. Earlier trade associations had tried to regulate production, distribution, trade practices, and labour relations, but the results had been less comprehensive. A joint-conference board was to administer the agreements, which Cohen hoped would make for future constructive relations.[41] Significantly, this dispute produced mechanisms and procedures for conduct in various sectors so that the garment industry could better regulate itself and reduce cut-throat competition as well as sweatshop conditions. These relationships would also facilitate administering minimum-standards legislation when the Industrial Standards Act was passed.

After the strike, Cohen informed Dubinsky of its success and shrewdly advised him that the new arrangements facilitated further organizing. As well, he praised Bernard Shane, an organizer from Chicago who worked with the Toronto Cloakmakers' Union and then, in 1934, moved to Montreal as manager of the union's joint board of locals to organize dressmakers' locals for the ILGWU.[42] Shane's 'energy and hopefulness,' Cohen wrote, 'never lagged for one moment and I attribute the result in a very emphatic measure to his own persistence.' Such praise was typical of Cohen. He genuinely admired the trade unionists with whom he worked, and just as they deferred to him on matters in which he was an expert, he respected their competence and democratic procedures and was careful to consult them or await their instructions. When they asked him for advice, he was an idea man and a strategist as much as a source of legal information. Cohen also spoke admiringly of Louis Fine, a friend who, as the government mediator, played an important role in the negotiations. 'His adroit manner captured them completely. Once the psychological contact was made, the rest was a matter of manoeuvring and bargaining.'[43] Fine would have a distinguished career as a mediator, industrial-standards commissioner, and conciliator, and in this early period he was honing his skills.

Cohen's own role was significant and went beyond legal advice. He wrote, 'During the last week of the strike particularly, my time was so completely absorbed that I was not able to be at my office for any more time than it required to draft the constant series of memoranda and agreements required during negotiations.' The conferences regularly lasted into the early morning hours, and this hectic pace embodied his life as a labour lawyer. Despite much responsibility, his charges were minimal, even by the standards of the day.

After 1930, there was a testing period. In 1931 an ILGWU 'general' strike among the shops on Toronto's Spadina Avenue failed because the union competed with the IUNTW (WUL) in the dressmaking end of the industry and because the Depression had begun to take its toll. Whether by chance, because Cohen was hired first by the ILGWU, or by choice, because he was irritated with the CLDL, in 1931 Cohen worked for the existing union leadership and not the oppositionists in the needle trades. In this instance and later in his career, even though Cohen was political and often sympathetic to the Communists, trade unionism for him took precedence over party politics.

Again, in 1933, an industry-wide strike resulted and in 1934 hundreds in the Toronto cloak and dress trades struck for one week. They included thirty-eight female non-Jewish dressmakers at Eaton's, recent ILGWU members, whose strike received widespread support from the community, partly because adverse publicity about the industry's low wages and sweated labour conditions had resulted from the 1934 hearings of the Royal Commission on Price Spreads, and also because Communist and CCF partisans were competing for working-class support. This strike revealed ethnic divisions between Jewish and non-Jewish needle-trades workers, but an agreement was reached.[44]

In 1935, as a familiar and trusted figure on both sides of the industry,

Cohen mediated and the Toronto Cloak Manufacturers' Association accepted new terms. Both sides wanted labour costs of production equalized among large and small producers and job classifications and quality standards of garments defined.[45] Thus, Depression conditions stimulated greater cooperation between the parties than in the past and created an environment that was conducive to both negotiated collective agreements and more extensive standards legislation. In 1935 the Ontario government passed the Industrial Standards Act, which covered male and female employees, unlike the women's Minimum Wage Act. Under this measure, the government could investigate an industry, call a conference of workers' and management representatives to agree on minimum standards in an industry, and nominate an advisory committee to administer these standards.

In the 1930s, opinions diverged over how to maintain standards, so the Ontario act was a political compromise. The public, influenced by Franklin Roosevelt's National Industrial Recovery Act (NIRA) codes in the United States, demanded government action to implement fair wage and fair price codes. Some businessmen hoped to eliminate unfair competition; some trade unionists wanted minimum wages enforced but feared that such standards might be interpreted as maximum rates. Other unionists worried that standards legislation would mean state competition with unions to improve conditions, which would retard union growth. They preferred government support for the union movement and recognition of workers' right to join unions of their choice. This, of course, was not the attitude of Hepburn's government. Quebec's Collective Agreements Extension Act of 1934 also influenced Queen's Park. It extended the terms of certain collective agreements to an entire industry so that 'unfair' employers could not undercut wages.[46]

Ontario's new legislation was ambiguous about whether it addressed 'fair wages' or 'minimum wages.' Arthur Roebuck, Ontario attorney general and minister of labour in 1934, appeared to favour the Quebec model. This approach relied on industries themselves to negotiate standards and relieved the government of having to develop independently a level of fair wages. The problem for the government was that it meant 'a quasi-official recognition of unions and collective bargaining,' which was a controversial issue that took a decade to resolve, with Cohen's help. Hepburn publicly objected to the CIO union movement from the United States, which began to attract Canadian workers. Thus, the original Industrial Standards Act of 1935 reflected several influences, and whatever standards emerged were set by the parties in an industry.[47]

The government also had to deal with low-wage industries (like textiles, for example) with little unionism but a wage problem.

The act's language and subsequent amendments in 1936 and 1937 spoke of employers and employees, not of unions. The parties, not the government, activated the legislation by petitioning the minister. In a different era, the legislation might have become moribund, but in the 1930s workers' pressure – often with Cohen's assistance – was used to raise minimum standards and also to press employers to deal with unions. Since the original intention of the legislation was unclear, its contradictions complicated its administration. Amendments engaged Cohen's attention in 1935 and 1936, but the act of 1937 remained essentially the same for the next twenty years, despite the changing climate of labour relations in Ontario.[48] Even before the legislation passed in 1935, Cohen examined it and recommended some changes which were implemented. The initial draft of the act contemplated several geographic zones with different rates, as in the Quebec legislation. Cohen favoured one minimum wage standard. He also pressed for a broad definition of employers, to include both small and unorganized companies and larger, unionized ones.[49]

After the legislation passed, the first schedule was negotiated with Cohen's assistance. Covering firms making women's coats and suits, it was later extended first to all women's clothing and then to men's and boy's clothing.[50] Legal minimum standards agreed on within the Toronto garment industry were imposed on the rest of the industry in the province. At the outset of this negotiation process, Cohen met the ILGWU and employees to work out their position. He had to educate them about the legislation's purpose and allay their fears about its effect on collective bargaining. The act, he explained, legally implemented an industry-wide arrangement agreed to by employer and employee groups and approved by the minister of labour – 'a minimum ... below which it would be illegal either to employ or be employed.' On the coexistence of minimum and higher rates, Cohen believed that 'a legal minimum' would not prejudice union standards in shops with collective agreements or the union's right to organize non-union shops. To ensure this, the first agreement stated that it covered *minimum* standards and acknowledged the rights of organized labour 'to strike for standards above the legalized minimum.' Once a minimum was decided, its enforcement machinery was independent and would not affect collective agreements, and 'the force of law' supported it.[51]

Cohen presented the employees' position to company lawyers. His relationship with management lawyer L.M. Singer involved hard bargaining and some sharp exchanges, because employers at first opposed any joint implementation of the legislation's provisions. Cohen applied pressure through Fine, the industrial-standards commissioner. He pointed out that Singer misconceived the legislation's objective, which Cohen saw not as 'a complete cureall for all industrial ills and maladjustments' but as protection for workers against undue exploitation. Once employers decided to participate, they promoted their own position. This bargaining process stimulated Cohen. He wrote to H. Langer, 'The day has really been altogether a very trying one, but quite satisfactory. I am now looking forward to the joy of the battle of tomorrow, and after that is over, I will complete this report.' But it was also stressful, time-consuming, and frustrating. He commented ruefully that 'the last week has been a considerable strain upon me and I am hoping that at some future time, clauses will be included in registered contracts for hours of work for the Union's lawyer. I will be very happy to agree upon a sixty-hour week spread over six and one-half days and nights.' Much of this sparring preceded the actual conference called for in the legislation.[52]

An additional complexity was that the standards legislation in Ontario and Quebec linked the two economies more than in the past. Often the union had treated the two markets separately for organizational purposes, but that arrangement could not continue with minimum standards. During negotiations, Cohen was continuously in touch with the union in Montreal; he studied the Quebec legislation in as much detail as he had earlier done the American NIRA codes, and solicited information from the joint committee of the Men's and Boy's Clothing Industry in Montreal.[53] Similar communications took place on the employer side. When the Ontario agreement was concluded, it went into effect simultaneously with the Quebec agreement. This approach introduced a precedent – 'that conditions prevailing in these two provinces as to wages, hours and similar matters must be identical.'[54] Cohen recommended that in future the union better coordinate action 'between these two markets.'

When a schedule of wages and hours for the cloak and suit industry was worked out, Cohen summarized its achievements and benefits. The agreement defined the work week as forty-four hours, and then forty hours as of January 1936; it set complex overtime provisions, which were not as good as those in collective agreements but which were enforceable in non-union shops; it defined the crafts, the employees, and employers (including jobbers, contractors, and the employer who also did his own work). The schedule covered all sectors – clothing for adults, 'juniors' and 'misses,' and children and infants, and all cloaks, coats, suits, and skirts, with a few agreed-upon qualifications.

Under the act, an advisory committee with equal representation from unions and employers monitored its implementation. Its duties and personnel, Cohen warned the union, should be distinct from any joint board operating under a collective agreement 'since the wage rates and other matters provided for in the two agreements are totally different ... There will be a natural tendency on the part of employers to regard this Industrial Standards agreement as being the basis upon which all matters are now to be considered and regulated,' but 'this must be clearly opposed' because the minimum rates did not replace union rates. Clear thinking upon this subject 'really determines the whole question of the use which will be made of the Industrial Standards agreement.'

This agreement began 'a new era' for the union, because from then on it not only represented workers in organized shops but also sat on joint bodies determining minimum rates for union and non-union workers. The legislation did not solve all problems, and Cohen advised the union to monitor the agreement closely. No wonder the union thanked him profusely, for he helped them make effective use of the standards legislation. Cohen was touched by their confidence and praised union personnel for their cooperation in accomplishing the complex task.[55]

Cohen worked with other needle-trades unions on their 'schedules,' which were reviewed annually under the Industrial Standards Act. He was at much of the millinery industry's conference, for example, which amounted to eighty days of continuous negotiating, and he represented the United Hatters' union in that industry's conference.[56] In the men's clothing industry, the procedures and results were similar to the ladies,' except that overtime provisions were calculated somewhat differently and there were two zones in the province of Ontario instead of one. In the women's industry, some tinkering went on after the schedule was concluded and usually was politically motivated, as in the case of girls' coats, where some producers hoped to avoid certain of the code's provisions, while other employers hoped to drive any manufacturers of girls' coats out of the business of making adult garments.[57] There were other negotiated adjustments but Cohen's skill with language often helped achieved consent.[58]

The 1935 round of discussions was the most important; for the first time it established procedures, defined the parties covered, and set goals and actual minimum standards. Because the government provided little money or staff to implement and administer the legislation, the industry itself paid many costs.[59] The problems in some meetings were detailed and complex, and not readily comprehensible to an outsider, but Cohen understood the industry thoroughly, knew the employers and unionists involved, and invariably was a reasonable and often conciliatory figure in what was sometimes a chaotic and excitable atmosphere.

His hard work and experience led him to defend publicly the standards legislation and process. In December 1935 he wrote a personal letter, not for publication, to Graham Spry, editor of the CCF paper the *New Commonwealth*, about an article entitled 'Industrial Standards Act of Little Use to Employees.' He told Spry that he was not an apologist for the government but his professional experience had shown him that the legislation's benefits were not properly understood. The paper's article was superficial, not constructive, and displayed 'a complete misunderstanding of the part which that legislation can play in trade union affairs.' It made a gratuitous reference to Fine, whom Cohen defended, and he made the telling point that articles in the paper often displayed 'a lamentable lack of familiarity' with problems that affected the labour movement. This weakness indicated 'that the C.C.F. approach is amateurish and academic.'[60]

Cohen also wrote an article criticizing several columns in *Saturday Night* by Dalton J. Little on the Industrial Standards Act. Informed criticism was valid, Cohen believed, but he objected to Little's superficial, inaccurate, and obviously prejudiced criticism, as well as his attempt to discredit the act without analysing its aims or the social problems it was intended to remedy. Little's series degenerated into an attack on union wages and a tirade against unions 'dictating' to business. Cohen concluded that Little did not oppose details of the act, as he had claimed, but any legislation that interfered with business. In Cohen's view, he should not 'under the guise of an objective survey ... indulge in irresponsible statements which amount to misrepresentations and ... substitute hearsay for research' in a national publication, when a serious, responsible discussion was required.[61]

The legislation was evolving in 1936.[62] When the government considered amendments, it approached Cohen, who told the minister, David Croll, that most changes were unnecessary.[63] When an amending bill was introduced, labour leaders, who were not consulted, hastily held a conference of the unions affected. With Cohen, they opposed the amendments and presented a brief to the minister. They threatened to withdraw cooperation because, they protested, the amendments substituted the minister in formulating schedules for the conferences of involved parties and transformed the legislation from a voluntary, permissive, and cooperative procedure to a coercive one in which, at the minister's discretion, a schedule could be arbitrarily imposed on an industry for an indefinite period rather than one year, as in the original act.

Cohen believed that the chief defects arose because the duties and powers of the advisory boards were not defined clearly, and because the act's administration was inadequate to ensure consistent enforcement of decisions. Rather than address these issues, the amendments reduced the role of the industry representatives to advisers, rather than decision makers. Labour supported schedules developed by agreement. The minister withdrew most amendments, conceding on points that affected the fundamental principles of the legislation, but maintained new appeal provisions, which related to the act's administration and were less serious. Cohen told a press conference, 'The whole proceeding was a demonstration of what could be accomplished by organized labour if properly organized and co-ordinated action is taken.'[64] He believed that 'the experience of the coming year' would provide the legislation's final format.

In 1936, when forty agreements covering sixty thousand workers existed, and sixty-three more were being discussed, Croll broadened the legislation's scope, increased inspections, provided for fair wages and hours in all government contracts, and increased fines for noncompliance. In a well-publicized study of the legislation, labour law professors Jacob Finkelman and Bora Laskin concluded that the act was beneficial. It allowed parties in many industries to discuss problems and find solutions; where schedules were adopted, the act had stabilized wages and 'eliminated the worst instances of exploitation;' the authors were uncertain whether it undercut or promoted unions. On the legislation itself they concluded that 'the original act was faulty; the amending legislation leaves much to be desired, but a beginning has been made in a development, the importance of which cannot be overestimated.'[65]

In 1937 leading Ontario civil servants discussed the new Industrial Standards Act amendments with Cohen. Ontario reorganized its Department of Labour to improve its administration of the act in response to a Privy Council decision which threw out minimum-wage legislation at the federal level and shifted the burden to the provinces. Ontario established an Industry and Labour Board to replace the Minimum Wage Board, which meant that minimum-wage legislation now covered men as well as women. The new tribunal of three government appointees was not necessarily tripartite, and labour protested its make-up.[66]

Cohen's work with the needle-trades unions included assisting them in annual talks to revise standards schedules and bargaining for collective agreements. After 1937, he continued this work, but as the unions gained collective-bargaining experience and became comfortable working on standards advisory committees, Cohen's role became more strictly legal than in the 1934–7 period, when he had provided leadership, strategy, and guidance. The needle trades' experience with standards legislation became a model for less organized industries such as textiles.

A GENDERED WORKFORCE

Needle-trades unions continued organizing in the late 1930s, and the relationship between the 'parties' and the administrators of Ontario standards boards helped to rid the industry of its worst abuses.[67] But neither development – minimum standards nor collective bargaining – eliminated inequities based on gender. Piecework, for example, became institutionalized, and 'all that was left to argue about was the price per piece and the question of who had the right to determine it.'[68] As Mercedes Steedman has pointed out, the issues and the process itself reflected the patriarchal context of the talks as much as the conflicts between labour and management.[69]

The sexual division of labour in the needle trades became formalized, segregating jobs, skills, and wage levels by sex. Recently, historians have sought to explain these gender issues, but in Cohen's time the subordination of feminism to both class and ethnic issues not only 'inhibited the development of feminist perspectives' among women workers, who sometimes were both active trade unionists and socialists, but also left unchallenged the gendered division of labour and the discriminatory wage structures in both union and non-union garment factories.[70]

Gender and skill were intricately related, and 'the notion of skill in the clothing industry often had less to do with the job itself than with the sex and the bargaining position of the worker in the production process.' Thus, clothing industry traditions perpetuated female subordination. Cutters were skilled, the highest-paid workers, and men. Work on men's clothing was considered more skilled than dressmaking, which was 'an almost entirely female occupation' and was viewed as 'light' unskilled work.[71] Men worked more frequently on coats, and women sewed vests, trousers, and skirts. The male positions were paid at an hourly rate, whereas females received piece-rates, which employers adjusted arbitrarily. The result was that women 'were systematically confined to the lower-paying jobs.' When employers challenged skill levels or standards to cut costs at the expense of their workers, unions, placed on the defensive, defended these traditions.

Unequal pay for equal work was a problem. In Toronto in 1936, the average female worker earned 53 per cent of the average male's pay.[72] Women were paid as unskilled, temporary labour, even when that was not the case. The implicit rationale was social and cultural – that men were the primary breadwinners – and women's subordination was based on the prevailing belief in the patriarchal family, where women's 'proper sphere' was in the home; in the labour force, they were secondary earners. This notion of a 'family economy' justified cheap female homeworkers, whose existence depressed the pay rates of women factory workers. For men, 'no comparable group served to depress their wages.'[73] Such practices perpetuated female subordination in contract shops and in the unions.

Cohen felt uncomfortable with unequal rates and in the most egregious cases did something about it. Shortly after the first standards schedule was negotiated in 1935, the union's Toronto and Montreal sections disagreed over the rate for female operators. The debate was resolved when Toronto submitted to Montreal and agreed to a lower minimum for female operators, but Montreal agreed that the male/female differential should exclude female section operators, who were as capable as any skilled operator. Those women received the same minimum as men so long as they were as productive.[74] Cohen thereby acquiesced in some but not all unequal rates. He sought some fairness for women and wage parity between the cities. The solution also ensured that employers could not replace male section operators with lower paid females.

Cohen also injected the factor of productivity into the discussion, so that in certain jobs, if women produced as much as men, they would be paid the same. This productivity notion was different from the 'family economy' argument, because it treated employees as individuals in the labour market and offered more flexibility when rates were set and greater potential for equity. This notion would re-emerge in the war years, when Cohen used it as a lever for change with male peers who did not believe in equal pay for equal work.[75]

paternalism in the workplace

While employers exploited women as cheap labour, male union leaders spawned a 'male culture of the union hall' that excluded women.[76] This culture and its assumptions persisted both in collective bargaining sessions and in the minimum-standards conferences, where men in companies and in unions advised the male officials in government. Occasionally, when a female representative was present, she was ignored.[77] The paternalism created by this arrangement of the world's work was mostly unstated and difficult to overcome because it was based not only on economic conditions but also on ingrained social traditions and cultural beliefs.[78] Men were the privileged who made decisions; the exclusion of women in the process maintained men's favoured position in the industry. In exchange for such privileges, men took on responsibilities that also were not questioned. Precisely because many women were not in a position to support themselves, theoretically men were to do so.

cost of success

The prevailing male culture was the framework in which Cohen both excelled and faltered.These were the 'good years' in his career, when he could think, work, and rise to an influential and respected position in the legal profession, but at the same time, the stress, pressure of work, and responsibilities that he shouldered would begin to ruin his health. Cohen worked with men all the time – employers, union representatives, other lawyers, judges. The women he met were workers, clients, and secretaries. Occasionally he met a woman organizer, and his wife was a professional, but they were the exceptions. In Cohen's personal life, he had supported from age thirteen his mother, his brothers and sisters, and, in adult life, his wife and daughter.

Cohen's approach to standards, like that of his union clients, was based on class, because gender roles were not as yet questioned. He often referred to meetings with union representatives as talking with 'the boys.' While trade unionists understood class and ethnic issues, they seemed blind to gender. In this milieu, Cohen's intense efforts won both parties' admiration, as he manouevred for settlements, cajoled participants, and drafted agreements. He shared their understanding of the industry, but intellectually he believed in equal pay for equal work for women. Occasionally, Cohen suggested that female rates were no longer necessary under the new legislation but often was not listened to on this point. Sometimes he turned a blind eye to female inequality because his clients insisted and in the larger interest of achieving fair standards for all workers in an industry. He wanted to assist people during the Depression by eliminating the industry's worst abuses. Even when schedules were negotiated successfully, since women and men mostly did different jobs, female rates were less; some schedules listed different rates for men, for women, and for juveniles. Hence, traditions about gender and ideas about skill, which were often rationalizations justifying different rates, remained unchallenged, and the customs of the trades were retained.

For Cohen and male union leaders, the central issues were class and ethnicity, and the goal was unity of all workers in the union – male and female, Jewish and gentile. They believed that they represented all workers and gave special consideration to none, even though women's conditions differed from men's. Because the cutters and pressers had a strategic position in the labour process, they were the key to union success; they called the strikes and asked the women to join them.[79] Until the mid-1930s, when the ILGWU competed with the Communist-led IUNTW, which had involved women more, the union was slow to hire women organizers or develop special policies to recruit women members (even though special policies existed to attract non-Jewish workers). As Frager has found, the women themselves were conscious more of class than of gender, were focused on total family income as much as the men, and identified with the men as fellow workers and as Jews.[80]

The development of standards legislation and unions meant that unionization limited the exploitation of women and men, but women's subordinate status in the industry persisted and unions kept issues that particularly affected them – homework, contracting out, piecework – from being dealt with effectively. By 1939, 'trade unions had integrated women, limited the use of contractors and homemakers and improved the condition of work in the trade,'[81] but despite Cohen's efforts, the sexual division of labour was perpetuated.

THE TEXTILE AND RUBBER INDUSTRIES

Building on his experience with the needle-trades unions and the Industrial Standards Act, Cohen adopted a slightly different strategy in industries where workers' organization was weak. In the textile and rubber industries, he encouraged workers simultaneously to organize unions and to push for higher minimum standards, and he applied pressure by publicizing their terrible working conditions through proceedings of the Ontario Industry and Labour Board (OILB).

In 1936 textile workers in Cornwall struck Courtauld's (Canada), and in 1937 they followed suit at Canadian Cottons. Agreements with some concessions were signed but the union was not recognized. The strikes were significant because they validated the idea of industrial union-ism.[82] Afterwards, textile workers in Cornwall, Peterborough, and Toronto joined a new coordinating body – the National Textile Council, affiliated with the TLC – and sought to organize eighty thousand textile workers in Canada. Textile workers in Quebec Catholic unions and those afiliated to the ACCL were not included. Hence, fragmentation among unions persisted in textiles which inhibited unionizing.

Though the union did not win recognition in the 1936–7 textile strikes in Ontario, it obtained some non-monetary benefits and the OILB was to resolve wages and overtime issues in a long, drawn-out process that involved Cohen. The Toronto Needle Trades Council paid the legal fees for arrested strikers, and the Toronto Trades and Labour Council hired Cohen to act as a 'legal adviser.' He handled the court cases, and when Premier Hepburn intervened to mediate a settlement, Cohen partici-pated in high-level meetings at Queen's Park. He and the company law-yer, R.G. Kellock, drafted the agreement that Cohen read out and explained clause by clause to textile workers, who ratified it in a vote.[83]

The OILB then began a province-wide investigation of the textile industry in 1937. The industry was under pressure at the time, because the federal government had just established a royal commission (the Turgeon Commission) to examine it and evaluate the level of tariff pro-tection it received in light of its publicized deplorable conditions. At the Ontario hearings, Cohen was the workers' counsel, and he exhibited a detailed knowledge of the industry's tasks, wages and accident rates, its capitalization, trade patterns, the effects of tariff policy, and relations between the American parent companies and their Canadian offices. On wages, Cohen observed, 'It appears that the $15 wage for a fifty-four hour week predominates in the Cornwall Mills of Canadian Cottons. Workers should not be expected to maintain themselves on such wages.'[84] Drawing on his experience with standards legislation, Cohen pressed for higher standards. Since the OILB was to determine wages generally, not only in struck plants, he used the hearings to publicize conditions, to begin defining systematic job classifications, to upgrade wages, and to encourage unionization.

After this inquiry ended, in January 1938 Cohen spoke to the National Textile Council conference about the OILB minimum-wage order for the industry, announced several days earlier. One good feature was that it eliminated zoning and set one minimum wage for adult women at

$12.50 per week. Since the OILB could not regulate all hours and wages, it established minimum rates. But, Cohen stressed, 'I have often felt that the minimum wage-earner is the unorganized wage-earner. It is now apparent that the workers must find their own solution to their own problem out of their own efforts.' Cohen encouraged his audience to use minimum-standards legislation, which provided a floor, to improve conditions further. Workers had to unionize and negotiate better conditions directly with employers 'to ... advance the organization work' and take action 'to obtain what the employers will not give.'[85] As always, his audience listened to Cohen with respect, attentiveness, and trust, and it praised his work during the OILB investigation.

Cohen was involved in a similar inquiry following strikes in Kitchener's rubber industry. In late 1937 Kaufman Rubber, a Canadian company owned by 'our friend Mr. A.R. Kaufman, the gentleman, whose socially minded birth control clinics were the subject of considerable court attention earlier in the year,' was struck for six weeks. Kaufman had refused terms reached with his competitors, Goodyear and B.F. Gooderich.[86] Cohen presented the ministry's settlement proposal to the employees, which called for a return to work at the old wage scale pending an investigation by the OILB.[87] With no wage gains, the Kaufman strike was a defeat for the union. When Kaufman had refused to deal with the union, he met the local union committee, J.L. Cohen, and a Department of Labour official. Cohen became the intermediary between the union and government mediators, and when Kaufman signed an agreement, it was because the union was excluded from the negotiating process.

The Ontario Industrial Standards Act empowered the OILB to inquire into the strike and the rubber industry generally. Cohen believed that the public inquiry would increase wages and 'stabilize the situation' and had advised the union that, if properly handled, it might give the union entry into plants where it had made little progress.[88] Cohen pursued his strategy of using the OILB to improve conditions and inform the public about the prevailing low standards. The hearings also facilitated informal contact between managements and trade unionists, with Cohen encouraging unions to organize more aggressively and pressing employers to deal with them.

The minister of labour thanked Cohen for 'his reasonable attitude' and assistance in settling the rubber dispute.[89] Cohen got about eighty police charges against strikers withdrawn through negotiations with the attorney general. In the end, the OILB decided not to deal with wages, so Cohen worked on overtime (which the company defined as after fifty-seven hours of work a week) and piece-rate problems.[90]

When the war broke out, Cohen offered his services in any capacity to the premier and inquired if any special war legislation would be introduced.[91] The province did not give him a wartime appointment, but Ottawa would do so in 1943, when Cohen was at his busiest and most productive both as a labour lawyer and as a policy adviser in labour relations.

Cohen was a socialist, appalled by the economic hardship in the Depression years and by the state's inadequate response, but his legal training enabled him to assist people in practical terms. In drafting legislation, he thought about major policy issues and advised the Ontario government on its responses to social problems. By 1939, he had worked with union clients, was well known and respected in labour-relations circles, and had profoundly influenced the administration of standards legislation.

Cohen's experience as counsel to the needle-trades unions in the 1930s was excellent training for his work with other labour organizations in the 1940s. His assistance in organizing drives and negotiations, in handling grievances and on conciliation cases, and in writing job classifications and pressing for uniform standards developed his skills and expertise in a familiar environment, among sympathetic colleagues in a union movement rooted in his own Jewish cultural milieu. In the late 1930s and during the war, workers in many industries faced much opposition in their campaign for union representation. In these circumstances, Cohen hit his stride as a labour lawyer, becoming an invaluable asset to unions, a fearless defender of their interests, the most prominent labour lawyer on the union side, and a leading adviser to the Canadian labour movement as a whole. In the war years, his preoccupation would be the achievement of collective-bargaining legislation and the development of strong, independent unions, and in 1943 he would help shape new labour policy.

PART TWO

Redesigning Labour Policy,
1936–1943

4

Labour Lawyer, 1936–1943

J.L. Cohen's emergence as the leading labour lawyer advising unions paralleled the growth from 1937 of the CIO (Congress of Industrial Organizations) industrial union movement in Canada. Cohen continued to represent old clients, but he gained new unions as well and assisted them in their formative years. Their congress – the Canadian Congress of Labour (CCL) – was founded in 1940, and it also provided him with work.

The organization of industrial unions in the mass-production and resource industries had been a dream of labour activists since the Knights of Labor movement in the late nineteenth century. The idea was kept alive in the twentieth century by the short-lived One Big Union (OBU), the ineffective All Canadian Congress of Labour founded in 1927, and the Communists' Workers Unity League set up in 1930 and disbanded in 1935 by order of the Comintern. These efforts were not successful, and all met with extreme employer opposition in the 1920s and 1930s. Periodically, brief organizing forays sprang up in the auto industry and other unorganized sectors, led by unskilled, sometimes immigrant workers, often stimulated by Communists. After the WUL disbanded itself, its experienced organizers worked among factory workers and restless unemployed both in industrial centres and in mining and logging communities.

The labour movement began to take off in the mid-1930s as Canadian workers became captivated by American workers' successful new CIO unions.[1] Fed up with low Depression wages, they, too, moved to create independent unions to represent their interests. This wave of industrial unionism, initiated in 1936 with the first sit-down strike at the Holmes foundry in Sarnia, accelerated when in 1937 the Canadian economy experienced a brief upturn. Ex-WUL organizers and young CCFers entered factories to organize the unorganized, and workers inside the plants began informally contacting each other. A workers' victory in the 1937 strike at General Motors in Oshawa encouraged other employees to organize, and subsequently, with the outbreak of war in 1939, the resistance of employers to unionization led to a further increase in industrial conflict.

J.L. Cohen was at the centre of this unrest. The issues involved in post-1939 strikes included union recognition, as in the Kirkland Lake strike of 1941–2; union security, as in the 1945 Ford strike; wage increases, as in the 1941 Peck strike; and wage controls, as in the 1943 steel strike and in the strike wave of 1946 that engulfed many industries. At first in 1936, employers and politicians nervously contemplated what might happen, but then many companies opposed employee intitiatives either directly or by sponsoring alternative employees' representation committees. The ensuing conflicts led to a new labour movement and a new system of industrial relations. Its framework recognized the right of workers to organize unions of their choice and to bargain collectively. J.L. Cohen influenced the legislative underpinning of that system and some of its administrative procedures.

Working-class Canadians were building a union movement in a hostile environment, and they urgently needed a good and experienced lawyer. In this industrial and political struggle, Cohen sided totally with the workers, both emotionally and practically. Committed and intense, he was engaged in almost every key dispute until 1945, counselling, sometimes guiding, and always defending his clients. He worked tirelessly, not only to develop his practice and build his reputation in the legal community, but most of all because he was deeply committed to the principle of collective bargaining in industry and to his belief that working people had a right to organize, to engage in politics, and to earn a decent living.

As soon as he became associated with the CIO movement, Cohen was labelled. In May 1937 Colonel George Drew, a leading conservative in Ontario, attacked CIO organizers in a radio speech as 'ruthless racketeers' and 'worthless parasites' and charged that J.L.Cohen 'was a communist.'[2] While such statements oversimplified the person they vilified, they contributed to Cohen's reputation as a radical lawyer, and the pub-

Equation of working class Cdns with union building

licity attracted union clients. His name even appeared in leaflets. In a 1940 dispute involving the National Union of Domestic and Industrial Workers (an ACCL affiliate), a pamphlet described Cohen as the man 'who has scored many recent gains for Canadian workers' and 'whose achievements on behalf of labour are recognized by everybody.'[3]

Space does not allow for a detailed chronicle of every case of Cohen's, but the events described here involved him in the development of labour legislation and revealed his personality. As legal counsel, he handled cases of discrimination, union recognition and certification, and picketing, and made court appearances arising from strikes and immigration issues. In addition, he advised union people at all levels and helped formulate policies. He assisted in negotiations and drafted collective agreements in which he inserted precise, lucid language. 'J.L.'s language was out of this world,' former UAW director George Burt remembered. 'I mean he was the expert. And his method of approach and his arguments were compelling.'[4] He handled grievances and educated local grievance-committee members. The Steelworkers' Organizing Committee (SWOC) hired him to write a book about evolving wartime labour policy, which was published in 1941. He assisted labour department officials in communicating with union members and generally was labour representative in labour-standards and conciliation proceedings. Thus his role was broader than is customary today for practitioners of employment law, and much of his work was groundbreaking.

Cohen was involved in the first, much publicized, sit-down strike in 1936, in Sarnia. The workers borrowed the sit-down tactic from the American CIO movement, which used it successfully. But in Sarnia, the workforce was divided, so while some, mainly immigrant workers stayed inside the plant, others – most of them born in Canada – raided the factory. The attack, conducted under the impassive gaze of a regional police force, which was unsympathetic to the strikers, ended the dispute. Cohen handled the resulting court cases for sixty-five strikers. When they came to trial in March 1937, one man was fined ten dollars and costs, while the others were released with suspended sentences. The judge noted condescendingly, 'I think you men are more foolish, stupid if you like, than you are criminal. I think that in doing what you did you were badly advised ... But you people who come from various parts of the world will have to learn to live according to our laws.'[5]

The union considered legal action against the raiders, since Cohen had documented proof that their action was pre-arranged with company personnel and with the knowledge of the police. Realizing that further repercussions against the strikers might result, and that Premier Hepburn's strongly expressed anti-union bias was receiving wide support in the province, Cohen instead made his evidence public to try to vindicate the strikers. Police had witnessed an attack on roving organizer Milton Montgomery, but they had not intervened when he was kidnapped. Montgomery could identify one abductor and the driver of the car used to convey him. Cohen prepared affidavits and wrote to the Amalgamated Association of Iron Steel and Tin Workers of North America, soon to merge with the CIO's SWOC, to apprise them of the situation. The Sarnia city council called for a public inquiry, but Cohen doubted there would be one. The day following the plant evacuation, Hepburn told the legislature emphatically that his sympathies were with those opposed to the strike, that sit-down strikes were illegal, and that he would fight the CIO in Ontario – a promise he kept.

Despite this defeat, Canadian workers were excited by the CIO movement. In February 1937 that movement won an important victory in a huge UAW sit-down strike at General Motors in Flint, Michigan. After the SWOC launched its campaign in the steel industry, CIO leader John L. Lewis and company president Myron Taylor announced in March 1937 an agreement between SWOC and U.S. Steel, 'the world's biggest industrial enterprise,' according to *Fortune* magazine. The signed contract created a sensation, because it recognized the union and granted a wage increase of ten cents an hour, an eight-hour day/forty-hour week, time and a half for overtime, the seniority principle, and a four-step grievance procedure with an appeal mechanism using an impartial umpire to settle disputes.[6] That year, Sidney Hillman, leader of the ACW union in the CIO, set up the Textile Workers Organizing Committee (TWOC) to organize the dispersed textile workers as employees in Akron Ohio, the 'rubber capital of America,' were sitting down in plants.

These conflicts, and others in the mining and maritime industries, resulted in a growing number of signed first agreements between large corporations and the new unions. As the CIO's success gained momentum, Canadian workers also organized and even Cohen received requests for organizational help. In June 1937, for example, Herb Grant asked Cohen if he could arrange for a UAW organizer to go to Chatham to organize International Harvester: 'We are very much in need of a union here. I don't think that it will be much of a job to put over a union in the shop, for ... the work-men are tired of overtime without time and a half. I read in the Detroit Times where J.L. Louis [sic], CIO, is getting ready to organize the I.H.C. plants in Chicago. I think that Canadian plants should be in on it too.'[7]

When the Oshawa auto workers at GM joined the UAW and struck for union recognition and wage increases, Cohen was off to Oshawa less than a month after completing the Sarnia-strike court cases. That two-week walkout at GM 'would change the direction of labour relations, give birth to industrial unionism, and push J.L. Cohen into the national spotlight as Canada's leading labour lawyer.'[8] Cohen's close association with the UAW lasted for many years.[9]

The strike was preceded by several short work stoppages after the company announced record profits in January 1937, implemented a wage cut the following month, and speeded up the production line. These actions precipitated the walkout of 250 skilled men in the body shop. Several Canadians contacted the UAW in Detroit for help, and in February, just after the Flint victory, organizer Hugh Thompson – 'slight, carefully groomed, and well-spoken ... [who] looked more like a clerk or a cleric than an experienced union organizer' – arrived in Oshawa. Within a month, he signed up nearly thirty-six hundred employees in the newly chartered Local 222 UAW affiliated to the CIO.[10] Charlie Millard was elected local president and George Burt treasurer, with stewards elected from each department as the negotiating committee.

Premier Hepburn had condemned the 'sitdowners' at Sarnia and during the Oshawa strike he charged that the CIO was foreign and communistic. While the company, for its part, was willing to talk to an employees committee, it adamantly refused to deal with the UAW, despite mediation attempts by Minister of Labour David Croll. On 8 April 1937, GM workers struck for collective bargaining through their elected representatives, company recognition of the UAW local, a grievance procedure, seniority provisions, a rest period, a forty-four-hour week, a wage increase with time-and-a-half pay for overtime, and no discrimination for union activity. A mass picket of four hundred surrounded the plant. During the auto strike, rubber workers in Kitchener in another CIO union, the United Rubber Workers of America (URWA), for whom Cohen also worked, walked out while others watched the unfolding drama at GM.

As soon as he was retained by Thompson as union counsel, Cohen set to work.[11] In early April, when Hepburn met Millard, he refused to talk to Thompson on the ground that he considered him an *outside* union representative. In consultation with Cohen, Millard sought another meeting. After communicating with the company, Hepburn invited Millard, Cohen, and GM management to his office, while a committee of workers and Thompson waited nearby. Cohen and the premier hammered out an agreement, sparred over the status of the union delegation, and agreed on wording to the effect that the committee represented the 'organized workers of General Motors of Canada.' Cohen received Hepburn's permission to call UAW president Homer Martin for his approval of the language. When further proposals were discussed, Millard and Cohen withdrew to review them with the others. Again they decided to phone Martin. But Hepburn then exploded about what he called 'remote control' negotiations and sent the union packing.

Cohen's role was valuable. Local union president Charlie Millard wrote to Martin that 'matters in Oshawa have considerably improved over the past week, due I feel in large part to the timely arrival and careful attention of Bro. J.L. Cohen. Bro. Cohen has very skilfully planned negotiations here in Oshawa to the point where I will be able, from now on to represent the negotiating committee and on behalf of the union be able to consult more freely with the management.'[12] Henceforth, Cohen would be 'damned often as the CIO mouthpiece' by a predominantly pro-management and anti-CIO press.[13]

The Oshawa strike was significant as the first large CIO dispute in Canada but also because Hepburn intervened aggressively in support of the company and against the CIO. He tried to break the strike by supporting the company's decision to move out parts and to hire non-union employees. He sent in the Ontario Provincial Police (OPP), put them on twenty-four-hour alert, and received Royal Canadian Mounted Police support from the dominion government. Hepburn considered the number of RCMP inadequate, so he organized his own special police force to supplement the OPP, which the press labelled 'Hepburn's Hussars.' He ordered the provincial Welfare Department to refuse relief to strikers' families, and fired two cabinet ministers, Arthur Roebuck and David Croll, who opposed his actions. The Department of Immigration was asked to prevent entry to CIO 'paid agitators,' but after investigating, it found no grounds for Thompson's deportation. Hepburn opposed the federal Department of Labour's offer to conciliate, and, acting as a mediator himself, he twice angrily broke off talks when he realized that the union remained part of the UAW. From his undercover agents, he knew that CIO organizing activity was increasing elsewhere in Ontario, and that the union had only verbal support from the UAW and so was vulnerable if the strike were prolonged.

Cohen's role became more prominent as pressure mounted. The men wanted to return to work, especially as non-union employees started a back-to-work movement. The union wanted an agreement, and, luckily for it, the company decided finally to resume production. It was Cohen who found a settlement formula that was acceptable to Hepburn. GM recognized the local union of Oshawa workers but not the UAW/CIO. The agreement was approved by both parties, signed in the premier's office, and ratified in a union membership vote, ending the fifteen-day strike. GM knew that its employees belonged to the UAW, but it ignored the connection. The auto workers won their other demands, but Hepburn claimed a victory because the UAW was not formally recognized. Millard and Cohen publicly declared, using Cohen's language, 'The agreement was so worded and the interpretation was so planned that there can be no doubt about the union's recognition.'[14] The workers reaffirmed their UAW connection at a public rally and their contract's expiry date was the same as the American agreement between GM and the UAW.

After the strike, union members thanked Cohen with a life membership in UAW locals 195 and 222.[15] Even though they were on opposing sides, Cohen won the premier's respect, for shortly after the strike he was made a king's counsel (KC), and in 1938 Hepburn hired him to draft a provincial unemployment-insurance act. It would be the first, but not the last, time Cohen worked as a 'hired gun' for Ontario's Liberal government.

As the first victory for Canadian workers in a CIO industrial union, the Oshawa strike inspired others to organize and sparked many union-recognition conflicts over the next few years. It stimulated membership in several unions in Oshawa and other communities. But until 1939, the Oshawa settlement was a model for corporations, whereby managements granted de facto recognition to a union, dealt with a local union committee, but withheld formal recognition. Often unions did not achieve the next stage of full recognition and legally enforced collective bargaining until the war years and only after a struggle.

The tasks that Cohen performed for the UAW in this early period he repeated for different unions. His assistance was invaluable, and his knowledge of the law and his mediating abilities were essential, as he influenced union policy and worked tirelessly with union committees. Increasingly, his practice was conducted at many levels – with union leaders and members, politicians and civil servants, lawyers and judges – as he established his place as Canada's pioneer and premier labour lawyer.

Between 1937 and 1939 in the auto industry, for example, when the UAW was emerging as a force in Oshawa, Windsor, and St Catharines, Cohen often negotiated for the union and signed contracts as the workers' representative. He tried to get the Oshawa formula – recognition of the local union but not the UAW – converted into full recognition, helped the union train shop stewards, and educated its elected negotiating and grievance committees. In 1938–9 for example, consultation between GM and the union's grievance committee became routine, and this process evolved into a mature company/union relationship.

Cohen's role was vital to the UAW and its new leaders leaned on him for the widest range of advice. A skilled negotiator himself, George Burt nevertheless remembered how much he learned from Cohen. 'I sat beside him and threw my two cents worth in,' he recalled, 'but I gained a lot of experience from just watching Cohen.' He used a blackboard during negotiations and was a habitual scribbler. 'He was a very friendly guy with the company but he wanted to dominate which isn't a bad thing in negotiations.' During the process, he would carefully draft eloquent contracts that protected workers. As Burt exclaimed, 'God, he was out of this world! He was an expert at drafting language' and even in today's contracts 'the seniority clauses still represent his draftsmanship.'[16]

In this work, Cohen perpetually rode the rails between Oshawa, Windsor, and St Catharines. In May 1938 he wrote to C.H. Millard, the Canadian UAW director, who was then in Detroit (international union headquarters): 'I will be in Detroit on Friday morning and it should be possible for us to deal with the Windsor situation on Friday night, St. Catharines on Saturday and finish up with Oshawa on Sunday.'[17] In providing advice, he also corresponded with UAW president Homer Martin and local leaders. Often, when union leaders were elsewhere, he proposed strategies for dealing with management to local union committees, something normally beyond the task of union counsel. He suggested policy priorities to trade unionists and counselled caution to frustrated and sometimes hot-headed members of the rank and-file. In performing such functions, he was careful not to interfere unless asked for advice and he never promised the membership anything unless directed to do so by the proper union authority. The men trusted him because he consistently respected internal union democratic procedures and the elected union leadership.[18]

Once collective agreements were concluded, Cohen became involved in the administration and interpretation of UAW contracts, and he worked with rank-and-file grievance committees in an instructional role. After the Oshawa strike, for example, he reviewed twenty-six individual complaints by GM employees and concluded that many were not legitimate. He wrote to Millard, 'Although I have asked the management for a report upon each case ... I explained to the committee at the same time privately, that they must be careful about dealing with such matters.' In April 1937 Cohen reported to Homer Martin about the educational work that would have to be done 'with a group of men as yet untrained in the trade union approach.' He found the union committee 'unprepared even for the mechanics involved in handling grievances. There had been no attempt ... to examine any questions prior to the sessions [with management] or to sift out undesireable [sic] cases.' Cohen explained the committee's functions to its members and suggested 'that they fix regular hours during the week for meetings ... at union headquarters, when grievances can be presented and discussed and the policy determined.'[19] In time, union members would learn to negotiate with the company and to administer collective agreements, but Cohen's assistance in the early stages was crucial.

In 1939 Cohen had cases that illuminated two important issues – signed collective agreements and protection from discrimination for union activity. SWOC hired him as counsel to General Steel Wares (GSW) employees in Toronto during negotiations with the company and a strike. In 1937 GSW developed a policy that lasted till 1939: 'The company is willing to bargain and discuss working conditions, etc., with any employee, or with any duly accredited Employee Committee representing our employees, *subject always to the principle that the right to work is not dependent upon membership or non-membership in any organization*, and subject always to the right of each and every employee to bargain freely in such a manner and through such employee representatives, if any, as he may choose.' The company believed that existing procedures and mutual trust were more beneficial than formal agreements, but its employees wanted collective bargaining and a signed contract.[20]

When the company insisted that the issue was whether the CIO should dictate company policy, four hundred workers struck for union recognition and improved conditions, while one hundred and fifty remained working. The six-day strike was supported by the Toronto Trades and Labour Council, whose secretary, J.W. Buckley, told the strikers that the conflict was not about the CIO but about their job conditions. Conciliator Louis Fine helped settle the dispute, told Cohen when the company was ready to talk, and after four days of meetings at the Department of Labour, the resulting agreement recognized the union and collective bargaining and granted grievance procedures, increased wages, and overtime rates.[21] This brief strike was significant because the company moved from opposition to collective bargaining in 1937 to, in 1939, a negotiated and signed collective agreement with the union, a change that reflected a trend, a new model for wartime agreements. Canadian workers, like their American counterparts, were on the move and their counsel, J.L. Cohen, was there to assist them.

A second case was not successful and involved a legislative issue. In August 1939 Parliament passed a new Criminal Code provision, section 502A, designed to protect workers against dismissal or other discriminatory treatment for trade-union activity. In November, Cohen wrote to dominion ministers Norman McLarty and Norman Rogers on behalf of Walter Camm, a gaugemaker and local union leader at John Inglis Company in Toronto, who was dismissed for union activity in what Cohen described as a 'gross act of discrimination against the IDI [Industrial Disputes Investigation] Act and the Criminal Code section.' When the majority supported a union, the firm announced that a company union, the Welfare Recreation Club, was starting up. Camm decided to run in the company union election; the firm first postponed the election rather than have him on the executive and then fired him.

Cohen at once sought government intervention, since Inglis was totally engaged on war contracts. McLarty responded that his Department of Labour was investigating, and if the company was guilty of an infraction, Ontario's attorney general would enforce the law. The company agreed to a meeting about Camm at which, Cohen advised McLarty, the company 'admitted quite definitely that there was no fault at all to be found with this man's workmanship or qualifications as a toolmaker,' with his conduct, or with his demeanour.

While the union maintained its pressure, Cohen and SWOC leader Silby Barrett met the minister of labour on Camm's behalf. Finally, Major Hahn, the company's senior executive, simply evaded the issue, telling the government that 'the best interests of the company' were served by this man's discharge. Since the firm gave no reason for his dismissal, Cohen insisted that its continued evasiveness as well as the circumstances corroborated the likelihood of an unfair and discriminatory discharge. He wrote, 'I have taken this matter up because personal contact with Camm impresses one so distinctly that something unfair has been done to him,' particularly given that he was blacklisted and could not get work elsewhere. After further delay, McLarty wrote to Millard that 'every effort has been made by myself and the officers of the Department to determine whether or not discrimination was exercised by the John Inglis Company,' that the president denied discrimination, and that his department had no authority to force the company to give a more adequate explanation.

In February 1940 Cohen signed off on the case, telling Silby Barrett that nothing further could be done. Millard responded by writing a furious article – 'Bren Gun Firm Flouting Labour's Bill of Rights' – for the CCF publication *New Commonwealth*. Here, he castigated John Inglis, with its profitable government munitions contracts, for deliberately ignoring the law that guaranteed workers the right to organize trade unions without intimidation or discrimination. On the company's application forms, employees were required to state past and present union membership, and when the union asked the Department of Labour to inquire into the questionnaire, the company responded that it was guarding against 'subversive influences.' Nonetheless, the union failed to get Camm reinstated, and the government, Millard charged bitterly, was virtually a partner in this unfair action. Union organizing at Inglis continued.[22]

Cohen concluded that workers needed more adequate legislative protection. His model was the American National Labor Relations Act (Wagner Act). In 1941, when Cohen wrote *Collective Bargaining in Canada*, he dismissed Canada's Criminal Code section as useless in protecting workers and demonstrated how its language rendered conviction 'practically, if not completely, impossible.'[23] By then he had had a number of frustrating cases of this kind, but only after unfair labour practices were spelled out in legislation and discharge 'without just cause' cases became fodder for arbitrators after the war did jurisprudence develop to protect unionized workers.

During the war, Cohen reached the peak of his influence and the range of his activities was impressive. Dedicated to the interests of working people, he consulted with governments about labour policy, ~~really~~ but until 1943 he expended most of his energy advising unions in organizing and strike situations. In 1940 Cohen acted for the Canadian Seamen's Union in its strike on the Great Lakes in which three hundred ships and five hundred men were idle, and he was also the union's nominee on the conciliation board. It was a significant strike in which the government interned union leader Pat Sullivan for sabotage against the war effort. Cohen would represent him before an appeal committee. On the conciliation board, Cohen sat with Mr Justice C.P. McTague, prior to their appointments in 1943 to the National War Labour Board.

Also in 1940, a year after the TLC expelled the Canadian CIO committee, the industrial unions created their own congress, thus duplicating the divisions between craft and industrial unions in the American labour movement. After negotiations, the ACCL merged with the Canadian CIO committee to form the Canadian Congress of Labour (CCL). Cohen knew ACCL leader A.R. Mosher well since he had acted for his union, the CBRE, and other ACCL affiliates and had handled the ACCL's legal problems in 1936 when its secretary, William Burford, tried to take over the congress before leaving to form the Canadian Federation of Labour (CFL). As we have seen, moreover, Cohen worked with C.H. Millard, leader of the CIO unions, during the 1937 Oshawa strike, when he was local union president. After that strike, Millard was elected Canadian director of the UAW for one term, but he was later defeated for re-election by Communists in the union who organized support for George Burt. Then, he was hired immediately by the CIO to continue organizing in Canada and was appointed a director of SWOC.[24]

While Cohen was immersed in internment cases concerning Jehovah's Witnesses, Mosher and Millard hired him to draft a memorandum that called for a founding convention of the new congress. Cohen then wrote the CCL's constitution and by-laws.[25] The new organization favoured industrial as opposed to craft unionism, welcomed members of both Canadian and international unions, and toned down the ACCL's nationalism. It adhered to Canadian autonomy on legislative and political issues, and as a result it would become a staunch supporter of the CCF (over the Communist minority's opposition in some affiliated unions), whose support would peak in the war years. The CCL assisted its affiliates to organize new members, and it became a forum for policy discussions among industrial unions.

For this early work for the CCL, Secretary-Treasurer Norman Dowd asked Cohen to reduce his fee, because the new congress had many expenses and little revenue. Such requests were characteristic of Cohen's practice. He usually agreed, for he knew that his services were essential, but once clients were on a sure financial footing he could be quite insistent on the prompt payment of his bills. Dowd astutely and prophetically commented, 'Apparently, you are going to have to do quite a lot of work for Congress unions in the near future and I need not add that, in our opinion, no one can do it more competently.'[26]

As the frequency of strikes increased in 1940 and 1941, Cohen defended many Canadian workers in cases brought forward by local police forces. For example, in the 1941 Weldrest strike in Toronto, the Canadian Hosiery Workers Union (CHWU) hired him to defend members including one, with the familiar name of John A. MacDonald, described as thirty-four, married, a knitter, a Presbyterian, and a Canadian, who was charged with assault by a police officer. Cohen got them off by arranging mediation between the Ontario Department of Labour and the parties in the dispute. He had trouble collecting his minimal fee of twenty-five dollars, because as union members joined the armed forces or moved to higher-paying jobs in the war industries, the CHWU had shrunk by July 1942 to three, relatively impoverished, locals. In such circumstances, the local's officer explained, 'I conduct the union business after I have finished my regular day work.' When Cohen learned of these reverses, he reduced his fee, which the conscientious official eventually paid, for, he assured Cohen, the union honoured its debts so long as it functioned.[27]

Collective bargaining became a major wartime issue partly because American workers already had protective legislation – the Wagner Act – but also because new unions needed such support in the face of employers' intense opposition. Despite labour's pressure, the dominion government delayed Canadian collective-bargaining legislation and instead used conciliation boards to try to resolve the many serious disputes. In June 1940 it did proclaim Order-in-Council PC 2685, a declaration of principles for the orderly conduct of wartime industrial relations, which stated that workers had the right to organize and bargain collectively and recommended that disputes be settled peacefully by negotiations and conciliation. But, because the order was entirely voluntary, it was ineffective. Engaged in war production, Ottawa recruited 'dollar-a-year' men from industry who were as anti-union as Minister of Munitions and Supply C.D. Howe, whom they assisted. Prime Minister Mackenzie King himself was ambivalent about collective bargaining because he feared that it would increase conflict, which he sought to avoid at all costs. Cohen's work as counsel to emerging unions and as their representative on conciliation boards gave him first-hand experience of the difficulties workers had with existing labour policy.

When unions applied for conciliation, they almost invariably nominated Cohen as their nominee. With his thorough knowledge of the law and his strong convictions, he greatly influenced other board members, which usually resulted in majority or unanimous conciliation reports, frequently drafted by Cohen. In other situations, he wrote his own minority report, hammering away at the issues of union recognition and collective bargaining. In June 1941, the same month that Cohen represented interned United Electrical Workers' (UEW) leader C.S. Jackson, Cohen completed a minority report for a conciliation board in the National Steel Car Corporation (NASCO) dispute in Hamilton, a dispute that had gained national attention. That conflict demonstrated polarized labour relations and made clear that the employer's anti-union strategy had government support.

The majority report of the NASCO conciliation board concluded in April that the parties should try to solve their own problems, but it recommended a plant-wide representation vote and reinstatement of discharged union president George Tanner. When the company refused to implement the recommendations, the workers struck in what became the first significant test of industrial unionism in Hamilton.[28] Immediately, the government appointed a controller, Ernest Brunning, a dollar-a-year man, to implement the conciliation board's suggestions. The minister asked Cohen to inform the union 'of the terms of the appointment of the Controller and of the relationship between that appointment and the functions of the Board of Conciliation.' On Cohen's assurance that a vote would be taken and Tanner would be reinstated, the employees returned to work. Tanner was rehired, and a vote on 8 May overwhelmingly favoured union representation. Instead of meeting with the union, the controller, acting on advice from C.D. Howe (which was unusual), told the board, which had briefly reconvened, that he did not intend to negotiate with the union. This was 'to the surprise, I would be inclined to suggest, of everybody,' Cohen wrote to labour minister Norman McLarty.

Brunning contended that union recognition could not be dealt with 'in view of the fact that the plant is being operated by a Controller appointed by the Government.' Cohen was outraged because such a position was 'contrary to established and accepted principles of collective bargaining and to the declared policy of the Dominion government. It is in clear conflict with the assurances given to the men and utterly inconsistent with the company Controller's concurrence in the plant vote.' The conciliation board thought it was an impossible situation and adjourned. As Cohen told the minister, the board had given the controller time to exercise responsibility, but for him 'to abdicate in favour of government opinion' was contrary 'to the mandate by which any tribunal is constituted' and to political and public policy which stressed democracy over bureaucracy.[29] The controller, as a company officer, was not simply to act on the instructions of the minister of munitions and supply, and nothing prevented him from dealing with union recognition, as the conciliation board recommended, particularly after the vote had been taken.

The controller did not negotiate with the union but instead met individual employees about their grievances. He helped establish an employees' committee, which met with him and considered *his* proposals regarding changes to hours and wages, changes that he then implemented. Cohen fumed that the entire procedure was contrary to collective bargaining and to the government's statement of principles, PC 2685. It also created an embarrassing situation for the conciliation board and ignored Cohen's minority report for union recognition, a negotiated agreement, and reinstatement with back wages for workers discharged for union activity. A second strike was threatened, but no negotiations with the union took place until a new controller was appointed. He held talks with both the union and the employees' committee, and, despite the representation vote, the union did not become the exclusive bargaining agent until it was certified in September 1945.

The distinctive feature of this case was that the government had intervened to support the non-union representation committee over the union, even after a vote that clearly chose the latter. The situation disillusioned workers, was protested loudly by the labour movement, and demonstrated problems with existing labour policy. As Cohen wrote to McLarty, 'There appears to me to be something incongruous in the suggestion that a government-appointed Board should be required to inform a government-appointed Controller that the principles and policy of an order-in-council [PC 2685] enacted at the behest of the government appointing both the Board and the Controller should be observed and lived up to.'[30]

Though defeated at NASCO, the union salvaged something from the first test case of the wage policy early in 1941, after a strike at Peck Rolling Mills in Montreal. The wage rates there were well below those paid in basic steel plants, and the union argued (rather dubiously) that the intention of wage order PC 7440 was to introduce uniform wage scales across the country. The conciliation board's majority report concluded that no national wage level existed in the steel industry and that rates were to be determined on the basis of *local* conditions. By the low-wage standards in Montreal, the Peck rates were not 'depressed.' Cohen's minority report argued that comparisons with other producers were pertinent, for neither the cost of living in Montreal nor the company's ability to pay warranted such low rates. A narrow interpretation of the wage order could condemn such workers to depressed pay rates for the duration of the war.

It was the first shot in a campaign that Cohen waged relentlessly in the years ahead over what he saw as built-in inequities in the wage-control policy. The Peck strike was lost, but those employees received a wage increase when the dominion government amended minimum-wage legislation.[31] The steelworkers' union took its cue from Cohen's report and reaffirmed its determination to establish a higher uniform basic wage rate in the steel industry by challenging the existing wage structure. At a conference in Ottawa in December 1941, the union decided that the wage differential in plants in Sydney and Trenton, Nova Scotia, was unwarranted, and it set a national minimum standard of fifty-five cents per hour plus a full cost-of-living bonus, which amounted to a minimum income of $1,750 a year. This goal became the issue in the 1943 steel strike.[32]

Cohen served on another important conciliation board in the 1941–2 Kirkland Lake strike of gold miners, and he performed many roles in that climactic dispute over union recognition. Since 1936, Mine Mill (IUMMSW) had been organizing the profitable mining industry in northern Ontario. In 1939 it had enough members to try to negotiate a contract with a single company, the Teck-Hughes mine. When the owners refused to talk, Cohen advised the union to apply for conciliation. The board was established, with Cohen as the employees' representative, and its public hearings highlighted the disputed issues, gave the union de facto status, and put pressure on the company. The Teck-Hughes dispute was lost, but from that experience the union decided that pressure on *one* company was insufficient. So Mine Mill decided to organize all the Kirkland Lake mines into one local, Local 240, and seek a master agreement. It signed up over 90 per cent of the workforce in twelve mines, and when the mine operators refused to meet the union, the dramatic strike of 1941–2 resulted.[33]

Before the miners could strike legally, the dominion government sent in an Industrial Disputes Inquiry Commission (IDIC), which meant delay. The commission had been set up on 6 June 1941, under P.C. 4020, and its major function was to investigate disputes prior to conciliation, thereby introducing another step in the dispute-resolution process. The government thought the commission might improve communication between parties in disputes and expedite settlements. Cohen argued

[handwritten margin notes: "public uninformed → working public not a union public, hence this is not about all working people."]

that this result was possible theoretically, but that, since the IDIC could both delay and deny conciliation, it was unlikely to accelerate the already overburdened conciliation process. He went further and described the IDIC's intervention in the Kirkland Lake dispute as a device to impose a government-sanctioned company union. The IDIC's report, Cohen later wrote, was a complete renunciation of trade-union recognition and representation.[34] He dubbed its solution of an employees' committee in this polarized situation, where union recognition was the issue, 'the Kirkland Lake Formula.' This 'formula' – which Cohen condemned as political expediency and a non-solution – emerged in other disputes as well.

To a public uninformed about labour relations, the labour movement's insistence on union recognition and adamant rejection of in-plant employees' committees, which some employers were willing to concede, was confusing. In an incisive and all-encompassing definition that distinguished between the two vehicles of employee representation, Cohen crisply clarified the issue and labour's objection to 'company unionism.' In 1941 he wrote in his monograph, *Collective Bargaining in Canada*, commissioned and published by the SWOC:

The essential feature without which it cannot be said that collective bargaining exists, is the independence of the bargaining medium operating on behalf of the workers so that it meets on *equal* terms with the employers. Anything which destroys that independence violates the first essential of collective bargaining. Any form of employee recognition which destroys the independence of the bargaining medium, and which is acquiesced in by the workers, not on their own volition, but only because of the influence or control or dictate of the employer, is a *collective bargaining form which emanates from the company and not from the workers*. That form of arrangement, whatever the variation is therefore a form of company unionism.[35]

In defining the issue, Cohen articulated the democratic basis of the CIO industrial-union movement. He opposed the paternalistic approach of Mackenzie King and the Department of Labour, of which the IDIC and its 'formula' was representative. Some officials remained sympathetic to non-union representation plans in individual companies, and King, who had formulated the Rockefeller Plan to defeat a union in the Colorado coalfields in 1911, was known afterwards in labour circles as the 'father of company unionism.' But Cohen spoke for wartime-production workers joining independent unions in droves, who sought a vehicle *of their own* to press their wage demands, their grievances, their pursuit of job security, and their desire for equality or at least equal opportunities in wartime and post-war Canadian society.

Cohen's analysis of the IDIC was part of his overall critique of Canadian wartime labour policy. He researched his book extensively, began to write in July 1941, promised the 'report' for Millard by mid-August, and suggested details for its printing.[36] While writing, he expanded his American contacts. David J. McDonald, SWOC's international secretary-treasurer, wrote, 'I hope that the opportunity will soon present itself for you and me to discuss the growing problems of collective bargaining in the Dominion of Canada because of the war effort.' Cohen's book was meant to publicize the inadequacy of existing labour policy and assist the labour movement in lobbying Ottawa to change it. After the study was completed on schedule, for which SWOC paid him $750, Cohen sent a copy to Lee Pressman at the CIO, with the comment that since the volume's publication in September the situation had worsened with the proclamation of PC 7307, which introduced compulsory strike votes and further restricted the right to strike, and PC 8253, which froze wages at existing levels 'more completely and drastically' even than before.[37] Pressman thought highly of the study and asked Cohen to keep him informed about Canadian developments, since the information was helpful to the Americans.

The book received widespread publicity and was read by many, including the prime minister. The *University of Toronto Quarterly*, which published an annual survey of Canadian literature, sent Cohen a request for information that normally went to writers and academics, and he responded, '*Collective Bargaining in Canada*, published by SWOC, sold for 50 cents' – not the usual sort of submission to an academic journal. Such attention indicated that Cohen's reputation as the leading labour lawyer was growing. He himself paid attention to academic writing in his area of interest. In August 1941, for example, he wrote to congratulate Professor Harold Logan on his recent article about government control of labour relations, but he could not resist providing Logan with some corrections.[38]

The Kirkland Lake dispute demonstrated labour-policy problems because the miners went through each prescribed stage to get the mine operators to recognize their union and, when that failed, went on a legal strike. It afforded Cohen an opportunity to criticize the inadequate policy. In August, after the IDIC report, the minister finally appointed a conciliation board, with Cohen as the miners' representative. The union's brief – lengthy, well researched, and written with Cohen's assistance – impressed the board. The companies presented less ambitious briefs and then dramatically flouted the conciliation process by withdrawing from the hearings. Such action was unprecedented, but it did not help their case, for the board's report was supported by the employer's nominee and was *unanimous*. The situation demonstrated the inadequacy of the conciliation process to settle a dispute whose central issue – the right to collective bargaining and union recognition – was not resolvable by compromise.

The report was publicized widely in the press. Mine Mill president Reid Robinson wrote to Cohen that he could see his hand in it and unquestionably, Cohen, as much as the mine managers' arrogant strategy, greatly influenced it.[39] The board recommended that the employers recognize the union; it accepted Cohen's argument that the IDI act was an inappropriate mechanism to resolve collective-bargaining disputes and issued a clear challenge to the government to intervene to compel negotiations where a union had the support of a majority of the employees. Thus, it repudiated the IDIC's 'Kirkland Lake Formula.'

Cohen had worked at a ferocious pace between April and August 1941, handling, for example, cases for the UEW at General Electric's Lansdowne and Ward street plants, for SWOC at Acme Screw and Gear, and for the Packinghouse Workers' Organizing Committee (PWOC) at Campbell Soup Company, all in Toronto, at the same time as he was in the spotlight because of his involvement in the NASCO, Peck, and Kirkland Lake cases. By August 1941, he needed a break at home, but even there, as he wrote M.M. Maclean, 'I have been spending a week or so here but much the better part of the time has been taken up with work. However, I think it has relieved the strain a little bit.'[40]

Following release of the Kirkland Lake conciliation report, Cohen performed other functions at different stages in the dispute. In October 1941, he accompanied Tom McGuire, the union's international representative, to a CCL executive meeting. The situation in the north was heating up as the two men presented a report on organization. Cohen told them that the mine operators' overly confident approach to the conciliation board had backfired. Employer opposition to Local 240 was the essential issue in the dispute, and Cohen believed that collective bargaining was a policy of national importance. He urged the CCL to give the union financial support, which it did.

Cohen's commitment to the miners' union and to collective bargaining as the basis for a restructured, modernized industrial-relations system went beyond his role as union counsel. His was a political commitment, which he pursued with great energy. A week after the strike began in November 1941, he travelled to Kirkland Lake and wrote to Reid Robinson, 'It appeared to me that no concrete steps had been taken to gear into the whole issue the support of the labour movement generally and particularly the Congress of Labour membership in Canada, to say nothing of the sister locals and affiliated unions in the United States.'[41] It was necessary, he believed, to mobilize such support to win the strike. Cohen had taken a similar approach during the 1937 GM strike in Oshawa, when he called on many unions to organize a provincial conference to provide 'a united front against Hepburn,' a gathering that apparently the premier's informers also attended.[42] In the miners' dispute, it was Cohen who urged the union to organize along these lines, told them how to do it, and acted as a catalyst in getting them motivated. The result was a national conference in Kirkland Lake of congress affiliates which focused public attention on the collective-bargaining issue.

It was Cohen who envisaged the role of local Kirkland Lake committees, established all across the country, to organize mass support for the strike and to educate workers and the public on the union-recognition issue. He wrote, 'These committees will constitute the nucleus of a national apparatus which, both from the standpoint of money and securing organizational support, will enable complete co-ordination of activity.'[43] He was deeply engaged emotionally and intellectually by this dispute, and his organizational efforts focused attention on the strike, helped raise funds, and instructed workers about the primary issue in the conflict. In the end, it was not enough, and the strike was lost. Then Cohen and the union sought government assistance to try to prevent the companies' blacklist of people, but they were unsuccessful. Many union activists were not rehired, moved south to look for work, and often served as the nucleus in union drives in the booming war industries.

Besides assisting the union and the CCL in mobilizing support, Cohen had plenty of action on the ground. Some mining companies tried to operate during the strike, to limit picketing, and to undermine the union's legitimacy with false allegations of union-instigated violence. Hepburn's government supported the mine owners with a large force of OPP. The presence of the police, who arrived one week after the strike began and marched down the town's main street every morning, made matters worse in an already polarized situation. Cohen believed that the police made it difficult for union men to lay charges against strikebreakers while they actively encouraged strikebreakers to complain about strikers. Cohen handled the court cases, and Mine Mill organizer Bob Carlin remembered, 'We got an awful lot of them off because we had the best attorney in the country – J.L. Cohen.'[44] A few men were convicted, and served time in jail, but the cases were not serious (though tempers on both sides had flared) or bore any resemblance to the *Globe and Mail* reporters' fantasies in front-page stories about the strike.

Cohen also handled an immigration problem and a libel suit connected with the strike. In October 1941 President Reid Robinson was harassed and jailed by immigration authorities when he crossed the border to meet his Canadian members.[45] Other CIO organizers were stopped at the border frequently during the war, and in each case Cohen contacted the federal government to remind it of an agreement between Canada and the United States which permitted infrequent but necessary trips by union personnel. He would acquire new papers to facilitate border crossings without incident, but new cases kept cropping up. Cohen also dealt with officials to overcome other barriers to union work when he got permission for organizers, who had to travel constantly in their jobs, to maintain cars and receive gasoline at a time when rations were strict for the civilian population. During the Kirkland Lake strike, President Robinson was so vilified in the press that he decided to sue. Cohen thought that the case might succeed, but in April 1942 Robinson had second thoughts and, against Cohen's advice, dropped the suit. Cohen feared that the case, if dropped, would cause bad publicity and hurt the union.[46] At one stage, Teck Township council suggested settlement by arbitration. Cohen advised the local to respond positively, discussed the proposal with council, and confirmed that the union would accept an arbitrated solution. CCL president Mosher even consulted the local on behalf of the newly appointed minister of labour, Humphrey Mitchell, who had become involved. After the minister met with the mine operators, he changed the proposal (as a result of their pressure) and then denied doing so. Mosher felt compromised with a member union, and Cohen was outraged by the minister's duplicitous behaviour. He was at his arrogant best when he scorned Mitchell, an unpopular minister with labour.[47]

After the strike was lost, labour was concerned about the future and, frustrated with both levels of government, thought of seeking joint AFL and CIO assistance to work out some viable Canadian legislative program. As these congresses were competing organizations and American, the idea was a pipe dream but it reflected the Canadian labour movement's political weakness. The CCL asked for Cohen's advice, and he cautioned them to be wary so as not to jeopardize the CCL's independence. The initiative came to nothing.[48]

In February, just after the miners' defeat, auto workers at Ford in Windsor walked out. Local 200 at Ford was founded in 1940 as the economy approached full employment. Its organizers met secretly at first and then announced the union's existence, as thousands of Ford workers signed up.[49] The company vehemently opposed a union and started an employees' association. Under pressure, Ford allowed the government to conduct a secret ballot and agreed to abide by its result. In November 1941 the UAW won representation with more than two-thirds of the vote.[50] By January 1942, the company had recognized the union grudgingly and signed a collective agreement that was better than GM's, but this victory did not change the way Ford operated.

While the union saw Local 200's contract as a beginning, the employer viewed it as the ultimate concession, for management barely tolerated the UAW as something to be endured during the wartime emergency. Relations remained rocky as the union established a shop-steward system in the plant, which the company foremen disregarded as much as possible. Tensions grew and three brief work stoppages occurred in the war years – 'preliminary skirmishes' before the 1945 conflict over union security.[51]

In November 1942 the men walked out to protest the hiring of thirty-seven women to do clerical jobs previously performed by men but not at the same wages. Cohen recognized the complexity of the issue: the men had conflicted feelings about working with women; the union had an increasing number of female members, whose interests it needed to protect to retain their allegiance; the company had a policy not to pay equal wages to women; and government policy makers seemed uncertain about equal pay for women. He crafted a solution for the union that recognized equal rights for women in principle but ensured men's monopoly of plant jobs. He argued that the dispute was precipitated by the issue of equal pay for equal work for women, contended that members of organized labour 'welcome the entry of women into war industry in order to ensure the maximum mobilization of our productive forces,' and argued that the nation's interest required that 'no discrimination of any sort should be permitted or practiced against women employed in industry.' Equal pay for equal work had repeatedly been pronounced as a national wartime labour policy. The company, however, was flouting it, Cohen argued, by employing women at Ford at lower rates, thereby damaging 'the existing wage structure in the automotive industry,' and by applying to the Ontario Regional War Labour Board (ORWLB) for a ruling to permit lower rates for women. The board refused the company's application on the grounds that it could not concede to its request 'merely because they are women.'[52] Once the 'equal pay' principle was adhered to, the case was over. The practical question then concerned the women.

The union agreed to persuade workers to return to work on three conditions: that an arbitrator determine whether any of the thirty-seven women were performing work under the collective agreement, for if they were they would receive equal pay;[53] if the company hired more women, it would first consult the union; and negotiations for a new agreement would commence and the company would respond to the union's submissions of November 1942. In the resulting arbitration decision, Mr Justice C.P. McTague of the Ontario Appellate Court ruled in favour of the company because 'clerical work performed by men was incidental to other duties not required of women.' In other words, they were doing different jobs. As the union was adamant that any women hired to work in the plant should receive equal pay, and as the company had no intention of paying them the same rate, the issue was resolved by firing the women. Throughout the dispute, Cohen was 'occupied these days, evenings and late during the night continuously with sessions with the Negotiating Committee, government reps, and company reps, considering proposals and preparing counter-proposals. Constantly engaged during these days analysing and dealing with [the] situation and with various documents and memoranda concerning the same.'[54]

When the strike was settled by the arbitrator, Cohen prepared a memo for George Burt about the settlement to use in the press and in the union. A column in the UAW paper, Ford Facts, urged workers to be disciplined and not strike 'even in the face of provocation' by Ottawa. It criticized the Department of Labour for approving a policy of equal pay for equal work for women and then not implementing it consistently. The paper, which supported the Communist policy of 'no-strike pledges' in war industries, also credited the Local 200 leaders for limiting the strike and Cohen for his mediation abilities. It applauded the new contract for its improvements but also because it made 'men's rights more secure.' While the union consistently presented the issue as one of principle over the issue of equal pay for women partly because 'considerable women are now employed in plants under contract with us,' it was obvious that the men were protecting their standards and did not want women in the industry.

An editorial in the *Midland Free Press*, which was widely reprinted, took a jocular tone towards McTague's arbitration award, noting that the result was that the women had been fired and that the company and union agreed not to have women engaged in production work. Cohen prepared a union statement to the effect that the union supported the hiring of women in war industries to release men for military duty, but its tone was defensive.[55] The union did some educational work on the issue with its own stewards. Thus, as in the needle-trades industry, Cohen adhered to the principle of equal treatment of women in the workforce, but in specific situations with competing demands from the men affected, the results favoured male workers. This Ford case demonstrated the ambivalence felt by men in the government, the company, and the union when dealing with the new situation of women in 'men's jobs.' Intellectually Cohen was more favourable to women than most, but he was at the same time part of the prevailing male culture and subject to its pressures.

Later in April 1943, Ford management locked out workers, and two arbitration decisions resolved the disputes. Relations continued to worsen, and in April 1944 another work stoppage occurred after the company suspended several shop stewards and disagreements over grievance procedures escalated.[56] Cohen was heavily involved in the 1944 round of contract talks and drafted much of the agreement, which was accepted only after the parties resorted to binding arbitration by the ORWLB. This was a very unusual approach in the private sector and indicated how dysfunctional relations between the parties at Ford had become. This arbitration became a precedent when in 1945 Ottawa hired Mr Justice Ivan Rand to arbitrate the Ford strike over union security. Until 1945, the NWLB had imposed on the company some concessions to workers such as vacations with pay, but Ford consistently refused the union's demands for union security, medical insurance, pension plans, and veterans' seniority allowances.[57] The widening rift between the company and the UAW was reflected in a growing backlog of unsettled grievances.[58]

Cohen worked closely with the UAW in all these disputes. Increasingly, the union leaders did more negotiating while Cohen gradually narrowed his role to legal matters, but this trend had as much to do with Cohen's leadership, his educational and mediation work, and his role as a model in early negotiations as with the increased experience of the trade unionists. The most significant strike at Ford over union security occurred from September to December 1945, and while Cohen performed important work brainstorming with the union leadership and doing legal tasks, he was not at centre stage as he had been in Oshawa in 1937, and indeed he finished the case in November, before the strike ended. The union had matured and its more experienced leaders were less dependent on him.

Another wartime client was the UEW. In a case involving Taylor Electric in London in July 1942, for example, workers asked the UEW to help them organize. When the plant was 90 per cent unionized, it sought an interview with the manager, who 'virtually threw the organizer out of the office.' The union applied for conciliation after the firm promoted a company union by holding plant meetings and firing the local union president. An IDIC commissioner recommended his reinstatement with full back wages, but the company stalled. The firm's president secured a letter from the Department of Munitions and Supply (DMS), which ordered him to cancel munitions production temporarily, and on this basis he discharged forty employees, including all the union leaders. A conciliation board ordered the reinstatement of the twenty-two union people and a representation vote. Most union members had left to secure better jobs, and the vote was lost. With no protection for union employees, the company used intimidating tactics to destroy union support. An unusual aspect of this case was the apparent collusion between DMS and the company, for the temporary cancellation of a war order gave the manufacturer a weapon it used 'to reduce the majority position of the union in the shop by lay-offs and dismissals arising out of the cancellation of that order.' As soon as conciliation ended, war production resumed. Cohen wrote, 'I have yet to contact a situation, and as you know I have contacted very many, which is so replete with shocking examples of anti-labour, anti-social, anti-Government and anti-war bias.' He urged the union to expose such conduct, which it did at the NWLB inquiry later in the year.[59]

Between the 1937 Oshawa strike and his appointment to the NWLB in 1943, J.L. Cohen was involved in virtually every major industrial dispute except the 1943 steel strike. He was the foremost labour lawyer on the union side in Canada. In the Kirkland Lake dispute, perhaps more than any other, his strengths were evident, as was his rapport with trade unionists. He understood the aspirations of the 'new unionism,' its young leaders, and members at a time when politicians, public officials, and journalists were wary and hostile. As a result of their mutual respect, his clients turned to him as one of their own and included him in their organizational and political decisions.

As a result of his association with trade unionists and 'radicals,' he gained notoriety. In November 1943, for example, cabinet minister Brooke Claxton was approached by writer Morley Callaghan and Neil Morrison, director of talks for CBC, for advice on 'liberal' speakers for the radio series 'Of Things to Come' on post-war Canada. Claxton thought the program was biased in favour of the CCF, and he was particularly incensed that J.L. Cohen, whom the prime minister had by then fired from the NWLB, was on the list. He instructed the CBC to change the program, bar Cohen, and fire or control Callaghan and Morrison. The CBC followed Claxton's 'advice.' The episode did not reflect well on the broadcaster's independence, but it did indicate how Cohen was viewed in certain official circles.[60] Claxton's reaction to Cohen related to his position on the NWLB. Though his job on the board had been brief, it caused him to cease his labour law practice and focus his attention on board cases, administering existing labour law and reforming national labour policy.

5

Designing Ontario Labour Policy, 1942–1943

During the war, J.L. Cohen was an outspoken critic of the federal government's labour policy. He opposed in particular the use of the compulsory-conciliation process as a substitute for collective-bargaining legislation because it delayed strikes, most concerning the union's status in workplaces, and hurt organizing drives.[1] Sometimes the obligation for both parties to participate in the conciliation process pressed managements to recognize unions, if only informally. Cohen had sat on conciliation boards partly to achieve this end, but by 1942, after Kirkland Lake mine owners had flouted conciliation by walking out with impunity, that approach was not satisfactory. Conciliation was not a solution to union-recognition disputes which required a decision, not mediation, and without a 'certification' mechanism employees could not establish lasting relationships with employers. Hence, Cohen deplored the refusal of the King government to enact collective-bargaining legislation. But his 1942 contract in Ontario to draft new provincial legislation and his appointment to the National War Labour Board in 1943 allowed him to influence policy.

Both labour's legislative needs and a changing political scene affected Cohen's work. After the Kirkland Lake strike was lost, both labour congresses (the TLC and the CCL) actively supported new labour legislation, as did the CCF. The CCF's electoral gains in the York-South national by-election in 1942 and in the 1943 Ontario election, in which it came from nowhere to capture thirty-four seats, led to growing public support which in turn stimulated politicians to accommodate labour.[2] Simultaneous pressure in the political and industrial arenas resulted in collective-bargaining legislation, first in Ontario and then nationally, that was central to the modern industrial-relations system.[3]

In 1937 in Oshawa and in 1941 in Kirkland Lake, Premier Mitchell Hepburn had used police against strikers to try to drive 'the CIO' out of Ontario. He lost credibility with many working-class voters, and in May 1942, to recapture support, he spoke in favour of a collective-bargaining act.[4] In August, Labour Minister Peter Heenan announced to the CCL convention that the legislation would 'force those employers who are still living in the past to recognize their men, give them freedom of association and then bargain with them collectively.'[5] Against the desolate mood at that convention after the loss at Kirkland Lake, the effect of his announcement was electrifying.

Hepburn retired abruptly soon afterwards, but by then steps had been taken to implement the new policy. His successor, Gordon Conant, despite his own conservative views, secretly hired J.L. Cohen to draft the bill, an action indicating that Cohen was a respected expert, known to officials from his work on standards and unemployment insurance. Cohen accepted the assignment after discussing the government's view of the proposed act.[6] He received a copy of departmental solicitor J.C. Adams' draft bill (which made unions suable and favoured company unions) and the assistance of legislative counsel Eric Silk. Cohen set to work, with a signed agreement giving him complete independence. The government had made no commitments to labour or management interests about the bill; he could draft a 'new bill' or could cease work and collect his fees if his and the government's views were incompatible.[7] Also, the government was not obligated to use his drafts.

Cohen spent two months examining the constitutional issues, other provincial legislation, and Andrew Brewin's draft bill for the CCF. He studied different legal language, did many drafts, and spoke with Heenan and Conant. By 25 January, his bill was ready. The cabinet liked his draft but did not adopt it. Cohen revised it again, faced more impediments, became frustrated, quit, and submitted his bill of $7,500.

We know from his study *Collective Bargaining in Canada* that Cohen favoured compulsory collective bargaining similar to that provided in the U.S. Wagner Act. Such legislation made union recognition by an employer compulsory where a union had the support of a majority of employees; it protected the right to organize by proscribing certain unfair labour practices; and it established an independent administrative tribunal to enforce the legislation. Cohen believed that a labour board (a tripartite, quasi-judicial tribunal that blended legal and policy-making functions) was preferable to ministerial discretion, which was subject to political considerations, or a court, which was slow, too formal, and unpopular with labour. If a board was rejected, Cohen preferred a court to ministerial discretion.

Nevertheless, Peter Bruce contends that, in his legislative drafts, Cohen was more bound by the precedents of other provincial collective-bargaining laws and by limits on reform which politicians would accept 'than by adherence to a model of the Wagner Act.'[8] Historians have offered several versions of the Ontario Collective Bargaining Act's evolution and of Cohen's role.[9] Some suggest that he was more accommodating in 1942 than he had been in his book the previous year, because he supported the post-1941 CPC policy of no-strike pledges to further an all-out war effort and tried to persuade the government that the legislation would encourage industrial peace. His politics may have affected Cohen, but so did his experience. When he had drafted legislation for the Ontario government previously, he took a pragmatic approach at variance with his unemployment-insurance book, so it was the same pattern again. His commitment to new labour legislation was consistent, but his practicality in Ontario and later his aggressiveness with the federal government represented shifting strategies to achieve desirable policy.

None of Cohen's drafts called for a labour board, because Labour Minister Peter Heenan wanted to exercise discretion.[10] The minister would define bargaining units and make certification decisions, which a privative clause exempted from review by the courts. Magistrates' courts using the Summary Convictions Act procedures would hear unfair labour-practice cases, but unions had to seek 'consent to prosecute' from the minister. One draft had judges of the Supreme Court of Ontario acting as a labour 'court' in certification cases.[11]

When his drafts were rejected by the government as going too far, Cohen resigned. On 5 February 1943, the Globe and Mail broke the story that Heenan had hired Cohen, 'the CCL's best lawyer,' to draft Ontario's collective-bargaining legislation. Business interests were outraged and labour criticized the secrecy of the process.[12] Once the news story broke, Cohen in public minimized his role and indicated that he did not know which of his suggestions would be in the legislation.[13]

Criticism led Heenan to persuade the premier to appoint a select committee of the legislature to investigate labour unrest and collective bargaining, to satisfy labour and give employers some input. Hepburn's political promise had to be kept to achieve industrial peace and to give the Liberals a chance of re-election.[14] The premier wanted a bipartisan committee of Liberals and Conservatives (there were as yet no CCF MPPs). When the Conservatives refused to participate, in order, they claimed, to protest the Liberal's secret dealings with Cohen, Conant appointed more Liberals, including two from Hamilton, an industrial centre, which satisfied labour. In response to CCF gains, the Conservatives had endorsed collective-bargaining legislation in their '22 Point Platform.' But the absence of Tories on the committee and its open proceedings provided a public platform for the identical reforms advocated by unions and the CCF.[15]

The appointment of the committee's counsel was difficult since labour lawyers were few and identified with one side. Cohen was eliminated because of his strong labour ties and recent notoriety. John Aylesworth was rejected because he was associated with auto-industry employers. The premier chose W.H. Furlong, who was acceptable to both employers and unions. Heenan suggested a labour expert to advise the committee, and Professor Jacob Finkelman of the University of Toronto Law School, a labour-law teacher, agreed to serve. John Willes noted, 'It was Finkelman's introduction to the administrative side of labour relations legislation.'[16]

Before the hearings, Andrew Brewin drafted a 'Trade Union' bill for the CCF which the CCL publication *Canadian Unionist* published.[17] It was submitted to four hundred local unions, approved by a conference of TLC and CCL locals, and widely publicized. Cohen studied it, as would his colleagues on the NWLB. The CCF model bill banned company unions and provided for compulsory collective bargaining, certification of unions, and procedures to deal with unfair labour practices. Based on the Wagner Act, it included an administrative board to ensure speedy decisions and a strong privative clause to prevent judicial interference with board decisions or delays through appeals to the courts (judicial intervention in the United States had delayed the board's work and weakened its impact). Some important features – compulsory check-off of dues and no conciliation or grievance arbitration provisions – were not in the Ontario act or later in the federal order, P.C.1003.

Ontario's legislative committee met in a changing political climate that made what was politically possible closer to what labour wanted, and this environment would affect Cohen's actions. In the process, politicians reached a consensus about the legislation. Business and labour presented their positions to the Ontario committee, which were identical to their briefs to the federal NWLB inquiry, so the Ontario exercise was a rehearsal, soon to be repeated federally. The labour movement demonstrated solidarity and maintained political pressure as industrial conflict escalated; business opposed legislation and was less united. With opinion on labour relations polarized, feelings were heated at the committee hearings.[18]

The hearings were scheduled so that legislation could be introduced before the session adjourned. In March 1943 the committee sat for twelve days and heard ninety-two witnesses 'representing all sections ... and all interests in the province who felt that they might be affected by collective bargaining legislation.'[19] Cohen followed the proceedings closely and counselled unions appearing before the committee.

Peter Heenan presented proposals similar to Cohen's drafts at the first session and told the committee that 'the chief source of dispute' was collective bargaining.[20] With no mechanism for achieving union recognition, workers had to strike. Existing procedures were outdated. When the Department of Labour was called into a dispute, any settlement was only a 'gentleman's agreement,' because there was no enforcement machinery.

Industrial conflict and political manoeuvring drove the hearings process. Heenan reported eighty-three strikes in Ontario in 1942, involving 27,248 employees with 171,442 lost workdays, a substantial increase from the previous year.[21] Unrest in the plants preceded the strikes, and disputes continued to increase. In January and February 1943, fifty-two applications for conciliation boards involved 49,581 employees seeking collective bargaining. Federal conciliators had helped achieve some agreements but thirty-two cases were pending. In these disputes, Heenan stressed, 'there was nothing about wages or anything else but collective bargaining, the right of collective bargaining.' Joint applications by employers and employees for conciliation or representation votes, and some amicable settlements, were positive signs. But sometimes, when a vote was taken, an employer would circulate a petition to find out how the employees voted and they felt compelled to sign. So, the minister concluded, 'it is not all harmony.'[22]

Complex federal procedures delayed strikes in Ontario and built up frustration so that workers approached conciliation 'with a clenched fist.'[23] Heenan expressed doubt to legislative committee members, as Cohen had in his 1941 book, that the conciliation process promoted stability. A collective-bargaining act that settled disputes quickly, Heenan believed – correctly as it turned out – could prevent strikes. He wanted legislation that was suitable also for the post-war period, since the province would resume jurisdiction over labour relations, and decisions should not be subject to review in the courts, except possibly on points of law.

Unions and employers presented their positions. The CCL brief laid out labour's demands: the right of workers to organize and join unions of their choice; the principle of majority rule to determine the exclusive bargaining agency; the right to strike; signed collective agreements; a ban on company unions (that is, unions influenced by employers); compulsory recognition of unions that had majority support, and compulsory collective bargaining between unions in this position and employees. A.R. Mosher argued that collective-bargaining legislation would settle the union-recognition issue and reduce strikes.[24] Unions wanted unfair labour practices defined to prohibit employers' interference with workers' right to organize and to ban spies, blacklists, and strike-breaking agencies. American unions had achieved these goals, and Canadian labour had articulated the same demands before, as had Cohen in his *Collective Bargaining in Canada*. But, for the first time, labour policy was the focus of a government inquiry.

After the CCL president Mosher, Pat Conroy spoke, Jacob Finkelman remembered, for most of the afternoon without a note and he impressed the legislators.[25] Collective-bargaining legislation was necessary, but to institutionalize it there had to be a mechanism, which, Conroy argued, should be democratic procedure – a secret ballot to determine whether or not workers voluntarily wished a union to represent them. A union that had a 51 per cent majority became the exclusive bargaining agent. Taking a moderate, balanced, and somewhat apolitical tone, which contrasted with the hearings' atmosphere of a political pressure-cooker, Conroy said that denial of rights stimulated irresponsibility, and that employers who refused to recognize labour were showing 'as much or a greater degree of irresponsibility by not having a proper perspective of the ... function of an employer in industry, as an irresponsible labour leader in trying to resort to a strike without proper negotiations. It seems to me that the things go together.'[26] Labour insisted on its right to exist. He wanted employer-dominated unions banned on the democratic grounds that they were not independent and did not reflect employees' interests. He favoured a board to administer the legislation, and not the judiciary, in a system that was primarily administrative.[27]

On 9 March 1943 D.W. Lang and K. Kilbourn presented the employers' position in the Canadian Manufacturers' Association brief. They expressed satisfaction with the existing methods of conducting labour-management relations, which included, since the last war, an increase in firms with employee-representation plans – the management alternative to unions. In 1942 the CMA had passed a resolution that favoured extending such employer/employee cooperation 'to achieve maximum production and an all-out effort to win the war.'[28] It opposed the American system, which had led to litigation and turmoil over bargaining units (not mentioning that such action was employer-initiated), serious strikes, and interrupted war production. Their brief opposed representation votes, with their attendant canvassing and pre-election promises that new, inexperienced workers in war industries could not evaluate.[29] It acknowledged existing agreements between employers and craft unions of skilled workers, and John Aylesworth for the auto industry pointed out correctly that craft unions, which represented a minority of workers in many industries, would be disadvantaged by the proposed certification procedures which favoured industrial unions. The CMA estimated that only 15 to 18 per cent of Ontario's workers were unionized, a figure disputed by the Steelworkers' lawyer, Andrew Brewin, who believed the rate was 25 per cent and would be higher but for employers' strong opposition.[30]

Instead of compulsory recognition, the CMA favoured the British model of voluntarism, where collective bargaining was left to the parties. Business wanted unions to be incorporated so they could be sued; and they similarly wanted unions to be required to register with the labour department and to file their constitutions, by-laws, and financial returns so they would be legally accountable for the enforcement of contracts. Any wording involving discrimination, they maintained, should be applied to employers and unions alike. Bora Laskin, representing the Amalgamated Clothing Workers, pointed out that, though unions were legal organizations, they opposed incorporation for fear that employers would involve them in expensive legal proceedings which would undermine their representation role.

The CMA brief to the select committee favoured company unions on the grounds that an employer should be able to influence the type of union in his workplace. It opposed the closed shop in favour of the open shop; it rejected the check-off of union dues. In general, employers favoured a free-market economy in which they could act as they wished and workers would remain largely unprotected. In addition, since employers realized that some legislation would be recommended, they argued that business should help determine its content along the lines they suggested.[31] In contrast, advocates of a new labour policy, like Cohen, favoured state involvement to establish ground rules in labour relations with enforcement mechanisms, because employees alone could not always get a reluctant employer to deal with them and they had no recourse if fired. Finkelman noted the many cases where employers refused to bargain, which was a problem that could not be solved without legislation.[32] All wartime labour-relations issues that Cohen addressed repeatedly in strikes and on conciliation boards were discussed at the proceedings.

On 2 April 1943 the bill was introduced and immediately aroused vehement opposition from employers. During its second reading, fifty-four 'of the most powerful and influential manufacturers of Hamilton' addressed a letter to every MPP opposing the act, which would mean 'a complete disruption of the existing economic balance of power.'[33] Nevertheless, on 14 April 1943, the Ontario Collective Bargaining Act passed easily, with support from all parties. It was 'the first attempt in Canada to enforce on employers in positive terms a duty to bargain collectively' and it indicated that Canadian legislators were moving towards the concept of 'administrative law.'[34] Business interests that normally had considerable influence on legislative change were, in this case, ineffective in their opposition. Vehement though this opposition was, it was thwarted by the pressure of the electorate.

Similar in many respects to the U.S. Wagner Act, the Ontario Collective Bargaining Act was distinctive in that it provided for a labour court, instead of a board, to administer the act. The Ontario Labour Court was to be a separate division of the Supreme Court of Ontario and was 'the first administrative body in Canada to be charged with the enforcement of collective bargaining.'[35] The judges, who were not specialists in labour law, would take turns in this court, which was given wide powers to handle recognition disputes or any matter arising out of a collective-bargaining relationship.[36] The act was an advance over earlier provincial legislation because it included an enforcement mechanism and, to preclude judicial intervention, a strong privative clause. The labour court – not the regular courts – was to make law and policy, and in this sense it was specialized, though the judges themselves were not experts.

Those who favoured a labour board criticized it. Cohen had introduced such a concept in only one of his drafts, which is probably where the idea came from. The court could establish rules to simplify procedures and create an informal atmosphere, but, as it turned out, it

In early days Cohen
favoured the Court
idea

Designing Ontario Labour Policy, 1942–1943   117

retained the familiar, formal court procedures and traditional rules of
evidence, and legal counsel had to represent the parties on both sides,
which galled labour. The CCF and the labour movement supported the
legislation but disliked the court's formality. According to Finkelman,
the judges were not enthusiastic about the court idea either, because
they worried that the act would subject the judiciary to too much publicity and criticism from partisans on both sides of labour disputes.
Andrew Brewin believed that the government, faced with employers'
hostility, had opted for this idea to 'exploit the prestige of the court to
mollify opponents of collective bargaining.'[37] After the act was implemented, the judges sometimes were rattled when workers at the hearings broke into applause or boos, depending on the cases' results. The
CCF, the labour movement, and Cohen continued to press for a board,
but despite the controversy, the labour court became the 'first attempt
by a provincial government to introduce a legal procedure to deal with
what had often previously been a disruptive power struggle between
employers and unions for bargaining rights.'[38] As it turned out, the
Labour Court would last less than a year, being superseded in October
1944 by a labour board under P.C. 1003.

The Ontario Liberals enacted the statute to improve both labour-
management relations and their political fortunes. The legislation took
effect in June, which was too little and too late to prevent their crushing
defeat in August 1943. The provincial election resulted in a minority
Conservative government and the CCF as Official Opposition. Apparently George Drew's Conservatives presented a credible alternative to
the Liberal Party, which had flip-flopped on labour issues between 1937,
when Hepburn campaigned against the CIO, and 1943, when the Liberals piloted the new labour bill through the legislature. The CCF, captur-
ing most labour votes as a result of extensive organizational work by the
industrial unions, and went from zero representation to thirty-four
seats. Twelve trade unionists were among its members, including leaders like Charlie Millard and Bob Carlin, whose election was unprecedented in Ontario's history. The election results indicated not only
greater support for the CCF and the effectiveness of labour/CCF cooperation but also extensive discontent about labour policy, which had
been an issue in the contest. The new labour legislation, the political situation surrounding its enactment, and continued high levels of industrial unrest all contributed to the Liberal defeat and the great increase in
CCF support. Cohen, for his part, realized that combined CCF/CCL
pressure had influenced the content of the Ontario Collective Bargaining

but the Tories, who
had boycotted the committee,
won the minority.

Act, which was an advance over his own legislative drafts for the Liberals and was closer to the legislative proposals in his 1941 book.

Despite its imperfections, the Ontario Labour Court ended recognition strikes. In the brief period it operated, J.L. Cohen presented thirty cases before it, all of which involved certification.[39] In its first six months, it received one hundred and thirty certification applications affecting about eighty thousand persons.[40] The predominance of certification cases indicated the large numbers of workers joining unions. The Labour Court began to develop its procedures. It determined, for example, whether or not a union had majority support by examining membership cards against employers' records, and most often the court registrar, Jacob Finkelman, administered a representation vote even when there was no intervenor. In cases where a union and an employee association competed for certification, the court ordered a vote. In a few cases, it simply listened to evidence and counted the union cards submitted – an approach used often by later boards.

The Labour Court frequently certified employees' associations that it considered 'independent,' even if unions viewed them as employer-dominated. In general, it failed to deal effectively with the company-union issue because the definition of such organizations was left vague. This was an area where employer pressure had some effect.[41] It was difficult to prove employer intervention, so managers who deliberately set up or influenced employees committees to defeat unions sometimes could do so with impunity.

Between July 1943 and October 1944, Cohen represented various unions that reflected the range of his practice during the war.[42] Unions sometimes competed with employees' associations for certification, so in twenty cases Cohen represented the applicant union, and in ten cases his client was the intervenor in an employees' committee's application. Three cases were withdrawn, two without explanation, but presumably because Cohen decided the union did not have enough support. One case was delayed because by the change over from the labour court to the labour board. Altogether, Cohen won fifteen certification cases and lost eleven to employees' associations.[43]

In these early cases, the Labour Court made decisions that contributed to developing a new jurisprudence in labour relations. In October 1943 Cohen represented the UAW, which was certified at Massey-Harris Company in Toronto and Brantford. In a secret ballot, the union won handily over the industrial council. The court concluded that the old employees' council, founded in 1919 and revived to compete with the union, was not independent and hence not certifiable. In this historic changeover, the union replaced an industrial council, which had negotiated agreements with the employer intermittently for twenty-four years.

Unions were expected to approach the court with considerable membership support, for in November 1943, after the UEW sought certification at York Arsenals in two applications, the court dismissed the case as 'frivolous and vexatious' because the union could not prove that it represented a clear majority. In January 1944, when Local 240 UAW, at Ford Motor Company in Windsor, won a majority in the representation vote, the court denied the certification application because the intervener – the Formocan Employees Association – proved to its satisfaction that 'electioneering' had taken place and that the union had used propaganda to 'coerce' votes. Thus, the parties were alerted about the boundaries of behaviour preceding and during a vote. In March 1944 the Lakeshore Workman's Council in Kirkland Lake applied for certification at Lakeshore Mines, and Cohen, representing Local 240 Mine Mill, was the intervener. The case involved two votes, both easily won by the union; the second was made necessary because the electioneering issue was raised again, but this time the judge ordered the union certified.

Another case was interesting because Cohen aroused the ire of Judge Wilfrid Daniel Roach. Prior to the certification application, the applicant – an employees' association at Donnell and Mudge – had bargained a cost-of-living agreement and a vacation-pay clause that were being reviewed by the Ontario Regional War Labour Board. Cohen wrote directly to that board requesting it to deny the implementation of the two awards until after the vote. Judge Roach was furious about Cohen's intervention, demanded that he retract his letter, and ordered a new date for the vote, which Cohen's client, the Fur Workers' Union, won.

Cohen was kept busy with miners' cases because they continued to struggle for union representation after the Kirkland Lake strike, but the mine operators set up employer-dominated industrial councils to thwart them. In May 1944 Local 240 Mine Mill, as an intervenor, lost at Wright Hargreaves Mines following a secret ballot, and the employees' council was certified. Altogether, Cohen represented that local in eight certification applications in 1943–4, in which five awards went to local councils and three to the union. The union was making a slow comeback, but it had to fight all the way and would not win until 1945.[44]

That same month, Cohen presented the UEW's application at Canadian Westinghouse against the Employees Independent Union, which intervened over two issues: the scope of the bargaining unit, since the application covered both the Toronto and Hamilton plants, and the jurisdiction of the Labour Court. The court dismissed the first issue. The firm then got an injunction and took its case to the Supreme Court, where it argued that the Labour Court had no jurisdiction to order a vote in a munitions company because such businesses were not covered by the Ontario Collective Bargaining Act. The Supreme Court dismissed the injunction and the Labour Court's registrar ordered the vote, which favoured the union.[45] Cohen's cases before the Labour Court often reflected inter-union fights for representation and demonstrated that local plant councils – an intermediate and not necessarily independent form of employee representation – remained active players at this stage.

It was perhaps too early for the Labour Court to be setting important legal precedents or developing meaningful jurisprudence, but it did gain experience in defining bargaining units, union jurisdiction, and procedures (both union membership cards and votes), to determine representation. It decided the basis for run-off votes, and despite employers' opposition, it determined that majority representation amounted to a majority of those voting rather than a majority of those eligible to vote. In many instances, its decisions took account of Cohen's cases and his input.

Cohen's role in the Labour Court was that of an aggressive advocate on behalf of workers and their unions. He appeared on the union side more than any other lawyer. He consistently sought employee representation in independent unions, despite employer resistance. In appearances before the court, Cohen was sharp, intelligent, and knowledgeable about unions, health, safety, and wage issues, and, in some cases, even the company's situation. He occasionally got entangled in the interplay between dominion regulatory intervention and the workings of the Ontario Labour Court, but Cohen was always professional, a stickler for proper procedures, clear and forthright with all parties. His tenacity, aggressive pressure for decisions, and occasional unsolicited advice about which procedures to follow often irritated the judges and opposing lawyers. Bob Carlin remembered that what he described as the Toronto legal establishment did not like Cohen because he was outspoken, criticized government labour policy, and publicized civil-rights issues. Carlin believed that 'there is a little jealousy in every profession. Cohen stood out. The Labour Court is where they really got to hate him.' There, up against leading lawyers representing employers, 'he made asses out of them and they didn't like it.'[46] Despite his expertise, he won only slightly more than 50 per cent of his cases; his record was partly a reflection of a new court developing its procedures but mostly was the result of employers' opposition to unions and certification procedures.

Cohen was intimately involved in events surrounding the introduction of collective-bargaining legislation in Ontario from the time Premier Conant hired him to draft a bill. Throughout the legislative committee's public hearings in 1943, he was a presence when the minister put forward the contents of Cohen's drafts in his statement on the need for legislation. The unions presented briefs that reflected theirs and Cohen's demands as set out in his 1941 publication on labour policy. After the legislation passed, Cohen appeared more often than any other lawyer before the Labour Court and displayed his talents as the leading union counsel, even as he favoured legislative improvements. The experience gained was excellent training for his stint on the NWLB. His awareness of the fluid political situation as the CCF gained support made him more forceful in Ottawa than he had been in Toronto. But, just as he irritated other members of the legal profession in the Labour Court, he would infuriate colleagues and the prime minister when he served as a member of the NWLB.

6

National War Labour Board Service, 1943

In 1943 Prime Minister Mackenzie King invited J.L. Cohen to serve on the National War Labour Board. Originally set up to administer wartime wage-and-price controls, the board was reconstituted in February 1943 in the settlement of a national steel strike. An independent chair was appointed to replace the minister of labour, Humphrey Mitchell, and the board became a tripartite panel of legal experts: the chairman, Mr Justice C.P. McTague, from the Ontario Appellate Court, represented the public interest; J.J. Bench, a corporation lawyer, was the business appointee; and Cohen sat as the labour representative.

The government intended to delay a new labour code, but several factors would convince Prime Minister King to enact a collective-bargaining policy, including Ontario's legislative initiative, the high incidence of strikes, the CCF's growing popularity and support from labour, the Liberal Party's declining fortunes, and the NWLB's public inquiry and reports, which perhaps inadvertently activated the policy-making process.[1]

The government consulted labour about the NWLB appointments, and Cohen was recommended. McTague advised the prime minister that, because Cohen enjoyed the confidence of both labour congresses, his participation on the board Cohen would assure labour's support. Cohen was delighted, and his friends were pleased that his talent, expertise, and stature as the leading labour lawyer was recognized. Cohen wrote to Pat Conroy that he hoped 'by tangible results' to merit the praise 'which is now being so unreservedly expressed.'[2]

The prime minister assured Cohen that the new board was independent and would 'be given power to deal in broad terms with the question of labour relations, as well as wage control.' McTague was confident that the NWLB could solve contemporary problems and Cohen saw an opportunity to shape new labour policy.[3] His thinking was evolving after the Ontario act, for he realized that more was now politically possible. On the NWLB, Cohen adhered to the views he had expressed in *Collective Bargaining in Canada* (1941) rather than to the ones embodied in his legislative drafts preceding the 1943 legislation in Ontario. He would champion U.S. Wagner Act principles – 'industrial democracy' – at the NWLB inquiry because the CCF and labour had injected them into the public debate.

Justice C.P. McTague chaired many conciliation boards during the war attempting to resolve labour disputes. He knew Cohen from panels that included the 1940 CSU strike on the Great Lakes ships and the 1941 Kirkland Lake strike with its unanimous report in favour of union recognition.[4] He thought the conciliation policy and statement of principles (P.C. 2685) were inadequate, and that compulsory collective bargaining would introduce rules and 'responsibility' into labour relations. J.J. Bench, at thirty-eight the country's youngest senator, was a corporation lawyer from St. Catharines who specialized in employment law and was a founder of the Niagara Industrial Relations Institute. An 'enlightened' employer representative he believed that collective bargaining would introduce stability and that 'freedom of association' would permit workers to organize non-union associations.[5] Despite different perspectives, the three men agreed that collective bargaining was necessary.

Cohen received media attention; one article depicted him vividly as conveying by his physical compactness an impression of a concentrated energy, as though 'considerable nervous forces instead of being diffused, were here focussed and controlled. His movements are quick but smooth, with an economy of motion and sureness of direction.'[6] At forty-five, this family man, who lived in Toronto in a large Georgian home, had a legal career that spanned thirty years. He viewed the law as a body of principles that was influenced by socio-economic factors and was subject to change and that could be an instrument for reform.

Given that Cohen was selected because of labour's support, unions expected attention from him. C.S. Jackson, for example, sent Cohen a list of problematic UEW cases and asked him to get them heard quickly.[7] Cohen himself told an audience at a dinner held for him by the Montreal

Trades and Labour Council that his mandate was from 'the working people of Canada,' as represented by organized labour. With this duty to his constituency and to his country at war, he summed up his role in an epigram, 'Serve labour and thereby serve the nation; serve the nation and thereby serve labour.'

Cohen saw the NWLB as an independent, tripartite tribunal with expertise, which would also receive advice from representative interests. McTague's position was essentially the same, but, unlike Cohen's it favoured independence not only from government and the courts but also from contending parties. While McTague stressed the board's judicial role, Cohen focused on its administrative functions and relations with the public. The nature of the new NWLB was gradually clarified, and in the process Cohen and McTague experienced ups and downs in their working relationship, until it broke down. What would evolve by the end of the war were dominion and provincial labour boards that were specialized, independent, and quasi-judicial and that mixed policy making and adjudication in a way that was different from the courts or governments' legislative and executive procedures. During the war there existed a mix of ideas and experiments, which eventually came together in the modern framework, but in the Ontario Labour Court and this early NWLB, the mix was not yet set. Thus, Cohen experienced tension between his roles as advocate of labour interests and a quasi-judicial adjudicator required to take a 'balanced' approach.

The day of the appointments, the three men issued a statement of intent; the board wished to establish consistent jurisprudence, hold public hearings, and publish its decisions. Neither government policy nor the order reconstituting the board required a narrow, legalistic approach, so it would implement *existing* policies flexibly to correct injustices within the scope of the controls policy, especially where wage rates were inadequate or depressed.[8]

Almost at once, French-Canadian pressure led to internal discussions about the reconstituted NWLB. While Quebec labour circles welcomed Cohen's appointment, it was not applauded universally. One paper wrote that Cohen was 'un avocat juif de Toronto qui, grâce à ses sympathies pour les communistes non moins qu'à sa science légale, était devenu leur représentant juridique dans leurs procès et leurs démarches.'[9] Because he spoke only English, the anglophone makeup of the NWLB caused French Canadians to lobby for a representative. *L'Action catholique* noted that the board had 'pas un seul canadien français. Pas un seul representant de la province de Québec.'[10]

Gérard Picard of the Canadian and Catholic Confederation of Labour/ Confédération des Travailleurs Catholiques du Canada (CCCL/CTCC), a member of the old board's advisory committee, was asked to continue on the new board's smaller committee. He resigned, because the CCCL was not consulted about the new NWLB. Picard raised a constitutional question about Ottawa's enhanced role in labour relations. He noted that Wagner Act principles might work in English Canada where local collective agreements were the norm, but in Quebec provincial legislation was unique since collective agreements were often extended sectorally in an industry or a zone.

Cohen told King that he regretted that no French Canadian was on the board and he favoured having one on its advisory committee, but that he opposed this 'political interference with the character and purpose of the NWLB.' Such interference, he wrote to McTague, 'will destroy the Board's essential usefulness – certainly it destroys my own.' He did not want Picard setting 'terms and conditions.' Pressure-group intervention could jeopardize 'any aspect of independence and judicial detachment which this Board has,' for Cohen took a class view of the situation and believed that he represented all workers, not just English Canadians. It was appropriate for employers' and employees' interests to be represented by 'experts,' but it was 'interference' to appoint 'special interests' which lobbied for 'political' influence. Politicization of the board in this sense would undermine it. He also was wary of a working-class representative unknown to him, particularly one from the Catholic union movement which the TLC and CCL considered conservative politically, an opponent of international unions, and not independent of employers or the Quebec government.[11] To Cohen, independence was the reason the board was reorganized; it was approved by 'the largest portion by far of Quebec's organized workers,' by which he meant those outside the Catholic unions, and he opposed unilateral changes 'which do not arise *inherently out of its operations.*' He and McTague both reacted to press comments that treated the board as an administrative arm of the Department of Labour, since they wanted no association with it or with Humphrey Mitchell, whom organized labour disliked particularly after the Kirkland Lake strike. To some government officials, Quebec's criticism was valid on representational grounds and because its unique culture, environment, and institutions resulted in a different viewpoint.

Briefly, there was talk of expanding the board to five members, which Cohen opposed because he favoured a tripartite panel with equal representation of employer and employee interests. He also sought to maintain his position to ensure that labour's legislative aims would be achieved. He threatened to consult labour over the issue, but did not, for fear of harming the new board.[12] Nevertheless, he demonstrated his dependence on labour and his view of himself as a delegate of that constituency. A similar debate over 'representative' versus 'delegate' status periodically erupts over the position of MPs. Since Justice McTague also supported a three-person board, expansion was dropped. Eventually Quebec's pressure resulted in Senator Bench's resignation and his replacement by Leo Lalande. LaLande was a French Canadian corporate lawyer from Montreal who had once worked for McTague's law firm in Windsor and shared his views.[13] He was a solicitor for the Ration Administration within the Wartimes Prices and Trade Board (WPTB). French-Canadian intervention and the consequent reshuffle of personnel confirmed Cohen's view that the board must be independent and tripartite.

Others expressed discomfort over Cohen's NWLB appointment. Some cabinet ministers had vigorously opposed his nomination, as did *Globe and Mail* and *Financial Post* editorials. Dr Herbert A. Bruce, Conservative MP from Toronto's Parkdale riding, attacked Cohen for being the CIO lawyer – in his view, a union congress of notorious trouble makers in the war industries.[14] Clearly, Cohen was in the spotlight as a member of an important national body. He set up an office in Ottawa, where he had a supportive junior to assist him in making new law, and their enthusiasm was reminiscent of the atmosphere in the early days of the American NLRB.[15] With board work, Cohen had no time for some old clients such as *Canadian Tribune*, but he was also scrupulous about avoiding conflicts of interest. In a Ford case over a five-cent bonus for the night shift, for example, Cohen excused himself from the case, since he had been the lawyer in the matter. It was heard by the other two board members, and the bonus was granted.[16]

In April 1943 Cohen gave an interim account of his 'trusteeship' to a union meeting. McTague had tightened control over the regional boards and treated the NWLB as an industrial court that developed jurisprudence. Such changes, Cohen told the union, permitted appeal cases from regional boards to the national board. The new board was more flexible and adjusted bonuses to correct unfairness. Cohen affirmed his commitment to collective bargaining and to more union organizations and he commented, 'I have come more passionately to accept' unions as fundamental 'for a sensible approach' to wartime labour relations, and as necessary for sound and constructive social policy.[17] His view was unique.

It was not held by employers, it was not an approach encouraged by government, and it would get him into trouble on the board.

Cohen's 'trusteeship' reflects some early dilemmas about tripartism, as well as the problem of staffing a regulatory agency. Were board members to be mouthpieces or independent analysts? People with expertise were required, but how could such persons perform without bias, given their past associations, or, in Cohen's case, continuing links and self-proclaimed role as an advocate? At a time when employer and labour interests were polarized over collective bargaining and the administration of wage controls, it was perhaps inevitable that the situation would create tensions. And, without as yet a community of 'professional neutrals' who in a later period would come to act as board nominees, mediators, conciliators, and arbitrators, no role models existed. Cohen saw his stance as a labour advocate as necessary, but it limited his ability to be judicious despite his efforts to avoid direct conflicts of interest. His partisanship collided with the chair's view, which favoured a more formal relationship with employer and employee interests.

IMPORTANT NWLB CASES

During Cohen's brief tenure, the board dealt with several important cases.[18] One was the steel case, which again raised the issue of the NWLB's autonomy, one affected the wages of women and youths, and all illustrated inequities in the administration of wage controls, the persistence of low wages paid to industrial workers in general and to women in particular, and Cohen's consistent efforts to raise wage levels and support fairness.

Workers were frustrated by wage controls, which the federal government adopted to avoid the galloping inflation of the First World War.[19] Labour opposed the policy, because it was not consulted, and because wage controls were the antithesis of free collective bargaining, were inflexible, and were administered inconsistently. Some frozen wages perpetuated substandard wage levels and regional disparities. Labour advocated collective bargaining for workers earning below the minimum wage of twenty-five dollars per week.

The conflict over wage controls climaxed in a steel strike of workers at Algoma in Sault Ste Marie and DOSCO and Trenton Works in Nova Scotia, but not the Steel Company of Canada (STELCO) in Hamilton, which was not well organized. The steelworkers' union wanted to raise wages, rationalize the industry's wage structure, and in the process organize new members; it sought fifty-five cents an hour plus a cost-of-living bonus (a minimum income of $1,750 a year) as a uniform base rate for the entire industry. For Ottawa, the strike was a challenge to its policy, because wages were adjusted in comparison with local standards, which conflicted with the union's plan for a higher, uniform national base rate.[20] After months of delay, the Ontario Regional War Labour Board and a royal commission majority report rejected the wage increase above the ceiling, and in January 1943 thirteen thousand steelworkers struck. The government immediately acted because steel was essential to war production.

Prime Minister King disliked union leader Charlie Millard, an active CCFer, but he also believed that steelworkers were underpaid, and though the strike challenged the wage-stabilization policy, he knew the union had considerable public support. He sought a solution that appeased workers, maintained controls, and was acceptable to business and his conservative cabinet colleagues but also took account of the political tide turning left. At several meetings, King, Millard, and the cabinet negotiated a 'memorandum of understanding,' which was embodied in war order P.C. 689. The settlement reconstituted the NWLB on a new basis, removing the unpopular labour minister as chairman, converting the board into an independent tribunal, and authorizing it to implement the 'memorandum.' Thus, the government achieved 'its limited aim of raising wages slightly, as a sympathetic gesture, while preserving the integrity of its control policy in the rest of the economy.'[21] The settlement ended the strike, but the steel case then went to the 'new' NWLB.

As the labour representative, Cohen was in a ticklish situation because the case was important to labour, and the steel 'memorandum' was interpreted differently by the two parties. The union argued that the board had discretion to set a base rate and cost-of-living bonus along the lines it demanded, but the companies contended that the rates were set and the board could examine only the bonus to be paid.[22] The board heard the arguments and reserved its decision.

Cohen analysed the language in the 'memorandum of understanding' and sought the prime minister's clarification.[23] While ordinarily the board would interpret the documents and decide the case, in this situation Cohen requested more information about King's agreement with Millard. To Justice McTague he wrote, 'There can be no doubt that these people were told in effect that they would now be in the category of national employment, and whatever reasoning we use I am very much

law vs. policy
a victory for law?

afraid that there may be a tendency to construe our judgment as a reversal of what was already promised.' On the wage rate, 'it appears to me
that once an irreducible rate of 55 cents has been acknowledged – and
the settlement certainly does that – we perhaps have no right to alter it.'
The board was troubled about a settlement that seemed to permit a ceil-
ing above the wage-control order. For a tribunal concerned about its
independence, its desire for consultation before deciding the case was
unusual. But with a collision possible between the law and the 'memorandum,' its members apparently felt awkward, even though a court,
when faced with a conflict between the 'law' and a deal negotiated by
politicians would have implemented the 'law.'

After some delay, the NWLB released its unanimous decision which
reinterpreted the memorandum. It gave the workers an increase in the
cost-of-living bonus at Algoma and an increase in the base rate at Sydney,
so in essence it 'split the difference,' a common approach of arbitrators.
Everyone received over fifty-five cents in total but in effect some steelworkers had their base rate reduced. It did recognize the principle of uniform payments at Algoma and Dosco, but it did not challenge the wage-
control policy or acquiesce in the union base rate of fifty-five cents for all
plus a bonus. The board also refused to designate steel as a national
industry but agreed to reconsider the issue of the industry's status,
should the union bring a new case, under the new by-law allowing appeals
of regional board decisions to the NWLB. So long as STELCO – the
other major employer – was not unionized and part of the negotiations,
it noted, 'certain practical difficulties' might result 'from designating
only two employers as national employers in an industry which admittedly contains, at least, one other extensive employer.'[24] The board had a
point, the union realized, and it increased its organizing efforts at Stelco.

The decision was significant because the board did not decide for
either party but compromised. It was a victory for the 'law,' for the tribunal's independence, and for the prime minister, but a defeat for the
union. Millard felt betrayed and was displeased with Cohen's agreement with the decision. He had been outmanoeuvred by King, whose
response was to uphold the reconstituted NWLB's 'independence' and
refuse to intervene further in the case. Millard continued to allege that
an understanding with the government existed which the NWLB had
failed to implement, but the steel strike did not resume, partly because
the board had by this time announced its public inquiry which the
union did not want to disrupt.

The union asked the minister to enforce the memorandum. Mitchell apparently considered intervening, but Justice McTague, with Cohen's support, bluntly informed him that if he tried to review the board's findings, he would resign. McTague also suggested that, if the government had a 'secret understanding' with the union, it should say so, but, 'the National War Labour Board knew of no such understanding at the time that it took on the reference.'[25] To the prime minister, he wrote, 'Either the Board must be supported unequivocally ... or a public statement must be made that Mr. Millard had reason to believe the allegations which he has been making so forcibly.'[26] The government told Millard that nothing would be done.

The government's support for the NWLB's independence conveniently served its political purpose. Cohen found himself defending the tribunal's independence, but at the expense of the union. The experience taught Millard that the unionization of Stelco was a top priority. In 1946 in the next conflict over steel-industry wages, the union ignored the NWLB and the ministry altogether, and the parties themselves decided the issue after one of the most dramatic strikes in Canadian working-class history.

Cohen also dealt with a policy concerning wages paid to women and youths, who were hired to relieve the wartime labour shortage and do what was considered 'men's work.' Cohen had experience from the Ford case (UAW) in the application of minimum-standards legislation in the needle trades, as well as with grievances that unions initiated over the principle of equal pay for equal work. A consensus existed among public policy makers and corporate leaders that women were filling in for men during the crisis but at the end of the war the labour market would return to 'normal.'[27] There are indications that the day-to-day administration of a labour force in which women were not in their usual places created confusion among the nearly all-male administrators. When unions were involved, the principle of equal pay for equal work often was adhered to, but otherwise there were anomalies. For example, in August 1942, INCO applied successfully, without consulting its employees, to pay lower rates to women and youths. The company argued that such people were less skilled and experienced than men, though it provided no evidence to support this contention. The board asked the company to file statistical information, but it never did so. On 12 May 1943 INCO again requested reduced rates for more job classifications at Copper Cliff and Port Colborne. With no justification for the proposed lower rates, and the issue arising in more cases, the board needed a policy.[28]

[handwritten margin note: views about women or women & their relation to union power?]

The NWLB recommended that wage order P.C. 5963 be amended so that where employers currently paid a single rate to all, or where training and productivity were the same, all employees would receive equal pay for equal work. Otherwise, females and youths during a probationary period would receive 70 per cent of male wages and later 80 per cent as permanent employees. The minister of labour drafted a long, complicated order with opaque language, which allowed the NWLB to fix lower rates for women and youths, on the grounds that they produced less and 'out of recognition of the social responsibilities of adult males.' The order was discriminatory; it reflected genuine perplexity over women's productivity levels, as well as prevailing male cultural attitudes and social customs.

Cohen's response to the draft order was testy because his views were in advance of other male public officials. He and the labour movement agreed that equal pay for equal work for women should exist out of fairness and so as not to jeopardize wage levels in men's jobs at the end of the *[handwritten margin note: exactly]* war. But, in the predominantly male policy-making environment, Cohen faced colleagues whose attitudes were unfavourable to females and who were ambivalent about an issue that signified change. The order should be a simple, flexible provision, which Cohen drafted cleverly in one clear sentence: 'that where any employer proposed to engage females on work formerly or usually performed by men, the National Board ... should be empowered to fix a lower wage, if it should be established to the satisfaction of the Board that such female worker would not produce the same output as a male performing the same work, such lower wage to prevail so long as such differential in production prevailed and to be adjusted from time to time as the differential varied or disappeared.' He criticized the order's 'rigid rigmarole' and 'recitals' about matters 'which must be dealt with objectively in each plant, in each industry, and even in each province as they arise,' with discretion left to the administrators. Any other approach involved 'serious trouble.'[29]

At the NWLB, Cohen focused on labour policy rather than his law practice. The change came at a good time in his career for two reasons: politics, and competition within the legal profession. As the labour movement's internal conflicts between the Communist and non-Communist trade unionists escalated, Cohen lost clients. He was legal counsel to Mine Mill, the UAW, and the UEW – unions that had considerable Communist influence. C.H. Millard, national director of the Steelworkers' union (USWA), became fed up with Cohen's close association with the Communists, and even before the NWLB decided the steel case,

Millard no longer hired him.[30] Though Cohen was not a CPC member, his professional and personal contacts with that party continued when he acted for wartime internees and for banned groups. But his service to the Communists hurt his labour practice, not because the unions did not support civil liberties, but because this work demonstrated his continued association with the radical minority in the labour movement at a time when it presented a real problem, particularly for CCL leaders.

Thus, for the first time, Cohen faced competition from other labour lawyers. As the major industrial unions and the CCL became pro-CCF, and the CCF's popularity rose dramatically between 1942 and 1944, labour leaders turned to Ted Jolliffe, the USWA's lawyer until he became Ontario CCF leader and in 1943 leader of Official Opposition.[31] Cohen was furious at Millard for using Jolliffe during the steel strike,[32] but that union also sought political and legal advice from David Lewis, national secretary of the CCF, and John Osler (after the war Jolliffe, Lewis, and Osler practised labour law together in the same firm).[33] Cohen did work for the CCL, but so did Andrew Brewin, who drafted the CCF's model collective-bargaining bill. A civil libertarian, he also was outspoken about labour policy and helped draft Saskatchewan's Trade Union Act, 1944, when the CCF assumed office there.[34]

Under pressure from these competitors, Cohen focused on the NWLB job, but he began to exhibit personal problems, which were exacerbated by his hectic, pressured life. Ted Jolliffe remembered that Cohen acted rather peculiarly at times, and some people thought he was on drugs.[35] Later, in 1945, his behaviour would get him into serious legal trouble which contributed to his ill health. But in 1943 he was already personally vulnerable and professionally insecure as he manoeuvred to achieve a new public policy on labour relations.

THE NWLB INQUIRY AND REPORTS

The steel decision established the NWLB's independence. It then announced a public inquiry into labour unrest, which in 1943 left a quarter-million workers on strike with over a million lost workdays. Between April and June 1943, the board held public hearings in Ottawa to investigate labour relations and wage conditions and recommend new legislation. Like Ontario's public hearings, labour, business, and other organizations made over a hundred presentations and put labour issues on the national stage. As in Ontario, workers simultaneously applied pressure on the industrial and political fronts, while business,

with a few exceptions, promoted industrial councils in lieu of independent unions. Company and union briefs repeated their basic positions,
often referring to their earlier Ontario submissions.The difference this
time was that union briefs were before a tripartite board, and Cohen's
position probably gave union presenters confidence. The unions'
themes – employers' intense opposition acquiesced in by government,
the problem of company unions, unfair administration of the wage policy, and the need for collective-bargaining legislation – intensified the
atmosphere of working-class grievance and class polarization.

Cohen played an active role questioning witnesses and raising issues,
as did Justice McTague. Both men believed the existing labour policy
was ineffective, sought change, and occasionally challenged those
employers who strongly endorsed company unions. The procedure was
formal as delegations read their briefs, but there were asides, pauses,
and elaboration. The hearings were dramatic because company representatives were belligerent towards unions which they viewed as
interlopers in industry. Labour representatives of varied political persuasions and organizations displayed remarkable unity in pursuit of
legislation which they believed would promote organizational growth.
They gave examples of employers' manipulation of employees and their
arbitrary behaviour; they criticized government delay and collusion
with anti-labour businesses and vividly described workers' low standard of living.[36] The evidence amassed increased public support for collective bargaining as a solution to unrest; opinion would influence the
new policy's introduction, for in 1943, with 53 per cent of the country
supporting 'compulsory recognition,' politicians understood that a consensus was emerging.[37]

While the NWLB drafted its report, Cohen referred to 'unusual proceedings' in the chair's office and decided to confer with labour representatives. It is unclear what concerned him, though it seems he
suspected McTague of receiving advice from politicians and not confin-
ing himself to evidence from the hearings and discussions with his
board colleagues. As a result, Cohen, worried that any delay in the publication of the reports might jeopardize the introduction of new legislation, decided to draft his own minority report and leave the board when
the reports were completed and submitted to government. Apparently,
differences over the role of board representatives and tripartism had
resurfaced.

On 17 August 1943, Cohen submitted his minority report to the government, before the majority report. Besides internal disagreements,

Cohen probably wanted to write a separate document so that his views would receive national attention. His report, in addition to his 1941 book, made his reputation as the leading critic of federal labour policy. It was clearly written, without legal jargon, but expressed a definite perspective. He placed proposed policy changes in the context of Canada's national development, which, with its expanded diversified economy, was at a turning point. To secure continued prosperity after the war with full employment and high productivity, he called for a national program involving all Canadians. Employees' physical welfare, morale, and sense of security were important, as was their representation in industry. Though patriotic, labour remained excluded in wartime policy making by government and industry, and the result was an ineffective labour policy which damaged the national interest, because workers distrusted the government's motives.

Cohen wrote that the spectre of the Depression made workers determined to avoid its repetition. 'It must not be forgotten that the worker acutely remembers the want and suffering which he and his family have undergone during the last twenty-five years. To him, it is a tragic contradiction that the years of peace spelled depressions, mass unemployment, starvation relief, and a callous indifference to the waste of human lives; while a ravaging war brought work and opportunity and a miraculous display of the productive powers of the nation.'[38] Canadians had learned from the war that, with political will, all people and resources could be included in a national program. A comprehensive labour policy was needed, and Cohen linked collective bargaining to industrial democracy.[39]

His seventy-six-page report made sixteen recommendations, including the enactment of a Dominion Labour Code with broad coverage, compulsory collective bargaining, a list of unfair and hence forbidden labour practices, an end to discrimination against workers for union activity, and a ban on company unions. A national tripartite board, with effective enforcement mechanisms, including penalties such as fines and remedies such as reinstatement, would administer the legislation. Cohen favoured the compulsory arbitration of disputes over unresolved grievances during the life of a contract. His proposal for voluntary conciliation by permanent boards, which reflected his negative view of the IDI act's application during the war, was rejected in favour of the status quo of compulsory conciliation by impermanent boards prior to a legal work stoppage.

Cohen recommended joint management-labour production councils for political reasons, which came to nothing. The government sometimes referred to these voluntary committees but did little to institutionalize them. The labour movement favoured them if that ensured consultation about post-war reconstruction. The Communists strongly favoured them as part of their support for an all-out war effort. Both the majority report and Cohen's supported the labour movement's repeated demand for greater representation on government bodies.[40]

The two reports differed primarily over wage controls. Like the labour movement, Cohen opposed inflation because it was harmful to the war effort, but he criticized the administration of wage controls as unfair. He favoured a flexible policy, recommended a mandatory cost-of-living bonus for male workers at the maximum rate across the board, and advocated equal pay for equal work for female workers and younger males. He proposed revision of the cost-of-living index and changes in the tax laws so that industrial workers would benefit. These recommendations were not implemented.

Cohen's report was partisan and neither tactful nor ingratiating. He condemned the wartime labour policy and charged the government with failure to implement suitable legislation or to cooperate with unions. Concluding with the national-economy theme, he stressed that these issues were 'as important to our time as were the struggles for representative government' in an earlier era. In this 'gigantic industrial system' with its 'modern working class,' workers should unite to play a substantial role, but employers should cooperate with their employees in bringing about a modern industrial-relations system. The government should 'lead and guide and, above all ... equip the nation, so that we can march, integrated and strong, to win the war and to guarantee the peace.'[41]

Cohen's left-leaning intellectual perspective was uniquely his own. He supported the Communist position for an all-out war effort and no-strike pledges to maintain industrial peace. This no-strike policy was contentious; it was held by a minority in the labour movement, separated labour's Communists and non-Communists, and was criticized strongly by CCFers, who insisted that labour had to maintain its strike weapon even in war, so long as there was no legislative support for collective bargaining. But Cohen also backed the unions' and CCF position on collective bargaining and wage controls. Despite his opposition to wartime strikes, in his law practice, he constantly assisted strikers in his law practice. On the NWLB, he both sought to solve workers' problems with new legislation and to reduce conflict.[42] His pro-union position and his urgent plea to enhance workers' roles in an inclusive post-war society was distinctive. It resulted partly from his immigrant working-class background, which taught him the need for unions to protect workers and raise their living standards, and partly from practical experience as a labour lawyer which demonstrated to him what workers could accomplish with strong organizations behind them and sound legal advice.

The majority report was submitted after Cohen's and was less than half its length. Both recommended collective-bargaining legislation, but McTague and Lalande did so not as proponents of industrial democracy but on the basis that 'contractual relations would increase responsible unions, diminish the appeal of militant tactics and insure industrial stability.'[43] The majority report was written in measured language, except for its hostility to militant labour leaders whom it blamed for unrest. This criticism was unfair, given the respectful union presentations at the hearings, but may have been intended to reassure business, even as the board adopted labour's major demand. The majority report placed less emphasis than Cohen's on labour-management cooperation, but it nonetheless favoured this practice, noting that voluntary workplace committees had been adopted in a limited way. It mildly criticized Canadian business leaders, urging them to take a more modern approach to labour relations.

The majority report had a different perspective on wage controls. The labour movement, it said, really did not understand their purpose. In a paternalistic tone, it emphasized how disastrous inflation would be for the 'common man' and advised the government to educate the public about the program. It endorsed labour's proposal that collective bargaining without wage controls should exist for workers earning up to fifty cents per hour, but it qualified this recommendation in two important respects, which reflected contemporary attitudes. First, while it was unfair to control substandard wages, labour, the report noted, assumed that all low-wage workers were heads of families. But, with more women working, families increasingly had two wage earners. The 'family wage' concept had affected wage rates for years, supporting higher rates for male workers as family 'breadwinners' and excusing unequal and low pay for female workers. Though challenged by the Depression and war experiences, the notion persisted in all-male policy-making circles. On the subject of women in industry, the majority report made the extraordinary suggestion that female wage levels should be handled separately by a different board, as in Australia – an idea the government did not adopt. Second, if the government thought that leaving substandard wages free of controls would lead to inflation, it should consider introducing a system of family allowances to the head of a family for each child below the age of sixteen. This recommendation linked the two policies – wage controls and family allowances – publicly and the labour movement reacted with suspicion and ambivalence.

The majority report recommended the conversion of bonuses to base wage rates and, as Cohen had, a revised cost-of-living index and tax system, with labour involved in the process. Like Cohen, it favoured simpler wage controls and incentives to bolster production and morale. Finally, it introduced the odd notion that the board should use the Defence of Canada Regulations (DOCR) to administer penalties, a point Cohen strongly contested, since his experience with those regulations led him to favour strongly a board with its own administrative mechanisms.

The majority report was an authoritative, but understated, document compared to Cohen's. Justice McTague was offended by Cohen's written comment that his report was independent, implying, in the chair's view, that the majority's was not, and thus the tensions between the two men were made public. The tone of the two reports was strikingly different, for Cohen used urgent, didactic, and even hectoring language. He discussed the national interest very much as a political outsider, whose appointment was the result – notwithstanding his ability and expertise – of political pressure rather than his own connections in government. Justice McTague's report had a moderate tone, and its language was persuasive, constructive, and even ingratiating. He got along with the prime minister, with whom he shared similar views on industrial relations (including King's distinction between 'responsible' [conservative] and 'irresponsible' [militant] unions). Well connected, with a successful corporate law firm in Windsor before his appointment to the bench in the mid 1930s, and in touch with informal male social circles in a way that Cohen was not, he was a team player.[44] He had been appointed because of his abilities to be sure, as evident in the report, he had a conciliatory personality which was capable of detachment.

It is conceivable that if Cohen had not been on the board, the majority report still would have recommended compulsory collective bargaining, because McTague, too, was critical of existing labour policies. But Cohen's appointment ensured the recommendation of new policy. The labour movement remained outside the power structure and was regarded with suspicion in governing and business circles. Cohen's appointment did not change that. But his presence meant that labour's view on crucial questions was presented clearly, at the top level, by its own trusted representative. That situation helped move the government to act on collective bargaining, in February 1944, with its proclamation of P.C. 1003.

Concerning wage controls, the government would not remove them until 1947. It did adopt the majority report's recommendation of family allowances, also recommended by Leonard Marsh, in 1945 as a partial, relatively inexpensive, first-step measure towards a social-welfare state.[45] Some Liberals, such as J.W. Pickersgill and Paul Martin, believed that the program would increase working-class families' incomes without raising wages. The labour movement, which supported a welfare state, opposed family allowances as a substitute for better wages.[46] In 1946 confrontation between labour and the national government over post-war wage levels erupted in a strike wave.

COHEN IS FIRED FROM THE NWLB

For weeks before submitting his report, Cohen and McTague sparred. Cohen read the draft majority report, suggested changes, and expected the government to have it in hand by mid-August. He was suspicious of McTague's reasons for delaying the submission of the majority report, fearing that 'the Chairman's tactic ... has indicated an attitude of hope that the whole matter would be forgotten in the 'limberlost' of casual activities.'[47] Meanwhile, the passage of the Ontario legislation followed by the outcome of the provincial election in July was continuing to place pressure on the federal government, until then impervious to labour's demands, to enact a national labour code. On 18 August, Cohen alluded to the contents of the as yet unreleased reports and publicly refused to participate in board cases until the government received the reports, made public their contents, and implemented their recommendations, for otherwise, under existing legislation, the board members had 'to depart from the principles enunciated in our own public statement' on the day of their appointment and render unjust decisions. Angered by a communication from the Department of Munitions and Supply telling contractors on war work not to make joint submissions with labour to the NWLB, Cohen interpreted this as an 'official command to management, not to co-operate with labour, even when management is agreed on the merits of the application.'

To this, McTague responded that he had not yet submitted his report, which Cohen apparently did not realize, and that Cohen should not have issued statements to the press before both the majority and the minority reports had been made public. He offered to accept Cohen's resignation and got to the crux of the matter:

Cohen is concerned about political boards yet he is overtly political

It has seemed quite clear to me ... that our job was to administer Government policy as to wages and cost of living bonus in a fair manner under the law. We were also empowered to conduct an inquiry into the general problems of labour relations and made what recommendations we saw fit. I have never felt that there was any guarantee on the Government's part that it was bound to accept any recommendations which we might make ... I can have no political interest on account of my position. Naturally I assumed when you became a member of a Government Board that as long as you remained in the position any political interest on your part would cease as well.'[48]

McTague took the position of an independent adjudicator in an arm's-length agency, who felt uneasy about Cohen's use of his board position to lobby the government. Once a tribunal becomes political, a government may treat it that way and make political appointments, something that both men had resisted earlier in response to pressure from Quebec.[49] McTague and LaLande heard cases without Cohen, who had refused to participate in the board's work.

Cohen was not a man to waste his time, and he was arrogant enough to think that no one, even the prime minister, should expect him to. Also, he was deeply committed to the changes recommended. At such a critical time, he had no intention of playing the role of a 'neutral' administrator applying the law as it was, while making recommendations for change which might not happen. As the labour appointee, he was a partisan, who participated in the inquiry to further the adoption of new legislation. While Justice McTague feigned surprise at Cohen's position, which was politically inconvenient, it is likely that the only thing that startled him was the extent of Cohen's dogged determination to embarrass the government enough that it would act. Cohen had also observed the government's behaviour in the steel case and may have resolved not to be manipulated as Millard had been. He had experienced working behind the scenes to draft the Ontario Collective Bargaining Act, where his conciliatory position had not worked. He knew the government felt pressured by the CCF and by high levels of industrial conflict, and the inquiry had revealed how polarized labour relations had become.

Without offering his resignation, Cohen told McTague that, if the government had not yet received the reports, the fault was his. McTague now approached the functions of the NWLB in a manner 'entirely different to that which was represented to the public and certainly to me, when the reconstitution of the Board was first announced.'[50] Cohen recalled, 'You and I were both agreed before I stepped on the Board that the government labour policy was bad,' and that 'it would be our job as a Board to change this, so far as possible, firstly by interpreting the laws themselves in a temperate manner, and secondly by recommending changes or additions to legislation which would conform to our concept. You were most emphatic in your expressed viewpoint that such recommendations would be accepted and I entered into this responsibility upon that basis. I have not deviated from that viewpoint.' Cohen believed that McTague had changed in the face of government inertia.

To ensure the quick publication and implementation of the reports, Cohen was taking the openly political stance of consulting the public and labour to press for action. He understood that calling press conferences to criticize both the board and the government, while he was still a member of the panel, would provoke a strong reaction, but his drive for new legislation was more important than his appointment. On 19 August, Justice McTague referred publicly to Cohen's refusal to adjudicate cases as a sit-down strike, a comment that Cohen characterized as 'a typical 'smear' tactic adopted by anybody with an employer mind.' Relations between the two men deteriorated into nastiness, but Cohen noted that his 'one man strike' at least had resulted in the judge's promise to submit his majority report shortly, which was an achievement. Deputy Labour Minister Arthur MacNamara informed Cohen when the government had both reports; he also observed that the government considered the reports important but that 'until the government has the opportunity to do so, the reports will not be made public.'[51]

The day before Cohen spoke to the TLC convention in Quebec City, Prime Minister King made a surprise visit to the labour gathering. Privately he assured TLC President Percy Bengough that he would study the reports but would not release them until after the CCL convention, so that neither congress would be placed at a disadvantage. King had already read the reports, confronted the existing policy's shortcomings, and decided to act, for Paul Martin, a rising young member and the parliamentary assistant to the minister of labour, who had worked with Lalande in MacTague's law firm, was pressing the point. On 1 September (the day of Cohen's speech to the TLC), King told the cabinet that 'I [have] not ... given my life to better the conditions of labour in order to end it as one who had gone back on all the principles for which he had fought ... I [propose] to fight openly for labour having its just dues.'[52] With strong objections from some cabinet ministers to overcome, it would take nearly six months to table P.C. 1003 in Parliament.

By now, Cohen already had decided that he would leave the board. In his address to the TLC convention, revealed his concern that the government might not act on the reports.The speech cost him his NWLB job, for afterwards McTague met with King. The prime minister recorded in his diary that McTague 'could no longer sit with Cohen, that he was a political intriguer, had changed his attitude on the night of the Ontario election, when he saw how the CCF was turning out, mentioned his different moves as to announcing his decision. Spoke of his treachery of going to Quebec [to the TLC] and making the address he did, etc.'[53] The cabinet discussed the situation; King met a delegation of labour leaders who had urged Cohen to resume hearing board cases.[54] When they complained about the reports' delay, King told Mosher of his assurance to Bengough that the reports would not be released until after the CCL's convention. He promised to consider them soon and warned that he would not interfere in the McTague-Cohen dipute since he viewed the board as a court. In fact, he had already told Labour Minister Mitchell that he 'would not be a party to reinstatement of Cohen.' On 8 September, King reported this meeting to cabinet and Finance Minister J.L. Ilsley complained that the government was losing face by not dismissing Cohen.

When McTague learned that Cohen had agreed to hear cases again, he told King that Cohen's contribution, particularly during the inquiry, had been constructive until recent events but that all this had now changed; he refused to sit with Cohen any longer and requested his dismissal. On 9 September, Cohen was dismissed by an order-in-council. The reconstituted NWLB was an industrial court, it stated, whose members were to hold independent, judicial attitudes; the chair had written the prime minister that Cohen's attitude was inconsistent with the board's principles; Cohen's public statements before the release of the reports 'indicate an attitude incompatible with the proper exercise of the functions to be performed by the members of the Board.' The prime minister therefore revoked the appointment.[55] Cohen had lost an influential job; it was probably a personal blow, though he denied it to the press. In adopting the tactics of confrontation, he chose to apply political pressure to achieve collective-bargaining legislation.

In a press release, Cohen characterized his firing as 'a fresh manifestation of its [the government's] hostility to the organized labour movement in Canada,' because labour was denied representation on the NWLB.[56] King was 'prepared to sacrifice labour's interests ... to blind partisanship of the present administration.' He accused Justice McTague of evading his responsibilities by defining the board as a non-partisan industrial court which would continue to function before new legislation was passed. He publicized his report's recommendation for the continuation of a tripartite board, because, as he astutely commented, 'the practical experience which such representatives could carry with them on such a Board is indispensable for its successful operation. It is idle to talk about judicial application or a judicial approach until practical standards have been established by which judicial action is to be governed. The establishment of these practical standards is a creative and important aspect of the administration of a Labour Code, and the active participation of direct representatives of management and labour is a prerequisite to a realistic and successful treatment of the whole problem.' The point of the code was to bring management and labour closer together. As he pointed out accurately, he had been consistent with the NWLB and the government about his views on the proper composition of the board. Cohen's reasoned support for tripartism is important, since this element would persist in many future labour boards, which would function much as he had foreseen.

Cohen's repeated public demands for the reports' release led King to note in his diary that Cohen was 'trying to create prejudice against myself personally for his dismissal, putting it on my anti-labour attitude. This is all part of the political game of the CCF. They have not dared to attack me personally while seeking to have Cohen create prejudice.'[57] Cohen told the press a day after his firing that the notion that the board 'clearly envisaged an independent and judicial attitude on the part of its members' was simply 'another piece of hypocrisy. The quarrel with me is just that I insisted on being independent of Government influence. What the Government sought was a servile government instrument ... They are not disappointed with my lack of independence. What they have been troubled about is my insistence upon being independent.'[58]

The *Globe and Mail* approved of the government's action to end what it regarded as an impossible situation at the NWLB. Its editorial, entitled 'Mr. Cohen Is Out,' asserted 'that Mr. Cohen could continue to remain a member of the Board while refusing to perform his duty upon it, and at the same time indulge in polemics against the authority which appointed him and the laws he was assigned to assist in administering, was an absurdity which must surely have been apparent to everybody but Mr. Cohen himself.' The paper adopted McTague's view of the board and that board members, like judges, were to 'observe, maintain, administer and help enforce the law,' not rewrite laws. King had granted labour *his initial election over the plaudits speaks to his need for approval.*

representation, but no individual had the right to ob-struct the board and Cohen's behaviour had set back labour's interests.[59]

Two weeks after the TLC convention, Cohen addressed the CCL convention in Montreal in another partisan political speech. Well known to delegates, he was viewed as a labour statesman. Delegates probably saw his demand for the reports' release as that of a principled man fired for his outspoken beliefs. Cohen had never regarded the board position as a career stepping stone, though he had become interested in public life. His speech was his report to delegates and the nation on 'the discharge of the functions and responsibilities' of the NWLB inquiry.[60]

He again called for public reports, because delay was not in the public interest. He refuted editorials that discussed the NWLB's function as solely to interpret and administer existing laws, and he reminded the convention that the reconstituted NWLB was to ascertain what labour laws and what labour policy should exist. 'It was upon *that* basis that I was invited to become a member of the Board. It was upon *that* basis that I agreed to accept, and did accept the appointment.'[61] The board had conducted its own inquiry, which was supposed to correct an existing policy that was unsound and injurious to the war effort.

Clearly, Cohen saw his role as that of a policy maker. The government had appointed the board in response to demands for labour-policy changes but also to delay immediate legislation, and Cohen had been frustrated. He was consciously using his constituency to pressure the government. The man was self-propelled; he had his own agenda, which meant ultimately that he could not be controlled. He would work within the system (as he had in Ontario drafting legislation and on the NWLB) if that served his purpose of achieving a labour code. But, as a partisan, he was equally capable of publicly embarrassing the government, if that tactic achieved the desired legislative goal. Eugene Forsey once described Cohen as a man of 'genuine devotion to the labour movement ... [who] did not think of himself as a mere adviser but rather as a force, a guru, a leader,' behaviour, of course, that enraged King and McTague.[62]

Cohen did not want his report ignored, as Leonard Marsh's 1943 report to the government on a comprehensive system of social security had been. He respected the law, which he used as an instrument of reform, and had influenced the making of new law, but just as the crisis in the steel industry had resulted in a new board and its inquiry, he deliberately provoked another 'crisis' to get the reports released. 'How regrettable that crises are needed,' he said, 'in order to bring about effective government or management action on matters of essential public interest.'[63] It was not a politician's approach of seeking compromise to accommodate different interests. The kind of flexibility Justice McTague exhibited, of which the prime minister was a master, could not work for Cohen on this issue of new labour policy. Cohen praised workers' contribution to the war effort, repeated his call for 'proper' labour law, and, as in the past, urged labour to unite to force the government to act. His speech was a remarkable, unprecedented performance by a union counsel.

Cohen had become nationally known, but he remained an individualist, whose influence was primarily outside governing circles. His understanding of the legal system was practical and profound, and his sense of urgency over labour policy reflected his political goals and his view of the country's future. His pressure of course did not win him any friends in government.

King, meanwhile, was engaged in a complicated strategy to undercut the CCF's growing support by moving the Liberal Party left while at the same time placating conservative business interests and cabinet ministers who had coordinated the military and war-production efforts. The political compromise that emerged was to focus on reconstruction, introduce some social-welfare legislation, make concessions to labour on the collective-bargaining issue, but hold the line on wage controls. The order of the new policies was revealing. First, the government introduced family allowances, which labour opposed as an inadequate substitute for wage increases. Next, a new order confirmed continued wage controls, and finally the government proclaimed a collective-bargaining policy. Accordingly, on 4 December, the prime minister stated that the reports were being 'carefully studied;' on 28 January 1944 the reports were tabled in the House of Commons.[64] McTague was consulted about legislative drafts and, in February, P.C. 1003 inaugurated collective-bargaining legislation in Canada.

The press interviewed Cohen about these developments, for he retained a high profile. Family allowances, though an admirable social-security measure, were in the current context 'a means of avoiding the necessity of dealing in forthright, direct fashion with the question of wages.'[65] He criticized the new wage-control order, which King delivered 'in his usual unctious manner' in a speech on 'the Battle of Inflation.' The order was not based on the two NWLB reports, as King implied, Cohen declared, because it did not leave the lowest wages free of control but instead dealt with cases of 'gross inequities' as the ground for wage adjustment, considered an employer's ability to pay, and did not take account of workers' productivity.

AFTER THE NWLB

When P.C. 1003 was proclaimed, Cohen's NWLB position was filled by J.A. Bell of the Order of Railroad Telegraphers. Early in 1944, McTague left the board to chair the Progressive Conservative Party, much to King's disgust, since he had considered asking him to be his labour minister. His successor was Justice Maynard Archibald of the Nova Scotia Supreme Court. Only Lalande remained, and when the new NWLB reverted to interpreting wage-controls policy narrowly, labour's animosity was renewed. When wage controls ended in 1947, the NWLB disbanded.[66]

After Cohen was fired from the NWLB, he returned to practice, but he also made public speeches to various groups, including the Rotary Club of Toronto and the Business and Professional Men's Club. On these occasions, he spoke as a 'labour statesman,' using moderate language about the national interest and the post-war period. In all his scenarios for the future, labour policy and a modern industrial-relations system were important. He put behind him his 'purely political,' not personal, differences with Justice McTague.

Cohen seemed to move closer to the CCF, for when his name was mentioned in 1944 as a possible federal candidate, he did not stifle the rumours. In a speech on the 'complicated' steel case, he referred to Ted Jolliffe as 'our friend, the Leader of the Ontario Opposition,' who 'played an effective role for the union.' Cohen was flirting seriously with entering politics and his public addresses were political. He pointed out, for example, that collective-bargaining legislation might have been introduced when employment was increasing and unions could use it effectively, but the government was 'hesitant and doubtful and studious and dubious.' After much delay, it promised legislation when 'layoffs mark the industrial scene from one end of the country to the other.' On a statement of George Drew's that current politics was about revolution or reform, Cohen countered that the issue was between reform and reaction.[67] In the midst of this active public life, Cohen injured his arm. He clearly needed rest, but, as David Lewis, CCF national secretary, noted, 'you don't carry out the instructions of your doctors.'[68]

CONTEMPORARY ANALYSES OF P.C. 1003

P.C. 1003 – the Wartime Labour Relations Regulations – proclaimed in February 1944, marked a turning point in the Canadian industrial-relations system. In the brief Cohen/McTague period, the NWLB had helped bring about that change. By pressing for a labour policy that facilitated union organization, the new board became a vehicle for popular pressures and 'used its jealously guarded independence, industrial relations experts, and expansive powers to push collective bargaining to the top of the national agenda.' While McTague and Lalande were liberal pluralists seeking to end wartime industrial conflict, Cohen was 'intent on winning industrial democracy for workers,' but despite their differences they used their positions to convince Mackenzie King to move beyond conciliation mechanisms.[69] The combination of pressure from a grass-roots social movement with widespread support and a sympathetic board stimulated policy makers to act and resulted in this major policy breakthrough.

'For the first time in Canadian history, a federal law compelled employers to recognize and bargain with the representatives of their employees choosing,' writes historian Taylor Hollander.[70] It thereby curbed managements' prerogative and adopted the major recommendations of both NWLB reports: the right to organize and bargain collectively, certification of unions with majority support, and the principle of exclusive bargaining agency. It defined unfair labour practices and outlawed company unions. It established a tripartite administrative tribunal (rather than a court) with powers of enforcement, thereby incorporating U.S. Wagner Act principles but at the same time maintaining the distinctive Canadian policy of compulsory conciliation prior to a legal strike. Unlike the American legislation, a Depression measure designed to encourage economic recovery, the Canadian order-in-council contained no preamble stating that collective bargaining was in the public interest and a desirable method of conducting labour relations, for the government's motivation was simply to eliminate industrial conflict.[71] Workers in Canada, unlike American employees, could not strike nor could employers lock them out during the term of an agreement, and to maintain the language of even-handedness, even though it bore no relation to reality, the Canadian legislation outlawed unfair labour practices for *both* employers and unions.

Cohen's response to the order received widespread publicity. Despite some shortcomings, in his view, P.C. 1003 marked 'in many respects a satisfactory beginning of a new labour policy.' He wrote to CPC leader Tim Buck, 'The voice of labour and the threat of the CCF ... in B.C. and other areas had been crucial to forcing the Liberals to grant the new labour code ... The gains should be enlarged [by] ... the same processes and forces.'[72] Cohen advised labour to be energetic in gaining the full benefits of the legislation, so that it could solidify its position and power, contribute to public affairs, and advance national policies. The improvements in labour laws and their administration had not come 'as manna from heaven' but from the 'combined influence and insistence of labour and generally the progressive forces within the country' and decisive action at strategic times.

Despite defects in the policy, David Lewis observed that 'you [Cohen] and Eugene [Forsey] feel relatively pleased with it.'[73] The Department of Labour asked Cohen's advice about P.C. 1003's regulations, which he suggested should be simple.[74] Labour welcomed the protective legislation that eliminated recognition strikes. Employers' opposition to trade unionism continued, but certain practices became illegal. The dominion legislation superseded provincial legislation in 1944, and in Ontario, for example, the government repealed its provincial act and established a board to replace the labour court.

Though delighted to have collective-bargaining rights, the CCL established a committee of its leaders to recommend amendments to both P.C. 1003 and wage order P.C. 9384.[75] It retained Cohen to identify weaknesses and prepare a report, which in 1945 was sent to the Department of Labour and all congress unions.[76] The most important defect in P.C. 1003, he concluded, was that the order did not certifiy trade unions but 'bargaining representatives.' The motive behind this procedure may have been to assist employees committees, but for Cohen, 'the existence of a continuing entity which can and does review and shape negotiations as they are carried on is the first essential of any bona fide collective bargaining process.' The committee recommended that a trade union or a genuinely independent employees' association be certified for bargaining purposes, a change the government adopted.

Labour wanted a clearer disqualification of 'company unions' but did not achieve the total ban of sections 8(a)(2) and 2(5) of the Wagner Act, since Canadian boards certified non-union representation committees so long as they appeared independent of employers, and employer-dominated groups could exist without certification. After the war, unions grew and non-unions declined, but the greater flexibility in Canadian legislation may have prevented employer backlash, which in the United States resulted in the Taft-Hartley Act 1947.[77]

The committee advocated simple, prompt certification procedures to avoid lengthy hearings.[78] It recognized that representation votes were often occasions when employers used subtle tactics of intimidation. It supported grievance procedures for in-contract disputes with binding arbitration as the final stage of settlement, and a ban on strikes during the term of a collective agreement. It advocated a provision whereby the board could incorporate a union-security clause in a collective agreement and enforce it. This proposal reflected a concern over the future status of unions which erupted in the Ford strike of 1945. The committee sought simpler conciliation procedures and, surprisingly, recommended that if conciliation boards' reports were unanimous, or if the chair and the union representative agreed, the reports should be binding. This suggestion, like the union-security proposal, was not implemented, but it reflected the strength and prevalence of employers' anti-union tactics at the time. After drafting these proposals, Cohen considered the new wage-control policy, P.C. 9384, to which he and labour remain opposed.[79]

Cohen also published articles praising the new collective-bargaining policy. He defended P.C. 1003 after Joe Salsberg, director of the CPC's trade-union wing, and George Grube of the CCF ascribed 'faults and virtues to the new federal legislation according to their own particular slant,' with the former being overly optimistic and the latter overly pessimistic about the order's effect. The Communists attributed the new government policy to international developments and ignored the domestic pressures of CCF growth, industrial unrest, and political pressure, which actually brought it about.[80] The CCFers minimized the order's significance, focusing on its inadequacies and the business opposition it had aroused.

Cohen was critical of both views. As a person who was in a position to know, he understood the political context in which the policy was introduced. As a pragmatic reformer, he wrote that 'the King government was both frightened and enlightened when it enacted P.C.1003;' the task of those who believed in collective bargaining was to analyze the legislation, and 'from the political realities known to us,' estimate what led to inclusion or exclusion of clauses, and then use the measure even with its shortcomings to promote adjustments which would further labour's interests, and possibly also those of the political left.[81]

Cohen used the order to his union clients' advantage in this way, and as he worked with the legislation, he decided that boards should be smaller, full-time bodies. In August 1944 he wrote to George Burt that company unions were still not illegal. 'I have just been able to get from Finkelman's Board for the first time a judgment ruling a company union off the ballot because of employer interference, but this is very new. In any event it stretches the regulations to its utmost.' He concluded ruefully, 'This, by the way, is a heck of a way to spend a holiday. I am supposed to be forgetting all this so that my mind can be fully rested and come back as good even as J.B. Aylesworth!'[82] But he loved the work and, knowing that his clients needed his advice, continued his furious pace. After the NWLB experience, he was back in the trenches as a working labour lawyer.

The political impact of P.C. 1003 reduced labour's opposition to the dominion government, decreased conflict, and increased union membership. Strikes declined and, between March 1944 and July 1946, the new labour boards granted 76 per cent of all certification applications, while the failure rate for contract negotiations was only 3.5 per cent. Thus, the new environment created a 15 per cent increase in total union membership.[83] Because the legislation was a temporary order-in-council, workers at the end of the war, felt uncertain about the future and worried about the permanence of their wartime organizational and legislative gains. Their insecurity resulted in a massive strike wave in 1945 and 1946. In 1945 a federal-provincial conference agreed that provinces would resume their constitutional jurisdiction over most labour matters and in 1948 the Industrial Relations and Disputes Investigation Act implemented P.C.1003's provisions permanently in federal jurisdiction. Similar legislation was passed in the provinces. All these statutes incorporated the collective-bargaining principle won during the war, as well as some CCL amendments drafted by Cohen.

By then, Cohen was no longer involved. After he assisted the CCL in analysing the new policy, Cohen's most influential and public years as a labour lawyer were over. His life began to unravel following his NWLB appointment, and Mackenzie King inadvertently struck the first blow when he fired him from the board.

Part Three

War and Aftermath,
1939–1946

7

Defending Wartime Internees, 1939–1943

The midnight knock at the door. A visit from the secret police. And suddenly a political dissident is hauled off to a concentratio ̸amp. No charges are laid, no lawyers are allowed, no jury ever renders a verdict. Labour leaders disappear in the midst of negotiations. Religious organizations have their buildings seized, their publications suppressed. All in the name of national security.[1]

Lister Sinclair

IMPLEMENTING THE POLICY

J.L. Cohen was a lawyer deeply involved in disturbing occurrences, such as the ones described in the above quotation. He defended many internees, criticized the process, and demanded that the government amend it to protect civil liberties better. Two days after the government passed the War Measures Act, in September 1939, it proclaimed the Defence of Canada Regulations (DOCR), which gave it sweeping powers to arrest and detain without charge both alien and Canadian-born persons, considered to be a threat to national security.

Since 1938–9, government officials had discussed what security problems were likely to arise in a war. After several false starts and a period of inertia, policy decisions were made in the atmosphere of crisis following Hitler's invasion of Czechoslovakia. In September 1938 the Committee on Emergency Legislation (CEL) revised a First World War order to

produce Defence of Canada Order (DCO) 1938.[2] The RCMP and the
Department of National Defence (DND) wanted broad powers of arrest
and detention for non-aliens as well as enemy aliens. The Naturalization
Act revoked the citizenship of naturalized British subjects engaged in
seditious acts, making them eligible for alien internment. Additional
powers of prosecution were in the Criminal Code, and officials examined the severe British Defence Regulations before the arbitrary-deten-
tion regulation was included in the revised 1939 DCO. That
controversial clause provoked disagreement in the CEL and the cabinet
about the proper balance between state power and individual civil liberties. It was ultimately passed with Minister of Justice Ernest Lapointe's
support, but it was the only Defence of Canada Regulation that did not
receive unanimous cabinet approval, and during the war it would provoke discussion and amendments.[3]

The policy was relatively liberal towards Europeans, in that each
enemy alien was judged as an individual. This seemed appropriate
since only a small percentage of Germans and Italians in Canada
belonged to right-wing extremist groups; most had arrived before the
rise of the right in Europe in the 1930s and thus were distanced from
contemporary politics in their homelands. The policy suited the RCMP,
which was so unconcerned by Nazi organizations in Canada that not
until mid-1939 did it seriously consider the security threat they posed.[4]
In contrast, from 1931, when Communist leaders were convicted under
section 98 of the Criminal Code, the RCMP focused on them and would
target them for arbitrary detention.[5] The approach to Asian enemy
aliens was illiberal, sweeping, and influenced by a history of racism
towards such immigrants and fear of Japanese militarism. Well before
Pearl Harbor, government officials were prepared to deal with Asian
aliens collectively and severely, and even Canadian-born Japanese were
targetted for internment camps.[6]

When the DOCR were proclaimed in September 1939, the arbitrary-
detention clauses, Regulations 21 and 22, entitled the minister of justice,
on advice from the police, to arrest and intern individuals deemed dangerous to the nation's security. Alien internment was covered in Regulations 24 to 26 but was not the focus of Cohen's legal efforts. Though an
internee could appeal to an advisory committee and receive reasons for
the arrest, the burden of proof was placed on the accused, reversing normal peacetime trial procedures. The committee could recommend the
internee's release to the minister, but he could reject its recommendation. In William Kaplan's view, the regulations were an 'extraordinary

infringement on the civil rights of an individual' and only tolerable for the country at war,[7] and Ramsay Cook has written that the DOCR 'represented the most serious restrictions upon the civil liberties of Canadians since Confederation.'[8] Officials who favoured broad powers of arrest and detention had won a bureaucratic struggle against liberal elements 'hoping to preserve as much individual freedom as possible.'[9]

The war crisis affected everyone, not just soldiers and munitions workers. Public attention focused on the battle in Europe, but the media also warned citizens to look for spies, members of Hitler's fifth column, seeking to undermine Canadian security by trading secrets to the enemy or by sabotage.[10] Internees included Adrien Arcand, a fascist in Quebec; neo-Nazis and neo-fascists, many of German and Italian origin; thousands of Japanese who were rounded up after Pearl Harbor and sent to separate camps; and even the mayor of Montreal, Camillien Houde, who, after advising non-cooperation during the registration of manpower under the National Resources Mobilization Act (NRMA), was interned in Camp Petawawa in Ontario and in one month lost fifty pounds sawing logs.

Internees almost invariably sought out J.L. Cohen. In addition to his growing labour-law practice, Cohen, as an exponent of civil liberties, represented three groups – the Jehovah's Witnesses, the Communists, and the Ukrainian Labour Farmer Temple Association (ULFTA).[11]

REPRESENTING THE WATCH TOWER SOCIETY

The Jehovah's Witnesses, known also as the Watch Tower Society, opposed organized religion and were virulently anti-Catholic. In 1939–40 an opponent, Cardinal Jean-Marie Rodrique Villeneuve, a church leader in Quebec, wanted to suppress the Witnesses and found Ernest Lapointe sympathetic.[12] In June 1940, in the fearful atmosphere following the fall of France, and as a result of political pressure from Conservatives and right-wing Liberals in Mitchell Hepburn's Ontario government,[13] P.C. 2363 expanded a DOCR regulation to suppress over thirty 'subversive' organizations. The order banned the CPC for its anti-war stand, several left-wing organizations, the Jehovah's Witnesses (the only religion), three allegedly pro-fascist German organizations, and left-wing ethnic clubs such as the Finnish Organization of Canada, the Polish Peoples Association, the Russian Workers and Farmers Club, and the Ukrainian Labour Farmer Temple Association (ULFTA).[14] Anyone in such organizations could be arrested and interned.

When CCF MP Angus MacInnis asked why the Jehovah's Witnesses were banned, the prime minister replied that its literature disclosed 'that man-made authority or law should not be recognized if it conflicts with the Jehovah's Witnesses' interpretation of the Bible; that they refuse to salute the flag of any nation ... and ... they oppose war. The general effect of this literature is ... to undermine the ordinary responsibilities of citizens, particularly in time of war.'[15] No other public information was forthcoming, but an internal memo described them as a group 'whose activities aimed at 'stirring up animosity between all religions' and governments. In a war its program was 'subversive' for it viewed other religions as 'rackets,' described the Red Cross as doing 'the Devil's work,' and favoured pacifism. Its activities were a nuisance, its literature prejudicial to the war effort, its teachings anti-Catholic, and its ideas tantamount to 'ecclesiastical Bolshevism.'[16]

Immediately prior to the ban, the Watch Tower Society hired Cohen and sent him a $5,000 retainer, which was a welcome change from his experience with less affluent clients. It knew that he supported unpopular causes and was an effective counsel. Cohen may have accepted partly because the Jehovah's Witnesses were one of the few groups in Germany defying Hitler.[17] But he knew relatively little about them, and so he contacted a clipping service for information and read their literature to educate himself. As he wrote to E.J. McMurray in Winnipeg, the order could not be reversed because in Ottawa 'the sense of apprehension here ... dominates every thought and consideration.' The parliamentary committee established to review the DOCR refused to hear from any banned group, and thus Cohen could not appear on behalf of his client.[18]

Cohen had conflicts with this client. Kaplan has written that Cohen 'had a sympathy for the underdog and he was in his own way a straight shooter. He refused to accept cases without any prospect of success and he went into court and argued law; any other instructions Cohen refused to accept.' Charles Morrell,[19] an active Jehovah's Witness, wrote privately in 1943 that they had difficulty in getting Cohen to do 'what we want the way we want.'[20]

The Jehovah's Witnesses were given no specific reasons for the ban. Only a few members were actually interned, but over five hundred were prosecuted for DOCR violations. Provincial crown attorneys would request their respective attorneys general for consent to prosecute members of the illegal group. In Ontario, Attorney General Gordon Conant was particularly zealous, and police arrested, searched, questioned, jailed, and charged scores of Witnesses in 1940–1 for membership, canvassing, possessing literature, not saluting the flag, or not joining the armed services. Conant even surveyed Ontario government employees to determine how many were Jehovah's Witnesses and threatened them with loss of employment and/or a court case if they did not break with their church.[21]

Cohen travelled by train throughout the province seeing to the Witnesses' legal needs.[22] He could not represent everyone charged, but he did defend many. In August 1940, for example, George Bottomly was picked up in Beaverton while distributing literature and found guilty of membership. The county court judge only reluctantly allowed an appeal, since the Watch Tower Society, he stated, was an unpatriotic, illegal organization. Cohen corrected him, saying that, while he himself did not support its point of view, their religious concepts had brought them into conflict with military service; 'there was no suggestion that they were unpatriotic' even in the House of Commons.[23] The church encouraged individuals to represent themselves in court, plead not guilty, opt for jury trials, and go to jail rather than pay fines. Some were refused bail or were released after large bail payments, which the Watch Tower Society raised and Cohen recorded.

Other clients were charged with possession of illegal literature, such as Edward Cambridge of Fort Erie. In May 1942 the police raided Jack McDowell's home in Stratford and charged him with possessing a copy of 'Children,' a Jehovah's Witnesses booklet. He was eventually acquitted, with the judge ruling that having an interest in the organization did not prove membership. Delighted, McDowell thanked Cohen for 'your effective manner in court.'[24] E. Spalding, owner of a printing company, was charged, remanded on bail, and later convicted of printing subversive literature that was likely to prejudice recruiting.[25] Almost all those prosecuted were convicted, but the number of charges declined as the war continued.

Several cases concerned schools, for children of Jehovah's Witnesses were suspended for not singing the national anthem or refusing to salute the flag.[26] The first time parents were prosecuted involved Cohen in a case in Kitchener. They received a suspended sentence and the children were permitted to return to school if they followed the rules. But the situation escalated; a boy in Tillsonburg was expelled, as were two girls in Tavistock.[27] In Hamilton, twenty-six students were suspended. Clarence Leeson and his wife had instructed their two children not to take part in opening exercises because it conflicted with the family's religious beliefs. The parents were arrested, held for ten days in jail before being charged, released on bail, found guilty in county court, and sentenced to four months in jail plus a fine and costs. Cohen appealed the case on the ground that the evidence did not support the conviction. During the trial, the teacher who had sent home the children (aged seven and nine years old) agreed that they could be excused from religious exercises but had to sing the anthem and salute the flag. Throughout the trial, Cohen's objections were overruled, and he lost the case.[28]

Eric Ellison wished his son Arthur to attend school and be excused from class during opening exercises. Instead, Arthur was charged under the Juvenile Delinquents Act for being unlawfully absent from school. Cohen decided to make his a test case, in what became 'one of the more important religious liberty trials in Canadian history.'[29] Cohen's brief attacked Regulation 14, which required singing the national anthem, in every primary school. He argued that it did not say that a student was obligated to sing, and further that the regulation was subject to a conscientious-objection provision of Ontario's Public Schools Act, which was as old as the school system itself. Arthur was not unlawfully absent, but was excluded from school, despite his persistent attempts to return. Cohen wanted the charges dropped. His reasoned presentation should have won the case, for the prosecutor made a weak but patriotic argument, but Judge Burbridge ignored Cohen, decided that all children should sing the national anthem, and found Ellison guilty. He also expressed extraneous, unfavourable opinions of the sect.[30] The court removed Arthur from his family and placed him in foster care, and thereafter similar orders were issued for other children.

Cohen appealed the case to the Supreme Court of Ontario, where Justice Hugh Edward Rose quashed Burbridge's judgment and ordered the parties to settle out of court. In January 1941 the Department of Education directed Ontario school boards to allow children to absent themselves from opening exercises, but despite this policy, in Hamilton, instances persisted where non-conformist children were expelled from school. In March 1944 Cohen repeated his arguments in the Donald case, the judge dismissed it, and the Donald brothers (one in primary and one in high school) remained expelled.

The DOCR permitted indefinite detention of persons considered a threat, but sometimes abuses and mistakes occurred. In June 1940, for example, Cohen took the case of Aurelio D'Appolonia for the Watch

Tower Society. It was a mix-up from the beginning, but it revealed short-comings both in the internment policy and in Cohen. He wrote to W.R. Jackett, director of internment operations, to inquire about the charge, which he presumed, since his client was Canadian-born, was under Regulation 21. After the Department of Justice checked with the RCMP, Jackett confirmed that assumption. When Cohen received the charge in July, he was non-plussed, for it read, 'Representations have been made that you are a member of the Fascist Party, a subversive organization which is opposed to the interests of Canada. It would appear that you are disloyal to Canada.'[31] Cohen asked for an interview with his client before the hearing, and told Jackett that 'I may state that I am somewhat shocked at the charge made with respect to this man and ... if, on inter-viewing him, it appears to me at all that there is basis for the charge made, both those who have instructed me and I personally will regard it as our duty to withdraw completely from the matter.'[32] While Cohen upheld civil liberties, his commitment apparently did not extend to defending fascists.

Cohen heard from a Mina Brodie that D'Appolonia, whose friends called him 'Ral,' was very downhearted in the camp and had lost fifteen pounds. She told Cohen that the Watch Tower Society was not an illegal organization when Ral was its caretaker, suggested two people who would provide supportive affidavits, and even wrote to Prime Minister King concerning Ral's arrest, which was part of 'the round-up of Italians in Toronto.' She pointed out that no other employees had been interned, that Ral was a labourer and not responsible for the society's policies, and that 'some malicious person has given false information about the boy.'[33]

Cohen met Ral at the July hearing before Judge James Duncan Hynd-man. He realized that the charge was absurd and asked a R.M. Hearst for a statutory declaration vouching for Ral's character, hoping to obtain his immediate release. Hearst stated that D'Appolonia was 'a quiet, peace-able, law-abiding young man of the highest principles,' was never a member of the 'Fascist Party,' had no connection with either pro-German or Communist movements, and had 'definitely shown a dislike for all such radical movements.'[34] Others corroborated this view, and Cohen sent their testimony to Judge Hyndman.

In August, Cohen wrote to Jackett that his client's arrest was an error and that he wanted to speak to Hyndman. The judge was out of town hearing appeals, but after waiting three months, Cohen wrote a coldly furious letter, recounting the times he was put off and repeating that the charge was 'fantastic and grotesque.' Ral was ill and Cohen demanded his immediate release. Six days later, the minister freed D'Appolonia.[35] Later still, Cohen received an explanation for the injustice. Apparently his surname had appeared on an Italian organization's list, but it almost certainly belonged to his cousin, A. D'Appolonia, a young priest in Toronto in 1941, who might have joined a fascist organization without intending to get Ral into trouble.[36]

As the war continued, the arrests of Jehovah's Witnesses gradually decreased. Cohen then spent time negotiating property matters with the custodian of enemy property for the disposition of the sect's Canadian assets, and arranging for bail money in many cases.[37] When the Jehovah's Witnesses ceased operations in Canada, their debts were paid by the custodian's agents, while surplus funds were held by a bank under the custodian's control and disposed of by the government. The Witnessess's Toronto building was managed by a trustee at their expense until the custodian and the sect agreed on its disposal. Cohen contacted the group's lawyer in the United States, who arranged that books, literature, printing equipment, and furniture be sent to head office in Brooklyn, New York. When a shipment from Vancouver to Seattle was stopped at the border, Cohen got permission for it to proceed to its destination.[38]

In 1944, when Cohen was counsel to the United Mine Workers during the royal commission hearings on the coal industry, he ceased representing the Jehovah Witnesses. In the autumn of 1943, the organization was removed from the DOCR's list of banned groups, but some of its publications remained outlawed. Nevertheless, despite government repression, it actually increased its membership from 3,000 in 1939 to 15,000 in 1945.[39]

DEFENDING COMMUNISTS

Cohen became involved with interned Communists. The CPC's policy had many twists and turns between 1935 and 1939, but with the growing threat from the right, it adopted a 'popular front' policy to work with other left-wing groups and within existing trade unions.[40] When unexpectedly, in 1939, Stalin and Hitler signed the Nazi-Soviet Pact, the CPC opposed Canada's participation in the war. In the 1940 national election, the CPC's manifesto condemned British imperialism as just as responsible for the war as German imperialism, and accused the Canadian government and ruling class of depending on the hegemony of

British imperialism in Europe and of seeking war profits. This stand angered many and made the Communists unpopular. In June 1940 the government decided that the CPC's activities were inimical to the national interest and banned the party. The RCMP began arresting its members, including some trade unionists. When Germany attacked the Soviet Union in 1941 and the Soviets joined the Allies, the CPC immediately flip-flopped and favoured an all-out war effort. It lobbied the government to release Communist internees, which it did gradually.

The Cases of Pat Sullivan and C.S. Jackson

Pat Sullivan, head of the Canadian Seamen's Union, was the first and most prominent trade unionist to be arrested following an early important wartime labour dispute. In 1940 the CSU had notified several companies that it intended to negotiate new contracts when the Great Lakes shipping agreements of 1938 expired. The employers stalled, and the CSU was obliged legally to apply for conciliation. Fearing that conciliation would cause delay and favour the companies, the union called an illegal strike. On 14 April 1940, six thousand seamen ceased work and tied up two hundred ships. Violence erupted as the companies imported strikebreakers, CSU members were arrested, and the federal minister of labour ordered the union to end the strike. He provided for an interim wage increase and a conciliation board chaired by Justice C.P. McTague, on which J.L. Cohen sat as the union's nominee. After the board's report recommended that the shipping companies recognize the union, the CSU was entitled legally to strike against those that would not negotiate. The strike affected about fifty ships – a small part of the Great Lakes fleet – employing six hundred seamen, but since it was wartime, shipowner Scott Misener asked the labour minister to declare the CSU 'subversive' and 'illegal.' He refused, but at a time when Hitler was conquering Europe and the Allies were dependent on Canadian supplies, the government was greatly concerned about the disruption. Many Canadians viewed the strike as unpatriotic and an example of the CPC's opposition to the war.

The RCMP had kept CSU leaders, whom its undercover agents confirmed in 1939–40 belonged to the CPC, under surveillance. It reported to the justice minister that a CPC plan existed to use Great Lakes ships to smuggle banned literature from the United States. It claimed that Communist seamen were to relay timetable, destination, and cargo information to the party leadership, which could use it for sabotage and espionage. On the eve of the 1940 strike, an agent reported that the CPC viewed the conflict as a 'trial balloon,' and that if it succeeded, the party planned other stoppages through unions it controlled.[41] The strike ended, but when the government read the agent's report, it banned the CPC and interned leading party members including Sullivan.

The other CSU personnel picked up included David Sinclair, editor of the union paper *Searchlight*, Charles Murray, who organized fishermen in Nova Scotia and in 1939 was in an unsuccessful union-recognition dispute in Lockeport, J.S. Chapman, and Joseph Cline. All became Cohen's clients. They joined 112 labour activists (union organizers, local politicians, and journalists) arrested without warrants or charges and interned as Communists.[42] Not all were party members, and those who were, denied it. They included Winnipeg alderman Jacob Penner; Pat Lenihan, a mining organizer and Calgary alderman; Dick Steele, an early CIO organizer in Ontario, who would die overseas in battle; Bill Walsh, who organized rubber, auto, and electrical workers; and Kent Rowley, involved with lumber, garment, and textile workers. Later, UEW leader C.S. Jackson, who was prominent in the Canadian Congress of Labour, was interned briefly, and like Sullivan, a leader in the Trades and Labour Congress, he too was represented by Cohen. All were arrested on the basis of evidence the police submitted to the minister of justice.[43]

Cohen's role as counsel in these cases was to learn DOCR procedures, try to represent his clients as best he could given the restrictions, and, as he did so, raise issues concerning the rights of individuals and the inadequacies of the tribunals. The RCMP arrested Sullivan at the St Regis Hotel in Toronto in June 1940. He spent a day in a police station and then went to Don Jail. He was moved to the Canadian National Exhibition Buildings, a temporary barracks, where he stayed for a month. He had a miserable time, since about sixty Italian and German Fascist/Nazi party members were there, arrested shortly after Italy had declared war on the Allies. A strict army major was in charge and each day internees exercised by picking up garbage from sidewalks, under armed guard. Next Sullivan went to Camp Petawawa, which C.S. Jackson later described as 'a large barbed-wire compound with sentry towers at intervals on the perimeter, and one dining hut for over 700 internees.' A reserve corps guarded the camp, which Sullivan said contained '15 huts, each capable of housing from 45 to 70 persons.' The small wooden structures had double bunks and straw mattresses, and in the middle of each was a large barrel stove. One hut was for Germans exclusively; two were occupied by Adrien Arcand and members of his Parti de l'Unité

Nationale, whom the RCMP had arrested belatedly, long after their underground printing press produced pamphlets blaming the war on the Jews, and whose party headquarters contained swastika banners, German propaganda, and a plan for a Canadian Nazi army of seventy thousand.[44] Sullivan said that 'the remainder, with the exception of hut 7, were occupied by Italians. Hut 7, of course was our hut and became known to the camp inmates as the International Hut.'[45] It was crowded with nearly one hundred people in it.

Lieutenant-Colonel H.E. Pense, whom Sullivan found strict but fair, was in command. The food was army fare, and prisoners wore prisoner-of-war clothing; they could receive packages from outside and one letter a week, which was censored, as were any books that they were permitted. Jackson was the most fortunate; he received packages from local unions and distributed their contents through the hut committee. The camp day began at 5:30 A.M.; prisoners laboured in work parties from 7 A.M. until about 5 P.M.; lights went out at 10. Jackson recalled, 'Each hut had to supply a quota of workers every day for work inside the compound, latrines, cleanup of grounds, etc., and another quota for work outside the compound on road building, wood cutting, etc.' Outside work gangs were paid twenty cents for an eight-hour day, and Jackson claimed that the contract for outside work was held by James Franceschini, an ex-internee, who received three to five dollars an hour for their labour. Each internee rotated between inside and outside work, which amounted to three days per week. They received a small amount of cash and eight-dollars-a-month worth of coupons to spend in the canteen on cigarettes and candy. In their leisure time the Communists held study sessions, though they had few books or magazines to read and newspapers were severely censored. They helped each other prepare for their appeal hearings. Some worked on crafts and produced some beautiful woodworking.[46]

Cohen faced the same problems and frustrations with all the Communist cases, but since Sullivan was their most prominent internee and the Communists organized committees all across the country to publicize his case, demand his release, and raise money for the Sullivan Defence Fund, it is emphasized here to demonstrate the process, though Jackson's case at the hearing stage is also discussed. As soon as Sullivan was arrested, the union contacted Cohen, who was catapulted into the silent, murky world of internment administrators. He immediately wrote to Justice Minister Ernest Lapointe to enquire about the charges against Sullivan; he also asked 'what procedure, if any, has been provided in respect to appeals in connection with matters of this sort.' He did not know where Sullivan was being held, but he wired Lapointe for permission to interview his client.[47]

Lieutenant-Colonel H. Stethem, assistant director of Internment Operations, eventually replied that an appeal could be made under Regulation 22 of the DOCR but that Cohen could not interview his client until just before the hearing.[48] Cohen had to apply formally for an appeal. He sent Sullivan the appeal form, on 6 July, wired Internment Operations on the twelfth, phoned on the thirteenth, and wrote the next day in a frustrated mood to the Department of Justice that it was 'totally impossible' to discover if the formal notice had been filed.[49] On 19 July he was informed that the advisory committee wanted to proceed soon; it asked when he could be at Petawawa for a hearing, and told him to contact Internment Operations if he wished to interview his client. Cohen still did not know the charges. Meanwhile, the advisory committee informed Sullivan that his hearing would be on 29 July, that he should be ready to present his case, and that he had been detained 'because representations have been made that you are a member of the Communist Party of Canada, a subversive organization which is opposed to the interests of Canada. In view of this, it would appear that you are disloyal to Canada.'[50]

Cohen interviewed Sullivan at Camp Petawawa, six weeks after his arrest. He told authorities that he was anxious to proceed but was indefinite about a time for Sullivan's hearing since he was worrying about the process. To Sullivan he wrote, 'I am quite concerned about the conditions governing these proceedings and I am very seriously considering the position which I, or any client represented by me should take in respect of the matter.' Because the government had refused to furnish details, 'I personally doubt [the] advisability of our proceeding with [the] type of enquiry proposed.'[51] Cohen faced the same predicament in Charles Murray's case. 'Beyond the blunt assertion that you are a member of the Communist Party of Canada,' he wrote to Murray, 'no particulars were forthcoming of the charges ... against you ... It did not appear ... that under such circumstances anything in the nature of a fair trial or hearing could be anticipated' and no preparation was possible without an indication of the nature of the charges.[52]

From the time Sullivan was arrested, a public and political dimension surrounded these internment cases, and thus Cohen worked on two levels as counsel to internees, concerned about their well-being, and as a public critic of the regulations. He disliked the DOCR's imprecise procedures, and he believed that his clients were arrested for being trade unionists as well as Communists. He publicized the cases on this basis, as did the CSU. Ernest Lapointe, however, told the House of Commons on 27 February 1941 that trade unionists who were interned were arrested because they were Communists, not because of their labour activities.[53]

The labour movement was concerned about the lack of protection for individual rights under existing internment procedures and 'the danger to the organized labour movement if its leaders can be apprehended in this way and held arbitrarily without trial,'[54] but it was also supportive of the war effort. Trade unionists, CCFers, and civil libertarians tried to balance their perceptions of the need for civil-defence requirements in wartime with their concern that protection of civil liberties in a democracy be safeguarded.

Labour politics were a factor as well. The labour movement had to be free to function effectively, but Communist trade unionists would not be defended if they were arrested for Communist, as opposed to trade union, activities. The TLC was bombarded with requests from affiliates to 'protest' the arrest of responsible labour officials. But TLC President Tom Moore eventually accepted the government's word that Sullivan's activities as a Communist, not as a trade unionist, had precipitated its decision to detain him, and while the timing of his arrest was unfortunate, the McTague conciliation report had favoured the union.

CCF leader M.J. Coldwell was less sure of the government's motives, and as a member of the committee reviewing the regulations he could monitor their administration. As late as May 1942, CCF MP J.W. Noseworthy, newly elected in an upset victory over Arthur Meighen in the York South by-election, spoke of a lingering suspicion, despite the government's reassuring statements, that 'men have been interned because of their work in labour organizations' and such doubts were 'a deterrent to our war effort to-day.'[55]

Moore articulated his position as early as August 1940 to W.R. Eggleton of the Port Arthur labour council in connection with Bruce Magnuson's arrest. He wrote, 'The reason for Magnuson's detention was that he was not only a member of the Communist Party but had continued activity in it knowing it to be an illegal organization. His arrest had nothing to do with the fact that he was an officer of the Trades and Labour Council and I am assured that the same action would have been taken if he had no connection whatever with the trade union movement.' The Congress's duty was not to protest DOCR detentions but 'to assure ourselves that persons are not being arrested because of anything done by them in carrying out trade union duties.' Unless evidence indicated that Magnuson was detained as a trade unionist, 'there would seem to be nothing we should do except allow the law to take its course.'[56]

Moore's positon differed from that of the radical labour minority, which viewed the internment of Communists and trade unionists as an 'undemocratic, un-Canadian procedure,' destructive of civil liberties, using methods that resembled those 'used to destroy the trade union movement in the Fascist countries.'[57] Years later C.S. Jackson wrote about his own experience and linked the internment of trade union leaders to a government attempt 'to head off the rising demands of the working people for the right to collective bargaining and union contracts, encouraged by the tremendous growth and successes of the CIO movement in the U.S.'[58] The Communists took this staunch civil-libertarian view, peppered with rhetoric about democracy, because they wanted to be free to operate politicially without restraint, both before and after the Soviet Union's entry into the war. When the Communists' line shifted to support for an all-out war effort, their position moved closer to the government's, though for different reasons, and restrictions were relaxed. Left-wing internees were released slowly, however, because mistrust and resentment remained for those who in 1939–41 had opposed the war.

The debate among trade unionists about the government's motives was a matter of perspective. Moore, who was probably being naive, was not too concerned that Communist activists who criticized Congress leadership had been removed from the scene temporarily. Cohen's direct experience with government administrators made him sceptical of government motives, and he was suspicious of the timing of Sullivan's arrest in the midst of a labour dispute. When the advisory committee questioned Sullivan on union matters, Cohen decided that the procedures were improper. Jackson, whose internment related directly to his trade-union work, confirmed Cohen's suspicions, but in the Jackson case the Toronto *Star* and the Civil Liberties Association of Toronto also thought the government was out of line. In contrast to Moore or other non-Communist trade unionists, Cohen's view was influenced also by his sympathy for the Communists' political activities. He believed strongly enough that the government's motives in interning Communist leaders were questionable that he wrote to CCL Executive Secretary Norman Dowd after he heard that Dowd had expressed little sympathy for Jackson's predicament in a private conversation with a friend at the 1941 Couchiching conference, an annual gathering on public affairs. Dowd responded with surprise and provided Cohen with an excerpt from his conference address in which he criticized the timing of the trade unionsts' arrests, the review process for internees, and the government's handling of the cases. He told Cohen that Congress officers had urged the minister of justice to give interned trade unionists a proper trial and that they had protested 'strenuously against the practice of arresting Labour leaders in the midst of Labour disputes.' He concluded, 'I have not now, and never had, any desire whatever to prejudice Brother Jackson's case.'[59] In response, Cohen backed off, saying that he did not think the rumour was correct, in view of the CCL's position on the matter.

Nevertheless, within the CCL, conflict between Communist and non-Communist trade unionists, which after the war would climax in the expulsion of several unions, was heating up and one month before C.S. Jackson was interned the CCL executive board suspended him. His internment experience did not heal his rift with the Congress, for Jackson believed, unfairly, that the CCL leadership was so steeped in anti-communism that it did not lift a finger to gain the release of the interned labour leaders. As Lapointe told the House, all parties involved – the police, trade unionists, politicians – knew that the level of Communist organizing activity and propaganda remained high.[60] The labour movement took a carefully considered position, supporting the DOCR as necessary in time of war but also supporting Cohen and other civil libertarians in their efforts to protect the rights of individuals by improving the appeal process and by ensuring that the regulations were administered without interference with lawful trade-union activities.[61]

With respect to the Sullivan case, Cohen bided his time while waiting for the DOCR procedures to become clearer. At first, the public favoured the ban on groups, but gradually the regulations came under close scrutiny and members of the opposition, particularly the CCF, out of concern for civil liberties, criticized the arbitrary process. The cabinet could alter the regulations and did; for example, on 5 June 1940 it added new illegal organizations.[62] In response to criticism, the government agreed to a special committee of the House of Commons to review the DOCR and, if necessary, revise them.

The House Committee

The members of the all-party committee changed each year, but in 1940 they included such luminaries as Brooke Claxton, M.J. Coldwell, and

John Diefenbaker. Over the summer, the committee met in camera for security reasons, and in August it released its report. The contents were not revealed, but the justice minister implemented amendments in 1941, which included changes to Regulation 21. Henceforth, the minister had to report all cases where he did not follow the advisory committee's recommendations on an appeal, and he also had to report every four weeks when the House was in session about the numbers of detainees and the status of their appeals.[63]

The establishment of the committee each session prompted debate, as did issues that touched on the regulations or on appropriation bills concerning the costs of their administration. Such debates were long and often quite good, though predictable, with Conservatives praising the police, Liberals applauding the minister of justice, and the CCF agreeing that the regulations were necessary in time of war but insisting that internees, including Communists – with whom, they always pointed out, they had serious differences – should have proper appeal procedures. Diefenbaker, whose maiden speech in Parliament was on the DOCR, and Coldwell in particular distinguished themselves. The committee's recommendations changed certain procedures in 1941 and consolidated the regulations, but its 1942 report was not adopted and by 1944 action under the regulations was rare.

One of the first submissions to the parliamentary committee was an unsolicited brief from J.L. Cohen. In William Kaplan's view, Cohen's brief was 'simple but profound' because it focused on the principal objection to internment procedures – the advisory committees – which replaced a trial in court and were one-person committees, not impartial quasi-judicial tribunals.[64] Cohen acknowledged the need in war to deny to certain persons a public trial, but he recommended that a proper board be appointed to hear internment appeals, since a broader mechanism was more likely to be impartial and thorough in its review of cases. The legislation had intended committees with several well-known and experienced individuals to compensate for the denial of a trial. The appointment of 'one-man' tribunals of unknown officials was inadequate. He recommended advisory committees with three persons who were capable administratively and whose stature made them identifiable to the public.[65] Cohen's call for amended appeal procedures was 'sensible' and 'eventually implemented.'[66]

Cohen also recommended that, under regulation 39C of the DOCR, which declared groups illegal, there be a right of appeal and third-party review of decisions, both at the time of the initial ban and as circumstances changed. While individuals could appeal internment, organizations whose property was subject to confiscation immediately after the ban had no appeal procedures. Some process should ensure that orders were in the community interest to prevent instances of injustice or excess. As it stood, proscribed organizations could be removed from the banned list only by executive order, which, in the war, was nearly impossible to obtain.

Orders against groups were issued because of complaints, with no representation allowed from the proscribed organizations. Cohen criticized, for example, the decision to ban the Jehovah's Witnesses, which resulted from information received from its critics only, and he later made the same argument about the Ukrainian Labour Farmer Temple Association (ULFTA). While government needed to act quickly in wartime, there was also 'a social need' to ensure goodwill and promote public understanding of the regulations. An illegal group should be able to demonstrate its actual situation if it differed from the supposition on which the order was based, and Cohen requested a review committee for his clients, the Jehovah's Witnesses and the ULFTA.

Cohen's brief was applauded in *Saturday Night*: 'It is improbable that the right of review would lead to the reversal of any considerable number of declarations of illegality, but its mere existence would tend to make the original tribunal considerably more careful in the exercise of its immense powers.'[67] TLC President Moore praised Cohen and offered to endorse his proposals if that 'would strengthen your hand.' A report on the DOCR that endorsed Cohen's proposal for review of Regulation 21 cases would be tabled at the next Congress convention.[68] The government ignored Cohen. In 1940–1 public criticism of internments was muted, so there was no pressure on government to change its policy.

But Cohen had allies. Concern about the state of civil liberties in wartime led to the formation of associations in Toronto and Vancouver for the first time, and groups established in Winnipeg and Montreal in the late 1930s to protest Duplessis's Padlock Law became more active.[69] In July 1940 the parliamentary committee listened to B.K. Sandwell, editor of *Saturday Night* and president of the Canadian Civil Liberties Association, and F.A. Brewin, its young counsel, criticize Regulation 21.[70]

In the next two years, as internment under Regulation 21 became more controversial, the committee would hear from groups and individuals with different political viewpoints. A. Lloyd Smith, for example, who represented the United Church of Canada, criticized the regulations because they rejected British principles of justice, accepted information from unreliable informers, relied too heavily on the minister's decisions, and gave the police too much power. But the Canadian Legion thought that all aliens in Canada from enemy countries automatically should be interned.[71]

In early August 1940, Cohen told Tom Moore that he was pleased with progress made in the Commons committee, particularly the acceptance of the TLC's proposal to amend the regulations so that 'such particulars are to be furnished as are, in the opinion of the committee, sufficient to enable him (the objector) to present his case.' He decided to let the Sullivan matter sit until this change was put into effect. Soon, however learned that the House's acceptance of the committee's report would not have immediate results, because it would take time to have its recommendations implemented as amendments.

Going Public

Though the situation remained as before, Sullivan and Internment Operations pressed for a hearing date, and Cohen was in a quandary about what to do.[72] Finally, he agreed to a date, provided that he received 'sufficient particulars ... to enable proper preparation and presentation of the case.' Jackett's response was a copy of the new order (the House committee's recommendation to furnish more information to internees) plus a RCMP memo to the minister, which listed persons it recommended be detained.[73]

Cohen decided to go public. In September, he spoke about the Sullivan, Chapman, and Sinclair cases to the TLC convention to 'point out the necessity of this congress protesting vigorously the arbitrary arrests and internment of Trade Union Leaders.' *Searchlight* reprinted his speech, which Moore sent to the minister of labour. The delegates demanded a full examination of Regulation 21 and supported the right of any person arrested to a trial and hearing.[74]

Cohen's concern about internees' rights enhanced his reputation as a civil libertarian, as did his work with the Civil Liberties Association. In October, its executive invited him to discuss the procedures under Regulations 21 and 22, and Cohen addressed the association's public meeting the following month. He focused on the Sullivan case to clarify the DOCR procedures. After an internee formally objected to detention, he received a communication providing grounds, which in Cohen's view 'gives the conclusion reached by the Minister of Justice, but fails to indicate in any way upon what the conclusion is based.' In effect, the arrested person had to prove that the minister's order was not supportable. In such a situation, Cohen could not advise his client, since a simple denial of the assertion was the only conceivable reply. Cohen had avoided a hearing in Sullivan's case until the parliamentary committee reviewed the regulations and recommended that a detainee be given sufficient particulars to enable him to present his case.[75]

Cohen reviewed the amendments. 'One would have thought,' he said, 'that it was reasonably clear that the detained person was to know specifically why he was held, so that he could direct his defence, or objections, to specific allegations.' When Cohen again asked why the department had detained Sullivan, it claimed to have provided additional information, which 'in the opinion of the committee' was sufficient to prepare the case. So, despite representations to the prime minister and the minister of justice, the report of the House committee, and the resulting amendment, Sullivan's situation remained the same in November 1940 as in July when he was informed that he was detained for being a Communist. Cohen could not prepare for the hearing, and 'so far as I know, the position of the Department taken in the Sullivan case ... represents its general policy.'

In concluding, he criticized Regulation 21 and wondered if this use of arbitrary power was related to class, economic, or political interests. He argued publicly that the timing of Sullivan's arrest, just as the seamen's conciliation board completed its public sessions and was about to try to mediate a settlement, assisted the employers. The Department of Justice insisted that such timing was a coincidence, but Cohen told his listeners that if they were seamen they might feel differently. Cohen pointed out that, when David Sinclair, editor of the CSU's paper, was interned as a Communist, a representation vote ordered by the labour department resulted in 95 per cent of the men backing the union. Sinclair's story on the vote's results, filed with Canadian Press in Montreal, never appeared. In October, Charles Murray, who had organized the CSU's only fishermen's local in Lockeport, Nova Scotia, was also detained. The previous June, after trying to negotiate with several fish companies, Murray received a threatening letter from the Nova Scotia minister of labour accusing him of Communist associations and warning him 'to desist from your efforts to create industrial trouble' and 'get out of Lockeport and stay out.' Cohen told his audience, 'I do not suggest that Murray's subsequent detention is in any way connected with this intemperate letter' and its attitude towards an organization of fishermen. But 'many fishermen in Nova Scotia ... refuse to believe anything else.' A number of people in the labour movement were concerned that union activities accounted for these arrests, but, he contended, the use of arbitrary power was of concern to all, for those who acquiesced in injustices against people they disliked might find themselves subjected to similar treatment in the future.[76]

Cohen's powerful speech received extensive publicity. CCF leader M.J. Coldwell asked Cohen's advice about handling the issue in the House of Commons,[77] and Unity (United Front) MP Dorise Nielson read it into the public record.[78] In November, Cohen published an article in *Saturday Night* entitled 'Is Canada Setting Up a Gestapo?' in which he called for reform of the DOCR.[79]

Despite growing public support, he was discouraged. He brought an application of habeas corpus as a test case before the courts, attacking the regulation's procedure and arguing that the order to arrest Sullivan had been improperly issued. The lower court held that the war could not be fought according to the principles of the Magna Carta, and the Ontario Court of Appeal in January 1941 dismissed the application in a decision that the leader of the Official Opposition, R.B. Hanson, cited in the House of Commons. The court proceedings did not obtain more information,[80] and the judgment, Cohen told Sullivan, was based entirely on the court's technical interpretation of the regulations. The decision left Sullivan with no recourse but the regulations' appeal procedures.[81]

In February 1941 the government reconvened the Commons committee, where pro-Communists and civil libertarians again expressed their concerns. The internees' supporters organized a conference that called for an 'open and fair trial for "Pat" Sullivan and other interned trade union leaders.'[82] In March, the committee again received a high-profile delegation from the Civil Liberties Association of Toronto.[83] Brewin presented its brief, in which Cohen's influence was apparent. It noted that, of fifteen hundred persons interned, about half sought review but few had obtained release. Serious delay in the disposition of cases arose, partly because only two advisory committees existed – one French and one English. The association recommended more advisory committees to deal promptly with cases. It supported Cohen's earlier recommendation for high-profile, three-person advisory committees, and specified that one appointee should be a labour representative because many labour people, whose arrests were controversial, were detained.[84] The brief relied heavily on Sullivan's case; it recommended that a committee should furnish a detainee with particulars, not as the committee saw fit but from the minister, which included the grounds for detainment and the facts that justified it.[85]

Brewin noted in his presentation of the brief that the advisory committee had a departmental file on the detainee, the contents of which were not divulged but whose very existence might make it difficult for the committee to be impartial. All information supplied to the committee should be available to the applicant for review. Such amendments were necessary, Brewin concluded, to reassure the public and especially the labour movement that detainees' rights were respected.[86]

In April the parliamentary committee heard from the Wives of Interned Labour Leaders delegation, which opposed the internment of Chapman, Magnuson, Murray, Sinclair, Sullivan, and Taylor – mostly Cohen's clients. Norman Penner (years later Manitoba's attorney general) represented the Committee for the Release of Labour Prisoners. Such delegations reflected increased organizational activity against the internment of Communists.[87]

In May, Alexander Patterson, the commissioner of prisons for England and Wales, spoke of British procedures regarding the internment of enemy aliens and others suspected of subversive activities. The Communist Party had not been banned there. In a breezy talk to the rather earnest Canadian committee, Patterson explained that 'there was not much trouble in Britain with Communists as the British sense of humour was somewhat inclined to view them as a joke rather than a menace.'[88] But the Fascists, and especially Oswald Moseley's followers, were taken seriously. Patterson spoke briefly about British internees transferred to Canada.[89] British internment hearings required a judge but the source of government information was never disclosed to prisoners and the final decision about cases was made by the home secretary. Thus, though Patterson was more lenient on the Communist party's legal status, he supported procedures already in place.

While the CSU concentrated on its public campaign for Sullivan's release, in 1941 the House committee's report recommended DOCR amendments to make the minister of justice more accountable to Parliament, and three-person advisory committees chaired by a person who currently or in the past held judicial office. The report further recommended that the committees inform internees of their right to object and provide them with the grounds for their arrest. If they made an objection, the committee had to inform them 'within a reasonable time before the hearing' of the 'full particulars' concerning their detention.[90] Cohen's brief and public efforts had influenced this outcome. He promised Sullivan that when the amendments were implemented he would proceed, if they were 'at all sufficient to enable proper preparation or a fair hearing.'[91]

As though his frustrations surrounding this case were not enough, Cohen received a letter from Sullivan about his health. It is difficult to evaluate this complaint, since in his memoir, published in 1955, Sullivan, then a healthy individual, writes at length about his internment experience but makes no mention of ill health.[92] In any case, in June 1941 he told Cohen that he had had five heart attacks since the end of March, had been in hospital for nine days, had lost weight, could not recover in the present circumstances, and wanted to see his personal physician, who had his medical records. After receiving several 'serious and disturbing' reports about his client's health, Cohen wrote to Lapointe to repeat the union's request that Sullivan receive outside medical attention. The request, he said, should not be seen as a reflection on the camp's medical personnel; the union simply believed that, when an internee had serious health complaints, he should receive attention from an outside physician.[93]

Also that month, after Germany invaded the Soviet Union, the CPC shifted its pro-Soviet policy from opposition to support for the war and began to agitate for the release of Communist internees so that they could participate in the 'all-out' war effort. Those in Hut 7 at Petawawa organized a petition for their release and pledged loyalty to the government.[94] The National Council for Democratic Rights (NCDR) was formed as a successor to the Canadian Labour Defence League, a banned organization, which, like its predecessor, was a Communist front headed by A.E. Smith. It focused on the civil liberties of interned Communists and organized a campaign for their release.

In this situation, Sullivan's health became a political issue because the CSU distributed a petition sent to Lapointe, which stated that, since Sullivan was seriously ill, he should be released on terms 'at least as favourable as those granted to James Franceschini, millionaire friend of Dictator Mussolini.' Franceschini, CSU Vice-President Dewar Ferguson wrote to locals, was released recently on 'compassionate' grounds with his contracting and shipbuilding companies returned to him at an enhanced value because of government contracts.[95] 'How different is the treatment accorded to trade unionists!' Aware of such agitation, Cohen distanced himself from it when he wrote to the minister, assuring him that he had checked all facts concerning Sullivan's health, noting that the release of some 'well-known individuals' was a coincidence, and making it clear that he had no desire to make capital out of such recent public events.[96]

Lapointe told Cohen in July that he had enquired about Sullivan's health and learned that it was 'fair,' but that, nevertheless, he had arranged for him to have a thorough medical exam. Meanwhile, after the DOCR amendments of 1941, Cohen again asked for particulars and the names of the people on the committee. Two advisory committees were set up under Regulation 22.[97] One was based at Petawawa, and Cohen appeared before the chair, Daniel O'Connell, a former county court judge, Robert Taschereau (later chair of the Royal Commission on Espionage), and William M. Dickson, a former deputy minister of labour, whom Cohen knew.[98] In practical terms the amendments resulted in little change. Cohen did receive a more detailed list of charges against Murray, one of which associated Sullivan with the Lockeport fishermen's strike.[99] The hearings would unveil some surprises.[100]

Cohen interviewed Sullivan before his hearing and again pressed Lapointe for a 'proper examination and treatment' for Sullivan's 'serious heart condition.'[101] Cohen also protested the camp conditions for the eighty persons interned for 'alleged subversive activities on the Labour front,' who were surrounded by over five hundred German, Italian, and Fascist adherents with alleged pro-Fascist associations. The labour group, he learned, was excluded from many camp activities, discriminated against in matters of food, and subjected to annoyances. With recent changes in the war situation, they were 'in actual danger of violence at the hands of the hundreds of Fascist adherents,' whose leaders had informed the camp commandant that they would not be responsibile for what might occur unless the labour group was removed. That group, Cohen told Lapointe, should not be subjected to constant threats of violence and risk of injury. 'It is incomprehensible to me that you will permit these conditions to prevail.'[102]

The left-wing contingent soon was moved to the Hull jail. C.S. Jackson remembered, 'The transfer arrangement[s] were high drama, indicating the government hysteria against progressive unions and unionists. We were moved in army vans, about eighteen to a load with two armed guards to each van, and a motorcycle armed with a machine gun between each van, to the railroad station at Petawawa and entrained for Hull, again under very heavily armed guards.'[103] Hull was an improvement, because, Sullivan remembered, the inmates had it to themselves; they cleaned their own cell blocks and did their own cooking, and there were no work parties. They secretly made a still which produced several gallons of alcohol a week and which was not discovered in the regular inspections, and a radio was smuggled in so they could keep up with world news.[104]

Lapointe reported to Cohen that two medical officers found Sullivan's condition satisfactory and that 'he should be able to carry on the regular life of camp,' but, as a result of publicity, Sullivan was examined by specialists. He was sent to Christie Street Hospital in Toronto and, according to his memoirs, was elated to get a medical check-up because it was a change in 'everyday jail routine.' Through a Toronto cab driver he contacted the CSU and received phone calls at the hospital, and Cohen probably visited him there. Demands for his release on grounds of ill health persisted, but Sullivan was returned to Hull jail to join his colleagues.[105]

Jackson's Internment

Between June and September 1941, Cohen was deeply involved in the controversy surrounding the internment of C.S. Jackson, international vice-president of the UEW. The RCMP arrested him on 22 June, the day after Germany invaded the USSR, and sent him to internment camp. At the time, Jackson was involved in a dispute at Canadian General Electric (CGE) in Toronto, where the workers, trying to get a meeting with the company, took a 'holiday.' The Department of Labour promised to appoint a conciliation board immediately if they returned to work, and on 20 June, at Jackson's suggestion, they did so. Jackson was at a UEW executive board meeting in New York City when he learned that the RCMP was waiting for him in Toronto. He flew instead to Buffalo and then took a small plane to Toronto airport, where members from the CGE plants were there to greet him. Scheduled to appear in court a few days later with his stewards in the strike, he decided to go into hiding until the court appearance, when he would try to fight the internment order. His plan failed, because the RCMP had removed the distributor points from his car at the airport, so it would not start. As he drove in UEW staff member Harold Kinsley's old Ford, towing Jackson's car, 'we were met on the airport road by armed RCMP and Toronto police, and I was taken into custody.' His car was impounded, and he went to his apartment while Detective Daniel Mann of the 'Red Squad' searched it and removed some books. He was then moved to police headquarters on College Street to be photographed, fingerprinted, and locked up until an RCMP escort took him to Union Station to catch the late-night train to Ottawa. Then he went to Petawawa and was issued a prison uniform. For two days he was placed in the hut of interned Italians, and indeed he occupied the bed recently vacated by Franchescini, the contractor. He then transferred to the hut which housed the eighty-three 'anti-fascists.'[106]

Cohen informed the Department of Justice that he was acting for Jackson, sought an interview with his client, and asked for specific charges, which he received on 21 July. The grounds for his detention were: his conduct in the illegal strike at General Electric which had obstructed the production of war materials; his association with CPC members; and his nomination of Tim Buck in the 1938 municipal election. Cohen asked for more particulars about the second item and was told that Jackson had associated with Harry Binder in Brockville in 1937 and Dick Steele in Toronto in 1940–1.[107] On 5 August, Cohen interviewed Jackson, and on 10 August in Hamilton he discussed the case with the UEW's district conference. As he collected evidence, he determined that the only serious charge concerned the strike. He advised the 'union defence committee' about 'the question of publicity, proposed line of defence, particulars received, nature of detention, effect of Regulations.'[108] Jackson benefited from Cohen's protest to the minister about camp conditions and moved with the others to Hull. After examining leaflets and advising the union defence committee on its publicity campaign for Jackson's release, Cohen prepared for Jackson's hearing, which began on 5 September 1941 for one day and resumed on 11 September.

Cohen was experienced in handling internments by this time, and the Justice Department itself had refined its procedures, so the delay was not as long as in Sullivan's case. Also, Cohen worked more closely with the union and concentrated on his public educational role in Jackson's case. He outlined Jackson's situation to the Civil Liberties Association's council, of which he was a member. The association held a public meeting, with most speakers from outside the labour movement, as did the union defence committee with union representatives and other groups to discuss 'a further programme of activity on the Jackson case.'[109]

In 1940 Communists had politicized the internment issue and were supported by other groups in 1941. With Jackson's arrest, public support for the release of left-wing internees increased. In Toronto, the Civil Liberties Association protested to the minister about the inadequate charge against Jackson – that he was interned 'because of subversive activities in organizing strikes.' The Toronto *Star* published an editorial on 'The Case of Mr. C.S. Jackson' and argued that Jackson's internment, so far without a hearing, should cause public apprehension, especially among organized labour, because the case revealed abuses in the DOCR's administration. The *Star* agreed with the Civil Liberties Association that 'the practice of interning labour organizers and others in this summary fashion' created distrust and suspicion in the minds of working people' and gave the impression that the government was using internment to hinder trade-union activity.[110] In September 1941 the UEW's international convention in New Jersey passed a resolution condemning Jackson's internment and calling for his release, and it sent the resolution to Prime Minister King and President Roosevelt. The union was so concerned about the inimical environment in which its Canadian district and its staff representatives operated that its executive board arranged with the U.S. State Department for 'a safe conduct pass for our Canadian delegation.'[111]

Jackson's hearing took place amidst the controversy. It was unusual and an injustice, in that he was, without question, on trial for his trade-union activities, which the committee probed almost to the exclusion of anything else. It did ask him if he were a Communist, which he denied. But the rest of the first day and all of 11 September were spent fishing for more evidence. The chair conceded to Cohen that 'in an extended inquiry of this kind, questions are frequently asked that are not really relevant to the subject and that are not of very much importance,' which was certainly true in Jackson's hearing.[112] Jackson was articulate and patient as the committee grilled him repeatedly and in detail in 'a somewhat sharp manner' about meetings during the CGE dispute. In discussions of labour law and wartime labour relations, Jackson was better informed than the committee. Cohen held his temper, as the committee raised fourteen new items that had not been in the original particulars. He wrote, 'I did not think it advisable to interfere too early with the questioning on these matters since this served to disclose more of the information in the files before the Committee.' Among the new charges were: that Jackson had publicly at UEW and CCL conventions criticized government labour policy, that he had attended a conference on civil liberties, that he had been 'charged' with loitering at a strike (even though the charge was dismissed), that he had in 1940 organized for the New Democracy movement founded by former ambassador to the United States W.D. Herridge, and that he had distributed leaflets, which in the opinion of the chair stirred up antagonism among different classes and promoted strikes. These issues were not grounds for internment.

Several times the committee's chair was high-handed, in Cohen's view, directing his questions like a cross-examination. When Cohen asked for a copy of the department's résumé of the case, on which the committee relied heavily, he was refused on the ground that it was confidential.[113] It is not surprising that the committee did not release the document to Cohen, for he would have learned that the department had picked Jackson up for being a nuisance. An internal memorandum noted that he was 'reported' to be a CPC member; at a UEW convention he said that trade-union leaders in Canada were imprisoned for expressing their opinions on war matters; in January 1941 he was connected with the Phillips strike in Brockville; and in May 1941 he was suspended from the CCL. The memorandum further asserted that Jackson was responsible for keeping the CGE employees on an illegal strike, and the RCMP described him to the minister as 'a dangerous individual whose activities are prejudicial to the public safety and welfare of the State.' In addition, C.D. Howe, the minister of munitions and supply, on 11 June had written to Lapointe about Jackson's activities, calling him 'one of the most active trouble makers and labour racketeers in Canada today.' He blamed him for several strikes; 'he is now boring in to the Canadian Westinghouse plant at Hamilton,' which Howe considered a most important war manufacturer. 'I cannot think why Canada spends large sums for protection against sabotage and permits Jackson to carry on his subversive activities,' he complained. 'No group of saboteurs could possibly effect the damage that this man is causing.' He urged Lapointe to take prompt police action. The next day, the minister of labour confirmed that Jackson was meeting workers at the Westinghouse plant and predicted that he would 'foment' a strike there within a week. Apparently it did not occur either to these ministers or to the minister of justice, who arrested him a few days later, that Jackson was trying to get the employer to recognize and negotiate with the union so that there would be no need for a strike.[114]

Jackson told the advisory committee that his detention was brought about by employers so that workers would be too intimidated to demand unions and 'industrial democracy.'[115] At the hearing's conclusion, Jackson condemned the committee's arbitrary war powers, saying, 'Whenever such power is placed in the hands of an individual or a group of individuals, it invariably results in injustices.'

The next day, Cohen addressed the second convention of the CCL in Hamilton and presented, in the words of the Toronto *Star*, an 'amazing report on the internment of C.S. Jackson.' Jackson's hearing was so unfair that the *Star*'s editorial – 'Can This Have Happened in Canada?' – condemned the Department of Justice as well as the entire process and concluded that the first charge – that Jackson took part in an illegal strike – 'constitutes no reason whatever for detaining him in an internment camp. If what he did was considered illegal, the obvious course was to try him in the courts.' The charge that he associated with Communists and had nominated Tim Buck for a Toronto controllership in December 1938 is 'ridiculous,' since Buck's candidature was perfectly legal and he received over forty-five thousand votes. For a government that had proclaimed its friendship with labour, its action was an outrageous 'violation of the lawful liberties of a labour organizer – or indeed of any citizen.'[116]

Continuing to work with Jackson, the Civil Liberties Association, and the union committee for Jackson's release, Cohen had two more hearing days – one in October and one in November. On the 'pivotal' charge related to the CGE strike, Cohen felt that 'we have clearly established that there was no culpability on Jackson's part with respect to the strike, that it was a spontaneous and determined action on the part of the men themselves, provoked by the adamant attitude of the company on the question of collective bargaining.'[117] The advisory committee itself seemed uncomfortable because on 19 December 1941 it recommended Jackson's release. The next day the minister freed him after six months' internment. Jackson announced that union officials still in the camp, like himself, wanted to assist the government in the war effort.[118] Cohen's modest bill to the UEW was $2,500, including disbursements of $630.

Sullivan's Hearing

Pat Sullivan's hearing was scheduled finally in Hull on 16 and 17 October 1941. Cohen booked two rooms in the Chateau Laurier Hotel in Ottawa, 'on the first or second floor on the court side' as usual.[119] He had just completed conciliation-board proceeedings in the Kirkland Lake gold miners' dispute, in which his role was crucial. Between 13 and 24 Ocober, Cohen argued four CSU cases, for J.S. Chapman, Charles Murray, David Sinclair, and Pat Sullivan, and represented C.S. Jackson.

J.A. 'Pat' Sullivan was forty-seven, an Irishman who had come to Canada in 1922 with his family. He had worked as a cook and steward on boats and in hotels and then was involved in the National Seamen's Organization (NSO) run by H.M. McMaster. Seamen's conditions were terrible and when the NSO failed to represent the men effectively, Sullivan started the National Seamen's Union. By 1937, 60 to 70 per cent of the unlicensed personnel on Canadian Great Lakes vessels were in the

Canadian Seamen's Union – the new name resulting from a merger – and it affiliated with the TLC.[120] The employers refused to negotiate, and the first strike in 1938 was against twenty-two companies. Sullivan also was vice-president of the Montreal District Trades and Labour Council and assisted the organization of meat packers, coal handlers, and truckers.

At his hearing, the advisory committee asked Sullivan about his relationship with the CPC. He denied under oath any association, but the committee produced documentary proof that he was a member. Several years later, in 1946, Sullivan shocked the nation when he revealed that he had been a Communist but was renouncing his party membership and leaving the CSU, which was dominated by Communists. He had joined the CPC in May 1936, since it seemed the only organization 'interested in the plight of workers in the hungry years of the 30s.'[121] He met Jack Munro, who was active in the Single Unemployed Men's Association in Montreal, and was introduced to Quebec CPC leader Fred Rose and to Joe Salsberg, who handled CPC work in the unions.[122] By 1935, the party had increasing influence among seamen, which probably motivated Sullivan to join it. The party contributed five thousand dollars to the 1938 strike, which resulted in wage increases and union recognition. In 1938 Sullivan was elected CSU president, with an executive board on which only one member was not a Communist.

The advisory committee called on Émile Côté to testify. A French-Canadian CLDL organizer in Montreal, he had seen Sullivan at a CPC trade-union commission set up to improve the party's contacts within the labour movement, at CPC meetings, and at one Communist 'fraction' meeting of Montreal labour-council delegates. The party expelled Côté in 1938 but Cohen established in questioning that Côté knew that the RCMP had Sullivan interned and wanted information about him. Côté prepared a four-hundred page report over five or six months and in December 1940 gave it to the police.[123]

Cohen's earlier public charge that Sullivan and others were arrested because they were unionists – a disturbing development since workers retained the right to strike during the war – was not a popular argument. Lapointe had denied the accusation, insisting that such persons were detained for being Communists. In Lapointe's mind, this was possibly true, but the internees' labour activities did not enhance their popularity with a cabinet that wanted to run a war effort without opposition and with little interruption in production and that contained businessmen such as C.D. Howe who opposed collective bargaining. Howe, as we have seen, had complained to the minister of justice about Jackson days before he was arrested.[124] TLC President Tom Moore, who got along well with Mackenzie King and was a veteran of internal labour conflicts with the Communists, believed Lapointe, but his position infuriated the left wing of the labour movement. In contrast to Jackson's hearing, where the advisory committee blatantly questioned him about his union activities, in Sullivan's hearing the committee members were more cautious. Yet even in this case they did not distinguish between Communist and labour activities.

The committee asked questions about the legality of a three-day Toronto strike in 1938 over workers' right to choose the CSU over McMaster's outfit, which Sullivan said had no members and was used by employers as a strikebreaker. Sullivan conceded that there had been no conciliation but he did not consider the strike illegal. The committee probed his union work until Sullivan blurted out, 'I cannot understand why the trade union movement is being tried here instead of Pat Sullivan.'[125]

Cohen was more aggressive in Sullivan's hearing. He was disturbed by questions on issues not contained in the charges, and he pointed out that for over a year he had pressed the department to disclose all particulars in advance of the hearing. When further details had been revealed, they included no mention of the strike, which, if it related to his detention, should have been on the list. After a procedural debate, the chair ruled that Sullivan had to submit to questions but could decide whether or not to answer them, and that if Cohen was taken by surprise and wanted more time to prepare, he could apply for further information. Cohen did not want a postponement but requested an exhaustive, detailed list of allegations. The RCMP and the committee continued the probe.

On 21 October five new allegations were raised as the committee questioned Sullivan about a 1940 strike which involved east coast fishermen. Cohen interjected, 'This is entirely new to me ... that the internment of Sullivan is in any way based on the 1940 strike.' The situation was 'incongruous' because William M. Dickson was deputy minister of labour at the time and had viewed the strike as illegal. Now he sat on the advisory committee. If the strike was a reason for Sullivan's internment, and if the committee was using Dickson's earlier opinion as evidence, Cohen protested Dickson's apparent conflict of interest. The Labour Department opposed internment based on labour activities, and the Justice Department had publicly assured labour leaders that 'Sullivan's internment had nothing to do with any of his trade union activities.' Cohen advised Sullivan to answer no further questions until they knew what was alleged against him.[126] These issues were not resolved, and the committee did not recommend Sullivan's release at this time.

Six weeks after their hearings, the CSU internees asked Cohen to work for their release, since 'our desire to join in the development of all-out production has been made known again and again.'[127] Cohen sent one hundred dollars for Christmas cheer for all the 'anti-fascist internees,' who thanked him profusely. He assured his clients that he was fully engaged in their cases.[128]

Ernest Lapointe's death delayed everything, but by January 1942, with the Soviet Union now an ally, the political climate had changed sufficiently for Ottawa to release a few internees at a time. Cohen used the new CPC policy of support for the war to get his clients released. He requested transcripts of Sullivan's hearing to pursue the procedural issue, and he saw Robert Justice Taschereau. But events were moving so quickly that, by February 1942 this advisory committee had heard eighty-three cases and recommended the release of forty-three internees.[129] On 27 February, Cohen also concluded his arguments before the House committee on the release of Communist internees and believed 'that the committee were sympathetically disposed' towards his argument.[130]

Pat Sullivan and others were released in March 1942, and thereafter had to report to the RCMP regularly. Sullivan thanked Cohen 'for the untiring efforts and the care that you gave in preparing our case.' Cohen charged the union fifteen hundred dollars for four cases. The union paid him only two hundred dollars at first – it had other bills to pay as well – but it promised to pay him the remainder as soon as it could.[131]

Gaining the Release of Communists

In May 1942 the government accepted the parliamentary committee's recommendation that Regulation 21 not apply in cases where mere union activity or participation in a strike was involved. In response to pressure, the minister established an advisory committee with a labour representative on it to hear the large backlog of cases.[132] That same month, the National Council for Democratic Rights pressured the government to release all Communist and trade-unionist internees. Their continued imprisonment, it argued, was inconsistent with war policies, the existing political situation, and national unity. In June it noted growing public uneasiness over the regulations' use against left-wing groups, recommended that the minister specify overt actions that constituted a danger to the state, and emphasized that the government should not intern citizens 'solely for holding political opinions which while not those of the Government, very definitely are for the maintenance and defense of the State and Dominion of Canada.'[133] It wanted all banned left-wing organizations legalized and speedy action on the remaining cases, and it noted Roosevelt's recent release of American Communist leader Earl Browder.

Pat Sullivan's release, the NCDR stressed, had led to cooperation among the union, the government, and shipping companies, his assistance in mobilizing thousands of Canadian seamen behind the war effort, and the CSU's 'Victory Program for Shipping' to maximize the shipping industry's contribution.[134] In Kaplan's view, it was an 'ill-conceived hastily constructed program for an industry which was operating quite well,' but, significantly, it included a no-strike pledge for the duration of the war.[135] This pledge, reflecting a Communist policy to accelerate war production, was a source of conflict between Communist and non-Communist trade unionists but had been implemented by the American labour movement. It was hotly debated in the two Canadian labour congresses, where the majority rejected the policy because, unlike American workers, Canadians had no collective-bargaining rights recognized in law; until they did, labour refused to relinquish the right to strike, despite its support of the war effort. Using the policy, Sullivan ingratiated himself with government leaders, in 1942 was elected national vice-president of the TLC, and in 1943 became its secretary-treasurer. His position increased Communist influence in the TLC and gained him both access to government circles and leverage with management to win more and improved contracts, so that 'just a few years after his internment, [he] had become one of the most powerful and influential union leaders in the country.'[136]

The NCDR used public sympathy for the Soviet war effort to demand the internees' release but also to press the government to legalize the CPC. The House committee in May 1942 heard the new justice minister, Louis St Laurent, on the internment of CPC members. In June the committee received a petition from the Communist internees still at Hull.

On 9 June 1942 Cohen accompanied a NCDR delegation to the House committee to argue for the CPC's legalization.[137] The committee listened to Cohen on DOCR revisions all day, all the next day, and all morning on 16 June. It was a fascinating, closed-door session, not only because of the issues discussed, but for what it revealed about Cohen's political views, about how he was perceived by politicians, and about politicians' anxieties about adjusting their policies to the changing war situation. They were slower than the CPC to change their position, since they distrusted the Communists for their opposition to the war between 1939 and 1941.

At the start of the session, the chair began, 'Mr. Cohen needs no introduction to members of this committee. He is well known to the public men of Canada.' Cohen spoke for the NCDR with only a few pencilled notes. Living at a frenetic pace during the war, 'catapulted as I have been in recent weeks if not for months and years, from one situation to another,' he apologized that 'it has been physically impossible for me to complete ... a ... statement in writing.'[138] His manner was respectful and even deferential as he repeated earlier arguments about the DOCR. Cohen noted that some men were detained under Regulation 21 for nothing more than having been at one time a member of a banned organization. Was such membership prejudicial to public safety? He wanted an amendment that mere membership in a banned organization was not grounds for action under the regulation. Organizations, like individuals, should be allowed to appeal, he said, but the chair responded that individual appeals reviewed the applicability of the law to the case while the status of organizations was a policy matter.

Impatient with so general an introduction, Ralph Maybank interjected that he thought that Cohen would say circumstances had changed and that the CPC should no longer be illegal. Cohen became obsequious and said that he was worried about the time he was taking but that, since the committee wanted to listen to him, he would come to the point. Section 39C had declared the CPC illegal; he represented the NCDR, which believed that the CPC's illegal status injured the war effort.

These proceedings revealed politicians' discomfort with the Communists' frequent policy shifts, which many saw as blatantly opportunistic. CCF MP Angus MacInnis, for example, commented that while the NCDR sought CPC legalization in 1942, it had not done so in 1940–1, and several members remained bitter about its early opposition to the war. Cohen noted that the CPC now supported the war. Two reasons were given for its continued ban – first, that it advocated force and violence, and second, that it had opposed the war and many still distrusted its support for the Allies. Committee member Thomas James O'Neill noted that gaining power by the sword was not popular in Canada and that the Communists should change tactics. Cohen agreed but said that many ideas associated with the term 'communist' came from the past. Using CPC documents, he revealed a detailed knowledge of Marxist theory and policy and the history of the party in Canada. He concluded that, if Marxian theory dictated use of violence to bring about social change, then the CPC had deviated from this position and the government should not adhere to 'the technical situation which operated in the Buck trial to bring about conviction' in 1931. The committee believed in secret Communist documents that contradicted the CPC's peaceful public position. Cohen replied that, if they existed, he would not be representing the NCDR.[139] Cohen returned to his main point – that many would not be interned under Regulation 21 were it not for Regulation 39C, and that the regulations should be amended to lift the ban on the CPC and other groups.

Committee members were curious about Cohen's own political views and his relationship to his client, and they probed him about whom he represented. He replied that not everyone identified with the NCDR was a Communist. The committee tried to get Cohen to admit that he represented the CPC and was possibly a member. It even suggested giving him immunity if he 'confessed,' but he would not. Instead, Cohen presented himself as a disinterested professional, and when the CPC's shifting position was noted, he replied, 'I suppose that applies to all of us ... Except lawyers. We never change because we never have any points of view; we merely present the point of view of others.' He was retained as a professional, and paid – 'of course, not enough, I never am' – but to reassure the politicians, he indicated that he would not take a case if he thought it against the war effort. Yet did not convince the committee, which regarded him as a radical lawyer.

Though Cohen refused to identify his political affiliation, he did reveal something of himself. He told the committee, and convinced some members, that when the Communists opposed the war 'I refused ... to represent any persons charged or associated with communist affairs,' even when the *Clarion* was attacked and copies of it confiscated. He accepted the NCDR cases 'because I personally was ... honestly convinced that the war effort was to be advanced by my arguing these cases.' He was not merely a mouthpiece. He exaggerated when he said that he was uninvolved with the party between 1939 and 1941, since he represented Communist internees then and it is likely that he knew that Jackson and Sullivan, who had lied at their advisory committee hearings, were Communists.

Committee members assumed that Cohen was knowledgeable about Communist activities and programs. He responded, 'I am only conversant in as far as I read and ... I act for many trade unions and very many other labour matters; so one necessarily is brought into an atmosphere and in contact with the whole subject matter.' When he argued that Communist support for the war could be relied on, he made a slip of the tongue and referred to the Communists as 'we,' which confirmed the committee's impression that, however professional and disinterested he wanted to appear, he had close ties with his client. And his knowledge of the history of the international Communist movement, including its policy shifts on Soviet foreign policy and even Stalin's internal policies, was evident in his detailed, informed analysis.[140] His perspective, which today sounds naive, probably sounded simply pro-Communist to the committee.

Cohen was opinionated; he disagreed with the Allies' appeasement policy towards Hitler, as undoubtedly some committee members did, but for different reasons. Cohen also revealed a view of the Nazi–Soviet Pact which was shared by many Canadian Communist sympathizers. 'I, for one, was so deeply shocked, confused and puzzled at the time of this Soviet German pact and so alive to the danger it presented to our cause that I sought constantly for facts which would pierce the gloom in which I found myself.' Spending days in a library, he devoured the files of the New York *Times* to try to understand the reasons for the pact. By 1941, the Soviet Union had moved closer to the Allies because, according to Cohen, the appeasement policy ended when Churchill became the British prime minister. Presumably Germany's attack was a factor, too, but not one that he mentioned. His lengthy, often theoretical discussion in a closed session of a parliamentary committee was unusual, sometimes bizarre, and frequently dramatic, but members listened intently.

Most members clearly believed that Cohen was a Communist, and his submission indeed revealed his sympathy for the Soviet Union, his knowledge of the doctrines and politics of the Communist world, and his personal difficulty in reconciling his support for the war with shifts in Communist policy. His lawyer-client relationship, which he portrayed as professional and principled, in fact was sympathetic and committed. On the politicians' side, these proceedings revealed their dislike of Communist opportunism, their lingering bitterness about Communist opposition early in the war, and their continuing unease about the sincerity of Communist loyalty to the Allies. Their attitudes partly explain the government's delay in releasing Communist internees after the Soviet Union became an ally.

Aware of the committee's ambivalence, Cohen persuaded it to interview internee Norman Freed on Communist policy, which it did in July 1942. Cohen advised Freed before his appearance about his presentation, and he was permitted to listen to Freed's testimony.[141] Evidently Cohen had made an impression on the committee for, though it split over legalizing the CPC, its report nevertheless recommended that the government lift the ban (thus responding positively to the one hundred and fifty telegrams, letters, and petitions it had received on the subject). On 5 July 1942 Cohen reported to the NCDR, and in February 1943 his speech to its conference appeared on the front page of the *Tribune*. The government turned down the House committee's report, partly because Quebec MPs were opposed, and the CPC remained illegal. But all interned Communists were released.

Also in June 1942, after Cohen's lengthy NCDR submission, the committee heard from the Jehovah's Witnesses on lifting the ban; they were represented by Charles Morrell, not Cohen, who affirmed his religious beliefs and thereby risked internment. The annual delegation from the Civil Liberties Association presented a brief that Cohen influenced. It praised recent amendments, particularly the provision eliminating the regulation's application to peaceful strikes, which, if added earlier, would have prevented C.S. Jackson's internment.[142] It supported removing the ban on the CPC, for the ban could 'no longer be justified by the need to safeguard the state from subversive influences.' The existing policy, it argued, might hurt the war effort by creating mistrust between Canada and its Soviet ally; Britain and the United States did not ban their Communist parties; and Canadian Communists 'are now wholly desirous of participating in the war effort.' The regulations' purpose was not to suppress unpopular opinions, and, in the view of the Civil Liberties Association, the CPC's inconsistent positions had so discredited it in the eyes of the public that those who feared its philosophy need not worry about its increased influence.[143]

During 1943, other delegations made similar arguments. One was led by Tim Buck, who in June 1940 had gone underground and then in August 1942 had voluntarily turned himself over to authorities, with Cohen at his side. He was interned for less than a month and was represented by Cohen at an advisory committee hearing in September 1942. Buck assured the advisory committee in writing that he would not behave in any way that would endanger the safety of the Canadian state, and was released.[144]

The issue of Communist Party status by then was mainstream enough that, after Communist internees were freed, Premier Hepburn wrote to Louis St Laurent to congratulate him publicly on their release. In supporting the decision, he expressed 'the feelings of the people of Ontario' who were indignant about the government's failure to lift the ban on the CPC, and he urged St Laurent to act to enhance national unity. He may have been trying to win friends on the left to bolster the Liberal's position in the upcoming Ontario election, but he failed; the CCF continued to pick up support. Even the *Globe and Mail* favoured removal of obstacles against Communists because the public supported it, the Soviet peoples were heroic in the war, and the British had removed a ban on a Communist newspaper. It also noted that the turnaround in public opinion resulted from revelations as the war continued about the 'complete impropriety of some of the administrative practices followed by the Department of Justice' which had 'aroused widespread public disquietude.'[145]

The government's refusal to remove the CPC ban annoyed Cohen very much.[146] After Buck was free, he told the press that he resented the minister's release of a distorted summary of the advisory committee's in-camera proceedings and wanted the full text of Buck's hearing published. He noted that, after the House committee recommended lifting the ban, St Laurent had attempted in Parliament 'to divert the issue' by asserting that the CPC was illegal under the common law and enabling legislation would be required to restore its legality. Cohen called this 'sheer poppycock.' St Laurent's maintenance of the CPC's illegal status was what Cohen bluntly labelled 'crass and class politics.'[147] The Communists themselves ignored their illegal status, which was mostly symbolic in any case, and in 1943 simply adopted a new name, the Labour Progressive Party (LPP), under which banner they continued their political activity and even ran candidates in the 1945 dominion and Ontario elections.[148] The LPP cooperated with the national Liberal Party, supported its re-election in the interest of the war effort, and thereby effectively continued its opposition to the CCF, as it had both inside and outside the labour movement for years.

THE ULFTA CASE

Cohen's other client was the ULFTA. The Ukrainian community in Canada had been divided politically since the Russian revolution. During the Second World War, non-Communist groups united in the Ukrainian-Canadian Committee to mobilize support for the war effort, while leftist Ukrainians belonged to ULFTA.[149] Nationalist Ukrainians had long opposed the left and favoured the deportation of radicals, while pro-Communist Ukrainians denounced the nationalists as Nazis. After the Nazi-Soviet Pact, even pro-German Ukrainians who admired Hitler's anti-communism supported the Allies, to prove their loyalty and in the hope that the war might lead to an independent Ukraine.[150] The willingness of the state to intervene on one side resulted in the Canadian government banning ULFTA, interning its leaders, and, through the Office of the Custodian of Alien Enemy Property, seizing ULFTA real estate (108 halls) and selling some properties to the Ukrainian National Federation, the Polish Alliance Friendly Society, and the Orthodox Church at bargain prices.[151] These actions were so biased that by 1941 even persons outside the Ukrainian community protested their unfairness.

In June 1942 the Civil Liberties Association told the House committee that the ULFTA case was 'one of particular hardship and unfairness.' The ban resulted from ULFTA's association with communism, but it was increasingly inappropriate and should be removed and the group's properties restored. Some municipalities, such as Lachine, Quebec, Crowland, Ontario, and The Pas, Manitoba, the committee was told, had petitioned the government for the return of ULFTA halls to its members.[152] While the 'labour group' of internees released between August and October 1942 included ULFTA leader John Boychuk, its former national secretary, and the internment jail in Hull was closed, ULFTA remained a banned organization. Well into 1943, the NCDR circulated petitions and organized rallies protesting the seizure of ULFTA's properties and their contents and the destruction of some of its libraries, musical instruments, and national costumes.[153]

Cohen had extensive correspondence with the Custodian of Alien Enemy Property to elicit information about the ULFTA property and to forestall its sale at a fraction of its worth. He was stonewalled and shuffled among the Department of Justice, the custodian's office, and the secretary of state's department. Finally, out of frustration, Cohen sought an interview with Secretary of State Norman McLarty, whom he had known when he was minister of labour. At first, McLarty put him off by saying that he could do nothing until the Justice Department changed ULFTA's status, but Cohen persisted and McLarty grudgingly sent him a schedule of ULFTA property. Cohen pressed for a more complete picture, including a statement of receipts, disbursements, rents, and taxes and received more details about some sixty-nine properties.[154] In January 1943 Cohen learned of an ULFTA property not listed that had been sold. His difficult relations with the custodian's office were included in his brief to the House committee.

In July 1942 Cohen told the committee that the Ukrainian organization's illegal status should be lifted and its confiscated property restored because ULFTA had a long and honourable record in Canadian affairs. With a membership comprised of workers, farmers, and small tradespeople, and youth and women affiliates, it was 'the best, the most constructive and the most representative expression of Ukrainian-Canadian life.' From modest origins, it had become an extensive cultural organization by 1940, with eighty-seven buildings worth close to a million dollars, 'built virtually by the pennies and energies and sacrifices of Ukrainians throughout the land.'[155] As with the Jehovah's Witnesses, ULFTA's ban was sudden, with no opportunity for it to hear or answer charges. Its support for the war from 1939 was consistent, and its anti-Fascist stand a matter of public record in its *People's Gazette*, from which Cohen read at length. He contended that it was difficult to understand the basis for the ban, unless false reports by rivals, as rumoured, had induced the authorities in June 1940, 'during the confusion and hysteria of those days,' to declare ULFTA illegal.

Its political opponents, who were pro-Fascist, Cohen charged (borrowing some rhetoric from his other client, the NCDR), 'exploit the Hitler technique of "red smear" as one means of attacking the Association.' The right wingers alleged that ULFTA was a CPC agency, but though it was undeniably working class in character, and three of its twenty-two member executive were associated with the CPC, ULFTA was an independent organization that formulated its own policies.[156] It had criticized the government, particularly during the Depression, but the allegation that ULFTA was a Communist organization, Cohen concluded, was false in fact and in substance. ULFTA's support for the war, its working-class character, even its advocacy of socialism, was no reason to ban it. 'It seems anomalous to say the least, and necessarily must injure the war effort, if the group within Ukrainian circles in Canada with the clearest anti-fascist record should remain under a ban of illegality while others – some of whom have seen virtue in Hitler's programme – remain undisturbed and by comparison even endorsed by the Canadian government.'

In October 1942 B.K. Sandwell wrote an editorial in *Saturday Night* that analysed the government's failure to lift the ban on left-wing groups even as it released Communists at the rate of a dozen a week. He surmised that one consideration was practical, for when the government had seized ULFTA's property, some real-estate holdings were turned over to rival, anti-Communist Ukrainian organizations. This action was an embarrassment and an 'extraordinary error of judgment,' because even if there were reasons to deprive ULFTA of its holdings between 1939 and 1941, it was a mistake to sell them to another group. Sandwell doubted whether the government would take remedial action, because the other Ukrainian group apparently was influential in Saskatchewan, the province of Minister of Agriculture 'Jimmy' Gardiner.[157]

In 1943 a campaign to restore ULFTA property gained greater support[158] as the Civil Liberties Association circulated a petition across Canada opposing the confiscation of ULFTA's properties and demanding their return or compensation for their loss.[159] Finally, in October 1943, ULFTA, the Jehovah's Witnesses and other organizations banned under the DOCR regained legal status. St Laurent announced an advisory committee to assist the secretary of state 'in making a proper return or accounting to the person or persons from whom property had been received' in a fair manner.[160] When little happened, the Civil Liberties Association in Toronto in 1944 published a pamphlet, *An Appeal for Justice*, to publicize the 'very grave wrong' the government had committed in the ULFTA case. It had offered ULFTA 14 per cent of their properties' value as compensation, and the custodian's agents, who 'completely misconceived their functions,' were guilty of gross negligence.[161] The association wanted halls restored, a fair tax settlement, claims for damage paid, compensation to temporary owners for improvements, and an inquiry into the government's actions.

These measures were not taken, but in 1945 the government finally and grudgingly returned most halls, that is, those not previously disposed of, and drastically undercompensated ULFTA for those it had sold off, so that the organization received a fraction of what its property was worth. The custodian charged it administrative costs for handling its expropriated properties and back taxes for the years its halls were held by government.[162] The government's arbitrary behaviour was political and cynical. Cohen summed up his frustrating years negotiating with departments on ULFTA's behalf as 'time and money wasted without the slightest likelihood, let alone prospect, of success or progress.'[163]

From the perspective of many persons who were subjected to the Canadian government's arbitrary and sometimes abusive power during the war, Cohen's efforts were not wasted. In political scientist Reg Whitaker's view, 'J.L. Cohen, the brilliant labour lawyer who had often in the past defended radicals under attack by the state, was a tireless defender of victims of wartime oppression.' Cohen's legal work and influence on public policy are an important part of the history of the legal profession and civil liberties in Canada.[164] His efforts were all the more remarkable in that they coincided with the busiest and most demanding phase of his career as a labour lawyer.

Graduation photo of J.L. Cohen, Osgoode Hall Law School, 1918. Cohen won the bronze medal for standing third in his class. He was shortly after called to the bar when he turned twenty-one.

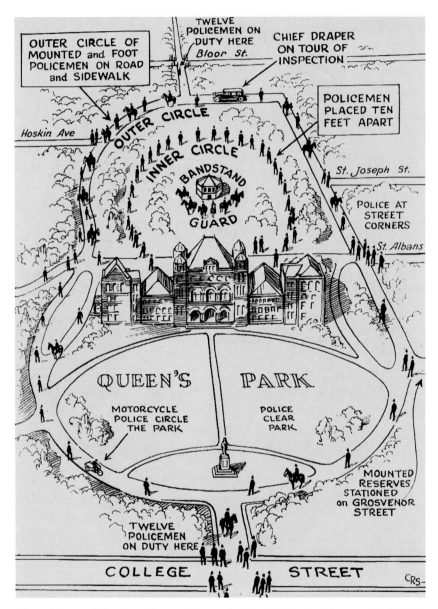

Map of Queen's Park and the positions of police during the Communist Party's 'free speech' campaign in 1929. J.L. Cohen defended those arrested at these demonstrations.

Leading Communists with whom J.L. Cohen worked in the late 1920s and 1930s
when he was legal counsel to the Canadian Labour Defence League. Left to
right: Tim Buck, Norman Freed, Annie Buller, and A.E. Smith. Cohen acted for
Buck and Freed, who were interned during the Second World War.

The body of Viljo Rosvall is found on 23 April 1930. Cohen, representing the Lumber Workers' Industrial Union, tried to get a provincial investigation into the disappearance of Rosvall and John Voutilainen, but failed. An inquest determined that they died of accidental drowning. Many workers believed they were murdered.

Phyllis Clarke was the only child of J.L. and Dorothy Cohen. Clarke was active in the Communist Party and in 1962 ran as a candidate in the federal election in Davenport riding, Toronto, but was defeated by the Liberal candidate, Walter Gordon. Clarke had a PhD in political science from the University of Toronto. She deposited her father's large collection of papers in the National Archives.

J.L. Cohen's mother, Esther, pictured here in the 1940s, was born in 1876 in Lithuania and died in 1979 in Canada.

Abraham Isaac Cohen, one of Cohen's brothers, was born in 1904. In his youth, he worked for several years in J.L. Cohen's office. He changed his name in 1938 to Alfred Charles Cowan.

Jane Cowan de Munnik, J.L. Cohen's eldest sister, born in 1899, and pictured here in the 1950s. She was Cohen's office manager and bookkeeper for years.

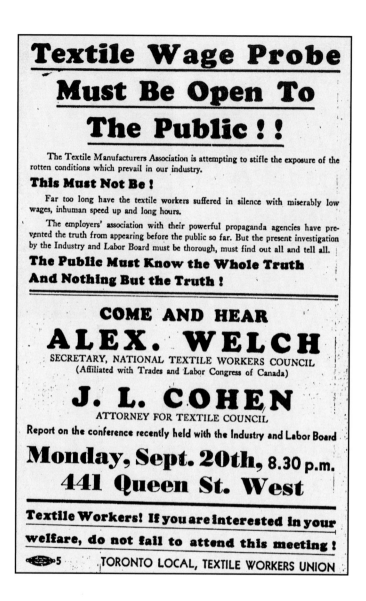

Textile Wage Probe Must Be Open To The Public ! !

The Textile Manufacturers Association is attempting to stifle the exposure of the rotten conditions which prevail in our industry.

This Must Not Be !

Far too long have the textile workers suffered in silence with miserably low wages, inhuman speed up and long hours.

The employers' association with their powerful propaganda agencies have prevented the truth from appearing before the public so far. But the present investigation by the Industry and Labor Board must be thorough, must find out all and tell all.

The Public Must Know the Whole Truth And Nothing But the Truth !

COME AND HEAR

ALEX. WELCH

SECRETARY, NATIONAL TEXTILE WORKERS COUNCIL
(Affiliated with Trades and Labor Congress of Canada)

J. L. COHEN

ATTORNEY FOR TEXTILE COUNCIL

Report on the conference recently held with the Industry and Labor Board

Monday, Sept. 20th, 8.30 p.m. 441 Queen St. West

Textile Workers! If you are interested in your welfare, do not fail to attend this meeting !

5   TORONTO LOCAL, TEXTILE WORKERS UNION

A leaflet published by the new Textile Workers Union urges its members to attend a meeting to hear its lawyer, J.L. Cohen, report on the Industry and Labour Board's probe into wages and working conditions in the Ontario textile industry in 1937. Cohen's public role was growing.

J.L. Cohen played a central role in settling the 1937 Oshawa strike at General Motors. He is seen here on the telephone in the midst of negotiations with the parties and a very interventionist Premier Mitchell Hepburn.

The parties arrive at an agreement in the 1937 Oshawa strike. Cohen is pictured on the right of Mitchell Hepburn. The local union president, Charles Millard, is on Hepburn's left.

In 1939, J.L. Cohen (seated at the top of the front table) was the labour nominee on a conciliation board in a test case taken by the Mine Mill union, which was seeking union recognition at the Teck-Hughes mine in Kirkland Lake. The board recommended voluntary recognition of the union by the company, but the company rejected this recommendation. Thereafter, the union decided to seek a master agreement with all the mining companies in Kirkland Lake, a decision that led to the Kirkland Lake strike in 1941–2.

J.L. Cohen in action at a hearing representing auto workers, members of the UAW, in one of the several disputes that broke out in the war years.

J.L. Cohen made front-page news on 25 September 1942 when Communist Party leader Tim Buck (shown here with Cohen) and thirteen others came out of hiding and turned themselves in to authorities with Cohen at their side. They were interned briefly. Cohen defended many internees, some of whom were incarcerated for years. He sought to protect his clients' civil liberties as much as was possible within the circumstances of the war.

Ford  Facts

LOCAL 200 · U.A.W. · C.I.O.

Vol. II, No. 59　　　　　Windsor, Ontario　　　　　July 20, 1944

J. L. COHEN TO RUN IN ESSEX WEST

Sent to Hospital Ford Dr. Says OK

Here's a story of how Dr. Langmaid, the Ford doctor, miscalculated and the man was saved only by taking matters in his own hands. Brother W. A. Rocheleau of Dep't 33 felt severe pains in the stomach. He went to see Dr. Langmaid who said he was O.K. and refused to give him a pass to go home. Feeling ill, Brother Rocheleau went home anyway.

When Brother Rocheleau arrived home, he called his own doctor, who ordered him to hospital at once since he had accute appendicitis. He was operated on the same day.

Brother Rocheleau was away from work from June 11th to July 10th, although his doctor told him not to go to work until July 16th. Upon appearing at work supervision did not

NOMINATED

NATIONALLY-KNOWN FIGURE NOMINATED BY UAW-CIO ON CCF-LABOR TICKET

Locals 200 and 195 of the UAW-CIO last week nominate J. L. Cohen, K.C., as labor's standard-bearer to run in th Federal Riding of Essex West on a CCF-Labor ticket. Th position was taken by the two locals, and endorsed by th Executive Committee of Ford Office Local 240, after matur consideration and consultation with the many political current that make up the UAW-CIO.

The above decision was finally arrived at at the last loc: meeting of Local 200, where considerable discussion took plac and the following two resolutions were overwhelmingly adopted, and which forms the basis of UAW policy

1 That we recommend that in the matter of the Federal Election that any candidate who runs in Essex West Riding run as a CCF-Labor

nominee to run as CCF Lab' Candidate

Union officials are confident th Mr. J. L. Cohen will carry the Ridu on a CCF-Labor ticket and theref secure outstanding representation

---

The front-page story in the 20 July 1944 edition of *Ford Facts*, the UAW's Windsor paper, sparked controversy about Cohen's possible candidacy in the 1945 federal election, resulting in a disappointing outcome for Cohen.

Members of the National War Labour Board, March 1943, Ottawa. J.L. Cohen is on the left; the Hon. Justice C.P. McTague is in the centre, and Senator J.J. Bench is on the right. Shortly afterwards, Leo Lalande, a lawyer with the Wartime Prices and Trade Board, replaced Bench.

NOTICE.

IN THE MATTER OF
THE LAW SOCIETY OF UPPER CANADA
AND IN THE MATTER OF
JACOB LAURENCE COHEN, of Toronto.

TAKE NOTICE that the undersigned who was disbarred as a barrister and struck off the Roll of Solicitors pursuant to a Report of the Discipline Committee adopted by the Benchers of the Law Society in Convocation on the 19th day of June, 1947, has submitted to the Law Society of Upper Canada an application for re-instatement as a barrister and solicitor.

AND FURTHER TAKE NOTICE that any person desiring to make any representations with respect to such application is requested to communicate in writing with the Secretary of the Law Society of Upper Canada, Osgoode Hall, Toronto.

DATED at Toronto this 29th day of June, 1949.

J. L. COHEN,
Applicant.

A notice in June 1949 in the *Ontario Weekly Notes* indicates that J.L. Cohen has applied for reinstatement into the legal profession, and invites interested persons to make representations to the Law Society of Upper Canada.

8

Politics and Espionage, 1944–1946

The years 1944 and 1945 were difficult ones for J.L. Cohen. In 1944 he was embarrassed and probably disappointed at losing a nomination to run for Parliament in Windsor, because local Communist and CCF factions conflicted over his proposed candidacy. The next year, Cohen was confronted with Ontario CCF/Conservative Party conflicts when he was counsel to several unions before the LeBel inquiry. By this time, Cohen was not well. Experiencing personal and work-related stress, he began to make mistakes, which judges and colleagues noticed.

NOT A CANDIDATE: WINDSOR, 1944–5

On 8 July 1944, three hundred UAW shop stewards in Windsor unanimously endorsed a resolution to sponsor a Labour-CCF candidate in the federal riding of Essex West.[1] They wanted J.L. Cohen KC to run for Parliament, and their members ratified the decision which was sent to the Windsor CCF.

Cohen's name had been circulating for months. Essex West was held by Liberal cabinet minister Norman McLarty, the secretary of state. He did not run in 1945 and, exhausted by the war, died several months after his retirement from politics. James D. Leach was the Progressive Conservative candidate. Earlier there had been talk of Cohen's running in Essex East against Paul Martin, MP. Martin was parliamentary assistant to the minister of labour, held more progressive views on labour matters

physical & emotional breakdown

than his party, and he and Cohen had developed a good association during the 1942 Ford strike.[2]

The consensus was that Cohen would be a strong candidate, since he was well known in Windsor, was national counsel to the UAW, and had support. He was 'nominated' from both large locals – 195 and 200 – and the idea was endorsed by the Ford office Local 240. Thus, labour in Windsor united behind Cohen, as 'a man who is thoroughly acquainted with labour's problems and who has fought like a lion for the adoption of genuine labour legislation.'[3] It wanted a candidate who could win, and even the Windsor *Star*, an anti-labour newspaper, thought that Cohen would.[4] 'The election of Mr. J.L. Cohen is a foregone conclusion,' enthused the *Canadian Tribune*, because, running under the UAW banner with the endorsement of both the CCF and the LPP, he would sweep the polls.

A larger political context influenced the proposal and affected the outcome. The CPC consistently viewed the CCF as competition on the left. Depending on what the Communist policies were – and these shifted – it either condemned the CCF as 'reformist' or advocated a united front between the Communists and the CCF. The party sought to dominate the united front in the late 1930s, when fascism was on the rise in Europe, and after the founding of the LPP in 1943. The CCF resisted unity because it was convinced, given the Communists' periodic outspoken hostility, that their aim was absorption and control of the CCF. Nevertheless, the unity idea appealed to many CCF members, so that, despite CCF policy, the issue caused debate and some divisions within its ranks.

From the time the Canadian Congress of Labour endorsed the CCF as its political arm in 1943 and established a Political Action Committee (PAC), the Communists tried to undermine that connection. The LPP was formed as a new Communist party to attract voters, and LPP supporters within the PACs of both congresses pushed for a policy of unity rather than endorsement of the CCF or non-partisanship. When they failed in the CCL, which continued to back the CCF, the Communists then supported the Liberal Party in the 1945 national and Ontario elections and convinced the TLC for the only time in its history to support the Liberals formally.

As early as March 1944, George Grube, a professor of classics at the University of Toronto and president of the Ontario CCF, reported on Communist strategy to the CCF's national executive and concluded that 'the Communist-Liberal alliance is very clear and definite. Their tactics are obstructionist.'[5] In Windsor, the CCF had considerable support in the community and within UAW locals, but because the locals' leadership and some members were LPP supporters, they pushed the unity policy, which resulted in their promoting a CCF-Labour label for Windsor candidates with UAW support.

The LPP was playing politics, jockeying for influence, and as a result both Cohen and the CCF were placed in uncomfortable positions. For Cohen, the idea of labour unity was appealing. During the war he had established good relations with both the Communists and the CCF. He supported the no-strike pledge put forward by the Communists, but he also worked for strikers and, like CCFers, had struggled for collective-bargaining legislation. Though he was always coy about his political views, many assumed that since he associated with Communists in a professional capacity, he was one of them, and indeed he did share their views on some issues. At the same time, particularly after his stint on the NWLB, he was comfortable with CCF leaders Ted Jolliffe and David Lewis and supported some CCF policies. Cohen was a 'radical' and an individualist, and for that reason he could not adhere to CPC discipline and would probably have been a maverick in any CCF caucus, just as Bob Carlin was at that time in Ontario, and Morton Shulman, years later, would be in the NDP.

The CCF had two problems with Cohen's candidacy. The first resulted ① from a wariness in its relationship with the labour movement, which probably was rooted in class tensions between working-class activists and middle-class reformers. The CCF wanted workers to become party members and participate in its constituency organizations, supported the affiliation of union locals to the party, and advocated cooperation between the CCF and labour – a successful combination that nearly brought it to power in Ontario in 1943. At the same time, it guarded its ② constituency associations' autonomy in decision making, much as CCF trade unionists, such as Charlie Millard, believed that unions should have a political policy made by the labour movement itself, not dictated by any party.[6] The Windsor CCF constituencies wanted UAW support but would not accept advice automatically from local unions. The CCF was unsure of Cohen as a candidate. The LPP was clearly anxious to endorse him, which made CCFers nervous, since they had decided not to cooperate politically with the Communists.[7]

When the UAW took the initiative, Cohen's potential candidacy became controversial. In a letter to the Windsor *Star* in July 1944, a reader wrote that the UAW had no right to choose the CCF candidate without its consultation and approval.[8] When the CCF provincial executive met, Eric Havelock reported on his visit to Windsor and the UAW proposal for a CCF-Labour candidate in Essex West. A motion passed to keep the Windsor situation 'under close scrutiny.' Ford Brand travelled to Windsor to organize more CCF members. Apparently the Windsor Central Club had taken over the jurisdiction of at least two or three of the Essex riding associations, and Brand was to help restore the authority of the individual riding associations.[9] The press referred to 'a lot of fuss' about the UAW proposal for Essex West.[10] Cohen's proposed candidacy evidently was wreaking havoc within the CCF, for it divided the party between its 'labour' and 'socialist' camps in the constituency and between those who favoured and those who opposed CCF cooperation with the LPP. The issue of local autonomy – from both the central party and the labour movement – was a factor, too. Some saw the CCF central office interfering in Windsor, and some union members who were active in the CCF saw UAW officials trying to dictate to the party. It was a political cauldron, and those alienated by the process began to talk of running independent candidates.[11]

In July 1944 Cohen's candidacy was discussed at the Ontario CCF-Trade Union Committee.[12] At the end of July, Fred Burr wrote to Cohen that the UAW had recommended him as a candidate: 'I have been asked by CCF riding associations in Essex East and Essex West to invite you to meet the joint executives and the Windsor Central CCF Club to discuss the local political situation.'[13] Cohen's secretary forwarded Burr's letter to him, since he was away, and told Burr that she expected a reply and would send it to him. With Cohen not available, the issue was unsettled and unsettling.

In the meantime, George Grube wrote to Burr and to the presidents of the two Windsor federal riding associations, Herb Henderson and E.L. Waterman, that he was concerned about 'misleading' reports and party harmony. He offered advice in his 'personal' letter. Because it was important for both ridings to build their membership as well as to have representative nominating meetings, he urged them to set up better-organized constitutency associations. In the specific situation, he affirmed the democratic right of CCF riding members to select a candidate. The action of the UAW to 'recommend' a candidate was unusual but not improper, and the riding should take the suggestion 'under advisement.' The 'recommendation' had been misnamed a 'nomination' by the press, but the party need not feel stampeded. As for Cohen, Grube respected him. 'J.L.Cohen is a man of very distinguished talents and experience, particularly in the field of labour relations. I have no doubt that if he were elected as a CCF Member of Parliament he would be able to make a considerable contribution and be of great service to the movement.'[14] This opinion was shared by Ontario and national CCF leaders. The constituencies were strong enough to be independent of outside dictation, and 'insinuations from political opponents should not affect your choice.' Grube concluded that he hoped they would not resent him clarifying some points. Clearly, he wanted to prevent division in what was a fragile situation. Grube also contacted Cohen, gave him a copy of his communiqué to the Windsor people, and told Cohen that if he became the candidate he should stand as the CCF candidate and *not* with the label 'CCF and Labour.' This was also the view of the national CCF leader, M.J. Coldwell, because the LPP, which advocated a coalition with the Liberals, was anti-CCF and was likely to exploit and confuse the Windsor situation if the broader label were used. Grube did not send Coldwell's internal party letter but told Cohen that he was welcome to read it at the CCF office.[15]

The CCF position was not news to Cohen, for he had also received a letter from David Lewis, the CCF's national secretary. Lewis had met Local 195 president Alex Parent, immediately prior to a joint meeting of Windsor UAW locals about political action in the coming federal election, and was informed that Cohen's name as a candidate was being considered. Lewis supported the idea, believing that Cohen would be a fine addition to Parliament, but he made it clear to Cohen, as he had to Parent, that 'I was certain that the CCF would not consider for a moment vacating the Windsor constituencies and that therefore if the foolish decision were made to run you on some label other than the CCF you would undoubtedly be faced with CCF opposition.' The local CCF organization would likely, and appropriately react that way, and the leadership would support it. A CCF candidate as part of a national movement had, in his opinion, a better chance of being elected than one running on an independent label. 'The argument of the Communists – who are undoubtedly responsible for the move – that if you run as an independent you would stand a better chance is, I am certain, pure nonsense.' He believed that the Communists would prefer to see Cohen lose on a non-CCF label than see him win as a CCF candidate, for 'this would be in line with their present policy.'[16]

Cohen's controversial candidacy put Windsor's UAW leaders – George Burt (Canadian director), Roy England, Alex Parent, and Dan Casey (presidents of Locals 200, 195, and 240 respectively) – on the defensive. They issued a statement that accused the Windsor *Star* of distorting the issue. The paper had made it appear that the union was trying to force a candidate on the CCF, whereas the UAW had 'recommended' Cohen as a candidate suited to represent labour and the CCF. The *Star* had also insinuated that the 'CCF-Labour' ticket was linked to the LPP. For Cohen to run on such a label was natural in a large industrial city, the trade unionists said, and they accused the newspaper of trying to create mischief.[17] Since the LPP faction in the UAW was strong, and Cohen was well known to the Communists, there was sympathy for the united-front idea and for his candidacy. If it stirred up the CCF internally, from the LPP perspective, so much the better. The *Star* had reason to report the story as it had. *Ford Facts*, the UAW local paper, had run a front-page story on the union's 'nomination' of Cohen for Essex West on a 'CCF-labour' label.[18] Editorially, the union paper noted that it represented twenty thousand people in the area, and that the union was politically involved and wanted a good labour representative to present the people's need for 'social security.'

The UAW had two motives for nominating Cohen. It trusted and admired him, and so on one level the endorsement was a genuine tribute to his ability, experience, and courage. *Ford Facts* praised Cohen as one who 'has greatly contributed in carrying to a successful conclusion many outstanding gains which Ford workers are enjoying every day. Without a doubt the most brilliant and forceful labour lawyer in the country, Mr. Cohen served labour's interests on the now reorganized NWLB.'[19] At the same time, the UAW, with its CCF and LPP factions, in broadening the candidate label, was adopting the LPP's approach. Editorially, *Ford Facts* argued that 'the CCF should recognize the political non-partisan set-up of the UAW just as the UAW recognized the affinity of the CCF to the labour movement.'

The CCF responded quickly and clearly. M.J. Coldwell stated that, when the CCF nomination meeting selected a candidate, it would be a CCF candidate. 'There will be no association with any other political party. That is definite.'[20] The UAW had helped elect three CCFers in Windsor and North Essex to the Ontario legislature in 1943, and the CCF wanted to maintain its support, but it rejected hyphenated candidates in the 1945 national and Ontario elections.

The CCF had reason to be on edge. In May 1944 UAW Canadian Director George Burt withdrew from the CCL's PAC, and in August, Local 195 president Alex Parent announced his support for Liberal Paul Martin in Essex East.[21] Parent, a long-time supporter of the CPC/LPP, was following the party line, and he himself would run provincially in Essex North in 1945 as a Lib-Lab candidate and win. Also in May 1944, the LPP national executive adopted a statement that favoured a Liberal-Labour coalition government. Its support for the Liberals was meant to undermine union support for the CCF, which it did, and it thereby exacerbated Communist-CCF conflict.

The LPP's enthusiasm for Cohen's candidacy not only worried the CCF, but it also sparked some 'red-baiting' innuendo, which was personally hurtful and impugned Cohen's professional reputation. On 1 July 1944, for example, the Toronto *Star* warned, 'The CCF had better watch out or it will wake up to find itself with a number of candidates who are Communists, who have disguised themselves as CCF supporters in an effort to enter Parliament.'[22] This was an oblique reference to Cohen. In mid-July the Windsor *Star* was more direct, snapping that one argument expressed against Cohen's candidacy was that he was an outside candidate, living in Toronto, who did not know where Windsor's city hall was. 'What Jakie does know is the location of the Prince Edward Hotel, all the UAW-CIO halls and the Politburo of the Vsosoyousny Kommunistuchisty Partei on Chatham Street West where he will find one Oscar Kogan alias Kayne in charge and maybe Fred Rose, alias Rosenberg hanging around. What more does a candidate need?'[23]

In August, Cohen travelled to Windsor, met the joint executives, was introduced by George Burt, and spoke for over an hour to a closed meeting of CCF members in the Essex West riding association.[24] Prior to this visit, CCFer Fred Burr warned him about the situation through an intermediary. He thought that Cohen would have made an excellent candidate 'had the situation developed differently,' but the local union leaders had 'bungled the whole affair' and the LPP had jeopardized Cohen's ability to win the nomination. In his view, 'Mr. Cohen has taken it 'on the chin' already in these parts too long and that he should know the situation before committing himself in any way further.'[25] If this warning reached Cohen, he nevertheless decided to meet the CCFers in Windsor. Cohen made a good impression, but the riding did not commit itself. On the issue of party label, Cohen left the designation up to the riding and suggested that the UAW's 'recommended action' was its way of getting in touch with the CCF. If nominated, Cohen promised to oppose Liberal policies, and if elected, to move to Windsor. Clearly Cohen wanted the nomination and thought that he would get it.

Cohen was to be disappointed and publicly humiliated as a result of UAW-LPP political manipulation and CCF internal politics, which were

· Cohen's aspirations

tactical and defensive but also parochial. In occasional Windsor *Star* articles about Cohen, comments – that he was a 'Jewish' lawyer being groomed for a cabinet position if the CCF took power, and that he was the counsel to the Communist Party – were meant to evoke fear and possibly anti-Semitism. There were several developments. In September 1944, UAW Local 195 wrote an open letter to the three CCF MPPs urging them to form a coalition with the Liberals against George Drew's Conservative government. This was straight LPP politics, and the CCF refused. Windsor CCFer Fred Burr, who in early August had told a correspondent, 'I know that a popular local man will definitely stand and poll a large vote at the convention' and that Cohen should be discouraged from running, a week later announced his decision to contest the nomination in Essex West.[26] Though responding to those CCFers who were uneasy about Cohen's being 'foisted' on the CCF by the unions, or worried that Cohen had ties with the LPP, Burr also was consistently self-interested. Liberal MP Paul Martin believed that 'the local CCF leaders regarded Cohen's views as too left-wing for their comfort and were very concerned about being chummy with anyone suspected of communist leanings.'[27] Cohen had said that he would run on a CCF label, so it was unfair to link him to UAW political factionalism.

In the meantime, Eamon Park, a prominent trade unionist and CCFer, spoke to Local 195 and condemned both the Liberals' record of anti-labour behaviour nationally and in Ontario and the LPP idea of coalition with the Liberals. He affirmed the Toronto Labour Council's support for the CCF and urged trade unionists not be sidetracked by 'LPP inspired manoeuvres which would sell out the interests of the labour movement.'[28]

The close relationship between the CCL leadership and the CCF did not mean that the rank and file was solidly CCF. The LPP knew this, and so did the Liberals. For years, Paul Martin had politicked at plant gates and in union halls to develop Liberal supporters in the UAW and he candidly admitted that he appealed to the workers over the heads of their leaders. In 1945 'it appeared,' Martin later wrote, 'as though my campaigning at plant gates and my progressive labour outlook had managed to prevent a solid bloc of labour support going to the CCF.'[29] Liberals in the UAW, like the Communists, argued that the union should be 'independent' politically. As Park recognized, CCF support could be eroded by either of them, and cooperation between them was potentially very damaging.

The open conflict in Windsor changed the situation for Cohen, and on 6 October 1944 he announced that he would not seek the Essex West nomination. In a letter to George Burt, copies of which he sent to the CCF and the press, Cohen said that the disagreement between the UAW and the CCF about a coalition in Ontario of the CCF, Liberals, and LPP had led to his decision not to stand. Originally, he had agreed to seek the nomination, he said, because he hoped that it would bring unity and 'rally the greatest possible agreement within labour in Windsor and its friends and associates.' He was wrong. 'The recent events and conflict' had destroyed the consensus 'upon which the whole proposal was based.'[30] In a private letter to George Burt, Cohen indicated that he had carefully thought over the matter before making his decision.

Though Cohen may have been politically ambitious at this time, he would not put himself in the anomalous position of opposing policies officially adopted by the union. He was willing to run as a straight CCF candidate if the union agreed or, as it suggested, on a coalition label if the CCF agreed. But he refused to run without UAW endorsement, because he put neither party (the CCF or the LPP) ahead of the union movement which was his first loyalty. Publicly, he referred to what the press mistakenly called Coldwell's disapproval of his nomination, stating that Coldwell had been positive with him, which he appreciated.

His open letter created turmoil among his supporters in the UAW and the CCF, but some in the riding association were relieved, and two days later E.L. Waterman, the riding's president, announced that he would seek the nomination. In early December, the schism between the CCF and the Communists was clear when Nelson Alles, CCF MPP for Essex North, resigned from the CCF because he believed that it had veered away from labour's interests and that its political manoeuvring had created disunity. Paul Martin believed that Alles resigned because the local CCF executives had not supported Cohen's nomination. The three UAW locals discussed their political policy.[31] Local 195 recommended nonpartisan political action and that the union ask Cohen to run as a labour candidate. There was no chance of that.

In the June 1945 Ontario and national elections, which were held one week apart, the CCF did poorly. In the provincial election, Drew's Conservatives won a majority government, the Liberals became the Official Opposition, and the CCF was reduced to eight cents from thirty-four. The Liberal and CCF leaders, Hepburn and Jolliffe respectively, both lost their seats. In Essex County, the Conservatives won three of four seats to displace the CCF, which had won the ridings in 1943. Only in Essex North did the Conservatives lose to Alex Parent, UAW Local 195 president, who was elected on the Lib-Lab label. His status in the union influenced the win, but his victory indicated that the union vote was split and that the CCF had lost support. In the national election, the Liberal government won a slight majority, while the Conservatives picked up over twenty seats for a total of sixty-seven, the CCF gained eight seats to bring them to twenty-eight but it was completely shut out in Ontario, even though its national popular vote in 1945 was 15.6 per cent, compared to 8.5 per cent in 1940. Paul Martin, newly appointed to cabinet, won Essex East for the third time. Immediately after the provincial-election results were tallied, his Conservative opponent, James E. Byrne, a farmer, charged that an unholy alliance was at work and that the 'Osgar Kogan-Paul Martin-communist machine' had defeated the Conservatives in Essex North. Martin followed the factionalism within the UAW and the controversy over Cohen with interest; he had kept open lines of communication with the Communists during the war, being careful not to alienate constituents from eastern Europe who were anti-communist. He rebuffed Byrne's smear but admitted that it had some foundation since the LPP opposed the CCF 'and undoubtedly some of Windsor's little band of communists would vote for me – as was their right in a democratic election.'[32]

The results in both elections were a disaster for the CCF and a short-term victory for the LPP's strategy, but that party would be eliminated by the Cold War. The real victors were Mackenzie King's federal Liberals and George Drew's provincial Conservatives. Neither government was pro-labour, so labour disunity over strategy in Windsor weakened the unions' political position. During the Ford strike in 1945 and the strike wave of 1946, the labour movement would have few friends in government.

How did Cohen feel about the controversy over his candidacy? While he tried to appear reluctant about running and waited to be invited by a united group of supporters, he seemed interested in entering politics. He never refused to run; he quietly visited Windsor, as the CCF had suggested, and no doubt canvassed support. In the end, he refused to throw his hat in the ring because he was offended on two counts. He was turned down publicly by some in the CCF and, with Burr's and Waterman's announcements, would have had to contest even a straight CCF nomination. He was subjected to considerable red-baiting in the press (which was both anti-CCF and anti-LPP). Far from uniting political factions in Windsor, his proposed candidacy had exacerbated conflict, a situation he did not want, because the LPP and its UAW supporters pursued their strategy of coalition to further their own and the Liberals'

Political aspirations

interests and to oppose the CCF. Cohen was publicly humiliated and probably personally disappointed. While he did not want to embarrass the union, Cohen realized that workers for whom he had done so much did not rally behind him in a way that would have allowed him to win the CCF nomination. He was stressful and told George Burt that he was going to slip down to Quebec for a few days 'to get a little relief from office strain.'[33] Inadvertently, Cohen had been caught up in the LPP-CCF rivalry within the labour movement, which spilled over into community politics. This rejection did not come at a good time in Cohen's career or life.

In 1945 Canadians celebrated the war's end but many feared the return of a depression as the war economy converted to peacetime production, thousands of workers were laid off, and returning soldiers claimed what looked to be too few jobs. Besides economic anxieties, the public was reeling from new knowledge about the war – the holocaust and the atom bomb – so concern about the future increased.[34] Politically, the world was becoming polarized as the Allies broke apart and their tensions escalated into the 'Cold War.' Closer to home, left/right tensions were readily apparent in the LeBel Commission Inquiry, investigating a CCF accusation made against Ontario's Conservative government during the 1945 provincial election – that it had set up a police 'gestapo' to persecute the left. Indeed, Cohen's possible CCF candidacy had interested Ontario's conservative government and he was the subject of an exhibit filed at the inquiry. Within six months, Soviet employee Igor Gouzenko shocked the public with revelations of Communist spies lurking even in Ottawa. Hence, in 1945 and 1946, politics were interesting but a bit fantastic, and those trends were reflected in Cohen's work, at a time when he was increasingly tired and less able to withstand pressure and the pace that he had set for himself during the war.

Cohen wanted to reduce his work and get some much-needed rest, as his doctors had advised. Yet in 1945 he became counsel to the United Mineworkers of America (UMWA) before the Royal Commission on Coal (the Carroll Commission). He was hired to draft its submission, which took longer than Cohen expected because he needed to do more research; eventually, union people drafted the brief, supervised by Cohen. He appeared several times before the commission to examine witnesses and in February cross-examined General Manager McCall of Dominion Steel and Coal Company (DOSCO). The union's position was that the coal industry was not a make-work project, since Canada

- the stress continues

needed its product and should not be dependent on American coal. As a national asset, it should be operated in the national interest, by a government coal tribunal with a management and a labour representative.[35] By autumn, it appeared that the commission would not make recommendations that were acceptable to the miners, and Cohen became discouraged. In November 1945, by mutual agreement, he concluded his work for the UMWA and the commission reported later.

The experience frustrated Cohen for it did not advance the miners' position in the industry or resolve basic problems. Because of the geographical distance, it also had meant a lot of travel for Cohen, and he had to back out of cases because he had no time to appear in court on behalf of clients.[36] In March, for example, he had to juggle his work in the Maritimes with that for the CCL revising P.C. 1003, which, of course, interested him very much. On top of all of this, both the UMWA and Cohen experienced regional and cultural differences as they adjusted to each other, which he was not accustomed to and had not expected. The union had consulted Professor G.V. Douglas of the Department of Geology at Dalhousie University to help it with its submission. To the union, Cohen referred to Douglas as 'this enigmatic academic colleague of yours.' But, ultimately, Douglas's assessment approximated Cohen's own view of the commission. Douglas wrote, 'These Royal Commissions have a way of blowing off a lot of hot air and then nothing happens ... If there is not going to be any follow through to this Commission anything which I may do will be a waste of time. Ethically you may secure a success, but if that win does not mean prolonged life, better living conditions, improved education, it is an utterly empty victory.'[37] One staff representative remarked that he was not used to the way Cohen worked, while a junior colleague of Cohen's found working in Sydney difficult. In July he wrote that union representative C. Wade was gathering material, that he and Wade had not started writing the brief, and that when it was drafted he would send it to Cohen. 'I find this community and its people very depressing,' he wrote 'so I won't plan to stay here longer than is absolutely necessary to get what you want.'[38]

Cohen also made himself available to the UAW and the Ford workers in Windsor as they moved inexorably towards confrontation with the large auto manufacturer. Relations between the parties at Ford had steadily deteriorated during the war, with the union holding to its demands for wage increases and union security and management refusing to deal with the union. Cohen's work there probably limited the conflicts at Ford, for he educated UAW members on how to conduct their committees and negotiate and tried to facilitate relations between the parties. But in 1945, they were testing each other, and the Ford strike over union security broke out in the autumn. In the course of this work in Windsor, Cohen met twenty-year-old Elizabeth Guenard. They became lovers and he hired her away from the UAW in May to work in his Toronto office. She travelled with him several times on business trips, including a trip in September to Nova Scotia.

Cohen was as usual too busy, and he had increasing difficulty keeping his appointments in order. In July 1945, for example, the UAW intervened on behalf of workers who wanted to remain in Local 200 UAW, and objected to an application for certification by Local 944 of the International Union of Office Employees. Apparently, Cohen had overlooked the notice of intervention and not received the date of a board hearing regarding a petition for leave to prosecute. In an affidavit, Cohen swore that he was at the LeBel hearings until 20 July and that he had not seen the notice but had communicated with the board on 19 or 20 July. He evidently was angry with his staff. But, as he explained to the board on the day of the hearing, after he arrived in Toronto from Windsor, within fifteen minutes 'I was drawn into the LeBel Inquiry, and I have been in it ever since.' That very morning in court, he had tried to review all two hundred and seventy exhibits but was only up to number 98 and had to appear at the inquiry that afternoon. 'I am engaged in an affair that has been keeping me going night and day literally ever since I last left my friends at Windsor,' and 'I have literally torn myself to pieces making the time to ascertain the situation and be able to appear before you and make my position and situation clear.' Company counsel John Aylesworth was unsympathetic, noting that Cohen had a month after the petition was filed and could have prepared the case in the time he had used trying to adjourn the hearing. Cohen reiterated that he had assumed the LeBel case before he knew of his appointment that day, and he had to finish it first, since LeBel was important and complex. Cohen told friends in Windsor that he intended to take a summer vacation, and in the board hearing he noted that as VE day had passed, 'we in this room have been working night and day during the war and should have a little rest.'

The oversight was very unusual for Cohen. He had slipped up, had to explain himself, and seemed frantic. The board decided to adjourn the case until autumn, and it ordered the union to publish in Windsor's press an explanation for the delay and then say nothing more. The company could publish its side of the case and the board would monitor the actions of both parties. Ultimately the union dropped the case and paid

Cohen his fee but there could be no denying that he had slipped up badly.[39]

THE LEBEL COMMISSION INQUIRY, 1945

The LeBel Commission Inquiry was an unsavoury experience for Cohen, and not simply because of its timing. On 24 May 1945, during the provincial election campaign, Ted Jolliffe, Ontario's CCF leader of the Opposition, in a dramatic radio broadcast charged George Drew's government with maintaining a 'special branch' of the OPP – 'a paid government spy organization, a Gestapo' – to spy on the CCF and labour unions in order to maintain itself in power. Jolliffe named William J. Osborne-Dempster as the man in charge of the operation and referred in detail to reports on CCF MPPs, on union meetings, and on other prominent Canadians. The purpose of such reports, Jolliffe claimed, was to link the CCF and unions to communism and provide information to anti-CCF propagandists Gladstone Murray and M.A. Sanderson, known as 'the bug man' because he also owned a pest-control company. The reports were signed 'D.208' and were delivered to the OPP commissioner, to Attorney General Leslie Blackwell, and to Premier Drew.[40]

The accusations dominated the rest of the election. When Drew angrily denied them and appointed a commission of inquiry headed by Mr Justice Arthur Mahony LeBel of the Supreme Court of Ontario, a known Liberal, the public apparently questioned the truth of Jolliffe's charges. In the campaign the CCF faced a number of challenges: Drew's fear-mongering, anti-CCF strategy, which encouraged a large turnout of mostly anti-CCF voters; the revival of Mitchell Hepburn as Liberal leader; and the LPP decision to cooperate with the Liberals and to split the left vote by running in twenty-seven of the thirty-two ridings held by the CCF. The result, as we have seen, was a debacle for the CCF in the provincial election and the federal one as well.

These defeats in June 1945 initiated the CCF's permanent decline. Ironically, regarding the anti-CCF propaganda campaign in Ontario, the electorate believed Drew and not Jolliffe. Yet the LeBel report's findings would later confirm Jolliffe's allegations and reveal that the OPP, which answered to the premier and the attorney general, had been used for political espionage at public expense against the Official Opposition.[41] Presumably these were improper purposes, but the report nonetheless cleared Drew and only mildly censured the attorney general. LeBel apparently believed the premier's testimony, in which Drew falsely stated that he knew Murray only casually, had never seen the Osborne-Dempster reports, and knew little about Sanderson's ads. Drew's papers in the National Archives reveal that Drew knew Murray well, had created the 'special branch,' had read many of its reports, and knew the identity of D.208. Much information in the reports was false and inaccurate and often was in the public record, but the reports' existence, not their quality, was the issue. In his memoirs, David Lewis called Drew's public denial and his evidence before the LeBel Commission Inquiry 'a deliberate lie' and a disturbing example of personal dishonesty. The only advantage of Jolliffe's broadcast was that the 'special branch' was shut down immediately after he made his accusations.[42]

The LeBel Commission was appointed by order-in-council under the Public Inquiries Act in 28 May 1945. Cohen appeared a few days later, announcing that he represented four unions on the attorney general's blacklist and demanding to be recognized. LeBel agreed, so long as Cohen promised not to waste the commission's time. Over two hundred exhibits were filed, some of which must have seemed both amusing and a bit grim to Cohen. For example, exhibit 12 was a report titled 'Communist Control of the CCF,' which purported to name CCF officials on the payroll of the CIO and CCL and added that CCF leader Jolliffe's law practice 'is mainly composed of retainers from CIO Canadian Congress of Labour unions. In this respect Mr. Jolliffe shares the C.I.O. business with Mr. J.L. Cohen, counsel for Communist and Communist-controlled organizations in Canada.' Exhibit 125 was a report by agent D.208 which discussed the CCL's PAC, indicated that three of its four members were Communists or Communist collaborators, and claimed that it controlled funds going to unions for political purposes. The PAC could 'dictate' nominations, and the report gave as an example the nomination of 'J.A.' [sic] Cohen as CCF candidate in Essex West. Besides mentioning that Cohen was legal counsel for the National Council for Democratic Rights, it claimed that the Civil Liberties Association had been partially infiltrated by Communists and gave as an example Cohen's membership on its board. Exhibit 184 recounted how two powerful UAW locals engineered Cohen's nomination as the CCF candidate in Essex West in 1945. 'Mr. J.A. [sic] Cohen K.C. holds the same position in regard to Canadian communists and communist activity as general counsel for such Communist sponsored organizations as the Communist Party of Canada, the YCL, the Labour Defence League etc., as Bedeaux (or Bedacht) the well known Communist lawyer does in Communist circles in the USA.'[43]

During the inquiry, Cohen acted for four unions – the UAW, the CSU,

Mine Mill, and the Packinghouse Workers (UPWA). He was aggressive, sarcastic, insulting, and very concerned. J.J. Robinette remembered Cohen at the hearings. 'He was very much an actor you see, and he would strut in, a little short man, and blare at everybody and make some eloquent extreme pitch.' As a result, Cohen got most of the attention at the well publicized inquiry.[44]

Cohen crossed swords with Joseph Sedgwick, the lawyer the government had appointed to assist the commission. Often such counsel do useful work for commission deliberations in examining and cross-examining witnesses and searching for relevant witnesses. Sedgwick, however, was a well-known Conservative who was antagonistic to Cohen. When Cohen wanted to cross-examine Osborne-Dempster, for example, Sedgwick opposed him and questioned Cohen's status at the hearings.[45] In addition, Sedgwick may have influenced LeBel's conclusions in that Premier Drew attempted to treat Sedgwick as his own lawyer. Years later, while researching his memoirs, David Lewis learned that in July 1945 Premier Drew wrote to Sedgwick that he 'wanted to have a chat with you about the final stages of the inquiry and any indications you had received of the attitude of the Commission.' He asked Sedgwick to drop him a line, though there is no evidence that Sedgwick did so. But in Lewis's view, this letter to Sedwick, 'coming from a premier, who was a central figure in the inquiry,' was scandalously improper.[46]

Cohen put on an aggressive performance at the hearings. He interrupted the court reporter to check facts; he quarrelled with David J. Walker, the lawyer representing M.A. Sanderson; and he tried to broaden the scope of the inquiry. Both Sedgwick and Robinette thought his behaviour obstructive, but LeBel restricted Cohen's interruptions. Cohen 'furiously' cross-examined Attorney General Leslie Blackwell, who testified that the many reports he received ceased in June 1944. Cohen retorted sarcastically and bitterly, 'Of course, you did not realize that you were by that means denying yourself the joyful experience of reading a report on the nomination of J.L. Cohen in Essex West. That came in just one month later. You cut yourself off at the wrong month' and should have read 'not nominated as CCF candidate or any other candidate in Essex or anywhere else.' Blackwell responded that he had not seen that report, but he commented rather ominously, given the course of events in Cohen's life thereafter, 'I am interested in you Mr. Cohen.'[47] Blackwell minimized the importance of the reports, saying that all police forces were interested in communist activity and he did not attach much value to such reports or see any harm in receiving them. The documents regularly included information from undercover agents about unions, but Blackwell denied such knowledge. He admitted to having lunch once with Gladstone Murray. Sedgwick complained that Cohen's cross-examination was taking too long. Cohen responded that he was trying to learn what, if anything, the attorney general considered improper or illegal.

From 18 to 20 July, the various lawyers, including J.J. Robinette for Leslie Wismer, H.L. Cartwright for Constable J.A. Rowe, and Andrew Brewin for E.B. Jolliffe, presented their arguments to the inquiry. Cohen spoke on the third day. He had not had a chance to review all the evidence, he began, but he did not think that the commission had conducted itself properly in terms of the amount of time it spent, its procedures, the order of witnesses, or its rulings concerning the scope of its investigation. Unlike his associates in the case, Cohen did not compliment LeBel as commissioner. He criticized commission counsel Joseph Sedgwick's methods in assisting Osborne-Dempster for example, whose evidence went into the record just as two written reports that contradicted Dempster were received from Inspector Edward Hammond, whom Sedgwick subsequently sharply cross-examined.

Cohen then outlined his theory of the case and discussed the commission's scope in a way that was different from Brewin, who focused on legality and the law of conspiracy. Cohen dealt more broadly with the issues and with the inquiry's process. He wished to determine whether any conduct of the nature that Jolliffe described was committed, whether such behaviour was appropriate in public affairs, and whether Drew or others were associated or identified with such conduct. In Cohen's view, LeBel was the jury; he had to be guided by the evidence and draw on his common sense, decency, fairness, and 'experience with men and affairs' to evaluate the testimony. He criticized the judge for failing to establish the premier's role. If LeBel believed that the premier's conduct was intended to help him maintain office, he should give his opinion. After Blackwell read a statement and concluded his testimony, Cohen concluded that he had failed to discharge his duty as attorney general. LeBel, Cohen thought, should say so. LeBel should evaluate the ethical character of the persons involved, their actions, and any information disclosed by the evidence which was of concern to the public.

To Cohen, Osborne-Dempster was a trashy, untruthful character, a secret spy, who was prepared to do anything and to serve any interest. Drew had acquiesced in his service and Blackwell had read the reports. Blackwell knew of D.208 and was prepared to have the government benefit from any information it received. He knew that the police were receiving the information and passing it on. Cohen believed that even an inexperienced minister would have ended the practice, or at least refused to receive the reports, but Blackwell did nothing, suspecting that the information would not do his party any harm. When Sedgwick examined the attorney general 'with that charming and delightful manner of his and that seductive voice and tone which I envy' about his luncheon with Murray, the talk was supposedly about bud worms, but really, Cohen asserted, a 'nice neat little blind was drawn down so that one could not peep into ... what was going on at this luncheon.' Cohen was blunt and harsh towards Blackwell; the attorney general was not being frank with the commission or the people of Ontario but was rather spinning alibis.

Cohen also discussed the change in the reports' content and tone following November 1943 – three months after the Conservatives formed a minority government and the CCF became the Official Opposition. He attributed it to a 'red' smear which had developed in stages during the war: first, it discredited the Soviet Union and the CPC until the latter was banned by the Defence of Canada Regulations; then in 1943 the LPP became a target; unions were also attacked as containing CCFers and Communists, and the CCF was slandered as 'the same as' the Communists. Cohen told LeBel that 'those processes are wrong;' they were distasteful, indecent, 'destructive of and subversive of the interests of this country, of the national interests, and that any Attorney-General reading a file containing that type of material at once had resting upon him the obligation of clearing up the mess.'[48] Instead Blackwell had ignored his responsibility and had continued to receive reports that might benefit the government politically.

The commission did not follow up contradictory testimony, Cohen noted, and there were questions about the exhibits not asked. Cohen referred to Drew's opening campaign speech on 14 May 1945 which was no different from Murray's propaganda, from Osborne-Dempster's reports, or from Sanderson's ads. All demonstrated the same charges, insinuations, and omissions characteristic of what Cohen labelled 'red smear' propaganda.

Cohen had seen similar material and attitudes before. In his remarks to LeBel, he noted parallels between the subject of this inquiry and his earlier submission to the parliamentary committee in which he advocated legalizing the CPC. This police project 'was designed deliberately and on the basis of falsehoods to create divisions' among people. He concluded wearily, at the time when the world was hearing about the holocaust: 'I think the world has reached ... a point where it has ... begun to understand that in terms of religion there must be tolerance ... and that all deplore even violence of expression, let alone the wars and ravages on the human race.'[49] Similarly, political divisions and ideological hatreds were not in the national interest. Drew's speech had appealed to prejudice, ignorance, and fear and had contained deliberate falsehoods. Cohen recommended that LeBel's report condemn the secret reports and fabrications, criticize the government's collection of such reports as being contrary to the public interest, find Drew and Blackwell motivated by political expediency, and rule that Jolliffe's statement was justified. LeBel did none of these things.

The experience of the LeBel Commission Inquiry was hard on Cohen. At one point in his summation, he said, 'I am beginning to feel that I have aged perceptively in this case.'[50] His performance was abrasive, adversarial, and dramatic, and his tone during the inquiry was severe, but he held consistently and eloquently to his past positions, which favoured the protection of individuals' civil liberties, legalization of the Communist Party, high standards of public conduct, accountability of politicians and police, and tolerance of religious and political minorities. He could not know that the kinds of accusations he deplored would increase exponentially during the Cold War. At the same time, his appeal to the commission that people learn from the war the danger of religious and ideological intolerance, and his stand against bigotry and discrimination, foreshadowed the trend in public attitudes in the 1950s and 1960s, which eventually led to a decline in anti-Semitism and to the establishment of human-rights commissions.[51]

Cohen undoubtedly alienated the other lawyers and made some enemies, including Leslie Blackwell, whom he accused publicly of being a liar. Four months after the LeBel Inquiry ended, the incident between Cohen and Elizabeth Guenard occurred. When Dorothy Cohen approached Sedgwick to act for her husband, he refused. When Cohen's own case was being considered by the Attorney-General's Department, Blackwell himself made the decisions, not his deputy minister, as was the usual procedure.

REPRESENTING SPIES, 1946

In September 1945, two months before the Guenard incident in Kirkland Lake, and unbeknownst to Cohen or Canadians, Igor Gouzenko, a cipher clerk in the Soviet embassy in Ottawa, defected with stolen documents. After an agonizing thirty hours in which he tried to convince the astonished Canadian authorities that he was serious, he was hidden for five months until the case finally was made public.

Having personally experienced political conflicts on the left over his nomination in Windsor, and witnessed ideological war between Ontario's Conservatives and the CCF at the LeBel Inquiry, in the autumn of 1946 Cohen appeared before the Royal Commission on Espionage, appointed to investigate persons accused by Gouzenko of being Soviet spies in what was later seen as the start of the Cold War in Canada. Before the commission, Cohen represented briefly Henry Harris, who was accused of issuing a false passport, and later in county court he appeared for David Gordon Lunan, who was charged with conspiring to violate the Official Secrets Act.[52] Shortly after, in June 1946, Montreal's Labour-Progressive MP Fred Rose was convicted of espionage on the basis of others' testimony. By the time Lunan was convicted, Cohen was ill, was facing charges on two counts of assault, and was awaiting his own trial, which occurred in December 1946.

In February 1946 Prime Minister King held a press conference to reveal the existence of a Soviet spy ring in Ottawa, involving Canadian civil servants who supplied confidential information to the Soviet Union. The RCMP had seized twelve Canadians and one Briton, and the government already had in place a royal commission investigating the situation, which in several interim reports would reveal the scope of Soviet activities and make headlines around the world. After Gouzenko defected, police interrogated him to evaluate his evidence. On the basis of his testimony and over a hundred Soviet embassy documents, the suspected spies were arrested five months later. In the intervening period, the Canadian government discussed with the British and American governments what it might do to promote better security, particularly surrounding information about the atomic bomb, without dramatically disrupting relations with the Soviet Union. It believed that the Canadian civil servants had given away only low-grade information but in doing so had broken their oaths of office and their motives were not known.[53] Once the story became public, the press ignored the quality of the information lost and indulged in sensational reports.

The RCMP opposed precipitous action, since it needed a royal commission to secure confessions and more evidence that could be used in court. All suspects had code names in the documents, but the police were particularly interested to learn that LPP MP Fred Rose and Communist organizer Sam Carr were involved.[54] The suspects had been under surveillance for months while the government studied Gouzenko's documents and the RCMP investigated to find corroborating evidence. On 15 February 1946, when the suspects were seized, no formal charges were laid, but they were taken to the Rockcliffe Barracks, held there for weeks incommunicado, and interrogated by two inspectors. Cohen's client, David Gordon Lunan, described the experience. They 'were kept isolated, one to a room, watched over by guards day and night. The windows were nailed shut and a row of overhead lights was kept burning all night.' Lunan's guard told him repeatedly that other detainees had attempted suicide, which was not true. Over two weeks, the police questioned Lunan six times and the royal commission called him five times before he was charged and given access to a lawyer. Others were incarcerated for as much as six weeks before being charged.[55]

On 5 February 1946, P 411 had established the Royal Commission on Espionage, under Supreme Court justices Roy Lindsay Kellock and Robert Taschereau, and provided it with the powers of the War Measures Act, the Public Inquiries Act, and the Official Secrets Act, 1939. Its legal counsel was E.K. Williams, the president of the Canadian Bar Association. When suspects were brought before the commission, they had to testify or face contempt charges if they refused. The commission made its own rules for the secret hearings and presumed that all suspects were guilty until proven innocent. The suspects were not permitted counsel, and they did not know how to protect themselves. When questioning resulted in self-incrimination, they were released, only to be immediately arrested, charged, and sent to trial.

As soon as Cohen heard that spy suspects were being held in Ottawa, he began collecting extensive material and researching the situation. He made notes on events surrounding the royal commission and on Igor Gouzenko's testimony, after it was revealed. He disliked the Russian and noted discrepancies in his testimony. He kept the prime minister's speeches on the matter in Hansard and press reports about Canadian-American consultations, and he speculated about a connection between the spy ring and the atom bomb. He even planned a study of the Gouzenko case from a civil-libertarian perspective. Cohen held a minority view that the spy cases raised serious civil-liberties issues 'arising from the nature of the charges which have been laid, the relevant statutes and from most peculiar procedural events which virtually deprived the accused of any possibility of a fair trial.' As with wartime internees, there were 'incommunicado' arrests, for the first time in Canada, 'third degree' statements, and the 'virtual conviction in the public mind of any potential accused before any charges were even laid against any person.'[56]

Cohen's interest was political, for he viewed the Canadian government's handling of the case and the delay involved as a way to divert attention from whatever else it was doing about post-war reconstruction. Cohen expressed sympathy for the Soviet Union as Canada's relations with that country became strained. He questioned the government's attempt to characterize the spy suspects as examples of the Soviet Union's selfish and aggressive motives, without at the same time questioning its own motives and placing the spy trials in some kind of context. He was critical of Canada's role in world affairs, with its apparent lack of independence from the United States, in particular, and Britain. He wondered specifically whether Canada should have withheld from the Soviet Union details about Canadian RDX manufacturing, a chemical process used in the production of explosives, at a time when that country was an ally and engaged in major battles with Germany. Dr Raymond Boyer of McGill University was found guilty and went to jail for telling the Russians about it.[57] Cohen's opinions ran counter to most of the media and public, for conflict between the Allies and the Soviet Union was leading to the Cold War, in which Canada sided with the Americans. Cohen's viewpoint was seldom expressed by others and was disregarded as the partisan rantings of a radical. The civil-libertarian aspect of his argument was listened to more closely but did not change the situation.

Lawyers for the suspects' families tried to interrupt the secret interrogations with appeals to the courts for writs of habeas corpus, but the commission fought the writs by arguing that under the Official Secrets Act habeas corpus did not apply. The means used – secrecy, suspension of civil liberties, and lengthy incarceration – became controversial and eventually were condemned by the Canadian Bar Association. In March, as a result of pressure from the prime minister, four suspects were released, then charged with violations of the Official Secrets Act and the Criminal Code, and jailed. An interim report became public. It revealed that two female civil servants had confessed to spying and would be tried. Emma Woikin of the Department of External Affairs and Kathleen Willsher, a secretary at the British High Commission, were convicted in county court and received two years and two and a half years in jail, respectively. Cohen prepared a list of the trials that resulted from the royal commission's investigation, which took several years to conclude.[58]

Shortly after the commission released a second interim report, John Diefenbaker protested in Parliament that suspects had been held without counsel until they had incriminated themselves, and 'Chubby' Power so opposed the government's conduct that he resigned as a minister to criticize it from the backbenches. The royal commission's proceedings must have reminded Cohen of the wartime internment hearings, which also were held in secret. There, too, the detainees were under the complete control of the RCMP and the minister of justice, the onus was on the individual to prove his of her innocence, and the procedure had the government's support. Once again, the rules of evidence were 'flexible,' to allow probing without protection for the accused.

Finally, when the last five suspects remained in custody, lawyers were granted access and Cohen had his first opportunity to get involved. He attended with his client, Dr Henry Harris, before the commission between April and June 1946. On 19 July, Cohen advised the Department of Justice that he was acting for Harris and should be kept informed. When Harris was charged for an offence arising out of the investigation – issuing a false passport – Cohen went to Ottawa to answer the charge and protest the trial's locale. He requested and received a transcript of Harris's evidence before the commission, and also obtained a transcript of the evidence in Fred Rose's trial. Cohen got in touch with J.J. Robinette, the prosecutor in Harris's case, and asked him which documents he would produce and when he could inspect them. The preliminary inquiry for Harris was to take place on 14 October before Magistrate Glenn Elford Strike, and to prepare for it Cohen received Gouzenko's evidence in the trial of H.S. Gerson, who had connections with the production branch of the Department of Munitions and Supply and who was ultimately convicted of giving secret information to the Soviets and sentenced to a penitentiary term. He and Robinette agreed to adjourn the case until after 16 December 1946. Ultimately, the case would not be heard until January, by which time Cohen himself was convicted of assault in a court in Haileybury and Harris decided to find a new lawyer. Since Robinette was by this time Cohen's own lawyer, he of course knew of the situation, but Cohen nevertheless formally advised him that he no longer represented Harris. As Cohen wrote accurately to a Russian translator in New York, whom he hired to translate some documents into English, 'I am sorry that these circumstances developed but they are beyond either your control or mine.' Cohen believed that Harris was innocent. Harris was convicted, but his case was appealed and he was acquitted.[59]

Cohen's chance to act in Lunan's trial came about indirectly and was short-lived, but he performed aggressively with his old fire. On 4 November 1946 H.L. Cartwright spoke to his client, David Gordon Lunan, and at his request invited Cohen to act as senior counsel in Lunan's trial. In his memoirs, Lunan recalls that he hired Cohen 'on the strength of his reputation as a scrappy labour lawyer and fighter for left-wing causes.'[60] Cohen came in at the last moment because Lunan expected Lucien Gendron of Quebec to represent him. On 3 November the Law Society of Upper Canada refused Gendron's request to be permitted as a courtesy to appear in an Ontario court. H.L. Cartwright of Kingston, who was Gendron's agent, told Cohen, 'The defense which I have advised and on which I thought my advice had been accepted by Lunan is not to be used. I therefore propose to leave the entire direction of matters to you from now on. If it were not for the fact that it would prejudice Lunan's trial I would now ask leave to withdraw from the case since I feel that I can be of very little further assistance to him.' He advised Cohen to deal with Lunan directly about fees, which he did. The trial was set for 12 November, a date to which Cartwright had agreed. He sent Cohen his documents and suggested that he seek an adjournment.

Cohen accepted the case and wrote to crown prosecutor John R. Cartwright, informing him that he would need two weeks to prepare. Cartwright rejected an adjournment on the grounds that Lunan had elected trial by judge without jury the previous May, there had been previous adjournments, and it had been made clear that the 12 November date was final. The trial would be that day.[61]

David Gordon Lunan, a former official of the Canadian Information Service, was charged with conspiring to communicate confidential information to the Soviet Union. He was thirty-two years old, of slender build, six feet tall, balding at the temples, and with a light brown moustache. He had come to Canada from England in 1938, worked in Montreal as an advertising agent, enlisted in the army in 1943, and from there was sent to the Canadian Information Service. At the time of his trial, eighteen persons had been detained and charged; five had been found guilty, three had pleaded guilty, three had been acquitted, and seven cases were pending. Lunan's was the first of five speedy trials before a county court judge.

Cohen conducted an aggressive defence. He first asked Judge A.G. McDougall for a dismissal, since the crown could not prove its case. Most of Lunan's evidence was in the public domain before the trial. Documents indicated that a Soviet embassy official known as JAN (Lieutenant-Colonel Vassili Rogov) gave Lunan, whose cover name was BACK, instructions about the information he wanted. Lunan received information from Edward Mazerall and Durnford Smith, both engineers at the National Research Council (NRC), whose specialties were radar and microwaves, and some oral information from Israel Halperin, a mathematician and former army ballistics expert, and reported it to the Soviets. Lunan was introduced to JAN by Fred Rose. He told the royal commission that its disclosure of the scope of the Soviet conspiracy in Canada had thrown an entirely new light on the situation. He had thought that he was giving the Soviets public information about military affairs, which would help them meet their international commitments.

In his somewhat confused statement to the commission on the reason for his actions, Lunan mentioned his aid to the Canadian veterans of the Spanish Civil War and his interest in left-wing organizations. He told the court that he met Rogov 'very much as a Canadian, who was acknowledgedly a communist in sympathy and a well-wisher of the Soviet Union.' He stated, 'It was only after a great struggle on my part ... that I could bring myself eventually to accept this kind of work as something which would in the long run advance the whole cause of international cooperation.' The latter was the basis of his political ideology. But then he said, 'I certainly did not think of it in terms of cheating Canada out of anything.' He claimed that he later decided to withdraw from such work but found that it was not easy to do, and that he was 'amazed' at the scope of the Soviet network. He recognized the 'dangerous' characteristics of his work, but in his mind the Soviet Union was an ally. When the commissioners asked him if 'you thought the Communist Party knew better what was in the interests of Canada than Canada herself?' Lunan answered, 'Yes.' Lunan's testimony was very important in incriminating several people, including Edward Mazerall, who was convicted and sentenced to four years; Durnford Smith, who was convicted and sentenced to five years; and Israel Halperin, who was innocent and was acquitted.[62]

When called to testify at his own trial, Lunan, in a light grey suit, white shirt, and blue and white tie, sat in a tall prisoner's box. Cohen objected to his placement, saying, 'I don't know if I can climb that high,' and requested that Lunan be allowed to sit beside him during the trial, 'so I may confer with him ... The way it is now I can just see the top of his head.' The judge had Lunan formally plead not guilty to the charge in the box, and then permitted him to sit with Cohen.

Cohen tried to prevent the admission in court of Lunan's testimony before the royal commission on the grounds that it was not given voluntarily but was acquired through intimidation after the offer of inducements. Cohen had an affidavit about Lunan's treatment while he was detained. He also argued that the royal commission's proceedings were improper. Cartwright retorted that the commission was lawfully constituted and that Lunan had testified under oath and under a statute that compelled him to answer questions. Lunan had not objected to answering questions, and Cartwright referred to Cohen's 'somewhat vehement recital' of the events during the detention period. The court ruled that such testimony was admissable, ignored the affidavit, and told Cohen to proceed with his argument.

Cohen then objected to the admission of Igor Gouzenko's testimony on the grounds that he had stolen documents from the Soviet embassy and was tainted by his criminal act, and that the documents should be given diplomatic immunity. Cartwright responded that the alleged illegality of the means by which evidence was obtained did not disqualify it. The commission had accepted Gouzenko's evidence and documents, and the judge in Lunan's case did not differ with it. Gouzenko was called as the crown's chief witness. Lunan smiled and took copious notes throughout his testimony, as Gouzenko explained that in the espionage network Lunan was a recruiting agent working with Fred Rose, who had already been convicted and sentenced to six years. The Toronto *Star* reported, 'The trial before the county court judge without a jury took a lively turn as Mr. Cohen began cross-examination of Igor Gouzenko.'[63] Cohen's vigorous efforts to discredit Gouzenko made for heated exchanges between the two men; Cohen demanded that Gouzenko stop arguing with him, and the witness charged that Cohen was twisting his previous evidence.

The conspiracy trial lasted four days but concluded abruptly. The court did not allow Cohen to call Prime Minister King, Reconstruction Minister Howe, or other government officials whom he had subpoenaed – they all made excuses for not appearing which the court accepted – but his attempt won him publicity. He submitted the evidence of RCMP Inspector W.H. Williams before the commission concerning Lunan's detention at Rockcliffe Barracks, and then he rested his case. He did not try to contradict the incriminating testimony and documents.[64] Cartwright placed the royal commission testimony on record, and neither lawyer gave a summary statement of their cases. Judge McDougall withheld his verdict and then convicted the accused on 18 November, in the eighth court case following the nine-month espionage probe, and sentenced him to five years in prison. The judge found that Lunan had committed the act as charged and had persuaded other government officials to give information to the Soviets, and that some of the information was 'of a highly secret nature.' Lunan was unrepentant at the end of the trial, saying, 'I don't consider myself guilty of the charge either in law or in fact.'

The next day Lunan was released on bail and left for Montreal. Cohen planned to appeal the case on the grounds that the judge had refused a request for adjournment and the crown had not made available testimony of alleged co-conspirators. He learned that his client had decided to hire another lawyer to conduct the appeal. Lunan was unimpressed with Cohen's performance, which, though headline-grabbing, he did not consider effective. He has left an unflattering description of Cohen at this time. 'It was depressingly clear that we had an emotionally sick man on our hands,' who scarcely left his hotel room throughout the trial. Cohen was partial to oysters and filet mignon, which room service delivered so that he could eat in bed. Part of his preparations in the bathroom before he went to sleep 'was the popping of a handful of downers.' Cohen would eventually pass out and, when Lunan woke him in the morning, 'his first act was to pop Benzedrine uppers which wound him up for the day ahead.' He would perform an elaborate toilette, dress in 'sartorial elegance,' and go to court. In Lunan's view, Gouzenko 'was in better shape emotionally and physically than J.L. and had had ten months of coaching and rehearsal,'[65] and Cohen seemed to have lost the thread of the proceedings. The other lawyers were embarrassed, he claimed, and one commiserated with Lunan that he would have been better off with nobody. Lunan obviously disliked Cohen; he probably exaggerated his condition, but if what he has written is only partially true, Cohen evidently was going into decline even before his trial.

When he learned that his client had fired him, Cohen expressed his appreciation to Gendron for his cooperation, particularly during the week of the trial, when he consulted in Ottawa with Cohen three times. Cohen commented that Lunan was completely within his rights to hire other counsel for the appeal, but he was clearly disappointed. He agreed to turn over his files to Lunan for the appeal but requested that the appellant counsel's record be sent to him later.

Because Lunan had not as yet paid him, Cohen wrote to the court reporter, D.J. Keele, that he was no longer acting for Lunan, 'and it is just possible that Lunan or some counsel on his behalf may attempt to circumvent me by ordering a new set of records from you.' Lunan had spoken to Keele in the courtroom after refusing to testify in Israel Halperin's case, and had told him that he had dissociated himself from Cohen for the appeal. Keele told Lunan that he had 'given up a gold mine for a dead horse.' He realized, he told Cohen, that it was none of his business, but he could not let the situation pass without comment. He promised to cooperate with Cohen in preventing 'any such circumvention as you have mentioned.' Three days later, Cohen told Keele that he had completed his accounts with Lunan.[66] Lunan's conviction was later upheld, and while he languished in jail, Cohen worked desperately and unsuccessfully to prevent his own conviction. Cohen's last struggle would be on his own behalf.

Part Four

Relations with the Law Society,
1945–1950

9

On Trial, 1946–1947

In 1945 Jacob Lawrence Cohen was the most prominent labour lawyer in Canada. Trade-union leaders sought his advice; workers struggling to form unions against obdurate employers admired Cohen's skill and commitment, and trusted him. Tim Buck remembered that Cohen was the first of a new type of labour lawyer, 'that is, the lawyer who understands the problems of the trade union movement far better than the average trade union officer. And understands the relations of the law to the trade union movement far better than the average lawyer.'[1] In Senator David Croll's opinion, 'nothing like him has appeared on the scene for a long time. There hasn't been anybody as brilliant in labour law' since then. George Burt, a past director of the autoworkers' union, recalled: 'Cohen was the smartest guy we ever used. He had a much more profound knowledge of the needs of the labour movement but he also had a real knowledge of the contractual matters that we used to put in our agreements ... and I think some of the language which is still in our agreements today carries the mark of J.L. Cohen, even yet.'[2]

But Cohen paid a price to become an economically secure and successful lawyer. He was a workaholic and a perfectionist who took on too much and spent hours mastering every detail of a case before he went into court. The demands on his time were unrelenting; he worked sixteen-hour days, travelled a great deal – mostly by train because he feared planes and did not drive a car often – and felt uncomfortable away from his home and office. He had no hobbies, except reading. He seldom participated in social gatherings and never involved himself in the Law Society, the university, or private clubs.[3] J.J. Robinette remembered, 'You'd never see him around anywhere. He never went to any gatherings. I can't recall seeing him at lunch at the two or three restaurants that anybody would bother to go to ... you'd never see him except when he would be strutting into court, or a union meeting, or an arbitration proceeding.'[4] His involvement in the Jewish community was limited. As he gained prominence, he was asked to participate in United Jewish Welfare, but his frank response conveyed a sense of his working life during the war. He wrote to I. Freiman, 'My own duties at the moment are so complex and take me out of town to such an extent that I cannot assume the responsibility of giving direction to any communal endeavour.' He offered occasional assistance but would assume no leadership since 'I am not,' he wrote, 'by any means, my own master as to my professional engagements.'[5]

Undoubtedly, Cohen's experiences as a labour lawyer affected his personality and manner and made him more partisan than he had been as a younger man. He was confronted daily with economic and political inequalities and class and cultural conflicts in Canadian society, which were sometimes exaggerated by the Depression and war. These divides could result in arbitrary and unjust treatment of vulnerable people because of the Draconian Defence of Canada Regulations and inadequate labour legislation. He sometimes displayed contempt for colleagues since he could not play the professional game. His daughter, Phyllis Clarke, confirmed that 'he was never a compromiser ... so people knew his views. People just didn't see him as another lawyer. It wasn't just that he was a lawyer on the other side and he and I go off to lunch because we are both lawyers. People knew that he was just not *on* the other side but that he *was* the other side.' As a result of demands, habits, and social isolation, Cohen only worked, and 'nobody could ever convince him to slow down.'[6]

In the war years, at the peak of his career, his demanding schedule began to affect him adversely. Other lawyers noticed that he was tense and edgy. By the summer of 1945, Cohen was suffering from nervous and physical exhaustion, yet he refused to stop. After a hard day he would drink scotch neat to relax and take sedatives to help him get to sleep. His daughter remembered, 'Every doctor he ever saw anywhere said that what he needed to do was try and cut back ... But workaholics don't cut back very easily and he would say, "Yes you are right, that's what I'll do!" But I don't think that constitutionally he could ever sort of relax.'[7]

THE GUENARD INCIDENT

In 1945 the Mine Mill union hired Cohen to prepare a brief to the NWLB requesting a wage increase and present it to the miners at their annual convention. It was an important job, because the government had retained wage controls, and Cohen was outspoken on the wage issue. With his health declining, he hesitated to make the long trip north to Kirkland Lake. In October he had visited a doctor in Montreal where he spent three weeks convalescing. Dissatisfied with the hospital, in mid-November he became impatient and returned to Toronto.[8]

The union pressed him to attend its convention. International union president Reid Robinson wired that his presence was important, particularly given that Robinson himself could not be there because President Harry Truman had called an emergency labour conference in Washington, D.C.[9] Union staff representative Bob Carlin pestered Cohen with phone calls. Dorothy Cohen fought and pleaded with her husband to stay home. She was concerned about his health, and because Cohen refused to fly, the train trip would be long and slow, with the cars full of returning soldiers. As Cohen could not get a berth, he would have to sit up all night for fourteen hours. Mrs Cohen resented the union's pressure, feeling that it was taking advantage of Cohen, and she was not convinced that his report was essential to the convention's success. Cohen's travels had been a source of conflict in the marriage. Moreover, Mrs Cohen probably sensed that her husband was having an affair with a young woman on his staff, particularly since his secretary, Elizabeth Guenard, had phoned him at home several times. But, as D.M. Estok recounts, 'as so many times in the past, Cohen placed everything else, including his health, aside. His work came first.'[10]

Elizabeth Guenard, who accompanied Cohen to Kirkland Lake, was an attractive twenty-year-old blond (she told Cohen she was twenty-two) whom Cohen had met in Windsor in May 1945. Formerly with the UAW, Guenard moved to Toronto to work for Cohen. The daughter of a French-Canadian lumberjack from northern Quebec, she was impressed by Cohen's lifestyle because he travelled first class, stayed in the best hotels, and dined in elegant restaurants. She found him 'charming' at times, though a demanding employer, and almost as soon as they met they were sexually intimate.[11] This was not a first affair for Cohen. Rumours had circulated for years about brief flings, usually with younger women. His marriage apparently was troubled and Cohen justified his sexual behaviour to himself as the result of a sexually unfulfilling marital relationship.[12]

Guenard was not a skilled stenographer, and after the two quarrelled in public at a Windsor hotel in June, Cohen fired her. He rehired her in September when she appeared at his hotel room in Montreal and pleaded for a second chance. Later in September, they quarrelled in public again when Cohen was returning by train from union business in Nova Scotia. Guenard gave a statement to the police; Cohen was put off the train at Rivière du Loup, was charged with creating a public disturbance, paid a small fine, and reboarded the train quickly, since he was anxious not to miss his connection in Montreal.

On Friday, 18 November 1945, at 11:30 P.M., Cohen and Guenard boarded the all-night train at Toronto's Union Station. Surrounded by boisterous, happy soldiers, Cohen was unable to sleep and arrived in Kirkland Lake nervous, exhausted, and irritable. At the Park Lane Hotel, a stone structure built in the 1930s in the centre of town, Cohen was given two adjoining rooms on the fifth floor.

Because he was unwell, Cohen made his report to the convention in the evening. The government's wage policy, he began, was out of date because the war was over. Its continuation was a way 'to keep wages down.' Only in the most outstanding cases were increases allowed, and 'every decision rendered by the Board was more and more restrictive.' The miners listened attentively to his lengthy presentation, for despite his illness, Cohen was a compelling speaker who communicated complex arguments simply and with wit. He outlined the great changes in the Canadian economy; the war had demonstrated that full employment with 'decent wages' for workers was possible, and he predicted a vital role for labour in post-war society. At the end, the miners burst into appreciative applause.

Cohen was up late, slept, worked all the next day in committee meetings providing advice on policy resolutions, and returned to his room exhausted. He told Guenard that he had hired a taxi to return them to Toronto the next morning, for delegates would be on the train and he did not want to sit up with them all night rehashing convention highlights. On 21 November 1945, four months after the LeBel Inquiry but before the spy trials, patrons sleeping in the Park Lane Hotel in Kirkland Lake, Ontario, were awakened by a woman's screams. Mine Mill's convention had ended five hours earlier, and Bob Carlin, a prominent union official, was just dropping off to sleep, after celebrating the conference's end late into the evening, when he heard the noise.[13]

In the hotel lobby, Maurice Doyon, the night clerk, at 2 A.M. had noticed a light flashing for the telephone in room 508, but then it stopped. Twenty minutes later, the light flashed from room 510. He went to the fifth floor to investigate, heard nothing, and returned to the lobby. A few minutes later, the light from room 510 flashed again, and he investigated a second time, but all was quiet. Around 5 A.M. the switch-board lit up with three or four telephone lights all at once. He answered one call from Wilfred Hardy, an auditor for the Hydro Power Commission, who was in 511. Hardy had been awakened by the screams and phoned the desk. He told the clerk that 'he should do something about getting the girl out of that room.'

In response to the commotion, Doyon rushed to the fifth floor and, sensing trouble, went to get the manager, Lawrence Mitchell. The two men returned to find patrons in their pajamas and robes gathered in the corridor. Mitchell rapped on the door of 508. Cohen opened it and spoke: 'Get the rest of these people back in their rooms; I can handle this,' he purportedly said. Doyon went back to the lobby, and when he returned a few minutes later, Mitchell, Elizabeth Guenard, and Cohen were in the doorway of 510. Doyon overheard Guenard say, 'I won't go back into that room, this happened before.' Doyon noticed that she was wearing a slip, 'her face seemed to be scratched and her lips puffed up,'[14] but she did not appear to have been drinking.

Doyon went downstairs but later received several insistent phone calls from Cohen demanding to know the whereabouts of 'the girl' who had left the scene with the hotel housekeeper, Mrs McLean. Cohen phoned McLean's room, 501, but she hung up when she realized who was calling. Cohen also spoke to Mitchell about a taxi he had ordered, so he could 'get the hell out of there fast.'

Before Cohen left Kirkland Lake, Bob Carlin thanked him for attending the conference, without mentioning the embarrassing quarrel he had overheard the night before, and warned him to watch his health. Earlier that year the Carlins had driven Cohen by Haileybury near Lake Temiskaming. Cohen had remarked to Kay Carlin, 'What a beautiful lake. I'd love to spend a holiday here.' Cohen would return to Haileybury about a year later for the most important trial of his life – his own.[15]

A few days after this incident, Elizabeth Guenard returned to work in Cohen's office. The hotel scene had lasted less than half an hour, but the events of that night, 21 November 1945, in Kirkland Lake were relived many times in the minds of those present. The sordid episode turned into a sensational case, involving persons at the highest levels of the

Ontario Attorney General's Department. The repercussions of the much-publicized trial led to the humiliation, ruin, and, a few years later, the death of J.L. Cohen.

LEAD-UP TO THE TRIAL

Cohen worked in his office occasionally in November and December 1945. Guenard continued as his employee with no complaints. But, as the trial revealed, unbeknownst to Cohen, the police approached Guenard in the office on Christmas Eve, 1945. She was driven to a station and questioned for several hours about the Park Lane Hotel incident by Detective John Nimmo of the Toronto police force and Sergeant Herbert Braney, an OPP officer from the Timmins detachment. They saw her again on 12 January 1946, when she signed a statement that was evidence at the trial. In February, she wrote an emotional letter to Braney, accusing him and Nimmo of forcing the statement out of her in the presence of her drunken, abusive father, said that it was all lies, and asked them to return it to her. She later claimed that no one had asked her to write the letter, which she sent just after Cohen told her he would not see her again, and after his sister, at whose place she was staying to avoid her father, told her she would have to find her own room.[16]

Cohen was having more trouble. In January 1946 he failed to appear in county court in a picketing case. This was unusual behaviour for a man who was a stickler for detail and organized in scheduling his cases. The frustrated crown attorney, E.C. Awrey, told the judge that Cohen's attitude in the case 'is almost bordering on contempt.' He learned at the last minute that Cohen would be absent because he had left Toronto suddenly to handle a case in Nova Scotia and had told no one. Judge E.A. Shaunessy made it clear that he would grant no more adjournments and considered Cohen's unexplained behaviour an 'abuse of the privileges of the court.'[17]

On 11 January, on the advice of his physician, Dr Jacob Markowitz, Cohen entered the Mount Sinai Hospital in New York City for tests and a medical examination. His doctors told him not to work for three months and to travel to a warmer climate. Cohen returned to Toronto briefly and then joined Mrs Cohen, who was vacationing in California. His erratic work schedule and increased medical treatments were creating financial problems and stress for both of them.[18]

While he was away, Cohen learned that the police were enquiring into the incident and had questioned Lawrence Mitchell and that Guenard had made a statement. In February 1946 Cohen asked a friend, Toronto lawyer Samuel Gotfrid, to visit Deputy Attorney General Cecil L. Snyder and tell him that Cohen was receiving medical attention, but if the crown or the police wanted to interview Cohen, he would return to Toronto. Cohen and Snyder had appeared opposite each other when Snyder was an assistant crown attorney in Toronto. Gotfrid told Snyder that he had heard from sources that 'this whole matter was being pushed by a group of mine owners in Kirkland Lake and Timmins' who wanted to discredit Cohen as a way of fighting the union. Snyder denied any knowledge of such pressure and said that the investigation arose because of gossip in Kirkland Lake, which resulted in a complaint. He did not name the complainant. The attorney general had been accused of not proceeding because Cohen was prominent and his department always tried to protect lawyers in trouble.

Gotfrid explained how ill Cohen was and said that he was probably not responsible for his actions. He also blamed Guenard, for Cohen's 'greatest difficulty was to rid himself of this girl who apparently had fastened on him like a leech.' Gotfrid wanted assurances that Snyder would not 'permit a charge to be laid unless he felt that an offense had been committed – regardless of what pressure had been brought.' Snyder usually decided which cases were prosecuted, but in Cohen's case the attorney general himself, Leslie Blackwell, would make the decision, and he and Inspector Stringer were simply carrying out instructions.[19] Blackwell was fair-minded, Snyder assured Gotfrid, and 'he wouldn't jump off the deep end,' but Snyder promised to keep Gotfrid informed.[20]

This procedure was unfortunate for Cohen. Blackwell was as ideologically on the right as Cohen was on the left, at a time when Ontario politics were highly polarized. At the recent LeBel inquiry, Cohen had cross-examined Blackwell as a witness and basically called him a liar. It is unlikely that Blackwell was sympathetic to Cohen and may even have felt vindictive. Snyder did not want to question Cohen and told Gotfrid, 'Tell J.L. to go and take a trip around the world; he has earned a holiday and should take one.' Snyder had himself earlier suffered from overwork, resorted to drugs, and recovered only after a rest. But he was not especially sympathetic.[21]

The OPP continued its investigation. On 12 March, Mitchell called Cohen's office for advice. Sergeant Braney had asked him to sign a statement that confirmed Guenard's. Mitchell was uncooperative, told the police that Guenard was lying, and asked why they were investigating a simple disturbance. When they replied that they had to protect the public, Mitchell responded, 'Well if you have to protect the public, there are much worse quarrels that take place here every Saturday night and if you want to follow them all up I can let you know all about them.'[22] After Mitchell's call, Gotfrid saw Snyder again. He realized that 'pressure is still being brought to bear' but thought that, without Mitchell's cooperation, there would be insufficient grounds for charge. He told Cohen not to worry or return.

Cohen heard nothing until 23 March, when Crown Attorney E.D. Wilkins, a Sudbury lawyer especially selected by the government, advised Cohen's office that he was charged with two offences, the unlawful assault of Elizabeth Guenard and a startling charge of indecent assault against Yvette Vallie, who had accompanied Cohen in a taxi from Kirkland Lake to Toronto immediately after the Guenard incident. Cohen's secretary called him in California.[23] A bill of indictment against him was presented on 1 April at the assizes at Haileybury, presided over by Mr Justice Keiller Mackay, and according to Cohen, 'this was the first intimation to me' that the crown was proceeding 'in respect to the Guenard matter, and the first intimation to me of any kind that there was even an allegation in respect to the second charge.' Cohen returned to Toronto by train, arriving two days after the bill of indictment went to the fall assizes. The crown and the police did not interview Cohen.

On another visit to Snyder, Gotfrid found him almost too busy to talk. He asked about the second charge, and Snyder said the evidence was that 'he had asked her to take off all her clothes in the hotel room, and on the trip to Toronto he had her go down on her knees and use her mouth.' The attorney general alone had decided to prosecute and 'felt that the weight of deciding whether to proceed should not be on the shoulder of a single Magistrate but left in the hands of the Grand Jury.' Believing that the evidence against Cohen was bad, Snyder confided that if he were defence counsel he would get it over with quickly and that Cohen should consider a plea of guilty before a judge with no jury. Gotfrid apparently thought his suggestion worth considering, and he himself proposed that Cohen's counsel go to Sudbury to talk to prosecutor Wilkins about what evidence he would present in court and what penalty he would demand. Gotfrid suggested that medical evidence be introduced to gain the court's sympathy and perhaps get a light punishment, and advised a quick decision so that Cohen would know what he faced and not have the problem hanging over him.

When the charges against Cohen became public in the local northern papers and all the Toronto dailies, 'the whole legal community was shocked.' According to Gotfrid, 'I'd never heard of it [preferred indictment] and had to go look it up in the Code.' J.J. Robinette thought that the bill of indictment was 'quite unusual' in that he could not recall being involved in another case in his forty-year career as a criminal lawyer in which the government took similar action. 'I don't know why they did it. They have a right to do it. They could prefer an indictment and cut you right out of a preliminary hearing.'[24]

Cohen needed a lawyer. Dorothy Cohen first approached A.G. Slaught, a leading criminal lawyer who was opposite Cohen in the Ontario Labour Court. Slaught refused, since he was solicitor for many mining companies in northern Ontario. She then asked Joseph Sedgwick, who turned her down because of his 'close political and professional ties with the Ontario government,' but he probably remembered Cohen's sarcasm towards him during the LeBel Inquiry.[25] J.J. Robinette accepted Cohen's case. He was known as a sound technical counsel, especially before the Ontario Court of Appeal, and two years earlier he had successfully defended Evelyn Dick in a sensational murder trial that made him famous.[26] He recalled thirty-five years later, 'I think that a lot of people thought I shouldn't have taken the case because they didn't like him [Cohen] but that's the worst thing a lawyer can do.'[27] Subsequently, Robinette gained a reputation as one of the country's finest counsel and had a long, distinguished career.

On 2 April 1946 the grand jury decided that the case should proceed, and the trial date was initially set for 7 August. Estok mentions that 'curiously, the *Globe and Mail* announced the decision of the Grand Jury twelve hours earlier in the bulldog edition of the April 2nd paper. How the *Globe* knew that a true bill would be presented was never discovered.'[28] Cohen refused to plead guilty, but without a preliminary hearing, Robinette had little information. He asked Wilkins for details about the two assault charges and requested copies of Guenard's and Vallie's statements, which Wilkins refused to supply since 'it would be a breach of confidence contrary to public policy to provide defense counsel with statements made by prospective Crown witnesses.' But, regarding the second charge, involving Vallie, Wilkins repeated what Snyder had told Gotfrid.[29]

The second charge, resulting from the intense police investigation, made the case against J.L. Cohen even more sensational, but apparently the prosecution had insufficient evidence for it was dropped after Cohen was convicted of the first charge. As to its plausibility, Cohen was concerned enough to ask the Kirkland Lake lawyer Edwin Pearlman to inquire about Vallie. Pearlman learned that she was living apart from her husband, 'is not exactly of the highest repute,' and was well known to the taxi driver, who had 'arranged for her services' (not specified, but probably to accompany Cohen in the taxi). The driver, J.A. Letourneau, indicated in an affidavit that his wife was a fourth passenger on the ride to Toronto. It is unlikely that Vallie's accusations were true, but the taxi driver and Vallie said in their statements that Cohen drank a bottle of whisky in the cab. Rumours circulated throughout Cohen's career that he was capable of reckless and indiscreet behaviour towards women, so it could have happened. Or it may mean that the crown was trying hard to convict Cohen.[30] After the trial, in January 1947, Vallie made a second statement, which contradicted totally what she had said before and confirmed that Cohen was tired and sick in the car. The statement may have been for an appeal, but it was not used, or useful, because the second charge was dropped.[31]

Robinette wanted the trial moved to Toronto but was refused. Since a jury in northern Ontario would not be sympathetic, he opted for trial by judge as quickly as possible to limit the damage to Cohen's professional reputation. J.B. Robinson, the district judge for Haileybury, was acceptable to both sides, but he disqualified himself because he had helped prepare the bill of indictment. Edmond Proulx and J.A.S. Plouffe were two other northern judges. Robinette recalled, 'Looking back I was undoubtedly thinking, I hope it's Judge Proulx because he was quite a worldly man.' At first, Proulx was scheduled to preside, but the crown delayed the case to October. E.C. Facer, Robinette's agent in the case, wrote that the deputy attorney general wished to proceed by speedy trial only with cases where the accused was in jail. Since Cohen was not incarcerated, the crown would wait until after the long break, and Proulx was unlikely to be the trial judge.

Robinette reminded the crown attorney that he had agreed to Judge Proulx and would not consent to Judge Plouffe.[32] Judge Robinson wrote that he wanted both parties to agree, but it was not necessary; in the absence of agreement, he would choose 'the Judge to preside without regard to the wishes of either side.'[33] With the trial two weeks away and no agreement, Robinette asked for an adjournment to November, which was granted, so he could appear at the Gouzenko spy trials in Ottawa, as indeed could Cohen. Cohen was concerned about the delay. In November, Robinette had to appear before the Supreme Court of Canada; he applied for a second adjournment, which again was granted. The new trial date was 12 December and Plouffe was selected.

Judge Plouffe was not anxious to hear the case, because 'he felt rather upset that he was, as he put it, "a second choice."' He did not want to be in the position of being specially selected by the attorney general to hear the case and he wanted Robinette's consent or at least no objections.[34] Robinette did not object further because he could do no more. Thus, after a nine-month delay, the crown won on the trial's location and the selection of the judge. Robinette was not overly confident. 'There wasn't much you could do for him. The best we could really do really was to say, well this is out of character.'[35] Robinette evidently believed that Cohen was guilty of assault.

Cohen had a long medical history, and his health was adversely affected by the case, but he refused to let Robinette introduce the health issue. After his return from California, he called his doctor, Jacob Markowitz, who had had Cohen as his patient since 1934 except during the war, when Markowitz had served with the Royal Army Medical Corps. During the time Cohen was under his care, he 'constantly suffered from ... claustrophobia and, sometimes, a fear of high places with periods of depression and he complained constantly of insomnia. All this was aggravated by overwork,' Markowitz later told the discipline committee of the Law Society. In December 1946, at the trial in Haileybury, the doctor realized that Cohen was in a state of depression and acute anxiety. As he later told the appeal court, 'I am certain that any period of imprisonment in His Majesty's gaols would be most disastrous to his health.'[36]

THE TRIAL AND JAIL

On 11 December 1946, over a year after the incident, Jacob and Dorothy Cohen entered the Haileybury district courthouse. Cohen sat in courtroom number one, 'almost oblivious to the large crowd of spectators and reporters,' who, along with Judge J.A.S. Plouffe, of North Bay's district criminal court, listened to several witnesses recreate the quarrel in the Park Lane Hotel. Cohen, then forty-nine years old, pleaded not guilty to both assault charges. E.D. Wilkins, Sudbury's crown prosecutor, handled the case instead of the usual Haileybury crown attorney.

Little information exists concerning the role of the Attorney General's Department, because the government file on Cohen's assault case has been destroyed. From the time the police investigation started, rumours persisted that inappropriate pressure either from the mining industry or from within the provincial government itself, or both, was brought to bear to make trouble for Cohen. Yet the gossip at the time was hearsay, the evidence available now is circumstantial, and, without a police report, or the Attorney General's Department's file, there is no proof.[37] But about three weeks before the trial, *Northern News* reported that OPP Sergeant Bert Braney from Timmins, and Inspector Franks of the OPP's Criminal Investigation Department from Toronto, were still in Kirkland Lake. Their movements were 'shrouded in mystery' until subpoenas were delivered.[38]

Cohen's highly publicized trial lasted two days. Dr J.M LeBlond, a doctor in Kirkland Lake since 1936, testified that at the Park Lane Hotel on 21 November 1945, at about 11 A.M., he examined Elizabeth Guenard. 'She had all signs and symptoms of a fractured nose, bruises on both arms, some on the face and shoulders, on the right maxilla bone and [was] scratched over the chin and lips. That was all.'[39] He treated her nose by putting packing in the nostril to lift up the bone and keep it as normal as possible, noted that the patient was nervous and in pain, and sent her for X-rays. In his cross-examination, Robinette tried to establish that the scratches were superficial, not numerous or serious, and that the bruises near the shoulders could have been caused by pressure on the arms, from being held tightly. According to the prosecution's next witness, Dr Robert Wellington McBain, a radiologist at the Kirkland Lake hospital, a fracture line in both nasal bones extended across the bridge of the nose; there was no depression, but a slight, not noticeable indentation on the right nasal bone. He thought that the bones would knit quickly, without disfigurement. He was not cross-examined.[40]

Maurice Doyon, the hotel's night clerk, gave his account of events in the early hours of 21 November. An important witness was Dora McLean, the hotel's housekeeper, awakened by the girl's screams, who entered the hall from her room, 501, just as Doyon and Lawrence Mitchell arrived upstairs. She overheard Mitchell speak briefly to Cohen and said that the girl was pounding on the door of 510 to be let out. When Cohen went into his room and through into Guenard's, McLean testified that Guenard 'started to scream again; she said "for God's sake let me out of here before he kills me."' Mitchell unlocked 510 and Guenard ran into the hall. In damning testimony, which Judge Plouffe later said he believed, McLean described her. 'She was hysterical, screaming, she was all blood and a terrible mess. She came to me and said, "for God's sake get me out of this room; he will kill me." Cohen said, "Get me a car and I will take this girl to Toronto." With that she said, "I don't want to go with him."' McLean described Guenard as wearing a slip, in bare feet, 'all bit on the chest, and her face was all bruised and on her neck was blood.'[41] She claimed that Guenard told her, in front of Cohen, that he had bitten and hit her and that she could not leave because he had the room key, statements that Cohen did not contradict at the time.

With difficulty, McLean continued, she got Cohen (who did not want to leave) out of room 510, collected Guenard's things, and took her to her own room; there, she washed and tidied Guenard and got her quietened down. She arranged a room for Guenard and told Mitchell not to tell Cohen where she was, since the girl did not want to see him. Later, Cohen visited McLean's room looking for Guenard; McLean told him that she was not there and threatened to call the police if he did not leave. She complained to Lawrence Mitchell, and when she left her room, Cohen was still in the hall and tried to slip in behind her to look for Guenard. She testified, 'I said there is no girl in there but you are not going in. So then he pushed me back to my room. I gave him a slap across the face. He came back and tried to shove in. I gave him another slap.'[42]

Later, Guenard asked McLean to take a train ticket to Cohen's room but he was not there. She noticed that 510 'was in a terrible mess ... The [bed]clothes were all over the place, blood all over the bed, and the telephone on the floor, clothing and towels in a terrible mess.' In her opinion, Cohen was drunk, 'but at the same time he knew what he was doing to a certain extent' and Guenard 'was perfectly sober.'[43] Under cross-examination, Robinette confirmed that Cohen wanted McLean to leave Guenard alone, that McLean saw no bottles of alcohol in 510, and that Guenard had no alcohol on her breath. He established that McLean saw no fighting or actual blows struck.

Wilfred Hardy, in the room next to Cohen's, confirmed McLean's testimony that Guenard was in a white slip and that she had red marks around her chin and cheeks. His statements differed somewhat about the positioning of the couple, but he heard Cohen tell the manager to get the guests back in their rooms and overheard Guenard say that 'she would not stay in the room the balance of the night and that he [Cohen] was biting her.'[44]

Evelyn Jelly, a chambermaid, confirmed McLean's testimony that the bed in 510 had blood on the bottom sheet, in the form of many spots about the size of quarters, and wet towels streaked with blood were on the floor. Room 508 was messy like an average hotel room in the morning. She had thrown out two bottles – one of rye and one of wine – the day before.[45]

Lawrence Mitchell, compared to previous witnesses, minimized the disturbance. He said that it was quiet when he reached the fifth floor; Guenard had not screamed or complained and looked normal; he had not noticed other people in the hall except McLean, and the door to Cohen's room was open. When he asked Cohen about the noise, Cohen told him that it was 'all quietened down now.' Mitchell mentioned that the previous day Cohen had arranged for a taxi to take him to Toronto; he asked Mitchell to call the taxi immediately, but it was not available for two or three hours. Mitchell testified that he saw Guenard through the connecting door, but because she was dressing he turned away. He viewed the situation as none of his business, so long as it was quiet, 'that was the main thing.' Cohen left the hotel by taxi between nine and ten in the morning, and Mitchell saw Guenard around midday. He gave her $25, which she later repaid, to go to the hospital, because she said her nose was sore.

Guenard was called to testify. According to her statement of 24 December 1945, she and Cohen had a few drinks on 21 November around 11 P.M., and then 'Mr. Cohen [seemed] to believe that I was his property, that he could do whatever he liked with me ... Mr. Cohen became very masterful, such as get me this, get me that, he wanted me to have some more drink, but I refused, so he hit me on the face, fractured my nose.' When she had a chance, she said, she ran naked from his room, locked the interlocking door, put on her slip when Cohen came through her front door, which was not locked, 'and started to punch me.' She began screaming and reached for the phone to call for help. 'Mr. Cohen kept on beating me until the manager arrived,' and then the housekeeper took care of her, the manager called a doctor, and for the next two days she was X-rayed and given medical attention. Cohen later called her, apologized for his behaviour, and told her to return to Toronto, where she remained at his sister's for a time.[46]

At the trial as a crown witness, Guenard sought to reverse her statement. She testified that around 4 P.M. on the twentieth Cohen had told her that he needed a rest and 'took a few sleeping pills and a small drink.'[47] He told her that he was too tired to return to Toronto by train and had ordered a taxi for the morning. Guenard had taken a bottle of whisky from Cohen's room to hers, had a few drinks, got depressed, and started to cry. Cohen asked her what was wrong and suggested she return home. She explained to the court that Cohen had not wanted to travel with her, that he had wanted her to take a course to become a better stenographer. In the past they had had a few quarrels: 'I occasioned them, like crying and yelling because I was unhappy.' She told him that she did not want to leave him, but she was afraid that he would send her away. He told her not to worry about it then and had returned to sleep in his room at about 8 P.M. After he went to sleep, Guenard had 'got in bed with him' and slept until she was awakened around four in the morning by Cohen murmuring his wife's name in his sleep. Guenard became angry and jealous, slapped him in the face, and jumped out of bed. She shouted his wife's name sarcastically, ran into her room, and 'was determined I would make a scene.' She took some liquor into her room and locked the connecting door. Cohen asked her what was the matter. She suggested he come in the front door and talk, and when he did she started screaming. Cohen put his hand over her mouth to quieten her, and she bit it. As he tried to get away, 'he sort of pushed his hand over my nose; I was kicking at the time and trying to scratch him and what not.' When Mitchell and McLean appeared in the doorway, Cohen unlocked the connecting door and returned to his room. McLean was alone with Guenard, who now testified that the housekeeper said: 'This was really a terrible thing that happened to me, a nice little girl like me; she couldn't understand such beastly things ... and that Mr. Cohen must be a very bad man. She threatened him in any event. I didn't tell her that I was the cause of the trouble.'[48] In McLean's room, the housekeeper kept threatening Cohen 'in a general way,' and Guenard asked to be alone, was given a room, and later saw a doctor. She did not want to leave the hotel or be seen. She was asked to demonstrate to the court how her nose got hurt, and she testified that she had no other marks on her body.

In the middle of her testimony, which contradicted McLean and her own statement, the judge and the two lawyers discussed an evidentiary point that became crucial to the verdict. Wilkins wanted to question Guenard about her statement to police, to show that she was a hostile witness. Robinette objected to questioning about the earlier statement and referred to cases which had concluded that 'before a contrary statement can be let in, it must be established that [the] witness is adverse or hostile,' defined as a witness whose manner in giving evidence shows that he or she is not desirous of telling the truth. He believed that the judge had to be satisfied that Guenard was hostile before receiving evidence about the statement. Both lawyers agreed that she was not yet hostile but disagreed about whether or not the court could admit the earlier statement in these circumstances. The judge decided that she had to be hostile first, before the earlier statement could be admitted.

Wilkins resumed questioning. He asked if her nose had bled, and she said 'No,' which was contrary to Dr LeBlond's testimony. Then he asked, 'When one's hand is over one's entire mouth, how can you open your mouth?' At first, she gave no answer, and then she said that it was hard to explain. She told the judge that she was not sober but was not so intoxicated that she could not remember what happened. When asked where her nose was hurt, she pointed to the top of the right side of her nose and then contradicted herself, telling Wilkins that it was Cohen's right hand that she had bitten, not his left hand, as she had stated earlier. She explained that Cohen was trying to prevent her from kicking and punching him; Wilkins established that she was wearing stockings but no shoes and that she was sitting on the edge of the bed. At this point, the judge decided. 'The evidence of this witness seems to be so unsatisfactory, and it comes into such flagrant contradiction with evidence of other witnesses which is more believable,' that 'I will permit you to treat her as a hostile witness.' Robinette's objection was overruled.[49]

Wilkins raised Guenard's statement to the police. Robinette insisted that Wilkins include the circumstances surrounding it, and he reminded the court that its contents could not be used as evidence against the accused. Guenard told a strange story of how on Christmas Eve in Toronto she was told to expect a call in the office. It came from a woman unknown to her, who said she was an acquaintance from Sudbury and would come by with a surprise for Guenard. When she showed up, Guenard did not recognize her. She invited Guenard into the next room to see the surprise, and Guenard went, thinking that it might be a Christmas present from her family. A tall man introduced himself as detective Nimmo and detained her, and a Sergeant Braney joined them. She wished to talk in the office, but they managed to get her outside into a car, which they drove to the police station on College Street. She was kept there for over four hours answering questions; her responses were put in a statement, which she signed without reading it carefully. Wilkins introduced a second statement (Vallie's), which was struck out.

At the trial, Wilkins noted that Guenard's statement said that Cohen fractured her nose, but in court she insisted that he just pressed it. Guenard admitted the discrepancy, swearing that the earlier statement was not true. She denied that Cohen had bitten her, and she stated that she had been intimately involved with Cohen since May 1945 and travelled with him often. She had been 'very much in love' with Cohen, and she repeated that she was the one who had made the scene. She admitted that she drank (half a bottle of whisky and some wine) on the night in question but said she was not drunk. She drank when she was unhappy, and alcohol depressed her. When the police came to her, she made the statement but had not lodged an official complaint. The two detectives urged her to 'put myself in a good light' and assured her that it was just for the record.[50] Her testimony seemed to assist Cohen's defence, but the judge clearly did not believe her.

Robinette recalled Mitchell, who confirmed Guenard's testimony. When he asked Cohen what the trouble was, Cohen said that he was trying to quieten Guenard and 'he said, "look what she did,"' gesturing to his hand. Mitchell was unconvincing because he hedged about whether he had seen a mark on Cohen's hand and about whether the hand was bruised or bleeding. His evidence was that he had little contact with Guenard; her testimony was that she had said things in his and possibly Cohen's presence, which unintentionally corroborated McLean's evidence and assisted the prosecution.

Robinette introduced a motion that the crown had not proven its case; there was insufficient evidence that Cohen had assaulted Guenard. Wilkins replied that the crown had proven bodily harm, provided evidence of a bloody sheet and towels, and produced Guenard's accusation. The judge refused the motion, suggesting that Cohen had not contradicted Guenard at the time, which was acknowledgment of his behaviour.

Robinette began his defence by calling Dr J. Markowitz, whom Cohen insisted was to be used in only a limited way. Markowitz had examined the X-rays of Guenard's nose and Guenard herself during adjournment and found nothing wrong with the nose, no serious injury, no scar or bony tissue. The X-rays showed 'a little crack in the nasal bone' but no displacement. The hairline fracture of the base of the bone was 'thin as paper' and could be caused easily.

J.L. Cohen was the main witness for the defence and was on the stand for nearly two hours. He began confidently, saying that he did not want to defame Guenard's reputation, especially since 'she has literally dragged herself up by the bootstraps' out of a sordid home environment, and that he found her 'trustworthy, estimable and with initiative.' His tone quickly changed. He portrayed himself as an innocent victim and blamed Guenard for the incident, describing her as a woman with a 'disturbing addiction to alcohol' who became abusive and created scenes. She had done so twice before, in Windsor and on a train, with similar embarrassing results. According to Robinette, the relationship followed this pattern, so that in Kirkland Lake 'what Mr. Cohen did was done out of apprehension – fear of what Miss Guenard would do.' After the first incident, Cohen had laid her off. In the second incident, Cohen was charged with contributing to a disturbance, pleaded guilty, and paid a fine.

Cohen's version of the Kirkland Lake episode refuted Guenard's statement that she travelled with him often; he said she was with him only when a stenographer was required. But then he indicated that he asked Guenard to accompany him because his wife could not bear the long journey north. He was busy and hardly saw Guenard until the convention was over. The manager had given him the only bottle he had. He confirmed the arrangements about the taxi. He took one sleeping pill and about two fingers of whisky.

He confirmed Guenard's testimony about being awakened twice, the first time by 'the most pitiful sobbing' in the next room. He called out to Guenard, who asked him to come in. She had drunk a lot of whisky and he realized she was having a 'crying jag.' She feared that he would not let her return to his office because she was drinking. He 'assuaged her fears and comforted her and got her all settled down.'[51] When she was quiet, he returned to his room, took another pill, and slept. He was awakened by a slap, with Guenard 'rushing across the room and calling out my wife's name in a sneering manner.' She then took a bottle of wine into her room and locked the connecting door. Cohen tried to calm her through the door and told her not to drink any more since she had consumed all of the whisky and most of the wine.

Guenard told Cohen that she would not open the connecting door and that he should enter by the front door. When he did so, she was sitting on the bed, lying on her elbow, and 'began letting out the most terrible screams.' He did not want to hurt her but to quieten her, so he put his hand 'perpendicular over her mouth. I did not exert any pressure.'[52] She bit his right hand on his smallest finger so hard that he tried to get it away. 'I pushed her on the shoulder, I then struggled to spread my hand over the greater surface of her face and pressed her down on the bed, thinking that if I hurt her or gave her some sense of alarm it would help.' He got his hand, which was bleeding, out of her mouth and washed it in the basin. She was violent, trying to kick him 'and I remember turning her around and holding her by the shoulders, and saying "look, stop this and be sensible."' He unlocked the connecting door, returned to his room, started dressing, and realized that the damage he had been trying to avoid was done. She announced that she was leaving the hotel at once, and he replied that it was no time to leave but that he would contact Mitchell and see if they could leave earlier than planned. Had he realized that it was nearly 5 A.M., he would have agreed to her departure.

According to Cohen, Mitchell and McLean walked in the open door of room 510. Cohen said that he was in 508 and that Guenard was in her room getting dressed. He denied saying that he could handle the situation; he merely suggested that Mitchell close the connecting door. He also denied that Guenard said anything to McLean in Cohen's presence that might be incriminating. Mitchell called about a taxi from 508 as Cohen finished dressing, and when Cohen returned to 510, Guenard was gone. He never found out where she was, and he was apprehensive that an unscrupulous person 'would use this information for a more sinister purpose.' McLean's testimony was wrong and the assertion that bite marks were on Guenard's chest after the alleged assault was 'grotesque.' He stressed that 'certainly no statements were made by Miss Guenard in my presence that I hit her or bit her or I would have contradicted them immediately, even though it would have provoked the girl further.' The only thing she said in front of him was that she was leaving the hotel, to which he responded that it was not a good time. He told Mitchell that Guenard had threatened a disturbance, that she had bitten him and screamed, and that he was embarrassed by the marks on his hand which were clearly teeth marks.

Cohen refuted McLean's testimony about events the next morning. After breakfast he walked around, not knowing 'where the girl was or what happened.' He went along the hall, heard someone, turned around, and saw McLean. She came to his side, 'flipped off my glasses,' and said, 'you dirty Toronto Jew.' He resented such treatment, said nothing – 'I felt it was beneath my notice' – and left. She did not slap him, and if she had, he would have charged her, since he found her attitude 'unfriendly,' perhaps because she believed that the girl had been abused.

Cohen left Kirkland Lake by taxi and arrived in Toronto about 3 A.M. on 22 November. Guenard returned to Toronto by train that evening and resumed work in Cohen's office the next day. Cohen did not return to work for two or three days, because he had caught a bad cold on his return trip as a result of the cab not having heat or a rug. Guenard made no complaint, and in Cohen's view 'if there would be any objection I would be the one to make it.' In the office, she was 'perfectly sober, none of this mad drinking; I just overlooked it and told my staff, my sister knew of it, to give the girl a chance.'[53]

During cross-examination, Wilkins probed Cohen about why Guenard was with him, particularly after earlier incidents of conflict and when he knew she drank. Cohen explained that he had been very tired, should never have undertaken the assignment, and 'I merely wanted someone to talk to.' Wilkins asked him if he was so tired that he needed a companion, and he replied, 'I was so tired my wife cried for hours and tried to prevail upon the labour officials so I would not have to come up here.' He had given up all work after 20 October to have his health problems diagnosed. Hints of his medical condition were sprinkled throughout his testimony but were not made explicit. The full story would not emerge until the disbarment hearings. He admitted that Guenard had been his secretary/companion several times, acknowledged sexual intercourse with Guenard, but said with a smile that the crown's reference to her as his 'mistress' was 'a rather extravagant term.'

On the issue of drink, Cohen admitted that a bottle was in his room in clear view and that he knew of Guenard's addiction, but he thought that she was cured. When he agreed to her returning to his employ, she 'was full of contrition and desire to be forgiven and so on; I am no believer in original sin. I do think there is at least a pretense of redemption.'[54] Wilkins reviewed Cohen's earlier testimony. Cohen denied Guenard's claim that, when he entered her room, he had covered her mouth as Guenard had demonstrated to the court; he repeated that she had bitten his finger and drawn blood and that he had the marks for weeks. When asked how her nose got fractured, he theorized that, as he extracted his hand from her mouth, he exerted a slight amount of pressure to cause a hairline injury.

He denied pounding on McLean's door. 'I may be aggressive in some efforts, but I didn't do any pounding.'[55] He acknowledged that he might have phoned the desk looking for Guenard, but not repeatedly. Several times he rang Mitchell, who assured him that Guenard had disappeared. Cohen by then was preoccupied with a premonition. 'I thought of the use that might be made of the whole incident.' He confessed that he might have called McLean in her room but he could not remember.

Cohen concluded that Mitchell had brought him a note from Guenard that said she was returning to Toronto by car with friends. Mitchell said the note had come by taxi, and when Cohen asked the kind of place she had been in, Mitchell told him that it was terrible. Shortly afterward Cohen left for Toronto, accompanied by a female passenger. Cohen denied asking for female company on the drive back but said, to explain the woman's presence, 'As I understand it, my sister in talking to Mr. Mitchell suggested that he secure a nurse.' Mitchell found Vallie, whom

Cohen understood was a married woman with two children. She made arrangements with Mitchell about her fee, which Cohen agreed to pay. He also agreed to the taxi driver's wife accompanying them. When they reached Toronto at 3 A.M., Cohen was 'almost in a semi-conscious condition' with a cold. Around 4.30 P.M. that day, he questioned his sister about Guenard, who, she told him, was still in Kirkland Lake at the Park Lane Hotel. He called Guenard and mentioned the discrepancy between her note and the fact that she was still there, and she said she was leaving 'almost at once.' He denied apologizing to her over the phone for his behaviour, particularly since his wife and daughter were in the next room. 'I would be very unlikely to engage in that type of conversation in her [his wife's] presence.' It was not his finest hour.[56]

Robinette recalled Mitchell, who confirmed that Cohen's sister called him. After their conversation, Mitchell had Guenard write a note that she had left for Toronto and he gave it to Cohen. At first, Mitchell could not recall telling Cohen that she was in a terrible place, but when pressed, he said, that he had told Cohen that the note had been delivered by taxi from, possibly he said a 'terrible place' since 'I was anxious to get things cleared up and get Mr. Cohen on the way to Toronto.' Mitchell thus confirmed part of Cohen's testimony.

What are we to make of Guenard's and Cohen's testimony? Guenard had a romantic interest in Cohen. Probably she understated her wounds to decrease the damage to him. It is likely that the reason she gave for making a statement to police was accurate – that she was ashamed of what had happened – and wanted to make her position look better than it was. She may still have been hurt and angry with Cohen, and she undoubtedly did not realize how serious his situation was. When it became apparent that his career might be at stake, she tried to undo the damage by blaming her own actions and minimizing his, as she reworked her story, possibly aided by Cohen's sister. Cohen was smitten or at least flattered by her attention, which made him vulnerable and caused him to act foolishly. Under normal circumstances, he probably would never have rehired her after the train incident, and he should not have asked her to accompany him to Kirkland Lake. Clearly, whatever the emotions or dynamics of their relationship, they were a disastrous combination.

Before his verdict, Judge Plouffe had harsh words for Cohen. He discounted his moral relations with the young woman, 'but the assault committed was of a very grave character and your conduct under the circumstances were [sic] of a man who is either drunk or mentally deranged, or what is commonly known as a pervert.' The judge lectured Cohen, in what must have been a very painful moment. 'When you were called to the bar,' he reminded the accused, 'you took an oath that you have not upheld. To some extent you have soiled the gown you sometimes wear.' Standing in the prisoner's dock with his hands on his hips, Cohen heard the judge say that he did not believe witnesses Guenard, Mitchell, and Cohen, whose stories were 'prefabricated,' but he accepted the evidence of Dr Markowitz. 'I have no doubt that the injuries inflicted on Miss Guenard were inflicted by the accused ... The accusations made by Miss Guenard were made to Mrs. McLean, and in the presence of Cohen, who heard the conversation and took part in it.'[57]

He found Cohen guilty of assault causing bodily harm. Cohen frowned when the verdict was announced but showed little emotion as the judge sentenced him to six months in the Guelph reformatory. Family members realized that it was a terrible blow to him. Judge Plouffe rejected the defence's request for a suspended sentence and explained his severity by saying that the publicity given the case was not adequate punishment, as Robinette argued, even though every major daily newspaper had carried a detailed account of the humiliating testimony in stories with sensational headlines. The judge wanted to make an example of Cohen, for 'men of your calibre may not be adequately punished by publicity alone. An example should be made to deter other people from conducting themselves as you have with this girl.' Wilkins dropped the second charge against Cohen.[58]

Robinette said that he would appeal the verdict on the grounds that the conviction was bad law and the sentence excessive. For the appeal, the judge would give fuller reasons for his judgment. Cohen was freed on $1,000 bail, pending an appeal hearing, but not before he had spent two nights in jail. He was taken into custody to the Haileybury jail, a massive stone building on top of a hill overlooking the surrounding lake. After his release, the appeal was launched immediately.

The next day the front page of the Toronto *Telegram* reported that 'J.L. Cohen, formerly a member of the National War Labour Board and well known Toronto lawyer, was sentenced to six months in reformatory today. He was found guilty at Haileybury of assault occasioning bodily harm to a Toronto girl, his secretary.'[59] Immediately, Cohen lost several clients. One was Dr Henry Harris, the Toronto optometrist who had hired Cohen to represent him against a charge that he issued a false passport to a Russian spy.

Sam Gotfrid was surprised by the conviction, and especially by the sentence. 'It wasn't the kind of case for a jail term.' He believed that Cohen 'got a bad deal' because 'he was very unpopular with the Establishment.' J.J. Robinette agreed that Cohen was unpopular. 'Let's put it this way, I don't think that they were unhappy about prosecuting. Well, he crossed so many people you know. He didn't try to be considerate of others at all. And because of his arrogance he offended a lot of people.' But Robinette thought that Cohen got a fair trial. 'I can't say the result was unjust. Maybe the way it was set up, unknown to me ... I mean, getting the particular judge and bringing Wilkins and the preferred indictment. I felt a little powerless after her [Guenard's] statement went in (the record) ... but I never felt that on what the judge heard, he could do much else really.'[60]

While awaiting the appeal, Cohen spent early 1947 in his study at home 'reviewing the details of his case ... writing notes on the trial, checking facts, and preparing affidavits.'[61] He also turned his hand to writing magazine articles on topical subjects. For the December 1946 issue of *Saturday Night*, he wrote of the dominion government's responsibility to develop peacetime labour legislation for the post-war period. In another article in January 1947, 'Are We to Be Bottlenecked?' he criticized former Ontario Attorney General Arthur Roebuck for his comments on the Rowell-Sirois report, a ten-year-old study of dominion-provincial relations, at a time when the war was past and the provinces were reasserting their powers.[62]

THE APPEAL

On 18 February 1947, the appeal case of *Rex* v. *J.L. Cohen* was heard. In an extensive brief to the higher court, J.J. Robinette argued that the evidence was contradictory about what Guenard said in the presence of others, no hard evidence existed that Cohen overheard any statement, and thus guilt was not proven and the conviction was not warranted by the evidence. The judge erred in declaring Guenard a hostile witness and in admitting and using certain evidence, particularly Guenard's statement to police, which in court she said was coerced. Her testimony to this effect was not disputed, and certain circumstantial evidence was treated, Robinette submitted, as proof of guilt. The judge ignored all the testimony of two crown witnesses, as well as the medical evidence. The sentence was 'grossly excessive' since 'the accused was tried, convicted and sentenced as a lawyer, and as a prominent lawyer ... not as J.L. Cohen, a *person*,' as was obvious from the judge's pre-sentencing remarks (which were omitted from the transcript of the trial) about making Cohen an example because he was a prominent barrister.[63]

Before the appeal, Cohen conferred with Robinette and lawyers working on the case in Kirkland Lake, including E.E. Pearlman, who advised that they stress several points: that Guenard made no complaint; that the trial judge had not considered this fact; and that the Attorney General's Department had interfered improperly before and after the charge was laid. Robinette did not pursue these points. In January 1947 Cohen asked lawyer H.R. Moscoe in Kirkland Lake to find information that might strengthen his case. He apparently believed that Evelyn Jelly, the maid, whose testimony about the number of liquor bottles and the amount of blood in the room was damning, had been prompted to give the story that she did, which he insisted was untrue. Yvette Vallie's second statement of 10 January 1947, which reversed her first, included a conversation with Jelly, who stated that a few spots of blood were on the bed in room 510 but said nothing about towels or bottles. Cohen also wrote to Mr Justice Keiller Mackay to try to learn more about the circumstances surrounding the presentation of the bill of indictment at Haileybury.[64]

Robinette presented the Supreme Court of Ontario with several affidavits in support of his arguments. He argued that the appeal court should consider some procedural irregularities. Before the trial, special Crown Prosecutor E.M. Wilkins had informed Robinette that the crown could not prove the charge against Cohen concerning Vallie and intended to withdraw it. He did not inform the court of that circumstance, however, until after Cohen had been convicted. Robinette argued that linking the two charges was an error that was prejudicial to his client. Wilkins also told Robinette that, if Cohen were convicted, he would ask for a fine, but in court he said nothing, and Robinette, who had relied on him, had not prepared any representations that might have affected the sentence.[65]

Robinette next argued that Cohen had a long medical history and that his frail health had affected his behaviour in Kirkland Lake. After Cohen's conviction, he was taken to the Haileybury jail, where he remained overnight, until he was released on bail. Apparently, though he had controlled his emotions in the courtroom, when he was left alone, the seriousness of his situation and the humiliation caught up to him. A guard, James Campbell, observed in an affadavit that around 6 P.M. 'J.L. Cohen began acting peculiarly by moving forward and backwards and then suddenly he tumbled into my arms and fainted.' With the aid of a prisoner, Kenneth Windover, they carried Cohen into a corridor, laid him on a cot, and summoned medical aid. Campbell reported that as Cohen fainted his body became rigid; white froth was coming out of his mouth, which was pried open to prevent injury to his tongue, and 'it was about 15 minutes before J.L. Cohen revived.'[66]

This curious seizure, like other occasional unusual behaviour of Cohen's which was gossiped about circumspectly by his contemporaries, indicated that Cohen was ill. His health was a factor in the situation, but, because Cohen had not allowed Robinette to question Dr Markowitz about it at the trial, Robinette could not do much at the appeal level. Consequently, the health issue came out only at the disbarment and reinstatement hearings, where the complexity of the man, who insisted on keeping his private life hidden, was revealed only behind the closed doors of the Law Society of Upper Canada. Cohen's health would continue to decline until his death.

In written reasons for judgment, which were lengthier than his oral statements at the trial, Judge Plouffe repeated his conclusions. He noted Cohen's efforts to clear the hall of people, to locate Guenard in the hotel, and to leave with her immediately by taxi for Toronto 'in order to cover up his actions.' Plouffe rejected Mitchell's evidence and concluded that he was trying to protect the accused. Plouffe disbelieved Guenard, whose testimony he described as a play-acting and whose evidence was so full of falsehoods and fabrications that he judged her to be a hostile witness because her story in court – that the trouble began when Cohen in his sleep mumbled his wife's name and she became jealous – was 'fantastic' and 'incredible.'

He did not believe Cohen's testimony that Guenard drank nearly a full bottle of whisky and two-thirds of a bottle of wine from one of the four bottles found in the two rooms. 'The liquor consumed in these rooms during these two days was mostly by Cohen and not by the girl.' He believed that 'whisky mixed with wine and sleeping pills may partly account for what has taken place on that occasion' but Cohen knew what he was doing. The testimony pointed to Cohen's guilt, and 'under the circumstances' he was as lenient as he could be.[67]

Despite Robinette's efforts and supporting evidence in the affidavits, the Ontario Court of Appeal upheld the lower court decision. Chief Justice Robertson dismissed certain technical objections about the jurisdiction and the procedure in the original trial, found that the judge in the lower court had 'reached the right conclusion upon the evidence,' and confirmed the sentence because 'we see no reason for disagreeing with his conclusions in that regard.' The higher court did not review the evidence but did remark that 'the girl was seeking refuge from attacks which obviously had been made upon her and the appellent [Cohen] was still pursuing her and continued to do so for some little time.' It agreed with Judge Plouffe that Cohen's behaviour 'upon this occasion in relation to this young girl whom he had taken away with him and who was peculiarly under his care' – and that 'as a man of some standing, conducting himself in a public hotel as he did' – warranted a substantial sentence and 'we think the learned trial Judge did not exceed the bounds of what was reasonable when he imposed the sentence that he did.'[68]

The courts' judgment was accurate, if we are to believe an interview with Elizabeth Guenard thirty-four years after the trial. After the verdict, she left Toronto, changed her name, moved across the country, and tried to forget the past, though 'the cloud is always there; there are always feelings and things you do remember.' Eventually, she married and raised a family. Guenard remembered Cohen as a forceful person and a demanding boss. He was a loner, she said, and overly concerned about his short height. Cohen did attack her that night in Kirkland Lake, and she was very scared and started screaming. Cohen was very ill and taking a great deal of medication. 'I didn't realize that as much as I would now,' she recalled. 'I knew that he had psychiatric care but that sounded a bit glamorous at the time; I was pretty naive.'

She had not intended to lay charges, but when the police contacted her she told them all the details, since 'I didn't realize that you didn't have to answer these things. I felt that if the police are questioning you – you answer.' The police tricked her into their car, but they did not use force or pressure her to sign the statement. 'I just felt that if they ask questions, I will tell the truth. Well then after that to save a man's life, not his life but his career, I tried the best I could to change it.' To assist Cohen's case, she exaggerated the coercive role of the police in a letter and at the trial 'perjured myself to try and save that man ... I said that I would do anything in order to save him. And I wasn't paid for it or anything like that believe you me. I was just stupid.' Despite his behaviour, 'he could be quite charming.' She did what she could, even though the letter made her look 'as if I was a liar and a cheat.' It did not work at the trial; 'I didn't do a very good job of it because it was against my nature' to fabricate and the judge 'apparently saw through it because the man was convicted.'[69]

The conviction set other forces in action. Family members worried about Cohen's six-month sentence, because his health was poor and his pride strong. His daughter recalled that the sentence upset him but he did better psychologically than they expected, for he 'adjusted to life at Guelph' and was 'much less tense about it than I think my mother expected. She was more concerned about how he was going to survive that – it wasn't easy for him – but he had a certain sense of humour about the whole situation.'[70] As soon as Cohen arrived at Guelph, he challenged the warden about the restricted reading list, and after much correspondence which kept him busy, he worked out a deal so that books sent to him would not be censored. He became fascinated with prison slang, and his papers include several sheets filled with such terms and their meanings. He told Bob Carlin that the prisoners 'had names for everything at the table and that amused him. They spoke a language all of their own and were intelligent.'[71] Carlin recalled that Cohen's attitude to his life in prison was fairly positive. 'He said the other prisoners had a sense of humour, they could laugh where I couldn't, they could curse out at the things they didn't like. I would look around and see what company I was in before I cursed.'

Privately, despite such comments, Cohen felt anguish in jail, and he worried about his future in the law profession. Immediately after the appeal court's decision, he wrote a note to himself on Chateau Laurier paper: 'Can they disbar automatically if one is convicted of a criminal offence?'[72] In prison, his physical health declined; he suffered from fatigue and anxiety and was seldom able to tolerate the rigorous prison routine. He later wrote to the Law Society, 'I am awakened, with all other inmates shortly before seven o'clock in the morning, am required to shave, wash, eat my breakfast, make my bed and then report for the duties, and they are extensive, which have been assigned to me here which, with a short interruption for a noon-day meal, keep me occupied until 5 o'clock in the evening and sometimes much longer, when I return to the Hospital Ward in which I am kept. Lights are out at 9.50 P.M.'[73] In fact, however, he remained in the prison hospital for most of his stay. Mrs Cohen made strenuous efforts and enlisted Robinette's support to make a case in Ottawa for his early release. Cohen told Robinette that he had a minor stroke. 'I am not going to indulge in tear-jerking phrasing, but I cannot overemphasize the seriousness of the whole thing and the effect on me. Will you please John, go out of your way if need be and carry out for me in respect of the matter Mrs. Cohen will be discussing with you. We both need your help and time is so important a factor that I cannot find words adequately to explain nor do I feel that with you there is any need to do so.'[74] On 10 April, Robinette wrote to the head of the clemency branch of the Department of Justice: 'Mr. Cohen has suffered over two months of his sentence in the Guelph reformatory and I am satisfied from the medical evidence that he is in dangerous physical condition.' He suggested that his client be released on a ticket of leave 'on the understanding he would go to the hospital where he can receive proper medical attention.'[75]

Dorothy Cohen asked Pat Conroy of the CCL to press for Cohen's early release. He spoke to Minister of Justice J.L. Ilsley, who did not know anything about the case, but 'in my presence he wrote a memorandum' and told Conroy that, as soon as he had investigated, he would decide the matter and advise him.[76] On 27 May 1947, after ninety-eight days in prison, Cohen was released on a ticket of leave and sent to a hospital. He was out of jail, but his ordeal was not over.

10

Disbarment, 1947

While Cohen was in prison, the Discipline Committee of the Law Society of Upper Canada learned that he had been convicted of 'having unlawfully assaulted and beaten a woman,' causing her bodily harm, contrary to the Criminal Code, and that an appeal was dismissed in February 1947 in the higher court. The committee decided to investigate whether he should be disbarred. It informed Cohen that his trial would be on 15 March 1947.[1] The committee was composed of benchers, mostly from Toronto; its chair was C.F.H. Carson, a distinguished commercial lawyer, and its members in 1947 were W.J. Beaton, J.R. Cartwright, W.B. Common, H.F. Parkinson, and J.W. Pickup. Benchers in the early twentieth century tended to be 'wealthy members of establishment law firms and to have something like life tenure once elected to convocation.' They were conservative, 'all male, white and Christian;' they met in convocation nine times a year in the morning until lunchtime, 'wearing morning dress or directors' suits.'[2]

Robinette recommended Toronto lawyer Arthur A. MacDonald, of MacDonald and Kennedy, to handle Cohen's case before the Discipline Committee, since 'MacDonald had practically a monopoly on that work because he had a great facility for arousing sympathy.'[3] Robinette felt that he was handicapped because of the conviction; all he could say to the committee was that Cohen was wrongly convicted, which Robinette probably did not believe. MacDonald accepted the case but met Cohen only once, the day before the hearing. Apparently, he was confident about its outcome, though it came out in the proceedings that he had not read Judge Plouffe's reasons for judgment.

The Discipline Committee prepared for the hearing by arranging with the Attorney General's Department for Cohen to attend if he wished. MacDonald sought to delay the proceedings so long as Cohen was in custody, but the committee intended to go ahead.[4] The secretary assembled for the committee's consideration the trial transcript, the reasons for judgment in the Court of Appeal, the appeal book, and Judge Plouffe's reasons for judgment. The committee chair, Carson, wrote to the secretary that he wanted 'everything certified with seals etc., as Cohen is a technical person.'[5]

On 15 March 1947 Cohen left prison to attend the hearing, which began at 10 A.M. and continued until 3 P.M. without lunch. Cohen's mental state was not good. That day he wrote to Robinette, pleading with him to spend a day or two on the matter. 'So John please enter this situation now – it's the last stage as to legal complications – as I know you will realize fully what it means to me.' His health was as precarious as his professional status, because he had spent over two months in the reformatory, mostly in hospital suffering from the strain, 'the thousand tortures of pain and anguish I go through every day and night.' He apologized that the matter had dragged on so, 'but neither of us could have foreseen that or the calamitous result.'[6] He was totally vulnerable. In April, Robinette worked on Cohen's behalf for his early release, a matter in which MacDonald told Cohen he would not intervene because Robinette would be more effective. Otherwise, MacDonald took over as Cohen's counsel and source of support as the ordeal proceeded.

The committee reviewed the material and heard witnesses who gave character references for Cohen. When the hearing began, MacDonald told the Discipline Committee that he had planned to seek a postponement until Cohen's release, but after conferring with Dr Markowitz, had decided that it was not in Cohen's interest (whatever the outcome) to have the hearing hanging over his head 'like a suspended sword.' His case preparation was hampered by Cohen's incarceration, since he had conferred with his client only briefly the day before. Cohen was present, but 'due to his condition' he would leave after his testimony.

It was not Cohen's first appearance before the Law Society's Discipline Committee. In 1924 he had been accused of writing affidavits on behalf of immigrants whom he did not know. He was found guilty of professional misconduct, but when Cohen admitted the charge and apologized profusely, he was reprimanded, not suspended. In 1928 a cli-

Cohen as his own worst enemy

ent accused Cohen of wrongfully misappropriating nine hundred dollars. The case proceeded to the committee, which decided that there was not enough evidence. In 1936, in a lengthy dispute that would involve the Discipline Committee in eleven days of hearings over three years, Cohen was accused of filing an affidavit that he knew to be false. Again, the committee found insufficient evidence, but he was censured for unsatisfactory conduct and had to attend convocation to be reprimanded. Compared to most lawyers in the province, Cohen's file at the Law Society was lengthy and not average.[7]

MacDonald intended to call doctors to testify about Cohen's medical condition, 'which I am going to submit has a very serious bearing here,' but first he asked Cohen to talk about himself. Cohen was permitted to sit while speaking, and his comments were surprising. The man separated his personal and public life to such a degree that he projected two rather contradictory images. While his papers in the archives are detailed, and record his professional versatility and excellence, they contain only gleanings of his personality, just as Cohen's confident public image and active life of achievement and intellectual pursuits seldom revealed the fearful, tortured inner spirit influenced by memories and harsh experiences.[8] But, before the Discipline Committee, he told all.

Cohen began by saying that he was forty-nine years old and had practised law since 1918. His testimony was similar to what he said at his trial, but for the first time he candidly revealed details of his personal life and health. In the second form at high school, when his father had died, 'I was obliged to leave the Collegiate, and took a position as office boy, and matriculated by taking courses extra mural.' He took his law training at Osgoode Hall, while working in J.P. White's office until after he graduated and began to practice. Soon after he married, around 1925, when he was twenty-seven, Cohen had 'a complete nervous breakdown' and was away from his office for about four years. He went to Atlantic City, New Jersey, because 'I thought perhaps the ocean would help,' but his condition worsened. When he returned to Toronto, he was plagued with phobias. He could not meet people or be in crowds, or go above a certain height in buildings, or stay alone. Some problems he overcame, but others, such as the height phobia, remained, which is why whenever he booked into the Chateau Laurier in Ottawa he always requested a room on the first or second floor. 'I could not possibly visit anybody who was above the fourth floor of a building,' so that solicitors sometimes had to go to Cohen's office to complete their business with him. 'I had a phobia about being on water. My father was drowned. The claustrophobia comes and goes; at times it is very acute.' Sometimes he feared being in a room or on the train from Toronto to Ottawa: 'I have had to ring for the porter on a train several times in the night, just to assure myself that there was somebody around – a sense of panic.'

The chairman asked Cohen why he felt such panic, and he replied, 'Just a general sense of insecurity, afraid of being alone. For instance, sometimes a bedroom was very small, and you feel yourself alone and there is nobody around, and you have no right to call upon anybody in an adjoining room, and you do not know them and they do not know you; and you have to be self-sufficient. That ability has been greatly weakened as a result of the nervous breakdown through which I went ... When stopping in a hotel, sometimes I have had to go down to the lobby, because I could not possibly stay in a room by myself.' At first, during the breakdown, he could earn a little money in practice, which he spent keeping up the office in the hope that he would return to it. Eventually he lost his office and his home, and Mrs Cohen, who had her own tensions, had to work as a social worker, but in time she too became very nervous and was obliged to leave her job. As a result, Cohen felt that he 'just had to return to the office.'[9]

He resumed practice 'still not cured' and opened a small office downtown. After he returned to work 'I was so nervous for months at a time that I could not cross Queen Street.' On one occasion around 1930, he had to call a colleague, Joe Singer, in the Temple Building. 'Somebody would have to accompany me, until I had the sense of security. If that sense of panic came on, I would have to have somebody with me.' Gradually he became more active in his practice; initially, he relied on his junior solicitors to do the court work, which involved too much strain for him, but increasingly 'I sort of grew out of that and got more poise.' But every three or four years, he had a relapse and felt a 'depressed sense of insecurity.' In 1938, for example, he took the summer off to go to the ocean, thinking that he was fully cured. He and his wife drove to New York and to Boston, but 'quite out of the blue' Cohen was seized by panic as he was driving and had to stop at a garage and hire a driver, 'as I could not drive it another foot.' Driving continued to be a problem. 'That sort of condition has prevailed more or less with me at all times; I could not possibly cross a bridge, for instance. If I have to cross the Bloor Viaduct ... I have to go down to Gerrard and along there in order to avoid the bridge.' The phobias about driving, heights, and bridges became more acute as he aged. One summer he could go nowhere at all.

Though he did not mention it to the committee, in 1938 he was trying to grapple with his condition. He read, taking extensive notes, about suicide, alcoholism, and melancholia caused by anxieties. He knew that he had psychological problems, addictive and self-destructive tendencies, which his reading informed him were characteristic of an immature personality. He sought reasons for his problems – his childhood, or his relationship with his mother, which he hinted was difficult. In these notes, there are glimpses of his stressful marriage and his sexual frustrations, which apparently led him into sexual promiscuity with numerous young women.[10] If he had a sense of doom about himself, he evidently tried hard to suppress it, and this became possible as he worked constantly from the time of the 'spectacular' Oshawa strike in 1937. In that strike, 'after some considerable difficulty,' he resolved matters but 'I would say for a period of about three weeks I had perhaps about three hours sleep a night. I had three telephones. It was a very involved affair.' As people in the labour movement needed him, he found a purpose in life, which distracted him from his inner tensions. At the same time, he had to repress his phobias, so that in the war, with increased professional demands and the necessity to submerge his personal fears in order to perform effectively, he told the committee, 'I was quite a tired person.'

When the war broke out, Cohen offered political leaders his services in any suitable capacity, to no avail. After the Nazi-Soviet Pact was signed, for about three months Cohen spent hours in the library. Disturbed by the war and the plight of German Jews, he was shocked by Soviet-German collusion, to such an extent that, he claimed, he took no Communist Party cases until the Soviet Union was on the Allied side. As the conflict heated up and thousands of workers joined unions, 'many problems were just hurled at me, carrying me to all parts of the country and under great stress and strain of travelling and hotel accommodation,' in trains, in airplanes (which terrified him), and in bad weather. 'I do not think that I touched on a matter, beginning in 1939, that did not in some way relate to the national interest as dictated by the war situation.'

He sat on many conciliation boards, which were not especially remunerative; in most cases the chair sided with Cohen, or he wrote minority reports. He developed an approach to wage policy in consultation with TLC President Tom Moore – there would be no wage increases unless there was an injustice – and he had to convince unions of this position. 'That [formula] is something which required a great amount of courage on the part of one who was serving many sections of the labour movement; in fact almost all of them as legal adviser.' Here, Cohen was making an appealing, patriotic argument to the corporate-commercial lawyers on the committee, for with a government wage policy in place during the war, wage restraint had not been voluntary. Also, Cohen had been motivated by his support of the Communist Party line, which from 1941 favoured an 'all-out' war production effort, but he did not mention this. Next, he told the committee of his NWLB service from February to September 1943, which he undertook at the 'urgent request' of Mr Justice McTague, during which time he dropped other labour matters to avoid any conflict of interest, at great pecuniary loss to himself. He was putting a bit of a gloss on this episode, for in truth he had basked in the limelight; he mentioned his 'unfortunate disagreement' with Justice McTague.

After the NWLB, his practice was so busy 'I did not even see my office' but consulted with clients while on the move. Working at a hectic pace 'had a rather damaging effect upon my health at the time,' but he did not stop and was obsessed with work. He took a break – a brief trip to Montreal and a spell at home chopping wood and being a handyman – 'and then came back for another load of work, work in the Labour Court settling industrial disputes, travelling all over the country, often at the unofficial request of the [Canadian] Department of Labour,' for a nominal fee.[11]

His fatigue and stress climaxed in May 1945, when he was in Ottawa working with the Carroll Commission investigating the Nova Scotia coal-mining industry. For four days he had argued and listened to the opposing lawyer. When he was rising to reply, 'I found, when I started, that my left hand was paralysed up to the wrist, so that I could not pick up a paper. I got up and I carried on my argument, and I could feel the sense of paralysis creeping up.' If the paralysis went beyond his shoulder he would have asked for an adjournment, which he was loath to do, because he did not want his condition known or his client jeopardized. Fortunately, it stopped at his shoulder, and so from 11 A.M. to 2 P.M. 'I argued with my whole left arm completely useless. But nobody knew that; but in my own heart and mind I was more than disturbed.'

From past experience he understood that his nervous system was exhausted and that he must disengage himself from other cases and seek medical attention. This proved impossible, because of demands on him and his need to work. Just before VE Day, he was involved with the dispute at the Ford plant in Windsor, which 'had been simmering for some time, and I do not think anybody who knows that situation, such as the

Officials of the Department of Labour, Paul Martin, the member from one of the Windsor constituencies, the trade union leaders, they would all agree that nothing but my insistence and constant attention to that problem prevented that plant going out on strike. It did, after the war was over, when I was no longer in touch with the situation.' He worked until June and planned to take off the summer but was drawn into the LeBel Inquiry, which carried on for about three and a half weeks. There, he was 'at the point of collapse' as he delivered his argument.

After a short break on Georgian Bay, he worked with the Carroll Commission, intending to withdraw from practice around Labour Day, rest, and get medical care so that he could resume work 'without such discomfort, pain and insomnia which had been influencing my life.' But, since a conciliation board was appointed in the Ford dispute, he spent about ten days assisting the UAW, immediately went to the Maritimes and Ottawa, and in October 1945 completed his work for the miners' union on the Carroll Commission. At that point he was so tired that he could not carry his own briefcase. The final matter was Mine Mill's NWLB brief and report to its convention.

Cohen told Dr Karl Stern in Montreal, who advised him to quit work, that it was impossible to quit because 'my position in industrial matters was such that I had a role to play which was a constructive one, and I could not desert it.' The doctor commented, prophetically as it turned out, that Cohen was like a Greek tragedy. Cohen replied, 'Some soldiers die on a field of battle, and I may die in a courtroom,' but he could not stop until he had fulfilled his commitments. He told his office not to accept new work, and briefly visited Montreal, where the doctor called his office to cancel all work for a week, but within three days Cohen was back at his desk. He tried to get out of the Mine Mill case by pleading illness and fatigue, argued with his wife about it, told her that his presence was indispensable, and decided to go to Kirkland Lake. His sister arranged his trip and suggested that Guenard accompany him.

The remainder of his testimony was similar to the trial, except in a few details. He denied any friendly relations with Mitchell, the hotel manager, which Judge Plouffe had mentioned. He took pills and a drink both at four in the afternoon and around ten, when he was awakened the first time. When he was comforting Guenard, they discussed Guenard's unfulfilled sexual desires. He stressed his apprehension about a scene being created; 'I felt that Kirkland Lake was the last place in the world where I could afford to have that sort of thing occur,' because some viewed his role in the strike of 1941–2 as that of a striker. 'Some people had been hurt financially in connection with the strike, and there might be an unfriendly disposition towards me; and I was very apprehensive.' A little later he repeated, 'I was afraid that somebody would use the girl and the incident in a way to damage me in some way that would be most distressing.'

When he returned to Toronto by taxi at 3 A.M., he 'was almost delirious from the cold.' He went to his sister's place, and then at 9 A.M. his brother drove him home, where he slept until four. Thereafter, he restlessly moved among hospitals. First, he went to Allan Memorial Hospital in Montreal, but he left it, since the accommodation was not acceptable, Stern's proposed treatment of insulin shots seemed 'rather extreme,' and he would be away from the office for an extended stay, not the two or three weeks that he had expected. Next, in Toronto, he consulted a Dr Blake, who recommended that he go to New York, which he did; there, a specialist told him that he had 'some deep-rooted anxiety neurosis' but that his insomnia should be treated first. Before a bed was available there, Cohen returned to Toronto, learned about the Institute of Living in Hartford, Connecticut, and travelled to Hartford. He stayed six days for an examination and tests, found that the facility catered to 'psychopat[h]ics rather than people with neuroses,' and returned to Toronto.

The report from Hartford, revealed in the disbarment hearings, concluded that Cohen was quite healthy physically but in a state of nervous exhaustion. After a week in Toronto, a bed was arranged at the Mount Sinai Hospital in New York. A Dr Wintrob wrote to Mrs Cohen that her husband 'was attending regularly and faithfully. He is making slow, but steady progress i.e. he is able to stay alone more and sleep with less sedative ... He is not so vehement and insistent as he had been in the past.' He advised Dorothy that 'you make the most of your vacation in order to be in the best condition to carry on with the problem before us.'[12] The physicians recommended a warm climate for Cohen, and he joined his wife in California. There, Cohen learned of the police investigation, but he stayed away because Gotfrid was reassuring. In March 1946 Cohen was told of the bill of indictment and he rushed back to Toronto, by which time the case was in the news and receiving enormous publicity.

Cohen then told the committee that he had expected an adjournment that day and so thought that he was not to testify. He knew nothing of Markowitz's advice to MacDonald to proceed. The committee asked why Mrs Cohen had not accompanied Cohen to Kirkland Lake, and he replied that she had high blood pressure and could not sit up all night on a train. It asked if he had always been a drinking man, and he responded that he had not been and was not, though in recent years he drank whisky when he was exhausted or to help him sleep. He also told the committee that he was addicted to Nembutal, which he took and could absorb quickly.

The use of drugs may partly explain Cohen's behaviour towards Guenard and why he had fainted in the Haileybury jail after his trial, when he was upset but probably also experiencing withdrawal. In the 1940s tranquillizers were prescribed, but the medical profession did not thoroughly understand their effects. Many but not all doctors knew that taking too many barbiturates could create behavioural problems out of keeping with a person's usual character, and that the effects were magnified when tranquillizers were combined with alcohol. This meant that some physicians were careful, while others were not, so a person who needed pills had access to them. To a point, for an anxiety-ridden person such as Cohen, alcohol and drugs could be relaxing and a kind of self-medication, but if the substances were abused they then became counterproductive.[13] Cohen's drug addiction was a well-kept secret, and it is not surprising, even if people knew, that it was not mentioned often, since addiction was considered a moral lapse rather than a disease; many of the behavioural effects were simply ignored, and often they were not recognized or understood for what they were. A professional such as Cohen obviously had functioned at a high level for years despite his addiction, and while the indications are that it had a disastrous impact on his personal life, it apparently did not impinge on his abilities as a lawyer.[14] The committee heard testimony about his drug use but did not really grasp it and obviously understood alcohol problems better.

Cohen had overruled Robinette, perhaps incorrectly, and opposed having Markowitz testify about his health at the trial, for he thought that it would ruin his reputation. After being found guilty, he continued to insist that he did nothing wrong but considered it his duty to serve his time 'with humble submission.' His income declined and virtually ceased in November 1945. Because the case interrupted his treatment, his health did not recover. His reputation was ruined and he had caused his family profound unhappiness. Though his wrongdoing resulted from bad judgment and ill health, he asked the committee to let him rehabilitate himself, and 'if I do not pursue a path that is designed to bring some credit to myself and to my family and my profession, to make up in part at least ... the Committee can act.' If he were not given that chance, 'anything that would deprive me of practising the profession in which I have grown up since I was a youngster of thirteen is certainly a death sentence for me. I do not mean that in any dramatic sense.

I am sorry I cannot go on.'[15] The committee hurriedly adjourned at 11:50 A.M. for ten minutes. Bob Carlin, who was waiting with Mrs Cohen outside the hearing room, remembered that Cohen was cross-examined for more than an hour. 'When he came out he looked washed up,' Carlin said, and when he met Mrs Cohen 'he just fell into his wife's arms and he said, "Oh darling, they murdered me. They pulled all the stops."'[16] Cohen later wrote to Robinette that at the hearing he 'was too overcome during my own testimony to be able to remain nor could I stand the strain ... of hearing of its details.'[17]

More details about Cohen's medical history were revealed, for Cohen hoped the new evidence would arouse the committee's sympathy and persuade it that extenuating circumstances explained his conduct. Though he allowed doctors to testify, it is not clear how much control his lawyer had over them. The medical testimony revealed much about Cohen, but not all of it was necessarily favourable to his case. To convey Cohen's medical condition, the evidence is presented here chronologically, in relation to his life, rather than according to the order of testimony.

Dr J. Markowitz's testimony was damning, though unintentionally, and was later disputed by Cohen. Markowitz graduated in medicine in 1923, worked in a laboratory for three years, and received a PhD, intending a career in physiology. In 1930–2 he was at Georgetown University but decided to return to Toronto, where he combined general practice with his position at the University of Toronto. From 1940 to 1945, he served in the Royal Army Medical Corps, was captured, and was a prisoner of war in Siam (Thailand).

Markowitz had known Cohen for fifteen years. 'When I first saw this man he was obviously a case of manic depressive.' He was 'markedly neurotic,' partly because he was on Barbaratol; in 1936 Markowitz put him on Nembutal, which he did not think Cohen would abuse. Ordinarily, it was acceptable to take four Nembutals a day, which is what Cohen took to counteract sleeplessness. In 1945 Markowitz refused to prescribe the drug after he heard about the Guenard incident; he told Cohen that he was addicted to barbiturates and should get off drugs. Cohen in 1936 had phobias and panic attacks, as well as some domestic difficulties with his wife – conditions that were still present in 1945. There are several theories about the source of such anxieties, which can be behavioural or cognitive, the result of conditioning or external stress, including relationships. Childhood traumas, such as the early loss of a parent, can contribute to phobias.[18] The doctor found Cohen an intelligent, good patient 'and a rather high-minded individual.'

After Markowitz returned from overseas, he received an urgent phone call from Mrs Cohen; he visited 'J.L.' and found him 'in a very bad state indeed. He was terrified of being alone; he could not sleep; he was incoherent and he had delusions of persecutions' – that everyone, including the government, was against him (a characteristic that Guenard also remembered). He told Markowitz about his psychiatric treatment in various places, including the Institute of Living in Hartford, Connecticut. Markowitz obtained its report, from which he read a paragraph to the committee. 'When in the company of girls he seems to show a rather affectionate disposition. He shows poor judgment in this respect. And it is felt that Mr. Cohen will probably get into difficulties if he continues to remain outside the hospital.' Later, the committee questioned Markowitz about Cohen's attitude towards 'girls,' and the doctor said that his wife, 'who is an attractive young woman,' had let Cohen into their home and went to tell her husband that Cohen had arrived, and she commented that Cohen 'had a wolf's look,' which Markowitz told the Committee, 'is part of his madness.'

Markowitz had contacted Robinette when Cohen was charged, because he thought that the Hartford report would interest the crown. Cohen, for obvious reasons, would not allow its release. Markowitz was persistent and apparently called Attorney General Blackwell to say that it should be in the evidence. Blackwell referred him to Robinette and advised the doctor that if he talked about it too much he might be sued. Markowitz wanted to testify at the trial, but Cohen was opposed. After Cohen's conviction, Markowitz briefly spoke to Judge Plouffe about Cohen's illness, but since such evidence had not been presented at the trial, it was too late. No new evidence was allowed at the appeal.

The committee asked Markowitz to describe Cohen's phobias, which had several forms, including fear of being alone. 'Children sometimes have that. But he would sometimes cry. I said, telephone somebody to be with you. That explains why he had to have a secretary with him ... on his trips. He could not possibly be alone.' The doctor's opinion of the Guenard incident was that, if Cohen had drugs and alcohol, intercourse was inevitable and he might not remember later. 'I think myself that this was a drunken brawl,' he told the committee, based on the evidence and Cohen's shame afterwards.

The committee tried to determine if Cohen was responsible for his actions. At first, Markowitz said that if Cohen mixed drugs and alcohol he would be completely irresponsible; then he contradicted himself and concluded that, after sedation, drink, and five hours of sleep, Cohen would recollect what had occurred. The committee enquired about Cohen's mental state. Markowitz could not commit him to a mental institution because two doctors had to sign an order and 'another man might feel that I was trying to pull a fast one,' but he could enter any centre voluntarily. In 1936 Cohen required treatment but not hospitalization, in 1937 'he had a complete mental breakdown,' which Markowitz diagnosed as depression, and currently he was 'manic depressed,' which the doctor defined as a condition when 'nothing is worth doing and he cannot do anything, and he goes into tears at any time and he may commit suicide.' Asked about such a person's future, Markowitz replied that the present treatment for depression was electric-shock treatment and that Cohen could be cured in a psychiatric hospital.[19]

Dr D.R. Blake, a psychiatrist since 1942, saw Cohen twice at his home in November 1945, just after his return from Kirkland Lake, because his family was upset about his condition. Cohen was in a hypomanic condition, 'abnormally overtalkative, extremely restless, rather grandiose – definitely he was grandiose – abnormally aggressive; definitely boastful; and I felt definitely lacking in insight and judgment.' The doctor convinced him to get psychiatric treatment. Cohen admitted that he felt tense and anxious, not surprisingly, after what had occurred with Guenard. Blake recalled, 'He felt the tension seemed to sort of get the upper hand; that at night, often after a day's work, he would have to resort to several drinks of alcohol to calm him down, and get him to his equilibrium; and also he told me he was taking sedatives at night.' The chair asked how many drinks Cohen took; the doctor thought it was several since Cohen had admitted that his drinking 'was excessive.'[20]

Blake thought that Cohen was sedated too much – he took three or four Nembutal barbiturate tablets per night, when one was the average dose. On the effect of mixing sedatives and alcohol, Blake replied that 'it was a very bad combination,' which led to intoxication, and if a normal person did it, they would become almost insane, with unintelligible speech, and would experience memory loss. Evidently, Cohen had mixed pills and alcohol off and on for years.[21] Blake prescribed a different sedative – only enough for a couple of days – and urged Cohen to leave and get psychiatric treatment. Cohen agreed and the doctor secured his admission to the Allan Memorial Institute in Montreal. When Cohen disliked the situation, he 'put on his hat and coat and left,' which annoyed Blake. Blake thought that Cohen's action demonstrated Cohen's lack of judgment. He did not see Cohen again but believed that he was very sick, 'on the border of a breakdown, not a nervous breakdown but a mental breakdown.' He was 'frankly suicidal, because there was, in spite of all his activity, an element of depression.' But Blake also felt that it was 'hopeless to attempt treatment while he was in Toronto, with his office in the background.'[22]

The family had told Blake about the Kirkland Lake incident, as did Cohen when he was alone with the doctor, but 'in his grandiose manner, he seemed to feel that there were more important things to talk about.' The committee asked if such behaviour compensated for feelings of inferiority, and Blake replied that it was common for persons who did not see themselves as psychiatric patients to act in this way, and that their conduct was entirely compensatory. 'But I feel that this man had that feeling to a degree which was abnormal and indicative of definite mental, shall I say, unbalance, and indicative of bordering on an actual mental condition.'

Dr Gordon Mellow, the physician at the Guelph reformatory, testified that on 25 February 1947 Cohen, who had just arrived, told him that he felt very nervous, had pains in his head, was accustomed to taking sedatives for insomnia, and wanted help to get to sleep. The doctor left him some pills. The next afternoon, the jail's hospital called Mellow because someone had a seizure. Cohen was collapsed on a bed. He was still in a convulsive state; 'the pupils were highly dilated, and the ball of his eye was insensitive to touch; that is to say unconscious.'[23] At first, Mellow thought that it was epilepsy, but he ruled that out after talking to Mrs Cohen and Dr Markowitz. Mellow concluded that he had symptoms – head pain, restlessness, insomnia – of 'cycloneurosis,' gave Cohen some sedatives, and told him he would 'help him out' but recommended that he stop taking drugs entirely.

Cohen was evidently worried about the disbarment proceedings, for, half an hour after receiving news of the Discipline Committee hearing, he visited Mellow and was 'very disturbed.' At the Guelph reformatory he was hospitalized almost the entire time. The hospital was a quiet environment for Cohen, but he was terrified of men in uniform outside the ward. Though he was given work when he asked for it and was assigned a clerical job, he was too nervous to continue it. He wanted to go to the prison's Sunday movie night, but when he saw the uniformed guards 'he started crying and said, I cannot, I cannot.'[24] His sensitivity remained acute and he had to take a blood test lying down, not sitting at a table. Cohen had confided his phobias to the doctor.

Dorothy Cohen had several character witnesses present who knew Cohen in his public life. They praised his work but knew absolutely nothing about the interior person, which Cohen had kept well hidden. T.W. Learie, secretary of the Men's and Boy's Clothing Industry advisory committee on standards, had known Cohen as its counsel since 1936. He read a resolution of appreciation for Cohen's excellent service. When asked about Cohen's character, Learie replied that he was scrupulously honest, consistently able, and conscientious. Though difficult to contact because of 'the overpowering pressure of work' flowing into his office, Cohen had never neglected the committee's business or declined a case.

Pat Conroy, CCL secretary-treasurer since 1941, had frequent dealings with Cohen, who worked for the Congress and its affiliated unions. Cohen was competent and confident about 'knowing his business and in handling labour disputes' and facilitating settlements. His professional conduct in terms of human relations was outstanding, and until the recent court case Conroy 'had no knowledge of the personal, private or public life of Mr. Cohen that was not a credit to him.' Because the labour movement was still relatively inexperienced in handling its legal problems, 'it is extremely important that a man of Mr. Cohen's experience and capabilities should be retained' to serve unions.[25]

J.W. Buckley, TLC vice-president and secretary of the Toronto Trades Council, had dealt with Cohen for over fifteen years and found him reliable and honest. The council hired him when its trust fund was stolen. The TLC had endorsed his appointment to the NWLB and had considered him its 'labour advocate' in courts or before the legislature. It was completely satisfied with his services and his fees. In both congresses 'the labour movement of Canada has had confidence in Mr. Cohen.'[26] R.H. Carlin, national director of the Mine Mill union, had known Cohen since 1939, as the union's lawyer. Carlin admired his honesty and reliability and had 'a great gratitude for what he has done for our organization ... I do not think there is any yardstick or scale to weigh his contribution to our organization.'[27]

The committee questioned Mrs Cohen. Trained at the New York School of Social Work, she had worked with some prominent men, including Harry Hopkins, who became President Franklin Roosevelt's top adviser. She also worked in public health for the New York Academy of Medicine. Married to Cohen for twenty-three years, to him she was 'Donia' or 'Donchka.' Her testimony was controlled, even impersonal. Regarding Cohen's relationship with Guenard, she insisted that he was sick and it resulted from his 'anxiety neurosis,' which peaked in 1945. She told Guenard in November 1945 to stay away from Cohen because he was ill. Guenard was calling him, and when Mrs Cohen objected, Guenard told her to mind her own business. Mrs Cohen opposed his trip to Kirkland Lake in 1945 and did not know that Guenard was accompanying him. She did not learn of the hotel incident until a week afterwards. She herself had offered to travel with him, but Cohen did not want her sitting up all night on the train. 'I assure you that in all my experience with J.L. Cohen no such incident had happened before.' As to his behaviour before the incident, 'the stories were fantastic,' though she apparently had heard them. The committee did not hear of other episodes concerning women, or of one occasion when Cohen was reputed to have gone 'streaking' through a hotel without any clothes on.[28]

Mrs Cohen was very professional. 'If I was just an ordinary woman who was jealous of her husband, I perhaps would have left him and applied for a divorce. But I am a social worker.' She believed that her husband was mentally ill and she would not desert him. 'I am sticking by him a hundred per cent, because I feel he is a useful member of society, who has played his part in the bargaining machinery, and in the good of industry. He has worked eighteen hours a day. I think this incident happened through overwork and complete nervous exhaustion.'[29] She seemed impersonal, talking about Cohen's service to his clients and his value to the profession and the community. She had urged Robinette to tell Blackwell about Cohen's health, assuming that, if the attorney general knew, he would not allow the case to proceed. Robinette thought that, if Guenard's evidence was withdrawn, he could get Cohen off without using medical evidence.

One committee member suggested that the doctors had presented conflicting evidence, and Markowitz thought that Cohen should be committed. MacDonald replied that no real conflict existed since all the doctors agreed that Cohen was very sick. MacDonald was concerned that the medical evidence be interpreted to prevent disbarment, not indicate an incapacity to practise law. The committee reconvened briefly to discuss the taxi, which Cohen swore he ordered the day before the Guenard incident. In his Court of Appeal brief, Judge Plouffe had said that he did not believe this story. MacDonald produced an affidavit from the taxi driver to confirm Cohen's statement, which the committee admitted as evidence.[30]

To bolster the medical testimony, MacDonald repeated that, Cohen had refused to have medical evidence presented, at the trial, fearing that it would harm him. MacDonald argued that had such evidence been presented a conviction might not have resulted. Two affidavits – from

A lawyer is his own worst client etc.

prison guard James Campbell and inmate Windover – confirmed that Cohen fainted after his conviction. A letter from Bob Carlin supplementing his testimony was admitted, which emphasized that Cohen in Kirkland Lake, 'from his personal appearance ... was in poor physical and mental health,' and many delegates noticed how tired Cohen was.[31]

MacDonald reassured Cohen that the committee was aware of the medical evidence 'and that it has been left with them in such a way that it will have a sympathetic and careful consideration.'[32] The committee had listened with 'great attention' to his submissions, but MacDonald cautioned, 'Don't get built up too high in your hopes, as we never know the outcome till the bell rings, but it could not very well have ended on a more hopeful note than it did. Keep your chin up.'[33]

J.W. Pickup wrote the Discipline Committee's report, though it circulated and all members signed it. Several wrote memos with their opinions. W.J. Beaton, concluded, 'There can be no doubt as to the conviction, as the judgment of Judge Plouffe has been confirmed by the Court of Appeal,' and the only question was whether or not the offence was 'within the definition of conduct unbecoming to a barrister or solicitor.' He thought it important that Cohen was a KC, an honour that accorded him 'a standing and precedence which, in my judgment, imposes upon the bearers of that distinction a correspondingly higher duty in respect of their conduct.' In his judgment, the evidence did not disprove the charge 'nor explain away, by medical evidence, Mr. Cohen's conduct.' He did not believe Cohen's version of events and agreed with Markowitz that it was a 'drunken brawl.' Referring to the *Weare* and *Hands* cases, which the committee considered precedents, he concluded, 'In my opinion, Mr. Cohen was convicted of a criminal offence of such a personally disgraceful character that the Benchers are bound to strike him off the rolls,' and he committed an act 'which does seriously compromise the profession in public estimation.'[34]

As soon as he learned of the committee's verdict, MacDonald wrote to Cohen to warn him. On 28 April 1947 the report was made public to the benchers of the Law Society. Cohen received a copy and was told that convocation would vote on it on 15 May 1947 and that he might appear if he wished. The Law Society again arranged for his release for a day.[35]

The report's language was straightforward but rivetting in its detail. Cohen had been convicted of assault, his appeal had been dismissed, and the committee had enquired beyond the conviction into the nature of the offence to determine whether or not it constituted conduct unbecoming a barrister and solicitor. In discussing the nature of the offence, it repeated the incident and the appeal court's description of Guenard as 'a young girl.' It noted that Cohen was in Kirkland Lake as a barrister representing a client and that, despite conflicting trial evidence, the judge believed witnesses McLean and Hardy. It highlighted the gruesome details including medical evidence about Guenard's fractured nose. The Court of Appeal 'did not disturb the Trial Judge's findings of fact' and the committee agreed with it.[36]

The committee then considered whether the offence had to be committed in the line of work as a barrister and solicitor if it was to be punishable. It concluded, using an English precedent – the *Weare* case (1888) – that it need not be, if there was a criminal offence and, as in this case, the conduct was 'closely related to his practice as a barrister.' The *Weare* case indicated that the question was 'whether it is such an offense as makes it unfit that he should remain a member of this strictly honourable profession,' whether the man is 'a fit and proper' person to be a lawyer.[37] The report repeated that Cohen was in Kirkland Lake on a case and was in the public eye. Because the Law Society had a duty to maintain standards of conduct, it found that Cohen's conduct 'should not be permitted or condoned in a member of the Law Society and finds the solicitor guilty as charged of conduct unbecoming a barrister and solicitor.' Thus, it censured Cohen.

Next, it discussed what action should be taken. It had discretion to admonish, suspend, or disbar. The committee noted that in the *Weare* case the solicitor – an owner of buildings who knowingly rented to tenants who used them as brothels – had been convicted in a criminal case 'of such a disgraceful kind that he ought to be struck off the rolls.' The court had decided that if a criminal offence was of a 'personally disgraceful character that he ought not to remain a member of that strictly honourable profession.' The judge in the *Weare* case distinguished between types of criminal offences – those that would compel the court to act or not – and gave an example: 'One can imagine a solicitor guilty of an assault of such a disgraceful character that it would be incumbent on the Court to strike him off the roll. On the other hand, one can imagine an assault of a comparatively trifling description, where in all probabilitiy the Court would not think its duty to interfere.'[38] Cohen thought that this precedent did not fit his case; the benchers on the Discipline Committee disagreed.

The report then revealed the doctors' testimony in detail, thus making Cohen's medical history public to the benchers, but did not find it compelling enough to excuse Cohen. Hence, the report added to his humiliation but did not help his case. The doctors testified that Cohen 'had for some time prior to the occurrence in question been suffering from a mental condition known as manic depressive psychosis brought on by overwork and followed by the excessive use of alcohol and sleeping sedatives.' This information was new and had not been presented in the trial. One doctor suggested that Cohen's condition might partially explain his actions, but in the committee's opinion Cohen knew what he was doing. It accepted the evidence about his nervous state and mental illness, 'but it is not at all satisfied that that accounts for or excuses the conduct of the solicitor at Kirkland Lake,' especially given that it was not the first time the couple had quarrelled. It recounted the earlier quarrels, and the committee concluded that it was difficult to determine whether the incidents were solely the result of Cohen's declining health, which affected his judgment. It saw a pattern, and 'after most careful consideration,' concluded that the only appropriate action for the Law Society to take was disbarment. It ordered that his name be struck from the rolls.

Convocation had to approve the committee's recommendation, which meant that the report's contents became known to many members of the profession. For a couple of months, Cohen's legal team scurried about to try and head off disaster. MacDonald was disappointed in the report and discussed with Cohen their 'line of attack.' Expecting a sharp division among members of convocation, he hoped to lessen the penalty.[39]

There were barriers. By May, Cohen, who had been in jail for nearly three months and was distressed by the 'urgency of my whole situation,' wanted to participate in the disbarment matter 'which involves my entire future.' He tried to get an adjournment and asked Robinette to help him get released early. Robinette requested a transcript of the hearing to use its medical evidence to get Cohen's sentence reduced, so that he 'might be admitted to some institution for proper treatment.'[40] The Law Society refused, since he had not presented the case and release of the transcript would contravene a 1946 decision of convocation.[41] The transcript was sent to MacDonald. As noted, Robinette's efforts for Cohen's early release eventually were successful.[42]

Cohen sought an adjournment to June. On 14 May, in a formal letter to the Law Society, which enclosed a memo written by Cohen, MacDonald stressed that his client sought an adjournment, for he felt handicapped consulting MacDonald under existing conditions. While Cohen's account and his own memory did not agree on some details, MacDonald could 'confirm a good deal of what he says in the enclosed document ... since I was first introduced to it.' The day before Cohen testified to the

Discipline Committee, 'he was in a very distressing state of mind. It was not easy to discuss the matter with him at all.' MacDonald did not discuss an adjournment. Partly on Dr Markowitz's advice, MacDonald had 'rightly or wrongly' proceeded, but after the fact, Dr Blake told him that Cohen was in no condition to testify and 'do justice to himself.' MacDonald wanted an adjournment at convocation.[43]

Cohen's memo pressing for an adjournment is a disturbing document. Conveying how the situation was affecting his life and his state of mind, it rehashed many events and issues in the case. His law practice had been totally disrupted, and his health continued to decline. Between April 1946 and February 1947, 'I was constantly engaged ... under great physical handicap,' first in trying to get the matter to trial, and then on the trial, and subsequent appeal.' Of his health, he wrote: 'I have been seriously ill since early in 1945.' He had had previous intervals of nervous and physical exhaustion, and this condition had become more serious because of events proceeding the trial, the conviction, and nearly three months in prison. In the Haileybury jail, until bail was arranged, he had suffered 'a serious nervous seizure,' had fainted, and had convulsions. After he lost the appeal, he surrendered himself to begin his sentence: 'I was transferred from Haileybury to Guelph, shackled throughout the night to other prisoners,' arrived in Guelph on 25 February, where the next day he suffered a seizure and was taken to the institution's hospital, where he remained.

Under unrelenting pressure, Cohen learned two days later, 'while still very shaky, nervous and in bed,' that the Discipline Committee would hear his case on 15 March. He told his wife to hire MacDonald and seek an adjournment, since he was in no condition to consult his lawyer. He assumed that an adjournment would be granted, but on 14 March he was told that he was going to Toronto to the Don Jail, where he was placed in the hospital ward. He saw MacDonald at 5 P.M. and learned for the first time that he would appear the next day before the committee. He thought that MacDonald would ask for an adjournment, but after a sleepless night he was escorted to Osgoode Hall 'under Gaol escort' and learned that, on the advice of Dr Markowitz, the committee would proceed and listen to him testify. He did not feel in the circumstances that he could object. He took the stand, 'spoke quite extemporaneously as sincerely and informally as I could, but broke down before I concluded my testimony.' He later learned that MacDonald had completed his argument and that the committee was deliberating.

After great difficulty, Cohen obtained a copy of the transcript of evia stroke is brain, not heart ??

dence before the committee and its draft report. With his limited time and energy, 'interrupted by spells of weakness and inability to concentrate,' he could spend no more than an hour or two in succession analysing the documents and writing his memo. He nevertheless critiqued the transcript and aspects of the proceedings, evidence, and report, to reiterate his desire for delay.

He did make some new points. He objected to the committee report's use of the term 'psychosis' and any suggestion of a link between it and events in Kirkland Lake. He confirmed that, while he was apprehensive at the time of the incident, and perhaps did not show good judgment, he knew what he was doing. 'The Committee cannot consistently deal with me on the basis that I was "calm" and "knew what he was doing" and then introduce psychiatric terms, and not altogether correctly I must say with respect, as part of the explanation of my behaviour.' He also objected to Markowitz's diagnosis of his behaviour as 'manic depressive.' He requested an opportunity to substitute for Markowitz's unscientific testimony the evidence of expert psychiatrists 'who knew me before and immediately after the Kirkland Lake events,' particularly since the committee might have been influenced by such testimony. Cohen had understood immediately that Markowitz's evidence, which was meant to evoke sympathy, was damaging.

Cohen condemned a report written in New York which said that he had a 'rheumatic heart.' 'I have never had rheumatism and have no heart problem' – a statement that is interesting both because he had earlier told Robinette that he had a stroke and because his early sudden death a few years later was supposedly occasioned by heart trouble.

Cohen suggested that different standards of conduct might exist regarding conviction and disbarment and should be examined. He rightly pointed out that 'the Committee has failed to consider the question of the Kirkland Lake incident as against the whole pattern of my life, public contribution and social usefulness and the extent to which I have unselfishly, despite its great strain upon my health, devoted myself to the public interest particularly during the War Period.' Had he detached himself more from his professional duties, as his doctors had advised, he claimed, the Guenard incident would not have occurred.

Cohen criticized the committee for stressing alcohol consumption over sleeping sedatives. He insisted that he was not 'a drinking man,' but then he admitted that a little alcohol had a considerable effect on him. His recent alcohol consumption resulted from severe strain and was intended to overcome insomnia and 'the possible disturbance resulting from habitually taking sleeping sedatives.' His admitted addiction to drugs was an important consideration, which was not well understood or stressed by the committee.

Cohen objected to the committee's citing of the *Weare* case, which, he submitted, did not apply to him since 'it deals with a course of anti-social and probably illegal conduct consistently and deliberately persisted in. The case affords no standard for dealing with one incident such as the events at Kirkland Lake.' Cohen objected to Markowitz's suggestion that he suffered from 'delusions of persecution.' Cohen said that he believed, as did 'tens of thousands of Canadians,' that the proceedings launched in April 1946 'emanated from interests opposed to me in political and socio-political terms, using the agency of the provincial government.' This government involvement may indeed have been a factor, but, because evidence was destroyed and the complainant in the case remains unknown, it cannot be proven.

Cohen was vulnerable, distressed at losing his legal credentials, and was reviewing his life. In the memo's final pages, he expressed his deep and sincere regret that convocation, the Discipline Committee, and the profession generally have 'been ... embarrassed by the most unfortunate, and to me most unpredictable, events upon which my conviction was based and these proceedings instituted.' He understood what was at stake, and he sensed that he would not live much longer.

On the 4th of June this year I will attain the age of 50. I have striven and worked – perhaps not always wisely but always honestly and zealously – since the death of my father when I was 13 years of age. It would only be trite to say that any such course as recommended by the Report would climax a life of labour and anxiety with shame and disaster. One does not at my age contemplate such a catastrophe with any equanimity nor in the face of it can one make any idle or opportunistic promises or gestures. Whatever may be [my] life span, I am entering into its final stages and as I stand at the brink I am conscious of one single determination – to redeem myself and prove myself worthy of the respect of my profession – bench and bar – of the confidence of my family and of the duty which rests upon every living person of discharging his social obligations to the full to the community of which he is an integral part. Any act which completely forecloses any opportunity of such redemption can only spell doom and disaster for me.

He 'should not have permitted fatigue, illness or any of the other contributory factors, to expose the profession, my family, and myself to such an unfortunate occurrence,' but failure on his part was not due to a deficient character or criminal tendencies. Extreme action such as the committee contemplated was appropriate only where there was no expectation of rehabilitation. He could not conceive that convocation would impose such a penalty. In his final plea, Cohen referred to the understanding, chivalry, and generosity that he and the profession believed should exist in people's treatment of each other. He hoped that such feelings would lead to mercy in his case, without understanding that it was precisely such sentiments that contributed to his peers' harsh judgment of him. In the public sphere, where he worked among men, a strong feeling of paternalism and protectiveness towards women existed. Sometimes this world view had the effect of subordinating women, as in the needle-trades conferences on standards. But, in Cohen's assault case, his peers felt that he had crossed the boundary of acceptable behaviour, and in such circumstances they expressed their sympathy and 'chivalry' towards the young woman, not Cohen.

Having spent painful hours contemplating his character and his future, Cohen was regretful. He promised 'most sincerely' to repare the damage he unwittingly but carelessly caused. Accepting blame for the situation, he concluded: 'I should be, have been and am being *punished* but [hope] that I should not be *condemned* to the life of frustration and despair which would inevitably follow if the course recommended by the Report is adopted.' This entreaty by a very humbled man was ignored.[44]

The Law Society records suggest that it was motivated to act properly and uphold the profession's standards of conduct, particularly in this widely publicized case. Traditionally, 'the benchers' responsibility was to articulate ethical standards of the profession and having satisfied themselves that a lawyer practised unethically, they disbarred without further ado.'[45] While this case was unusual and therefore was considered carefully, the Law Society was sensitive about the profession's reputation, and the benchers were neither lax nor generous in their treatment of Cohen. He was not well liked in the profession, for he was abrasive, and some were jealous of his abilities. Given the extent of anti-Semitism, some probably disliked him because he was a Jew. Others, who saw him as a fellow traveller or an outright 'red,' undoubtedly were antagonized by his left-wing politics, which were unpopular in 1947 Cold War Canada. The benchers would have been shocked to learn that some thought they were persecuting Cohen, for they were scrupulous in carrying out proper procedures, but the outcome of their deliberations contributed to Cohen's downfall. Cohen was vulnerable because he had enemies; he could not afford to make a mistake, and once he behaved recklessly, he had little support.

Convocation agreed to Cohen's request for an adjournment in May, and the report went forward to the June session.[46] In preparation for the June meeting, Dr Markowitz examined Cohen and found him 'fit and able physically and otherwise to practise his profession,' though he advised rest and limited work.[47] Cohen went over the evidence and had MacDonald contact the three doctors in case they were called, since he seemed to think that the evidence would be reviewed thoroughly. He hoped to reduce the decision to suspension and apparently thought that he had a chance. MacDonald doubted that Discipline Committee members would reverse themselves in convocation. A letter requested from Dr LeBlond stated that injuries on Guenard's neck and shoulders were not from bites and no blood was on her dress, though dry blood covered her scratches and was present in her nostrils.[48] The doctors' letters were submitted but were not in the oral presentation.[49] Cohen considered attending convocation but was weak and decided that his presence was inadvisable, though his wife was available to answer any questions.[50]

Nothing helped. On 19 June 1947 convocation confirmed the Discipline Committee's recommendation, disbarred Cohen for conduct 'unbecoming' a lawyer, and stripped him of his KC. The registrar of the Supreme Court of Ontario ordered that his name be removed from the rolls of the court.[51] Cohen was sent a registered letter of the decision. Such a penalty was a disgrace, since relatively few persons were thrown out of the profession and only a minuscule number were KCs.[52] For a man who had struggled to become a lawyer, built a successful practice, and was esteemed by his colleagues, the loss of his professional credentials at his stage of life was not only a disgrace but also a tragedy.

Cohen was a singular individual, and his disbarment was the exception rather than the rule. Between 1945 and 1965, ninety-three lawyers were disbarred in Ontario, and only six were reinstated or sought readmission to the profession. Most (83 per cent) were disbarred for misappropriation of clients' funds and related business activities. 'For the most part, the lawyers who were disbarred,' one study concludes, 'were what might be called "marginal" lawyers,' in the sense that they were in solo practice in real estate or general law. The vast majority of disbarred lawyers (85 per cent) did poorly academically, and quite a few either wrote supplemental exams because they failed a subject the first time or even repeated a full year in law school, so that they were marginal at school as well as in practice.[53]

Cohen was an exceptional law student and at the top of his field, and he was the only labour lawyer ever disbarred. Unlike most disbarred lawyers, who worked alone in general practice, Cohen was a specialist, an expert able to choose his work and clients, and hence he had a degree of independence. Also, unlike those disbarred for financial malpractice, he was imbued strongly with a sense of 'professional ethics.' While illness was a factor in his situation (as it was in other cases), Cohen refused to use it as an excuse but took responsibility for his actions, unlike many who blamed their deviant behaviour on the state of their health. Cohen's form of denial was to see his behaviour as less serious than the Law Society regarded it. He also blamed his treatment on the manipulations of political opponents (such as management lawyers and the Attorney General's Department). Whether this opposition was a factor, we do not know, but others besides Cohen believed that there was unusual intervention by the state in the case, so Cohen's concerns were possibly exaggerated but not a mere figment of his imagination.

Cohen shared certain characteristics with other disbarred lawyers in that he was in the category (73 per cent) of lawyers who had prior complaints laid against them and among the 15 per cent who had been reprimanded in the past, prior to disbarment. While he was older than the average age (forty-three years) of those disbarred, when the pre-war and wartime graduates are analysed separately from post-war grads, he fits the pattern of being about fifty years old and having practised an average of twenty-three years. In that group, he was among the eight disbarred lawyers who were KCs.

Cohen was not typical in terms of birthplace (he was an immigrant), religion, or class of father (blue-collar worker), for lawyers were predominantly Canadian-born and Christian and in his era the law was still a 'gentleman's profession.' He was similar to his peer group in that he was married. Like others, he was affected by 'life situation' stresses of middle age and was experiencing some mental and physical deterioration, but, unlike his colleagues, his medical profile was more complex than simple abuse of alcohol. Like other disbarred lawyers and unlike lawyers in large firms, Cohen was isolated in the profession because he did not have the same institutional supports, he did not get referrals from other lawyers (though he did not need them), he did not have extensive social contacts with colleagues, and he was not involved in the Law Society or in making the rules of the profession. In terms of achievement and prestige, he was a leader in his specialty and was imbued with the professional values of the legal community, but because of his background, specialty, politics, and personality, he remained a loner, outside mainstream circles, and vulnerable to them once he was in trouble.

Discipline imposed by the Law Society resulted in the most severe punishment for those whose behaviour threatened the profession's survival (Cohen's did not) or infringed on norms accepted either by the majority of the legal profession or by the majority of society (Cohen's did). The legal profession was sensitive to public criticism because its autonomy was at the pleasure of the government, which could amend legislation under which the profession regulated itself, and thus the publicity in Cohen's case hurt him. Lawyers were seen as trusted persons who provided a professional service, and those who betrayed that trust by stealing money or undermining the ethos of 'the professional' were punished.

Cohen's tragedy was compounded by his profound respect for the law and his profession. He took the rituals and trappings of the legal profession seriously. He had provided high-calibre professional service, yet he was judged 'unfit' because of his personal conduct. Even if one accepts that legal elites promulgate an ethical ideology that promotes their own interests, advantages, and status over an underclass (consisting of racial, religious, and ethnic minorities and women), Cohen's case does not quite fit. Despite his impoverished immigrant background, he was not a passive victim of prejudice. He had overcome discriminatory barriers because he was so able, and he retained professional independence at a time when there was concern that many lawyers were losing theirs to large corporate law firms representing their clients' views.[54] He did face impediments in the profession but his own behaviour also had brought on the penalties. Thus, Cohen's case was complex. It might have been decided the same way if he had been a rich, Protestant, Canadian-born, conservative corporation lawyer, even though there is evidence that the legal profession was prejudiced against Jews and Communists at this time and the Law Society of Upper Canada, like society in general, was disdainful of what it called 'alien' elements.

But there were other elements in the case, for in addition to being disliked as a radical Jewish lawyer, Cohen had alienated some peers who were professionally jealous of him. He evoked in some an exaggerated paternalism which was part of masculine culture of the day, because he had mistreated a 'young woman' and thereby stepped outside the bounds of respectable behaviour not only as a lawyer but as a man. Senator David Croll, in an interview many years after the Cohen case, hinted at these complex motives behind his colleagues' antagonism towards Cohen. He denied, probably incorrectly, that anti-Semitism played a role, but then commented, 'You didn't have to hate him because he was a Jew; you could hate him because he was Cohen. He could rub you the wrong way and you forgot his being a Jew. You see he was so brilliant that they didn't think of the Jewishness. People were jealous of his ability, of his capacity to catch an argument in the middle of it and twist it and turn it and deal with it.'[55] The Discipline Committee in Cohen's case did not have to display outright 'bigotry and ideology' to enforce its concepts of professionalism (which Cohen basically shared). As a result of the structure, culture, and biases of the profession, few of his peers were inclined to display sympathy towards Cohen once he got into trouble, even when it appeared that he was in a life-threatening situation.

11

The Struggle for Reinstatement, 1947–1950

In the *Weare* case (1888), which the Discipline Committee had cited, the English judge commented on the penalty of being struck off the roll. 'I know how terrible that is. It may prevent him from acting as a solicitor for the rest of his life; but it does not necessarily do so. He is struck off the roll; but if he continues a career of honourable life for so long a time as to convince the Court that there has been a complete repentance, and a determination to persevere in honourable conduct, the Court will have the right and power to restore him to the profession. His case, therefore is not hopeless.'[1] For the next two years, Cohen would endeavour to be reinstated – in his terms, to 'redeem' himself.

For some time, however, nothing could be done. MacDonald wrote to Cohen in October 1947 that 'I have heard nothing further except innocuous references to this matter of yours which do not in any way advance matters nor, on the other hand, militate against the fruition of your hopes.'[2] Cohen heard from George Newcombe Gordon of Peterborough that many thought that 'this Star Chamber Judgment is all wrong' and that 'the powers of these gentlemen who meet in secret and are chiefly corporation lawyers representing powerful employer interests, should have their powers very much limited, and all meetings should be open to the public.' He and 'a good many members of the Bar' encouraged him to seek review of the decision because 'you are the ablest and most competent counsel in labour law, and if you take this judgment lying down, I think it would be a mistake.'[3]

During the trial, jail term, and disbarment hearing, despite obvious humiliation, Dorothy Cohen had loyally supported her beleaguered husband. Once he returned home, she left for an extended period in 1948 and considered leaving him permanently and returning to New York. In the process, she and others were evaluating how 'Jack' was doing and what his future was likely to be. One friend from Toronto encouraged Dorothy to stay in California. 'You know Mrs. Cohen if I was in your place I would stai [sic] there and never com [sic] back to Canada no moor [sic] as I know there is not much happynes [sic] here for you ... I would not live a life like you ... you know that your husband [h]as not changed yet he is just the saim [sic].' She thought that he would never change, was sorry for the way Dorothy had to live, and hoped she was happier now that she was away. Another friend, Sarita Beals, a professor in New York, was glad that Dorothy was all right, 'despite all the pain and personal tragedy that seems to have met you everywhere you went.' She invited Dorothy to stay with her in New York before the summer heat set in and suggested that she look around for a job, since she might get a worthwhile position. 'You have a large acquaintance, excellent references and experience.' If Dorothy returned to Toronto, everything might go smoothly, 'but no harm is done in investigating the field.' As to Jack's cure, 'you are more optimistic than I.'[4] In the end, after four months in California with her sister's family, Dorothy returned home.

During his disbarment, Cohen's health was precarious, but he seemed to be improving, though he was as difficult as ever. When Mrs Cohen wrote to the Austin Riggs Foundation in Massachusetts for a reduction in its bill because of their poor financial situation, the administrator wrote, 'I was very happy to hear that Mr. Cohen is still improving and that his experience here helped him along the way. You must not at all feel apologetic for his behaviour while here for we did not feel critical toward him but instead tried to understand the nature of his demands and did our best to deal with them. He was an admittedly difficult patient but we did feel we were able to bring about a hopeful change in the course of his illness and point him in a new direction, even if we were not able to continue with him to full recovery.'[5] A Toronto friend wrote in February 1948 that Jack was doing some work, but outside of that 'I don't know very much as to how things are coming along. Jack told me he is feeling fine.' In March a sister-in-law in Toronto wrote anxiously to Dorothy, mentioning that Jack had visited their busy household. 'Jack has been very friendly. I believe he has called us as often as I have called him. He seems very cheerful. He has had long chats with

Louie at home as well as over the phone. Jack is quite enthusiastic about his work. He is apparently making excellent progress. He certainly feels more optimistic about himself. He always talks about you with fondness – Jack tells me you are returning home soon.'[6]

By December 1948, Cohen was already thinking of reinstatement. It was not an easy matter, since the Law Society viewed disbarment as permanent and restoration as possible only in 'exceptional circumstances and upon special grounds.' Only if the person had 'entirely purged his guilt,' had given substantial evidence that indicated 'that there is not probability of the Solicitor offending in the future,' had letters of support testifying to his trustworthy and unimpeachable character, and had proven over time that he was a trustworthy person 'and in every way fit to be a member of the Society,' would the Law Society review the case. It viewed reinstatement as a long, slow process.[7]

Cohen consulted MacDonald about its timing and procedure. He wrote a lengthy, lucid memo outlining the argument to be made before a future Discipline Committee meeting. The factors were: his case was not like the *Weare* precedent; the trial's delay and publicity worked against him; and the proven hostility of a Toronto newspaper (the *Globe and Mail*) and the northern press towards him because of his work with the miners was an issue. Other considerations were the harsh sentence, despite the incidental physical injury to Guenard; the marginal evidence on which he was convicted; the fact that he had not practised law since late 1945; and his professional behaviour in the past. He told Mac-Donald that 'even the R.C.M.P. who featured in many cases in which I acted, went out of their way to inform him, just before he came to Haileybury, that they held me in the highest esteem, and that I had always conducted myself with great fairness in respect to them, and that they certainly hoped that there would be no conviction.'

As to the 'medical phase' of the evidence, he was not consulted and did not agree with MacDonald's argument that because of his poor health he was not responsible for his actions. While his weakened, tired condition contributed, he understood that any medical testimony would relate only to the appropriate action the Law Society might take. He was not criticizing MacDonald, but 'the fact remains ... that we seemed to 'justify,' in a legal sense, the events of November 1945, upon medical grounds and that some, at any rate, of the so-called medical testimony given was harmful and, more importantly, was most unsound,' particularly that of Markowitz, who, though well intentioned, was unqualified. His evidence to the committee clearly 'will have to be dealt with and cleared up when an application is made for re-instatement.' Some reference had to be made to the Hartford report, in Cohen's view, a worthless, malicious document which Markowitz had only because Cohen did not want it left with the New York doctor.

After Cohen's disbarment, his anxieties seemed to lessen. His wife had been away and for the first time in twenty years he was able to rid himself of the fear of being alone. During visits with Dr Wintrob, he came to realize 'that I had permitted myself for years and years so to overtax myself that as a result my physical strength had been injured and my nerves and general sense of well being had been seriously damaged. I blame no one for this except my own inability to detach myself early enough from difficult and responsible work to secure the recuperation and rest which I needed.' But, after November 1945, he had developed, despite the continuing strain, 'a more balanced and temperate outlook,' had ceased drinking, had reduced his medication, intended to reduce his work, take less contentious cases, and write at home.

As his family (his wife, daughter, siblings, and mother) were all adversely affected by his disbarment, it would be tragic for them if he remained in disgrace. The Law Society had expressed its public disapproval, but further discipline might be seen as punitive and biased, whereas his reinstatement would demonstrate the absence of malice or undue harshness in its actions. On a personal note, he confided to MacDonald that 'continuing my disbarrment is virtually capital punishment – a death sentence,' and that 'the good must be considered with the bad.'[8] Cohen sent MacDonald a second letter, which raised darker issues that he might want to include in future arguments, namely, the attitude of Judge Plouffe, the actions of the police and the Attorney General's Department, the adjournments that the prosecution manipulated so that Plouffe, not Proulx, would be the trial judge, and 'the conduct of the "authorities" relating to the second charge' – conduct that was 'symptomatic of the spirit and yes, the purpose of the whole vicious proceeding.' In Cohen's view, the Guenard incident would never have gone to court had it not been 'for the industry ... of the Authorities, pressed by a Toronto newspaper' to develop a case which they could accomplish only by the extraordinary proceeding of the indictment, followed later by improper interference of the Attorney General's Department. That situation alone, Cohen thought, justified the Law Society's reinstating him. It was not an argument that MacDonald presented.

MacDonald thanked Cohen for his two helpful letters as the two men organized a reinstatement campaign. They drafted a petition as well as a

An ironic argument

list of supporters that included sympathetic benchers. MacDonald wrote to many of Cohen's associates on boards about the petition and requested letters from them that commented on Cohen's 'demeanor, conduct and treatment of the matter' in which they associated with him.[9] Cohen worked as a labour-relations consultant after his disbarment, and by May 1949 he had served on thirty-eight conciliation and four arbitration boards. He could not, of course, practise law, and MacDonald advised him about work he could do, cautioning him to keep away from jobs that the Law Society might consider to be borderline and to avoid totally any advocacy or counsel work in a court or before a tribunal. Both men kept track of his jobs as Cohen struggled to make a living.[10] MacDonald's request for colleagues' support of Cohen resulted by June 1949 in his filing the petition for reinstatement with the corroborative letters.[11] He inserted a notice of the application in two issues of *Ontario Weekly Notes*. Cohen regained his buoyancy and a renewed sense of humour, telling MacDonald, 'As it has been suggested in authoritative writings that the prayers of a sinner are more likely to be answered, this, I suppose, should better be left to me.'[12]

The Law Society received Cohen's petition, which went before convocation on 15 September 1949. The matter was forwarded to the Discipline Committee, which heard the petition on 14 October. The chairman of the committee, C.F.H. Carson, and five of its members were the men who had disbarred Cohen but eleven additional members reviewed the case.[13] The petition outlined the facts leading to disbarment: proceedings began in April 1946 with a bill of indictment to the grand jury in Haileybury, not by a complaint from Guenard; the trial, seven months later, resulted in Cohen's conviction; the Discipline Committee reviewed his status and recommended disbarment, which convocation confirmed in June 1947. It requested reinstatement on the grounds that, prior to the incident, Cohen was under medical care 'by reason of exhaustion and nervous fatigue resulting from the strain of overwork because of the volume of professional work which for a number of years your petitioner had performed.' The appeal and incarceration until May 1947 had interrupted Cohen's medical treatment, which, when it was resumed, Cohen had followed. He had recuperated and was now able 'to discharge the responsibilities and proprieties of the profession.' The petition attached letters regarding his condition from four doctors, who argued that Cohen's health would suffer if he could not resume work. Cohen's conciliation and arbitration work was described, and the petition stated that he had satisfactorily performed 'a constructive and useful function,' as thirty-three letters from colleagues on recent boards indicated. The petition concluded that Cohen was fifty-two years old, that he had caused his family grief and regretted the events that led to the Law Society's action, that he had done 'everything humanly possible to fit himself for restoration to membership in the Society,' and that he had not practised since his disbarment and indeed not since October 1945. On this basis, he asked for the Society's consideration of the matter.[14]

On 18 November 1949 the Discipline Committee met, with A.A. Mac-Donald again acting for Cohen. MacDonald was uncertain about the outcome but better prepared than at the disbarment hearing, for this time he had the benefit of Cohen's advice, though he did not take it in certain instances.[15] He had to convince the committee that Cohen was working effectively and that his physical and mental health was improved. He also had to reverse Markowitz's earlier damaging statement that Cohen was a manic depressive.

Among the doctors' letters, Markowitz's stated that he had seen Cohen several times between 1947 and 1949, that Cohen's mental health had changed completely, and 'that whatever there was in his temperament that led to his acts on which he was tried, is no longer evident.' Such conduct was unlikely to recur as 'he is not drinking nor is he taking nembutal. He is behaving like a rational member of a learned profession, and I have no hesitation in certifying to that effect.' B. Wintrob had cared for Cohen since September 1947 and found Cohen cooperative, improved considerably in health, and fit to work as a lawyer. Daniel Blake noted 'a tremendous change and improvement' in his condition and was of the view that he had recovered completely from his nervous condition and could carry on his profession.

Dr Robert Armour wrote of his three long interviews with Cohen – including one in his wife's presence – and indicated that he had studied the trial transcripts and other documents. In his opinion, Cohen had never suffered 'from any psychosis or any form of mental disease ... nor ... ever suffered from any constitutional psychoneurosis or any form of nervous disturbance which would have a tendency to recur.' He attributed his state of mind in November 1945 to prolonged overwork, too much responsibility, and excessive medication 'consisting of various barbiturates, chiefly Nembutol and Seconol, drugs that when used to excess, were demoralizing.' Cohen's habit of taking one to five capsules a day for many months, especially when combined with two or three ounces of whisky, would cause disturbed behaviour in any normal man and would have an undesirable effect in one so fatigued and under strain. 'I do not feel that Mr. Cohen took these drugs and the alcohol with them on account of any moral viciousness in him, but in all good faith,' since they had been prescribed by reputable physicians, though probably in smaller doses, and that he, in ignorance, increased the dosage, 'not being aware of the undesirable effects while he was under their influence.' When Armour examined Cohen, he found him composed, clear-minded, with good memory and concentration; he had no delusions or other abnormal mental processes and had 'a proper moral sense.' Cohen had benefited from treatment and had reduced his medication markedly. In his work, Cohen himself felt that he was acting more objectively, was less tense, and had 'not experienced the same drive to excessive work from which he suffered previously.' He could relax, take some recreation, and continue this approach indefinitely in the future. Dr Armour's report stated that Cohen could resume legal practice and would not exhibit any future abnormalities of conduct.[16]

Before the Discipline Committee, which sought assurances about Cohen's mental health, Armour elaborated on his letter. Cohen's nervous disturbance was attributable to 'undue responsibility and anxiety in his teens – the death of his father – and he had to take over too much responsibility – that he had worked unduly hard in putting himself through law.' His first depression and insomnia, in 1925, resulted from fatigue, not a mental disorder. In 1945 the problem was fatigue caused by overwork, which also was complicated 'by his use of excessive sedatives.' When the committee asked if Cohen had taken drugs in 1936, Armour suggested that Cohen began taking them as early as the first breakdown in 1925 and 'that he took them continuously all of those years.' He kept himself going with a moderate amount of alcohol, but the drugs were taken in 'grossly excessive doses.'

In June, when Armour examined him, Cohen knew that he had been 'grossly overworking' and overdosing on medication, but there was no evidence of abnormality in the functions of his mind. His problem was the need for some relief. He had moderated his work activities, was relaxed enough to drive a car – an activity he could not perform when he was tense. He had two new recreational interests, cabinet making and photography. Armour said that he was never a manic depressive, and that Dr Markowitz was not a psychiatrist. Cohen had completed things recently, 'and a manic depressive in the manic phase is greatly overactive mentally and physically but he does not accomplish anything. He does not finish it. All his activities end in blind ends or without purpose.' Cohen had learned an important lesson, that he had been overdoing things, and if he resumed practice, Armour believed that Cohen could be moderate.

Cohen appeared briefly before the committee. He was nervous and not as articulate as usual, but he discussed his medical treatment and his new hobbies and said that he was much healthier. He had changed his work habits while on conciliation boards. In the past, he explained, 'it would be common for me if I were to go to the office from court or conferences or even go from my home to the office to carry files with me on matters which have been touched upon that day and to continue working on them for the rest of the day and well on into the night and commence again at the very earliest moment the next morning, whether or not the matters necessarily had to be dealt with at once or not. There was no compulsion for me to continue delving into the files but I just felt that I had to do it until I had digested everything.' This compulsion was an inner drive that made for excellence but also exhaustion. Such habits had been automatic until recently, when he had analysed the way he worked. Since January 1948, 'I can come home and take a file out of my brief[case] upon which I have spent some time and put it down on my desk with other files ... and the file is not picked up or looked at again until the day upon which the hearings are to be renewed ... There is not the slightest inclination on my part to open up the file until the day upon which it must receive consideration.' He had been careful to select conciliation cases that were not complicated or fractious. He asked for the opportunity to make up for the injuries he had caused his family, friends, and the profession, 'in so far as I can in that portion of my life that is still available to me.' He was touched by the many letters sent voluntarily on his behalf, and by the support of MacDonald, who was his friend as much as his counsel.[17]

Many labour associates and lawyers supported Cohen's reinstatement petition. One who did not was Allan Bell, who, in a letter to MacDonald, spoke of Cohen's 'old arrogance.' He accused Cohen of an impropriety concerning a small payment in a case. An obviously agitated Cohen went through his old files to exonerate himself, though, as Cohen pointed out, Bell could have contacted him about the matter if there was a misunderstanding. MacDonald feared that Bell might contact the Law Society, so he wrote him a conciliatory letter and appealed to his sympathy. 'Mr. Cohen has passed through a pretty severely chastening experience since then, the turmoil into which he was plunged having endured from sometime in 1945 up to the present time and you can have some idea of the mental suffering he has undergone in that period, and it has not been without effect.' Cohen would not quibble about paying the account even now, but such action might be misinterpreted as trying to buy silence, and a payment 'on such a basis would be very highly improper' and could be costly. He invited Bell to talk to Cohen personally and thanked him for his candour, in what amounted to an abject apology. Bell wrote again to MacDonald to assure him that the chapter was closed, but he had not changed his view of Cohen one iota. 'I found Mr. Cohen to be a person who regarded obligations lightly. Even the few lawyers here told me of unpaid agency accounts,' and a few weeks earlier a judge had hailed him on the courthouse steps and asked Bell, 'Do you think I'll get my $27.00?' His story related back to an episode where Cohen and the judge had dinner at Cohen's invitation. Accidentally, Bell wrote sarcastically, Cohen forgot his money, and the judge had to pay. Later, Cohen included twenty-seven dollars in a bill of costs. 'As the bill came into Mr. Judge's hands for review, he put a red ring around it and sent it back 'sans comment.' This and other stories make interesting stuff. Waiters at the Prince Edward told me that when Cohen ordered meals brought to his room, the waitress would leave the meal at the door – knock, then run like the devil. I could regale you with dozens of yarns of a similar nature.'[18]

All other letters were sympathetic and, while conceding Cohen's earlier reputation as a difficult men, emphasized that he had changed. J. Wilfrid Teskey said that Cohen 'has been both chastened and humbled,' and if the Law Society reinstated him, he would work 'both ably and honourably.' Waldon Lawr wrote that, on a recent conciliation board, he and Cohen spent an evening together and discussed the Guenard incident and his disbarment. Cohen 'acknowledged that he had been very foolish; he did not minimize his conduct and admitted there was only himself to blame;' he was trying to rehabilitate himself and remarked that, at the time in question, 'he was sick and in a nervous condition.' Norman Matthews, a partisan management lawyer wrote of his several dealings with Cohen both before and after disbarment, stating, 'I have found a surprising difference in Mr. Cohen's general attitude in the last couple of years;' he was more cooperative, fair-minded, and courteous. Judge Egerton Lovering agreed that 'he is a changed man' since his difficulties, for earlier he had been 'most abrupt and almost arrogant. He was a difficult advocate with whom to deal.' Before he became a judge, he practised law, met Cohen, and found him 'so self-opinionated and ... 'ornery' but now I find him quite pliable, reasonable, willing to compromise and an excellent conciliator ... There is no doubt that Cohen is clever and an able counsel; I believe that the experience he has had has been of great benefit to him.' G. Marshall Ferguson of McCarthy and McCarthy wrote that in the past he was ambivalent about Cohen's conduct before labour boards, but at a recent hearing he had found him courteous, helpful, and cooperative. Many in the profession wished him well and he hoped that Cohen would be able 'to reestablish himself in the confidence and respect of the public and the profession.' Judge D.J. Cowan saw Cohen somewhat differently: 'He holds definite determined views on certain matters and is not afraid to express his opinion. This is a quality which I admire in anyone ... he has respect for the rights of others and a tolerance towards opinions of those who oppose him.' G.E. Collins thought that Cohen's great skill and experience were a loss to the bar; he noted that he had served with Cohen on a conciliation board which was chaired by the same Judge Plouffe who had convicted Cohen, but Cohen handled this difficult situation.[19] Thomas W. Learie of the Canadian Association of Garment Manufacturers had close contact with Cohen over the years and always found him honourable and trustworthy; in his experience, 'wherever he was engaged on matters which involved employers as well as employees' in the garment industry, he was impartial. Learie regretted Cohen's disbarment but informed the Law Society that the common view among his business associates was that 'Mr. Cohen has suffered and paid for any misbehaviour or mistake on his part' and that it would be fair and in the public interest to permit him to re-establish himself as much as possible.[20]

Two and a half years after his disbarment, the Discipline Committee reported that no unfavourable communications were received, except one anonymous letter, which it did not consider. Because many positive letters about Cohen expressed the view that he had rehabilitated himself, the committee recommended in November 1949 that Cohen be restored as a member of the Law Society. Convocation confirmed its decision on 19 January 1950, and the next day Cohen was reinstated as a barrister and solicitor by Mr Justice Dalton Courtwright Wells, but his KC was not restored.[21] After over four years of fighting a case that had destroyed his health, strained his family relations, and ruined his professional life, a much-chastened J.L.Cohen could go back to practising law.

Cohen received many letters of congratulations. Trade unionist Harvey Ladd wrote: 'We are aware of the very great contribution which you have made in the field of labour affairs and realize that your long experience and understanding of the trade union movement is invaluable in advancing our union organizations.' Judge J.C. Reynolds hoped that 'we will continue to be associated in labour disputes.'[22] Jack Fizel of the Sunshine Fruit Company reflected the views of some who thought there was a malicious basis to the case. 'I have always considered that the action taken against you was done purely through the selfish motives of various interests who were afraid of your ability and did everything they could to discredit you and shut you up.'[23]

Cohen's work at getting reinstated during 1949 had kept him going. Despite his improved health and more positive outlook, he had financial problems and had to swallow his pride and ask people for work. Some correspondence between 1947 and 1950 congratulated past colleagues on their successes – David Lewis on a speech, E.E. Sparrow on becoming chair of the Ontario Workmen's Compensation Board. They responded warmly to his good wishes, but they were moving upwards while Cohen was not, and he must have been frustrated in his isolation.

He tried to earn money by writing, and while some pieces, such as several articles for *Saturday Night* and *Canadian Forum*, were accepted and praised, others, including a small piece for the CCL paper *Canadian Unionist*, were not, and so he experienced another type of rejection.[24] He began various writing projects, including an autobiography, a book on the development of labour legislation in Canada, and an essay on civil liberties, none of which he completed. Some handwritten notes revealed his stressful state and were disturbing: a fictional story about a man who died of cancer, alone and frustrated with life; an essay called 'The Trick of Living'; and an angry, garbled, and increasingly illegible fragment, probably written under the influence of sedatives or alcohol, entitled 'The Hurdy Gurdy of Medicine,' which condemned psychiatrists. He wrote an essay Dostoevsky in which his comments about the Russian writer echoed aspects of his own life. 'Dostoevsky's power to instruct, to inform, to clarify, resulted from his unique intellectual ability,' but his exercise of that faculty was accompanied 'by his own misfortunes and physical ills.' The writer's genius resulted from the interaction of his intellect and his experience and was an instrument that 'supplied the heights from which he surveyed, not the depths to which he descended.' The law had been Cohen's instrument to reach intellectual heights, but his inner tensions, which he tried to overcome, threatened to overwhelm him, and thus he empathized with the Russian author.[25]

He corresponded with Eugene Forsey, the CCL's research director, who encouraged him to write.[26] They discussed constitutional matters when the jurisdiction of governments in the post-war era with regard to an expanded welfare state and new labour legislation was an issue.

Forsey was concerned about uniformity in labour laws and favoured an amendment to the British North America Act to centralize labour issues at the national level. Cohen had suggested that the Canadian Temperance Act provided a precedent. When Forsey praised his article in *Saturday Night* but asked for a specific case reference, Cohen replied that he should have referred to the Canadian Temperance case of January 1946 by name, but 'I have acquired an aversion to the fact that so many Canadian constitutional authorities centre around liquor legislation.'[27] Forsey also consulted constitutional law professor Frank Scott and former prime minister Arthur Meighen on these matters.

Cohen responded to Forsey's newsy letters, sometimes with humour; however, Forsey's sympathy was not enough to help someone as vulnerable as Cohen. Forsey wrote, 'I need hardly say how much I regret that circumstances have for the moment silenced your powerful voice and pen.' Forsey sent Cohen a *Bar Review* article and his congress reports for comments. When Forsey filled in for Pat Conroy at the Council for the Survey of the Legal Profession of Canada, he asked Cohen for ideas, as 'my ignorance on the subject is practically limitless.' He noted that F. Cyril James of McGill University and the new president of the Canadian Bar Association sat on the council, as did a Mr Carter of Saint John, 'who regards trade unions as emanations, not of the Crown but of the Prince of Darkness!'

After his reinstatement, Cohen had to start all over again. Much had changed in labour law since he dropped out in 1945. Unions – partly as a result of Cohen's efforts – had collective-bargaining rights and increasing membership and were negotiating improved collective agreements with employers who, in the context of a booming economy and large profits, were adjusting to the new system. Labour relations were more professional, and labour law was an expanding field with more bright young lawyers entering it on both sides.

Cohen wrote to his old clients to tell them that he was reinstated. Carlin remembered his letter. 'He wanted to know if I still had faith in him and his legal ability, his moral conduct and all the rest of it.'[28] Carlin had no work for him. By 1950, in the Cold War atmosphere, Mine Mill was expelled from the CCL, and Carlin, who had been a CCF MPP, was himself viewed ambivalently by some trade unionists and CCFers for being too close to the Communists. Cohen's past association with the CPC was not an asset. One of the first people to contact Cohen for legal help was Communist leader Sam Carr, who was in the Kingston Penitentiary. Cohen wrote on the letter, 'Forward!' and did not respond.

While Cohen was out of action, unions turned to other labour lawyers, notably Ted Jolliffe, the former Ontario CCF leader, David Lewis, and An drew Brewin. The UAW had no work for Cohen because by the 1950s it had its own full-time legal counsel. When it contracted out work, it used Jolliffe and Charles Dubin. Charlie Millard of the USWA had given Cohen work early in the war but disliked Cohen's association with Communists and was angered when in 1943 he voted with the majority in the NWLB steel case. Thus, the situation had changed considerably in a short period. Years later, Cohen's wife suggested that the labour movement, which provided some work, did not rally around sufficiently, probably because the reason for Cohen's disbarment remained a disgrace and an embarrassment for many. His daughter thought that 'he would have liked to have history repeat itself,' but the 1937 situation in Oshawa was not going to happen in 1950. 'I don't know that people were staying away so much as that things had changed.'[29] For all these reasons, he had little or no work after reinstatement.

Cohen had changed, too. He was still very capable, but at fifty-two, after a long ordeal with stress and humiliation, he lacked the stamina and energy that he had in the war years. He had shed his old arrogance, which had been a sign of his basic insecurity, but he had lost confidence as well and had no greater sense of self-worth. Cohen approached his old friend Sam Gotfrid about forming a partnership, but Gotfrid refused. He had a successful practice, and he knew that Cohen was demanding and might be a liability. As he said, 'With Cohen you were always second.' So Cohen opened a new office in downtown Toronto, but he had almost no clients, which must have been galling for him. Having been a labour lawyer for most of his career, it was too late to change specialties. Croll believed that Cohen knew his career was ruined. 'It didn't make any difference what happened because people were prepared to believe the worst about him.'[30] He also could not reconcile his tremendous professional success with his personal undoing, and he had no one to blame but himself.

His reinstatement came too late. In February 1950 Cohen wrote to Attorney General Dana Porter to enquire if, as a result of reinstatement, he had regained his KC. The Law Society was clear that he had not, but Cohen was not sure. He heard nothing and on 10 April wrote a short, sad note saying that, after thinking about the matter, he had decided not to ask for any ruling from Porter and would assume that his KC was terminated. He apologized 'that you were put to any trouble by me in regard to the matter.'[31]

In April, Cohen again had personal trouble when he lost his driving licence for three months for careless driving and was fined fifty dollars and costs in magistrate's court. Constable William Quennell testified that he was driving so fast and so erratically that pedestrians ran 'like sheep being chased by a wolf' and he 'forced automobiles on the sidewalk.'[32] The officer chased him for blocks, and when he caught up to his car he found Cohen groggy and dopey but not inebriated. Onie Brown, acting for Cohen, told the court that Cohen had taken cold tablets and was not wearing his glasses, even though 'he can't see two feet without them.' It is likely that Cohen, depressed and under stress, after being addicted to large doses of drugs for years, had resumed overdosing on medication for relief.[33]

Three years after losing his licence, and four months after his reinstatement in the legal profession, Cohen died suddenly at home on 24 May 1950. He was fifty-three. His conviction for assault ended his legal career. The physical and mental stress of the trial and jail term, as well as the strain of losing financial resources that he had worked so hard to acquire, exhausted him.[34] At the same time, the disbarment, his personal disgrace, and the lengthy struggle to be reinstated in the Law Society had humiliated him. The years of drug abuse at a period when its effects were not well understood, and finally his realization that he could not begin again, were other factors that contributed to his early death, probably a suicide.[35]

Epilogue

J.L. Cohen was an enigma, in that there was a discrepancy between his public life and his private behaviour. People who remembered him attributed his downfall to a range of causes from a nervous breakdown to drug abuse to an immoral character. Most admired him; many disliked him, but they all agreed that as a lawyer he was an effective professional and a committed defender of disadvantaged people, the working class, and trade unions. His obituary in the *Globe and Mail* described him as a dynamic, sharp-witted man, who rose from humble beginnings to become the most influential labour lawyer in Canada. 'Wherever there was a strike, wherever there were strike negotiations or wherever there was a labour dispute, almost invariably J.L. Cohen appeared on the scene, until he became known simply as the labour lawyer.'[1] Following the celebrated 1937 Oshawa strike at General Motors, Cohen 'appeared in almost every major labour dispute in Canada,' and, in addition to his growing labour practice, he argued many civil-liberties cases. The obituary concluded with what may be a fitting epitaph for Cohen, 'He championed all the wrong people in all the right things.'

The news of Cohen's death resulted in a flood of condolences from many quarters – unions, some employers, civil servants, and Charles P. McTague, former chair of the NWLB. Some letters were more personal than others. A Jannes Lee wrote to Mrs Cohen, 'The suddenness is so terribly shocking ... I understand why you could never give up fighting for him.' Alma Simpson remembered Cohen when he worked in

J.P. White's office, and agreed with the rabbi at the funeral that 'Mr. Cohen was a friend of man.' Seymour Hermant wrote, 'He was widely held in great esteem by everyone in the profession ... not only as the greatest Canadian Labour Counsel but also as a great man in general.'

Most people expressed shock at Cohen's sudden death. Rohama Lee, editor of *Film News* in New York, tried to understand the reason for it. She told Mrs Cohen that she had not seen him for years, 'but I remember him so well as a young Judaea leader and as a brilliant mind. Life is cruel to the brilliant minded man. It gives him something wonderful, then uses that very wonderful thing against himself.' Letters such as CCL leader A.R. Mosher's recognized the 'great debt of gratitude' that the labour movement owed Cohen for his service. The formal communication from the advisory committee of the Ontario Men's and Boy's Clothing Industry accurately recalled Cohen's role as its solicitor. 'Mr. Cohen's contribution to the establishment of the Industrial Standards Act and the procedure under it was of paramount importance to all those it seeks to serve ... He exhibited a knowledge of law that placed him in the category of Canada's outstanding members of the legal profession.'

One of the most touching letters arrived from Eugene Forsey, the CCL's research director, an inveterate letter writer to the *Globe and Mail*, and later a senator. He was genuinely shocked by Cohen's death, which he grieved, since he had not realized that Cohen's health was so precarious. Cohen probably had many friends of longer standing, he wrote, but he doubted that any 'liked and admired him more than I did.' Forsey had been kind to Cohen when his reputation was under a cloud, they stimulated each other intellectually, and they had long conversations on train journeys to Nova Scotia. Forsey spoke of his 'fine mind, richly stored'; he found Cohen a brilliant conversationalist, a charming and stimulating companion, with only one basic fault – 'he worked himself to death, literally and metaphorically. All the tragedies of the last few years came from that; and the greatest tragedy is that he did not live to regain and surpass his old position.' Forsey recognized his contribution and commitment to the labour movement and concluded, 'He was a great lawyer, a great leader, a great Canadian and a great friend.' He paid tribute to Mrs Cohen, 'the most devoted of wives,' who supported him in his career and 'in the great tribulations of his life.'[2] There were no letters from J.J.Robinette or Arthur A. MacDonald, those closely associated with Cohen in his troubled final years, although Sam Gotfrid did Mrs Cohen's legal work concerning the will.

Cohen's funeral service was held at the H. Benjamin and Son Funeral Chapel on Toronto's Spadina Avenue, the scene of so many of his cases in the 1920s.[3] He left his wife, Dorothy, who had stayed with him in the humiliating and heart-breaking final years, and his devoted daughter, Phyllis Clarke, who later deposited his papers in the National Archives in Ottawa and who, like her father, was political but more partisan, running in 1962 as a Communist Party candidate.[4] Cohen's mother and siblings also outlived him.

A PROFESSIONAL LEGACY

Cohen left a professional legacy that consisted of substantial legal jurisprudence in labour law, contract language in many collective agreements, grievance/arbitration decisions, conciliation-board reports, and Ontario Labour Court and NWLB cases and decisions. He influenced administrative practice in industrial-standards advisory committees, and articulated civil-liberties principles before wartime tribunals and standards of public accountability for politicians and police. The modern labour-relations system is administered by labour-relations boards and industrial-standards tribunals of which he was in part an architect. In the process, he educated many workers in local unions and trade-union leaders of growing organizations about a labour-relations system in which their role was expanding.

The industrial-relations system that J.L. Cohen helped create remains a part of our political democracy. Those who support collective bargaining – the labour movement, progressive politicians, public opinion, and labour-relations experts on mostly tripartite labour boards or in conciliation and arbitration processes – have developed a distinctive legal culture which supports workers' independent representation in the workplace and the regulation of employer-employee relations to promote harmony and fairness. Cohen would have approved.

He would have been surprised that as the system evolved constitutionally on a decentralized basis, the 'balkanization' of standards that Cohen and others feared did not develop despite some regional variations, which are largely the result of different provincial political cultures. The Canadian system has protected collective-bargaining rights better than the American system, judging by the levels of current union membership in both countries, because Canadian privative clauses have kept the courts at arm's length, whereas courts in the United States have undermined collective bargaining. Since the Charter of Rights and Freedoms, the courts have had the ability to become more involved, but so far they have been reluctant to interfere with labour-relations tribunals. Canadian boards have not been politicized, as has the American National Labor Relations Board, and have remained 'independent,' as Cohen argued the NWLB should be. The Canadian system may also have succeeded better in fulfilling its purpose than the American, in part, perhaps because of Mackenzie King's delay of collective bargaining until the public strongly supported it, and in part too, perhpas because King's insistence on even-handed language covering unions and employers in the legislation prevented the employer backlash that occurred in the United States after the war – a backlash that resulted in the national Taft-Hartley Act 1947 and states' right-to-work laws. This historical irony would have bemused Cohen.

Today, collective-bargaining legislation remains as essential for the labour movement as it did in Cohen's time, but it is being weakened by conservative politicians serving particularly hostile employers. Collective bargaining is still debated in the academy, where some oppose it or are ambivalent about it; some support it unequivocally; and others endorse it but are so pessimistic about its future in the United States that they are revisiting notions about cooperation in non-union representation plans that are reminiscent of Mackenzie King's Rockefeller Plan, which in essence aimed to displace unions. Cohen, of course, would have been appalled by such ideas.

Cohen's work and the historical origins of the Canadian industrial-relations system have been forgotten, neglected, or misunderstood, and this study has sought to rectify that loss of historical memory. This loss results partly from the theory of 'the post-war settlement,' a term not used in Cohen's day but developed by political scientists who have examined the role of the state and the emergence of the labour-relations system. With the benefit of hindsight, they argue that P.C. 1003 and its successor legislation undermined militant organization, deradicalized the union movement, and contained conflict because it sought to discourage strikes and institutionalize labour conflicts to ensure industrial peace. Workers, they conclude, in achieving certified unions and collective-bargaining rights, were confined and manipulated by legal rules and procedures, which restricted picketing and secondary boycotts, banned strikes during the term of a collective agreement, controlled and structured conflict, and co-opted labour to fulfil the objectives of capital. They minimize the role of employees and depict union leaders as 'agents of social control,' and they are critical of the human-resource-management approach taught in business schools and the increasingly legalistic labour-relations environment. Their views have not gone unchallenged. Paul Weiler, for example, has suggested that collective bargaining is more participatory than its critics concede. Those who 'dismiss the process as consisting only of a remote union bureaucracy negotiating a complicated contract with management, then hiring lawyers to fight grievances in front of professional arbitrators,' neglect to mention that workers are involved in union elections, in framing the bargaining agenda, and in strike and ratification votes and play a major role on deciding grievable cases.[5] Such participation was clear from the beginning, when J.L. Cohen taught local unionists about what he called 'the trade union way.'

Some Canadian working-class historians have imposed the 'post-war settlement' argument on the historical evidence, an approach that makes them selective about what they look for, report, and evaluate as significant.[6] The 'post-war settlement' analysis does not reflect workers' views during the war. They understood that, even when organized, they were not as powerful as employers. Nevertheless, they demanded greater consultation in industry, independent representation, grievance procedures on the shop floor, protective collective-bargaining legislation, and 'union security' to support the continuation of viable labour organizations after the war. They achieved these goals, which together they called 'industrial democracy.' With collective bargaining, employees were included in some decisions in industry, and with the new legal framework, they had some protection from antagonistic employers. The context was a society with a power imbalance between employers and workers, in which, briefly, the war economy created a labour shortage and gave organized workers some leverage to improve conditions. A generation that endured the Great Depression was motivated to act.

In any evaluation of what workers achieved, it is important to judge the worth of the system against the choices available to the participants at that time. Set against the example of the New Deal's Wagner Act, Mackenzie King's conciliation legislation without collective bargaining and employers' opposition to any unions were not acceptable alternatives. Historians need to consider whether the labour movement judged wisely its options, and whether the outcome was desirable in the context of the times and in light of the alternatives and the likelihood of achieving them. This approach is preferable to lamenting the lack of a radical labour movement or judging the worth of a system against some hypothetical model, which was probably unrealistic and unattainable. A factor that contributed to the permanence of these developments was the emergence after the war of greater state involvement in all aspects of the economy, including labour relations and the social-welfare system.

In stressing workers' containment and co-option, the 'post-war settlement' argument minimizes workers' struggles for change, the difficulties they faced when trying to organize, and existing power relationships. Employers, then as now, did not embrace the collective-bargaining system but battled it resolutely. Historically, industrial unions, in particular, could not achieve collective bargaining without legislation, which by 1942 both labour congresses advocated, and when workers took concerted action for admittedly 'reformist' goals through wartime strikes and political action, they sought to replace a situation in which workers had no rights whatsoever. Those who emphasize 'the incorporative aspects of industrial relations' and the desire of employers and the state to establish 'containable labour relations' seem to assume that volcanic working-class spontaneity that could usher in 'workers' control' or transform society was undermined, even though there is not much evidence of it. They overstate the inhibiting effect of the law, in that the legislative framework did not halt a strike wave in 1946 for higher pay and an end to wage controls. As Christopher Schenk told a conference on the fiftieth anniversary of P.C. 1003, 'As important as labour law is therefore, to see it as the determining factor in shaping modern unionism may well mean writing out of history some of the major struggles that occurred between workers and employers, and periodically between the union rank and file and its leadship.'[7]

During the Second World War, workers believed that they were making gains, not being contained, and that was certainly J.L. Cohen's perspective. If legal rights meant some restrictions, it was better than no rights at all, and union recognition by employers and written agreements were seen as achievements. As Schenk remarks, there 'needs to be some realization that written contracts ... were as much a product of rank and file activity in the 1930s and 1940s, as were sit-down strikes, other forms of work stoppage, stewards' organizations, seniority etc.'[8] 'Industrial democracy,' as Cohen defined it, increased consultation with management and workers' representation on tripartite committees and decreased managers' arbitrariness compared to the past. Management rights were retained, but collective bargaining and particularly the grievance procedure compelled the employer at least to share information and partly suspend the 'managerial prerogative' in the decision-making process in the shop.

Another aspect of the 'post-war settlement' argument is that, with a labour-relations framework, unions became bureaucratic (meaning larger, conservative, and inactive), although in the prosperous 1950s and 1960s other institutions grew as well.[9] Developments like increased union membership, union-security clauses, automatic dues check-offs, and purges of Communist-led unions during the Cold War strengthened a labour movement which, it is claimed, was committed to 'business unionism' (defined as taking a systematic approach to servicing members' needs, not as acting like a business). Yet the fact remains that in Canada many unions also remained involved in political and social issues.[10] Moreover, the bureaucratization aspect of the post-war settlement argument can degenerate into an unsubtle attack on 'labour bosses,' vocabulary that is similar to those who oppose unions and collective bargaining.[11] Politically, such scholars contribute to the ever-present criticism of workers' organizations by business and the media, and indeed, the language of critics of the left and right is often identical. Proponents of the post-war settlement do not take account of the historical reality that leaders of the industrial unions came out of the plant; they were workers too, not separate from their members, and they ignored the 'pressure of the membership' at their peril.[12] The question is, are unions bureaucratic and unresponsive to their members compared to other types of organization? Probably not, and certainly not in the historical period of the 1930s and 1940s.

Government regulation did lead to a more legalistic labour-relations system. Lawyers became more active players because the quasi-judicial character of the labour boards and arbitration panels and occasional appeals of board decisions to the courts created a growing jurisprudence in labour law. Insecure employers brought lawyers into negotiations, and unions that still utilized their own officials reluctantly but increasingly followed suit. Nevertheless, Canadian arbitral jurisprudence, particularly in discipline and dismissal cases, would define workers' rights, and the procedures and behaviour of arbitrators often contributed to educating management 'in good labour relations practice.'[13]

The law schools responded by introducing labour-law courses. Law journals published labour articles, commercial services reported board and court decisions, and a specialized bar emerged – divided between those serving employers and those working for unions. Collective-bargaining agreements developed from simple documents to longer and more formal contracts with guarded and technical language, but written union contracts – an outcome of working-class self-organization – remained important for developing protective practices, despite increased 'professionalization' of the collective-bargaining process. Finally, centralization should not be overstated, for the collective-bargaining system to this day maintains its local focus, which makes it less useful in establishing societal norms and may have to change in the new economy.

The existing collective-bargaining system has its limits, partly because it is a majoritarian model that sometimes overlooks individual or sectional interests, although the right to fair-representation clauses in most legislation seeks to protect minorities. The existence of collective agreements and labour laws could delay working-class conflicts, but to workers who lived through the Depression and war crises, the labour reforms represented an improvement from a time when there were no unions, contracts, or grievance procedures – a situation that also limited their actions. They had learned that, without legislation, employers could delay matters indefinitely and impede organizing efforts. Without a union or a collective agreement, workers could be as radical, militant, or spontaneous as they liked and get fired too with no legal recourse. Thus, it was important to workers that the government commitment to collective bargaining was maintained after the war and was relatively permanent. Their determination to ensure a continuation of wartime gains accounts for the strike wave of 1946.

In sum, the post-war settlement argument lacks historical evidence to make it supportable in its current form, and it also lacks an understanding of the labour-relations system as it developed in Cohen's time or as it functions now.[14] J.L. Cohen, like trade unionists of his era and those of today, viewed collective bargaining as a right and a legal framework as essential for workers to achieve improved conditions of work and a new social status.

And it is precisely because of his great contributions in making the labour-relations system a reality that the labour movement and the legal profession have remembered Cohen. Albert Hearn, a former Teamster's organizer, recalled, thirty years after Cohen's death, that 'Cohen left a real hole after he died because there was an awful lot of people who felt that if there was one guy who could present a case for you, represent you with feeling, as sort of a true representative of working class people, it was J.L. There was a lot of respect for other people, David Lewis, Charles Dubin, and others, but they were a different breed. They'd come out of law school, they hadn't been on the firing line in the tough old days of the thirties and early forties.'[15]

Personally, despite his incredibly active life, J.L. Cohen remained a loner within the legal profession, the Jewish community, and socially. He felt most comfortable in smoke-filled meeting rooms of men, counselling workmen and their leaders or arguing with businessmen and other lawyers on a client's behalf. His difficult, prickly, public personality only hinted at the neurotic inner person, which remained hidden until he had to expose it to win reinstatement in his profession. He suffered from obsessions and compulsions about his work; he lived with phobias about airplanes, heights, and being alone, partly because he was traumatized by the death of his father in his youth, which resulted in a difficult adolescence with many burdens. He abused alcohol and drugs and, in his last days, women. He was psychologically unstable, without balance or moderation, and when he tried to change his habits, he could do so only briefly. He struggled to regain his health, and his position in his beloved profession, but he failed to regain his reputation.

He was an imperfect character, but as a result of long, hard years of overwork, he made a formidable contribution to the growth of the modern labour movement, the development of labour law and labour relations in Canada, the emergence and administration of industrial-standards legislation, and the protection of civil liberties. His accomplishments were all the more impressive given that he undoubtedly faced discrimination and hostility from various sources because he was an immigrant, a Jew, and a radical. In the course of his career, he helped many people. One lawyer, who had refused to support actively Cohen's reinstatement as a solicitor, commented, 'It was too bad an otherwise brilliant man could have his whole career spoiled by something apart and separate from his vocation.'[16] But that something resulted partly from harsh experiences early in life, from the heavy responsibilities that all men in the culture of his day were expected to carry, and also from personality traits that prevented him from dealing constructively with his problems. As a result of his behaviour in 1945, he was ostracized in his profession and even by his clients in the end. He was an authentic tragic figure – the exceptional man with great talents whose flaws became his undoing.

We should perhaps conclude this story where it began. In 1953 J.L. Cohen's mother published memoirs of her early life, as she grieved over the loss of her eldest child. Esther wrote, 'There is always meaning to the destiny of each individual. Aspiration is part of being human. A human being is never satisfied with what he is or has. He always seeks something new. If he can't find it close by, he seeks it elsewhere. Sometimes he seeks it in distant lands or merely in another neighbourhood. But always he imagines that 'the grass is greener on the other side of the fence.' And sometimes it is. But I have always felt that whatever just precedes us, whether good or ill, can never be avoided no matter how we run and seek 'good luck' elsewhere. We carry our future in us.'[17] She was thinking of her roving husband, who drowned in Canada and left her with six children to raise, but the comment applied equally to her son's misadventure in the Kirkland Lake hotel, which set in motion events that culminated in his early death.

Notes

Introduction

1 On the relief system, for example, see James Struthers, *No Fault of Their Own: Unemployment and the Canadian Welfare State, 1914–41* (Toronto: University of Toronto Press 1983); on the Canadian social-welfare system, see Raymond B. Blake and Jeff Keshen, eds., *Social Welfare Policy in Canada: Historical Readings* (Toronto: Copp Clark 1995).

2 Old age pensions were enacted in 1926 in a minority-government situation when CCF leader J.S.Woodsworth manipulated them out of Prime Minister Mackenzie King; the Family Allowances Act passed in 1944; and Canada's medicare system, influenced by the medical plan in Saskatchewan under Premier T.C. Douglas's CCF government, took shape under the Canada Health Act, 1965.

3 Peter H. Irons, *The New Deal Lawyers* (Princeton, N.J.: Princeton University Press 1982), 10. A disproportionate number of these lawyers were Jews and Catholics compared to the overall composition of the American legal profession.

4 Politicians who focus on privatization, deregulation, and tax cuts have faced persistent public support for spending in areas of health care and education.

5 David Kettler, James Struthers, and Christopher Huxley, 'Unionization and Labour Regimes in Canada and the United States: Considerations for Comparative Research,' *Labour/Le Travail*: 1 25 (spring 199).176.

6 Alvin Finkel, 'The Cold War, Alberta Labour, and the Social Credit Regime,'

in L.S. MacDowell and Ian Radforth, eds, *Canadian Working Class History: Selected Readings* (Toronto: Canadian Scholars' Press 1992), 644.

7 Christopher Schenk. 'Fifty Years After P.C. 1003: The Need for New Directions,' paper presented at P.C. 1003 Conference, University of Manitoba, 1994, 4.

8 Catherine Hall, *White, Male and Middle Class: Explorations in Feminism and History* (New York: Routledge 1996). The historiography on masculinity is discussed in this work.

9 Michael Kimmel, *Manhood in America: A Cultural History* (New York: Free Press, 1996), 192; R.W. Connell, *Masculinities* (Cambridge, Mass.: Polity Press 1995), 28.

10 Michael Grossberg, 'Institutionalizing Masculinity: The Law as a Masculine Profession,' in Mark Carnes and Clyde Grifen, eds, *Meanings for Manhood: Constructions of Masculinity in Victorian America* (Chicago: University of Chicago Press 1990), 133–51; Cecilia Morgan, 'An Embarrasingly and Severely Masculine Atmosphere': Women, Gender and the Legal Profession at Osgoode Hall, 1920s–1960s,' *Canadian Journal of Law and Society,* 11, no. 2 (fall 1996), 19–61.

11 Gender intersects with race and class so that working-class masculinity may not be identical to middle-class masculinity. Borrowing the concept of hegemony from Gramsci's analysis of class relations, theorists of masculinity have developed notions of dominant and subordinate masculinities. Both categories of men are dominant in relation to women but those who are dominant because of their socio-economic position are more powerful than marginalized men who are subordinate because of their class, race, ethnicity, and so on. Viewed from this perspective, Cohen was subordinate (as a Jew from a working-class background) to his peers on the Law Society's committees (who were WASP and middle class). Connell, *Masculinities,* 77–82; Michael S. Kimmel, 'Judaism, Masculinity and Feminism,' in Michael S.Kimmel and Michael A. Messner, *Men's Lives* (Needham Heights, Mass.: Allyn and Bacon 1995), 42–4.

Chapter 1: The Making of a Lawyer

1 Author's interview with J.B. Salsberg, summer 1980.

2 Stephen A. Speisman, *The Jews of Toronto: A History to 1937* (Toronto: McClelland and Stewart 1979), 69.

3 Esther Cohen, *Esther's Story: The Reminiscences of Esther Kreengle-Bach Cohen* (Toronto: Arcadian Press 1953), 45. The references to her early life are covered in the first part of her memoirs, especially on pages 8, 13, 22, 24, 26, 32, and 39.

4 David Michael Estok, 'All the Wrong People: The Trial and Career of Labour Lawyer J.L. Cohen,' Master of Journalism thesis, Carleton University 1981, chap.3.
5 Esther Cohen, *Esther's Story*, 78.
6 Gerald Tulchinsky, *Taking Root: The Origins of the Canadian Jewish Community* (Toronto: Lester Publishing 1992), xxiv.
7 Speisman, *Jews of Toronto*, 71, 76n.5.
8 Ibid., 82; Tulchinsky, *Taking Root*, 173.
9 Esther Cohen, *Esther's Story*, 78, 83.
10 Tulchinsky, *Taking Root*, 173, 229.
11 Ibid., xvi.
12 Speisman, *Jews of Toronto*, 72.
13 Tulchinsky, *Taking Root*, 162.
14 Rosemary Donevan, *Spadina Avenue* (Toronto: Douglas and McIntyre 1985).
15 Esther Cohen, *Esther's Story*, 89.
16 Ibid., 94.
17 Esther Cohen, 'The Years Following the Death of Philip ...,' unpublished manscript, 8.
18 Esther Cohen, *Esther's Story*, 30, 31.
19 Ibid., 32.
20 Many left-wing Jews were secular in this sense, including Joe Salsberg and David Lewis.
21 Esther Cohen, 'The Years ...,' 19.
22 Ibid. On the subject of Zionism in the Canadian Jewish community, see Tulchinsky, *Taking Root*, xix–xxiv.
23 Speisman, *Jews of Toronto*, 73.
24 Esther Cohen, 'The Years ...,' 17, 21.
25 On a panel in the Law Society reception area, Cohen's name is listed for the year 1918 after that of H.A. Hall, who won the gold medal, and Benjamin Luxenberg, winner of the silver medal.
26 Esther Cohen, 'The Years ...,' 27.
27 Christopher Moore, *The Law Society of Upper Canada and Ontario Lawyers, 1797–1997* (Toronto: Osgoode Society and University of Toronto Press 1997), 196, 200.
28 Speisman, *Jews of Toronto*, 122. Speisman discusses the stereotype of an eastern European Jew as an exotic, poor, boisterous pedlar; Tulchinsky, *Taking Root*, 238. 'Antisemitism was part of Canada's general culture in the late nineteenth and early twentieth century.'
29 Moore, *Law Society*, 200.
30 Tulchinsky, *Taking Root*, 241. In 1920, 40 per cent of McGill's law students

were Jewish but the university reduced its percentage of Jewish students severely in the interwar years.

31 Speisman, *Jews of Toronto*, 119–20.
32 Moore, *Law Society*, 201.
33 R. Warren James, *The People's Senator: The Life and Times of David A. Croll* (Vancouver: Douglas and McIntyre, 1990), 12.
34 Speisman, *Jews of Toronto*, 304.
35 I. Abella, 'Anti-Semitism in Canada in the Interwar Years,' in Moses Rischin, ed., *The Jews in North America* (Detroit: Wayne State University Press: 1987), 236.
36 Tulchinsky, *Taking Root*, 239–40.
37 He went on to say, 'Laskin is not one of those flashy Jews, and the highest recommendation which I could give him is to say that, in the absence of any overwhelming prejudice and if I had control of a decent faculty, I would have no hesitation in placing Laskin.' Jerome E. Bickenbach, 'Lawyers, Law Professors, and Racism in Ontario, ' *Queen's Quarterly* 96, no. 3 (autumn 1989), 595.
38 Speisman, *Jews of Toronto*, 127. Two of Cohen's brothers changed their names probably to avoid discrimination. Lewis became Lewis Merrill and went to New York to live, and for some time organized in the CIO industrial-union movement. Abraham Isaac Cohen in 1928 became Alfred Charles Cowan after he was turned down for a job the previous year. (Conversation between the author and John Scott Cowan December 2000).
39 Bickenbach, 'Lawyers,' 593–5.
40 Ibid., 593.
41 Estok, 'All the Wrong People,' 36.
42 Esther Cohen, 'The Years ...,' 27.
43 L. Betcherman, *This Little Band* (Ottawa: Deneau 1976), 128.
44 C. Ian Kyer and Jerome E. Bickenbach, *The Fiercest Debate: Cecil A. Wright, the Benchers, and Legal Education in Ontario 1923–1957* (Toronto: Osgoode Society and University of Toronto Press 1987), 115.
45 Note, for example, the role played by Mackenzie King in a miners' strike; see William M. Baker, 'The Miners and the Mediator: The 1906 Lethbridge Strike and Mackenzie King,' in L.S. MacDowell and Ian Radforth, eds., *Canadian Working Class History: Selected Readings* (Toronto: Canadain Scholars' Press 1992), 383–407.
46 Finkelman also taught a course in administrative law. Calendars, University of Toronto, 1930–47; President's Reports, 1930–47, University of Toronto Archives.
47 File11, vol. 50, J.L. Cohen Papers, NA. The file is titled 'Mrs. Dorothy Cohen –

Personal Correspondence from the Soviet Union primarily in Russian 1923–39.' She sent a sister a loan so that she could buy a house.

48 Esther Cohen, 'The Years ...,' 29.

49 Stephen Speisman, 'Antisemitism in Ontario: The Twentieth Century,' in Alan Davies, ed., *Antisemitism in Canada: History and Interpretation* (Waterloo: Wilfrid Laurier University Press 1992), 118.

50 Moore, *Law Society,* 196.

51 Letter to Donia, 27 March 1926, file 11, vol. 50, J.L. Cohen Papers, NA.

52 *The Canada Law List*, 1920–35.

53 Esther Cohen, 'The Years ...,' 32.

54 J. Kerns(?), Santa Monica, California, to Donia, n.d., file: Mrs. Dorothy Cohen – Misc. Personal Correspondence 1938–51, vol. 50, J.L. Cohen Papers, NA.

55 File: Mrs. Dorothy Cohen–Misc. personal correspondence, n.d., 1938–51, vol. 50, J.L. Cohen Papers, NA.

56 Tulchinsky, *Taking Root*, 261.

57 Estok, 'All the Wrong People,' 40.

58 Carolyn Cox, 'J.L. Cohen Has a Philosophy,' *Saturday Night* (26 June 1943.

59 Nicola Sacco and Bartolomeo Vanzetti were convicted of murder and a payroll robbery in August 1920, although they protested their innocence. Many believed that they were being persecuted for being radicals and immigrant workers, and widespread protests lasted for seven years until their execution. New York *Times*, 4 August 1927.

60 J.L. Cohen, *Mothers' Allowance Legislation in Canada* (Toronto: Macmillan 1927), 4, 13–15, 20, 105–14. For a historical treatment of this legislation, see Veronica Strong-Boag, 'Wages for Housework: Mothers' Allowances and the Beginnings of Social Security in Canada,' *Journal of Canadian Studies*, 14, no. 1 (spring 1979): 24–34.

61 File 2, vol. 1, J.L. Cohen Papers, NA. It did not last long, since Cohen became too busy.

62 J.L. Cohen, ed., *Mr. Woodsworth's Speeches* (Toronto: Canadian Brotherhood of Railway Employees 1929), 6.

63 Estok, 'All the Wrong People,' 5.

64 William Kaplan, *Another Man's Salvation: Jehovah's Witnesses and Their Fight for Civil Rights* (Toronto: University of Toronto Press 1989), 79.

65 Betcherman, *This Little Band*, 69.

66 Estok, 'All the Wrong People,' 5; 6.

67 Kaplan, *Another Man's Salvation*, 60.

68 Estok, 'All the Wrong People,' 9.

69 Kaplan, *Another Man's Salvation*, 79.

70 Estok, 'All the Wrong People,' 7.

Chapter 2: Lawyer for the Communist Party, 1927–1931

1 In 1919 there were 378,000 union members in Canada. By 1921, the number had declined by 27, 000, and thereafter membership continued to fall during the 1920s. After 1919, with a decrease in strike activity, time loss due to strikes 'was practically back to the average of the past 20 years.' G.S. Bain and Robert Price, *Profiles in Union Growth* (London: Oxford University Press 1980), 14; *Labour Gazette* (February 1921), 164; (March 1922), 289.

2 H.M. Grant, 'Solving the Labour Problem at Imperial Oil: Welfare Capitalism in the Canadian Petroleum Industry, 1919–1929,' *Labour/Le Travail*, 41 (Spring 1998), 69–95; L.S. MacDowell, 'Company Unionism in Canada 1915–1948,' in B. Kaufman and D. Taras, eds, *Non-Union Employee Representation: History, Contemporary Practice and Policy* (Armonk N.Y.: M.E. Sharpe 2000).

3 Ian Angus, *Canadian Bolsheviks: The Early Years of the CPC* (Montreal: Vanguard 1981), chap. 7. Angus is critical of the twists and turns of Communist policy in the period from the late 1920s to the late 1940s.

4 The CPC was evicted without notice from an office building that it rented from the Sterling Trust, and Cohen looked into the matter. File 1, vol. 1, J.L. Cohen Papers, NA.

5 File 2, vol. 49, J.L. Cohen Papers, NA. Near the end of his life, Cohen began outlines for many writing projects. To my delight, when I had nearly finished this study, I discovered that he wrote out a table of contents for a proposed book on his own legal career and prepared a few pages on the early period. It was interesting to see what he considered important and the pattern of his practice from his perspective, and to my relief his outline was similar to my own but of course excluded his disbarment and reinstatement.

6 Lida-Rose Betcherman, *The Little Band* (Ottawa: Deneau 1976), 69.

7 Pat Sullivan, *Red Sails on the Great Lakes* (Toronto: Macmillan 1955), 118.

8 David Michael Estok, 'All the Wrong People: The Trial and Career of Labour Lawyer, J.L. Cohen,' Master of Journalism thesis, Carleton University, Ottawa, 1981, 49–50.

9 Author's conversation with Joe Salsberg, summer 1980.

10 Other progressive lawyers included J.G. O'Donoghue (1910s) and W.T.J. Lee, who later became a judge. In early twentieth-century Toronto, the firm of O'Donoghue, Harkin and Lee was known for its labour work.

11 In 1930 the CLDL hired Cohen to assist when Customs held up allegedly seditious CPC literature from Britain on the labour movement. Similar material had entered for years without interference. Cohen's intervention was successful. File 12, vol. 1, J.L. Cohen Papers, NA.

12 Fred Rose was convicted of vagrancy in 1929. File 7, vol. 1, J.L. Cohen Papers,

NA. He led the CPC in Montreal, was elected MP for Montreal-Cartier in a by-election in 1943 and re-elected in the general election in 1945, was convicted of espionage in 1946, lived in Poland for many years, and died there. Reg Whitaker and Gary Marcuse, *Cold War Canada: The Making of a National Insecurity State, 1945–1957* (Toronto: University of Toronto Press 1994), 294. His family was given permission to bury him in Canada. He was cremated abroad, and his ashes were shipped to Canada, where they remained in journalist Merrily Weisbord's cupboard until a suitable resting place was located. M. Weisbord, *The Strangest Dream: Canadian Communists, the Spy Trials and the Cold War* (Montreal: Vehicule Press 1994), preface. Harvey Murphy led the British Columbia district of Mine Mill in the 1940s.

13 Ian Angus, *Canadian Bolsheviks*, 261–2.

14 Estok, 'All the Wrong People,' 47.

15 Betcherman, *The Little Band*, 47.

16 Ibid., 48.

17 Ibid., 52; the United Farmers of Ontario/Independent Labour Party government was the first Ontario government that was neither Liberal nor Conservative.

18 Estok, 'All the Wrong People,' 49.

19 Betcherman, *The Little Band*, 70; trial transcript, 14, 45, file 11, vol. 1, J.L. Cohen Papers, NA.

20 File 5, vol. 1, J.L. Cohen Papers, NA; Betcherman, *The Little Band*, 71.

21 Cohen said, 'Waiving the right to put in evidence does not rule out the right to argue against the evidence of the crown.' Betcherman, *The Little Band*, 73.

22 File 7, vol. 1, J.L. Cohen Papers, NA.

23 Ibid., 75.

24 File 6, vol. 1, J.L. Cohen Papers, NA.

25 Betcherman, *The Little Band*, 76.

26 Estok, 'All the Wrong People,' 51.

27 Betcherman, *The Little Band*, 76, 77.

28 Trial transcript, 3, file 6, vol. 1, J.L. Cohen Papers, NA.

29 J.L. Cohen to J.S. Woodsworth, 15 November, file 6, vol. 1, J.L. Cohen Papers, NA. In court, Cohen told the judge that section 98 had been 'enacted in 1919 in a moment of panic.'

30 Files 8 and 9, vol. 1, J.L. Cohen Papers, NA.

31 Betcherman, *The Little Band*, 83.

32 Brief to the Royal Commission appointed to Investigate the Action of the Police in Toronto, 24 January 1936, file 2468, vol. 4, J.L. Cohen Papers, NA.

33 Betcherman, *The Little Band*, 85; file 8, vol. 1, J.L. Cohen Papers, NA.

34 File 6, vol. 1, J.L. Cohen Papers, NA; Betcherman, *The Little Band*, 112.

35 Ian Angus, *Canadian Bolsheviks*, 262.
36 Ibid., 270.
37 Betcherman, *The Little Band*, 84.
38 Ibid., 82; I. Abella and H. Troper, *None Is Too Many* (Toronto: Lester and Orpen Dennys 1982), discusses the anti-Semitic attitudes of Canadian officials and politicians, which adversely affected immigration policy concerning Jews in the 1930s.
39 Betcherman, *The Little Band*, 120; files 16 and 20, vol. 1, J.L. Cohen Papers, NA.
40 Betcherman, *The Little Band*, 121.
41 J.L. Cohen to G.R. Byers, 4 June 1930, file 16, vol. 1, J.L. Cohen Papers, NA.
42 Betcherman, *The Little Band*, 124.
43 Ibid., 125.
44 J.L. Cohen to CLDL, 30 August 1930, file 22, vol. 1, J.L. Cohen Papers, NA.
45 Section 98 was 'notorious' because it was passed during the Winnipeg General Strike to facilitate arrests. It was unpopular with persons on the left.
46 Estok, 'All the Wrong People,' 54.
47 Joel Seidman, *The Needle Trades* (New York: Farrar and Reinhart 1942), chap. 9.
48 Ronald Adams, 'The 1931 Arrest and Trial of the Leaders of the Communist Party of Canada,' Canadian Historical Association paper, 1977, 20.
49 Betcherman, *The Little Band*, 178.
50 J.L. Cohen to CLDL, 19 January 1931; J.L. Cohen to A.E. Smith, 28 April 1931; A.E. Smith to J.L. Cohen, 6 May 1931, file 22, vol. 1, J.L. Cohen Papers, NA.
51 Gregory S. Kealey and Reg Whitaker, *RCMP Security Bulletins: The Early Years 1919–1939* (St John's: Committee on Canadian Labour History 1994), 15–19; 438. J.L. Cohen's personal file was no. 2885.
52 Satu Repo, 'Rosvall and Voutilainen: Two Union Men Who Never Died,' *Labour/Le Travail*, nos. 8 and 9 (1981–2), 82, 83; the strike is discussed in Ian Radforth, *Bush Workers and Bosses: Logging in Northern Ontario, 1900–1980* (Toronto: University of Toronto Press 1987), 120–4.
53 Repo, 'Rosvall and Voutilainen,' 85.
54 Joe Farbey to A.E. Smith, 17 Dec. 1929, file 10, vol. 1, J.L. Cohen Papers, NA.
55 Ibid., 87.
56 Joe Farbey to A.E. Smith, 14 Dec. 1929, file 10, vol. 1, J.L. Cohen Papers, NA.
57 Joe Farbey to A.E. Smith, 14 Dec. 1929, file 10, vol. 1, J.L. Cohen Papers, NA.
58 Resolution to the attorney general of Ontario, seven copies from different groups, December 1929, RG4–32, 1929/3738, AO. The groups included the Toronto Women's Labor League; the Left Poale Zion, Winnipeg; the Polish Workers' Association, Winnipeg; the YCL, Winnipeg; several ULFTA groups

from East Kildonan, Manitoba, and Sudbury, Ontario; the LWUC, Vancouver. G.H. McCollum of the National Labour Council of Toronto sent Attorney General W.H. Price a more moderately worded resolution urging further investigation.

59 Joe Farbey to A.E. Smith, 14 Dec. 1929, file 10, vol. 1, J.L. Cohen Papers, NA.
60 Ibid..
61 Cohen to A.R. Mosher, 17 Dec. 1929, file 10, vol. 1, J.L. Cohen Papers, NA.
62 Betcherman, *The Little Band* 51, 162, 163.
63 Attorney general of Ontario to J.L. Cohen, 20 Dec. 1929; a copy of this letter is also in the Attorney General's Papers at the AO; Finlayson to J.L. Cohen, 17 Dec. 1929; 26 Dec. 1929, file 10, vol. 1, J.L. Cohen Papers, NA.
64 Cohen to attorney general of Ontario, 16 Dec. 1929, file 10, vol. 1, J.L. Cohen Papers, NA.
65 Memo to J.L. Cohen, 17 Dec. 1929, file 10, vol. 1, J.L. Cohen Papers, NA.
66 Cohen to Joe Farbey, 21 Dec. 1929, file 10, vol. 1, J.L. Cohen Papers, NA.
67 Joe Farbey to J.L. Cohen, 23 Dec. 1929, file 10, vol. 1, J.L. Cohen Papers, NA.
68 A delegate is a union organizer.
69 Affidavit of Erkki Haara, Aatu Pitkanen, Hjalmar Nummela, 26 Dec. 1929; affidavit of Paavo Vaananen, 26 Dec. 1929; affidavit of Oscar Maijala, 10 Jan. 1930; affidavit of Sulo Lahti, Vaino Pasanen, 26 Dec. 1929, file 10, vol. 1, J.L. Cohen Papers, NA.
70 Cohen to E. Bayly, 4 Jan. 1930, file 10, vol. 1, J.L. Cohen Papers, NA. There was a peculiar contradiction, he pointed out, between Maki's first story and what he later told the police. Twice, Maki told lumbermen John Vallenius and Edward Perkio that he 'was most positive in his assertions that the men did not fall through the ice.' Later Maki told the police that he had warned the men about the ice near the shore and to keep close to the edge. Further investigation would clarify Maki's comments, particularly because, if Maki had followed the two men as he claimed, they would have been in his view. The police investigation had not followed up on that point.
71 E. Bayly to J.L. Cohen, 7 Jan. 1930, file 10, vol. 1, J.L. Cohen Papers, NA.
72 E. Bayly to W. Langworthy, 14 Jan. 1930, RG 4–32, 1929/3738, AO.
73 W.F. Langworthy to E. Bayly, 22 Jan. 1930, RG 4–32, 1929/3738, AO; E. Bayly to J.L. Cohen, 30 Jan. 1930, file 10, vol. 1, J.L. Cohen Papers, NA.
74 Cohen to W. Burford, 11 Jan. 1930, file 10, vol. 1, J.L. Cohen Papers, NA.
75 E. Bayly to G.W. McCollum, 15 Jan. 1930, RG 4–32, 1929/3738, AO.
76 Cohen's notes, n.d., file 10, vol. 1, J.L. Cohen Papers, NA.
77 Repo, 'Rosvall and Voutilainen,' 88.
78 A.T. Hill to comrades, 27 Feb. 1930, file 10, vol. 1, J.L. Cohen Papers, NA.
79 A.E. Smith to Cohen, 28 March 1930, file 10, vol. 1, J.L. Cohen Papers, NA.

80 Constable James Higgins, report on the finding of the body of J. Voutilainen, 23 April 1930, RG 4–32, 1929/3738, AO.
81 LWIU to A.E. Smith, 23 April 1930; A. Hautimaki to A.E. Smith, 25 April 1930, file 10, vol. 1, J.L. Cohen Papers, NA.
82 Report, J.L. Cohen to LWIU, 8 May 1930, file 10, vol. 1, J.L. Cohen Papers, NA.
83 Ibid..
84 G. Sundquist to Cohen, 29 April 1930, file 10, vol. 1, J.L. Cohen Papers, NA.
85 Ibid..
86 Ibid..
87 Repo, 'Rosvall and Voutilainen,' 97.
88 Radforth, *Bushworkers and Bosses*, 124.
89 Repo, 'Rosvall and Voutilainen,' 99–100.
90 Cohen to A.T. Hill, 14 Jan. 1947, file 10, vol. 1, J.L. Cohen Papers, NA.
91 W. Burford to J.L. Cohen, 30 Jan. 1930, file 10, vol. 1, J.L. Cohen Papers, NA.

Chapter 3: Advocate for the Poor, 1927–1939

1 David Michael Estok, 'All the Wrong People: The Trial and Career of Labour Lawyer, J.L. Cohen,' Master of Journalism thesis, Carleton University, 1981, 68; vol. 5, J.L. Cohen Papers, NA. For more information on the Stratford strike, see Desmond Morton, 'Aid to the Civil Power: The Stratford Strike of 1933,' in Irving Abella, ed., *On Strike* (Toronto: James Lewis and Samuel 1974); and James D. Leach, 'The Workers' Unity League and the Stratford Furniture Workers: The Anatomy of a Strike,' *Ontario History* 60 (June, 1968), 39–48.
2 Estok, 'All the Wrong People,' 66, 67; vol. 5, J.L. Cohen Papers, NA. For historical background on the On-to-Ottawa Trek, see Victor Howard, *'We Were the Salt of the Earth': A Narrative of the On-to-Ottawa Trek and the Regina Riot* (Regina: Canadian Plains Research Center 1985); Ronald Liversedge, *Recollections of the On-to-Ottawa Trek*, Victor Hoar, ed., (Toronto: McClelland and Stewart 1973).
3 In York Township, for example, a Canadian Workers' Association of unemployed men in 1930 raised $5,800, which was given to a relief officer to distribute mostly to pay rent. Around the same time the St Catharines and District Workers' Association raised nearly $2,000. H.M. Cassidy, *Unemployment and Relief in Ontario, 1929–1932* (Toronto: Dent 1932), 181, 227, 245.
4 Patricia Schultz, *The Toronto East York Workers' Association* (Toronto: 1975), 14–15.
5 John T. Saywell, *'Just Call Me Mitch': The Life of Mitchell F. Hepburn* (Toronto: University of Toronto Press 1991), 264.
6 File 13, vol. 1, C.S. Jackson Papers, NA. On the ideas and policy surrounding

relief and unemployment insurance, see James Struthers, *No Fault of Their Own: Unemployment and the Canadian Welfare State 1914–1941* (Toronto: University of Toronto Press 1983).

7 File 11, vol. 1, C.S. Jackson Papers, NA.

8 John T. Saywell, *'Just Call Me Mitch,'* 267. The incident is covered in pages 264–7.

9 *Rex* v. *Panus*, in Estok, 'All the Wrong People,' 69; *Rex* v. *Veerman*, vol. 6, J.L. Cohen Papers, NA.

10 Norman Dowd would become the secretary-treasurer of the CCL, and M.M. Maclean would leave the labour movement for the position of director of industrial relations in the Department of Labour.

11 In a contract with Thomas Nelson and Sons, Cohen himself paid for one thousand copies and paid the publisher an additional $35. The publisher sold the book for two dollars a copy and publicized it. Cohen received 20 per cent of the selling price and review copies. The publisher provided an accounting quarterly and held the copyright 'in trust' for the author. File 2236A, vol. 3, J.L. Cohen Papers, NA.

12 Cohen to H. Langer, 19 Sept. 1935, file 2181A, vol. 3, J.L. Cohen Papers, NA.

13 Reviews are contained in file 2236A, vol. 3, J.L. Cohen Papers, NA. The *American Bar Association Journal* was conservative in the context of Roosevelt's New Deal, which was embattled in the courts until 1937 when the Supreme Court upheld the Wagner Act.

14 J. Pochna to Cohen, 19 Jan. 1936; J.L. Cohen to J. Pochna, 22 Jan. 1936, file 2236A, vol. 3, J.L. Cohen Papers, NA.

15 Windsor *Star*, 18 Feb. 1943.

16 The information is taken from extensive correspondence and materials in file 2690, vol. 12, J.L. Cohen Papers, NA.

17 H.C. Hudson to J.L. Cohen, 22 Nov. 1938, file 2690, vol. 12, J.L. Cohen Papers, NA. Hood thought that the legislation would cover about 500,000 insurable persons. Bennett's bill had coverage for an estimated 800,000 in Ontario.

18 Ruth Pierson, 'Gender and Unemployment Insurance Debates in Canada, 1934–40,' *Labour/Le Travail* 25 (1990), 77–104.

19 G.N. Sheppard's report, file 2690, vol. 12, J.L. Cohen Papers, NA.

20 Conversation with Toby Levinson Cole, 20 April 1997.

21 Estok, 'All the Wrong People,' 35.

22 H.G. Fester to S. Altman, 19 May 1932; J.L. Cohen to Hallman and Sable, 28 July 1933; and 23 Sept. 1932, file 1145, vol. 2, J.L. Cohen Papers, NA; Mercedes Steedman, *Angels in the Workplace: Women and the Construction of Gender Relations in the Canadian Clothing Industry, 1890–1940* (Toronto: Oxford University Press 1997), 112.

23 Estok, 'All the Wrong People,' 56; file 1451, vol. 2; J.L. Cohen to D.C. Draper, 19 July 1933, file 1632, vol. 2; D. Draper to J.L. Cohen, file 1688, vol. 2, J.L. Cohen Papers, NA; Steedman, *Angels in the Workplace*, 112.

24 D. Draper to Cohen and Rosenberg, 28 Aug. 1933, file 1680, vol. 2, J.L. Cohen Papers, NA.

25 Gerald Tulchinsky, *Branching Out: The Transformation of the Jewish Community* (Toronto: Stoddart 1998), 111–12.

26 File 1938, vol. 2, J.L. Cohen Papers, NA.

27 File 1937, vol. 2, J.L. Cohen Papers, NA.

28 Ruth Frager, *Sweatshop Strife: Class, Ethnicity, and Gender in the Jewish Labour Movement of Toronto, 1900–1939* (Toronto: University of Toronto Press 1992), 221. Tulchinsky's estimates are lower in 1931 for Montreal, where Jews accounted for 35 per cent of the clothing industry's workforce compared to 53 per cent for French Canadians. In the women's clothing sector, 32 per cent (of whom half were women) were Jews and 60 per cent were French Canadian (but 92 per cent were female). Tulchinsky, *Branching Out*, 96.

29 Ruth Frager, 'Class and Ethnic Barriers to Feminist Perspectives in Toronto's Jewish Labour Movement 1919–1939' in L.S. MacDowell and Ian Radforth, eds, *Canadian Working Class History: Selected Readings* (Toronto: Canadian Scholars' Press 1992), 507.

30 Erna Paris, *Jews* (Toronto: Macmillan 1980), 130. In 1931, Toronto had 45, 000 Jews.

31 Tulchinsky, *Branching Out*, 107.

32 Mercedes Steedman, 'Skill and Gender in the Canadian Clothing Industry 1890–1940,' in C. Heron and R. Storey, eds, *On the Job* (Montreal and Kingston: McGill-Queen's University Press 1985), 161. For different perspectives on the internal union conflicts, see Steedman, *Angels*, 129–36, and Joel Sediman, *The Needle Trades* (New York: Farrar and Rinehart 1942), chap. 9.

33 Tulchinsky, *Branching Out*, 90–1. Similar issues emerged in both the menswear and womens wear industries, including the newer dressmaking section, and in the 1930s the situation worsened.

34 S.M. Jamieson, *Times of Trouble: Labour Unrest and Industrial Conflict in Canada, 1900–1966* (Ottawa: Task Force on Labour Relations 1968), 224–5.

35 File 23, J.L. Cohen Papers, vol. 1, NA.

36 Cohen to Julius Hochman, 28 Dec. 1927, file 23, vol. 1, J.L. Cohen Papers, NA.

37 Cohen to James Watt, n.d., file 23, vol. 1, J.L. Cohen Papers, NA.

38 Cohen to J.W. Macmillan, 16 Feb. 1928, file 23, vol. 1, J.L. Cohen Papers, NA; Steedman, *Angels*, 112.

39 Irving Bernstein, *The Turbulent Years* (Boston: Houghton Mifflin, 1971), 80.

40 Cohen to David Dubinsky, 25 Oct. 1929, file 24, vol. 1, J.L. Cohen Papers, NA.

41 Steedman, *Angels*, 167; Cohen to David Dubinsky, 27 Jan. 1930; Cohen to L.M. Singer, 3 Feb. 1930; Cohen to Bernard Shane, 10 Feb. 1930, file 24, vol. 1, J.L. Cohen Papers, NA.

42 Tulchinsky, *Branching Out*, 97.

43 Cohen to David Dubinsky, 11 Feb. 1930, file 24, vol. 1, J.L. Cohen Papers, NA.

44 Steedman, *Angels*, 116. The first trade association was established in Montreal in 1908 by firms in the men's clothing industry. By 1919, 28 companies, or 15 per cent of the businesses in Montreal, were members.

45 Files 2095 and 2096, vol. 2, J.L. Cohen Papers, NA; Similar ILGWU strikes took place in Montreal in 1934. When an IUNTW dressmakers' strike was lost in 1934, and when the WUL disbanded in 1935, the ILGWU took over and began to make inroads among young French Canadian female workers. Steedman, *Angels*, 176.

46 Memorandum on the Industrial Standards Act of Ontario, 1935–61, prepared for the Royal Commission on Labour Relations in the Construction Industry, September 1961, 17. On the earlier legislation, see Margaret McCallum, 'Keeping Women in Their Place: The Minimum Wage in Canada, 1910–1925,' in L.S. MacDowell and Ian Radforth, *Canadian Working Class History: Selected Readings* 433–58. For clothing workers' testimony before the Royal Commission on Price Spreads, see Irving Abella and David Millar, eds, *The Canadian Worker in the Twentieth Century* (Toronto: Oxford University Presss 1978).

47 Memorandum on the Industrial Standards Act of Ontario, 19, 20.

48 Ibid., 11, 110.

49 Cohen to H. Langer, 1 April 1935, file 2181A, vol. 3, J.L. Cohen Papers, NA.

50 M. Steedman, *Angels*, 222.

51 Cohen to ILGWU, 10 Sept. 1935; J.L. Cohen to Bernard Shane, 18 Sept. 1935, file 2181A, vol. 3, J.L. Cohen Papers, NA.

52 Cohen to Louis Fine, 28 June 1935; J.L. Cohen to H. Langer, 18 Sept. 1935; J.L. Cohen to H. Langer, 25 Sept. 1935, file 2181A, vol. 3, J.L. Cohen Papers, NA.

53 Morris Hillquit, the ILGWU's counsel in New York, had sent Cohen a copy of the 'proposed code of fair competition in the coat and suit industry under the National Industrial Recovery Act' and the objections of the union. File 2096, vol. 2, J.L. Cohen Papers, NA.

54 Cohen to Alderman J. Shubert, Jr, Committee of the Men's and Boy's Clothing Industry, Montreal, 23 July 1935; Joseph Shubert to J.L. Cohen, 6 Aug. 1935; J.L. Cohen to Joint Board of the Cloakmakers' Union, 8 Oct. 1935, file 2181A, vol. 3, J.L. Cohen Papers, NA.

55 Cohen to Joint Board of the Cloakmakers' Union, 8 Oct. 1935, file 2181A, vol. 3, J.L. Cohen Papers, NA.

56 J.L. Cohen, '"Little" Criticism of the Industrial Standards Act,' 20, RG7–14–0–

96.1, no. 3, AO; Cohen's account with the United Hatter's Union regarding work on the Industrial Standards Act from 4 Oct. 1936 to 8 Feb. 1938, file 2641, vol. 10, J.L. Cohen Papers, NA.

57 Cohen to Bernard Shane, 6 Dec. 1935, file 2181A, vol. 3, J.L. Cohen Papers, NA.
58 Cohen to ACWU, 26 Dec. 1935; J.L. Cohen to Sidney Hillman, 31 Dec. 1935; J.L. Cohen to ACWU, 9 June 1936, file 2396, vol. 4, J.L. Cohen Papers, NA; Steedman, *Angels*, 222.
59 File 2494, vol. 5, J.L. Cohen Papers, NA. Correspondence in June 1936 between the Toronto cloakmakers' union and the cloak manufacturer's association argued about the expenses that they were contributing to maintain the schedule, including the cost of two inspectors.
60 Cohen to Graham Spry, 13 Dec. 1935, file 2236H, vol. 3, J.L. Cohen Papers, NA.
61 J.L. Cohen, '"Little" Criticism of the Industrial Standards Act,' RG7–14–0–96.1, no. 3, AO.
62 H.A. Logan, *Trade Unions in Canada* (Toronto: Macmillan 1948), 461. A special Court of Appeal quashed the conviction of an employer in magistrate's court for working employees on Saturday, contrary to the schedule. The remedy was an amendment, whereby the administrators could name not only daily and weekly hours of work but the actual days of the week. Later, the constitutional validity of the act was challenged, and it was upheld by the Privy Council in London in the *Tolton case*, in which Cohen represented labour.
63 Cohen to David Croll, 16 March 1936, file 2239, vol. 3, J.L. Cohen Papers, NA.
64 Press notice; J.L. Cohen, counsel to the delegation to David Croll; J.L. Cohen to J.W. Buckley, 14 April 1936, file 2521, vol. 5, J.L. Cohen Papers, NA.
65 John T. Saywell, '*Just Call Me Mitch*,' 257; Bora Laskin and Jacob Finkelman, 'The Industrial Standards Act and Its Administration,' 15, file 2363(2), vol. 4, J.L. Cohen Papers, NA.
66 File 2363, vol. 4, J.L. Cohen Papers, NA.
67 Canadian membership in the clothing unions rose from 3,000 in 1931 to 8,307 in 1938, Canada, *Report on Labour Organizations in Canada* (Ottawa: King's Printer 1939); McCallum, 'Keeping Women in Their Place: The Minimum Wage in Canada, 1910–1925.' The boards were the Minimum Wage Board in the 1920s and the Industry and Labor Board in the 1930s and 1940s.
68 Steedman, 'Skill and Gender,' 167.
69 Steedman, *Angels*, 220.
70 Frager, 'Class and Ethnic Barriers,' 507–8. For a more detailed discussion of gender issues in the needle trades, see Frager, *Sweatshop Strife*, and Steedman, *Angels*, (1997).

71 Steedman, 'Skill and Gender,' 152, 158, 159.

72 Frager, 'Class and Ethnic Barriers,' 509, 510, 512.

73 Steedman, 'Skill and Gender,' 162; Frager, 'Class and Ethnic Barriers,' 510.

74 Cohen to Sam Kreisman, 29 Oct. 1935, file 2181A, vol. 3, J.L. Cohen Papers, NA. In the same round of talks, the agreement included wage differentials between contract shops and inside manufactories, and between rural and urban shops. It also retained the sexual division of labour and lower wage levels for women.

75 It foreshadowed the 'second wave' feminist movement which argued that women should be treated as individuals in the labour force with equal pay and opportunities.

76 Steedman, 'Skill and Gender,' 157.

77 ACW Industrial Standards Act Conference concerning the Men's Cothing Industry, Minutes 1936, file 2396A, vol. 4, J.L. Cohen Papers, NA. The parties wanted to treat the pant industry separately from the coat industry because in the latter the majority of workers were men but in the former the majority were women and they did not want the same scale of wages for women. Cohen argued for as broad a definition of the industry as possible and one set of minimum rates, but he was overruled. A female representative from the National Clothing Workers of Canada argued that the pants industry should be treated separately and the women in it as a separate classification, an argument not likely to achieve equal pay.

78 Steedman, *Angels*, 254–5. Just as women moved from caretaking in the home to caretaking in the workplace, men moved from protecting and providing in the home into similar roles in the labour force. 'The social prescriptions for masculine and feminine behaviour further ensured that men and women would ... play out their destinies – men as protectors for the class and women as its caretakers.'

79 Frager, 'Class and Ethnic Barriers,' 514–15.

80 Ibid., 507–23.

81 Steedman, 'Skill and Gender,' 153, 165, 168.

82 The idea of industrial unionism was associated with the CIO movement, of which the United Textile Workers of America (UTWA), was a part. The Canadia CIO Committee was affiliated with the TLC until it was expelled in 1939. Thereafter, it united with the ACCL to form the Canadian Congress of Labour (CCL) in 1940; Cohen drafted the merger agreement.

83 *Globe*, 19 Aug. 1937.

84 File 2570, vol. 6, J.L. Cohen Papers, NA.

85 *Standard Freeholder*, Cornwall, 31 Jan. 1938.

86 Cohen to Louis Fitch, 2 Nov. 1937, file 2590, vol. 7, J.L. Cohen Papers, NA.

Kaufman's anti-union paternalism in the workplace was consistent with his reformist view on birth control, in that, as an employer of females, he felt he had every right to 'protect' them by intruding in their lives over both issues. See Mary F. Bishop, 'Vivian Dowding: Birth Control Activist,' in V. Strong-Boag and A. Fellman, *Rethinking Canada* (Toronto: Copp Clark 1986), 203–5.

87 *Kitchener Daily Record*, 3 Nov. 1937.

88 Minutes, arbitration board meeting, 4 May 1939, 7, file 2731-8, vol. 13, J.L. Cohen Papers, NA.

89 Kitchener *Daily Record*, 3 Nov. 1937.

90 N.H. Eagle to J.L. Cohen, 5 May 1938, file 2667, vol. 11, J.L. Cohen Papers, NA.

91 Memorandums, 17 July 1939, 6 Sept. 1939; file: Cohen, J.L. (Labour Lawyer), 1939, RG 7–1–0–250, AO.

Chapter 4: Labour Lawyer, 1936–1943

1 The Committee for Industrial Organization (CIO) was formed by John L. Lewis, head of the United Mine Workers union in 1935, as a committee of the American Federation of Labor (AFL). The CIO was suspended by the AFL in September 1936, and a rival Congress of Industrial Organizations was born at a convention in Pittsburgh in November 1936. Irving Bernstein, *The Turbulent Years: A History of the American Worker 1933–1941* (Boston: Houghton Mifflin 1969), 400–2, 425.

2 *Globe and Mail*, 21 May 1937.

3 File 2793, vol. 19, J.L. Cohen Papers, NA.

4 David Michael Estok, 'All the Wrong People': The Trial and Career of J.L. Cohen,' Master of Journalism thesis, Carleton University, 1981, 82.

5 Ibid., 75.

6 Bernstein, *The Turbulent Years*, 457.

7 Herb Grant to Cohen, June 193, file 2616, vol. 8, J.L. Cohen Papers, NA.

8 Estok, 'All the Wrong People,' 75.

9 The GM local in Oshawa was not the first UAW local in Canada. As a result of rank-and-file initiative, the UAW's first local, No. 195 in Windsor, was chartered in 1936, as was Local 199 at McKinnon Industries in St Catharines.

10 John T. Saywell, '*Just Call Me Mitch': The Life of Mitchell F. Hepburn* (Toronto: University of Toronto Press 1991), 305; see also Irving Abella, 'Oshawa 1937,' in I. Abella, ed., *On Strike* (Toronto: James Lewis and Samuel 1975), for a detailed account of the strike.

11 Cohen to M.T. Montgomery, 13 April 1937, file 2602, vol. 7, J.L. Cohen Papers, NA.

12 C.H. Millard to Homer Martin, 12 May 1937, file 2615, vol. 8, J.L. Cohen Papers, NA.
13 *Globe and Mail*, 25 May 1950.
14 Saywell, *'Just Call Me Mitch,'* 326.
15 Cohen to R.H. McCartney, 14 Oct. 1937, file 2616, vol. 8, J.L. Cohen Papers, NA.
16 Estok, 'All the Wrong People,' 84.
17 Cohen to C.H. Millard, 3 May 1938, file 2611, vol. 8, J.L. Cohen Papers, NA.
18 Cohen to Homer Martin, 24 May 1937, file 2614, vol. 8, J.L. Cohen Papers, NA.
19 Cohen to Homer Martin, 29 April 1937, file 2609, vol. 7, J.L. Cohen Papers, NA.
20 SWOC local president to A.C. Sutton, GSW general manager, 4 Oct. 1939; notice by F.S. Corrigan, general manager, 6 Oct. 1939; Sutton to president, lodge No. 1111, AAISTWNA, 30 Sept. 1939, file 2763, vol. 14, J.L. Cohen Papers, NA.
21 GSW agreement, file 2763, vol. 14, J.L. Cohen Papers, NA. The agreement included no discrimination for union activity, rest periods for female employees, and a new seniority system with separate, non-interchangeable male and female lists, except when workers of both sexes were doing the same work, when the list was combined.
22 Correspondence, file 2768, vol. 14, J.L. Cohen Papers, NA.
23 J.L. Cohen, *Collective Bargaining in Canada* (Toronto: Steelworkers' Organizing Committee 1941), 17. When P.C. 4020 created the IDIC in 1941, and P.C. 4844 extended its powers to investigate cases of alleged discrimination in employment because of trade-union activity, Cohen dismissed the change as inadequate in his book. Later, however, H.D. Woods saw it as an early example of government sanctions providing relief to individual employees, which foreshadowed the future system of legislated unfair-labour practices.
24 For information on Millard and his career, see L.S. MacDowell, 'The Career of Canadian Trade Union Leader, C.H. Millard 1936–1946,' *Relations industrielles/Industrial Relations*, 43, no. 3 (1988), 609–31.
25 Preliminary memorandum respecting the formation of a Canadian central body for the industrial organization of Canadian workers; file 2772, vol. 14, J.L. Cohen Papers, NA.
26 File: J.L. Cohen K.C. 1928–43, vol. 181, CLC Papers, NA.
27 File 2876, vol. 26, J.L. Cohen Papers, NA.
28 R.H. Storey, 'Workers, Unions and Steel: The Shaping of the Hamilton Working Class, 1935–48,' PhD thesis, University of Toronto, 1981, 277.
29 Cohen's minority report, 24 June 1941; E. Brunning to the conciliation board,

5 June 1941; Cohen to McLarty, 18 May 1941, files 2854 and 2854a, vol. 24, J.L. Cohen Papers, NA.

30 Cohen to Norman McLarty, 18 May 1941, vol. 38, CLC Papers, NA.

31 *Labour Gazette* (November 1942), 1228.

32 The wage-control policy is discussed in greater detail in L.S. MacDowell, 'The Formation of the Industrial Relations System in Canada during World War Two,' *Labour/Le Travailleur*, 3, (1978), 175–96; idem., 'The 1943 Steel Strike against Wartime Wage Controls,' *Labour/Le Travailleur*, 10, (autumn 1982), 65–85.

33 For a detailed study of the Teck-Hughes dispute, see L.S. MacDowell, '"Remember Kirkland Lake": The Gold Miners' Strike, 1941–42* (Toronto: University of Toronto Press 1983), chap. 3.

34 Cohen, *Collective Bargaining*, 54.

35 Ibid., 59.

36 He collected the current proceedings of the Conference on Industrial Relations, material from the Canadian Institute of Public Affairs, data on family income and expenditures, prices, and the cost of living index from DBS, and material on nutritional standards from the Department of Pensions and National Health. From the University of Toronto Press, he borrowed galleys of lectures delivered by Dr Bryce Stewart and Professor Taylor. He requested the CIO Defence Plan for the coordination of conditions in the steel industry from SWOC Secretary-Treasurer David J. McDonald. File 2877, vol. 26, J.L. Cohen Papers, NA.

37 D.J. McDonald to Cohen, 24 July 1941; Cohen to L. Pressman, 30 Oct. 1941; 13 Nov. 1941; Pressman to Cohen, 24 Nov. 1941, file 2877, vol. 26, J.L. Cohen Papers, NA.

38 Cohen to H.A. Logan, 29 Aug. 1941, file 2877, vol. 26, J.L. Cohen Papers, NA.

39 Robinson congratulated Cohen on the 'fine job of drafting' he had done. L.S. MacDowell, 'Remember Kirkland Lake,' 110.

40 Cohen to M.M. Maclean, 25 Aug. 1941, file 2856, vol. 24, J.L. Cohen Papers, NA. Maclean worked for the CCL and was one of the first trade unionists to make a career change and go to work in the Department of Labour.

41 MacDowell, 'Remember Kirkland Lake,' 127, 173.

42 Estok, 'All the Wrong People,' 80.

43 MacDowell, 'Remember Kirkland Lake,' 175.

44 Ibid., 168; Bob Carlin, transcript of taped interview with the author at Gowganda, August 1973.

45 MacDowell, 'Remember Kirkland Lake,' 132.

46 Ibid., 154, 170. The press accused Robinson of being a Communist. Robinson dropped the case so that there would not be too much prying into his politi-

cal activities, but Cohen feared that dropping the case would make it appear that Robinson had given into the press and conceded its point, which would look bad for the union.

47 Ibid., 201.
48 Ibid., 219.
49 Mary E. Baruth-Walsh and G. Mark Walsh, *Strike: 99 Days on the Line* (Manotick, Ont.: Penumbra Press 1995), 17, 19.
50 The workers voted by more than six thousand to four thousand for the union over the employees' association.
51 David Moulton, 'Ford Windsor 1945,' in I. Abella, ed., *On Strike* (Toronto: James Lewis and Samual 1974), 132.
52 The door was still left open to companies to apply to pay women lower rates on the ground that they were not as productive as men and that 'the average woman would produce less than the average man employed on the job.' Government policy provided a differential not on the basis of sex or age but only on the basis that the company was applying for a new job classification. Cohen interpreted the outcome of this Ford case as meaning that, after the board ruled, the company acknowledged P.C. 5693, which it was not doing when it made the application. It had contended that the order prevented the employer from adopting the principle of equal pay for equal work. The dispute was the first real discussion of the issue between the company and the union, and the board ruling meant that if women were employed in the future wages would be negotiated between the parties or would be the subject of an application to the wage board, and they would have to be in line with the equal-pay principle. Following the regional board's decision to reject Ford's application, the NWLB, in Cohen's words, 'climbed on the bandwagon' of 'equal pay for equal work,' but he regreted that the dominion Department of Labour had not made its position on the issue clearer earlier, since it might thereby have eliminated much of the problem at Ford. Cohen's view was technical and optimistic, but it was not the way much of the press interpreted the dispute.
53 It appears that the union expected the company to fire the women if the arbitrator ruled that the women were not in job classifications under the collective agreement. Handwritten note of Cohen's to Peter Heenan, 28 Nov. 1942, file 2969, vol. 33, J.L. Cohen Papers, NA.
54 Cohen's statement of account, 21 Dec. 1942, file 2969, vol. 33, J.L. Cohen Papers, NA.
55 *Ford Facts*, n.d.; 7 Jan. 1943; Roy England letter to press, 15 Jan. 1943, file 2969, vol. 33, J.L. Cohen Papers, NA. The Windsor *Star*, 1 Dec. 1942, had a column by W.L. Clark called 'Interpreting Ford Decision.'

56 Chronology of conciliation history with Ford and UAW Local 200, RG27, vol. 1772, NA; Baruth-Walsh and Walsh, *Strike*, 24–7.

57 Cohen handled the vacations-with-pay case for the union, did research that compared the union's proposal with what the other auto makers had already adopted, and urged that the decision be implemented as quickly as possible to avoid unrest. Cohen to A. MacNamara, 23 June 1944, file 3071, vol. 37, J.L. Cohen Papers, NA.

58 Stephen Cako, 'Labour's Struggle for Union Security: The Ford of Canada Strike, 'MA thesis, University of Guelph, 1971, 38, 40.

59 NWLB Proceedings, 829, file 2962, vol. 33, J.L. Cohen Papers, NA.

60 D.J. Bercuson, *True Patriot: The Life of Brooke Claxton 1898–1960* (Toronto: University of Toronto Press 1993), 120.

Chapter 5: Designing Ontario Labour Policy, 1942–1943

1 L.S. MacDowell, 'The Formation of the Canadian Industrial Relations System during World War Two,' *Labour/Le Travailleur* 3 (1978), 176. I want to thank Rick MacDowell, current chair of the OLRB, for his helpful comments on this chapter and chap. 6; the ideas and interpretation in these pages are, of course, strictly my own.

2 Gerald Caplan, *The Dilemma of Canadian Socialism* (Toronto: McClelland and Stewart 1973), chap. 7. In 1942 popular support for the CCF in Ontario more than doubled from 10 per cent in January to over 21 per cent by September.

3 'A serious steel strike in that year [1943] had led to serious discussion as to the need for compulsory collective bargaining legislation for Canada, such as the Wagner Act.' *Labour Gazette*, 50, no. 9 (September 1950), 1505.

4 Peter G. Bruce, 'Political Parties and the Evolution of Labour Law in Canada and the United States,' PhD thesis, Massachusetts Institute of Technology, 1988, in draft, chap. 6, 12.

5 L.S. MacDowell, ' *Remember Kirkland Lake': The Gold Miners' Strike of 1941–42* (Toronto: University of Toronto Press 1983), 228; at a conference of war labour boards in mid August, Heenan had moved a motion, which was seconded by L.D. Currie, the minister of labour in Nova Scotia, that collective bargaining was the public policy of Canada and that boards could direct the parties to disputes not to oppose public policy and could compel them to negotiate and recognize unions or associations. File 2973, vol. 33, J.L. Cohen Papers, NA.

6 John Willes, *The Ontario Labour Court, 1943–44* (Kingston, Ont.: Industrial Relations Centre, Queen's University 1979), 10; file 2973, vol. 33, J.L. Cohen Papers, NA.

7 Bruce, 'Political Parties,' chap. 6, 13. He suggests that it was not surprising

that Cohen, as a sympathizer of the CPC, agreed to work for the Ontario government at this time of closer elations between the CPC and the Liberals; file 2973, vol. 33, J.L. Cohen Papers, NA.

8 Bruce, 'Political Parties,' chap. 6, 14.
9 John A. Willes, *The Ontario Labour Court*; F. David Millar, 'Shapes of Power: The Ontario Labour Relations Board 1944–1950,' PhD thesis, York University 1981; Bruce, 'Political Parties.'
10 Bruce, 'Political Parties,' chap. 6, 18.
11 Ibid., chap. 6, 25.
12 Ibid., chap. 6, 20, 54.
13 File 2973, vol. 33, J.L. Cohen Papers, NA.
14 Willes, *The Ontario Labour Court*, 11, 12.
15 Bruce, 'Political Parties,' chap. 6, 44.
16 Willes, *The Ontario Labour Court*, 12,13.
17 Ibid., 32.
18 G. Burt to P. Heenan, 6 Feb. 1943, file 2973, vol. 33, J.L. Cohen Papers, NA.
19 *New Commonwealth* (March 1943), 1, 14.
20 Ontario, *Proceedings of Select Committee re Bargaining between Employers and Employees*, testimony of Peter Heenan, Ontario minister of labour, 2 March 1943, 10, Legislative Library, Toronto.
21 Ibid., 25. In Canada, the level of industrial unrest climbed from 1940 and peeked in 1943. In 1941 there were 231 strikes involving 87,091 employees and 433,914 workdays lost. In 1942, 354 strikes involved 133,916 workers and 450,202 lost workdays. In 1943 there were 400 strikes involving 218,404 workers with a loss of 1,041,198 workdays, after which industrial unrest declined for the remainder of the war. Canada Department of Labour, *Strikes and Lockouts in Canada* (Ottawa: Kings Printer 1941–43).
22 Ibid., 23–6.
23 Ibid., 27.
24 Ontario, *Proceedings*, testimony of Aaron Mosher, 3 March 1943, 148.
25 Willes, *The Ontario Labour Court*, 14.
26 Ontario, *Proceedings*, testimony of Pat Conroy, 3 March 1943, 210.
27 Ibid., for example: the UEW brief, 4 March 1943, 336–56; testimony of Tom McClure, president local 1005, USWA, 8 March 1943, 533. Unions' mistrust of the judiciary was related to their conclusion that the courts were an inappropriate forum for resolving labour disputes; however, unions also believed that judges were removed from day-to-day industrial relations and that courts had a long history of making decisions that did not favour workers. Eric Tucker, 'The Law of Employers' Liability in Ontario 1861–1900: The Search for a Theory, ' *Osgoode Hall Law Journal*, 22, no. 2 (1984).

28 Ontario, *Proceedings*, testimony of D.W. Lang and K. Kilbourn, 9 March 1943, 456. Many manufacturers introduced voluntary joint management-labour production committees. According to the dominion minister of labour's statement to Parliament on 22 February 1942, there were then to about 631 such committees representing 327, 000 employees, most of them in Ontario. Communist trade unionists were interested in these joint production committees as a way of increasing production, which was consistent with party policy at the time. Business and government did not make much use of them except as rhetoric to show their good intentions, and trade unionists intent on organizing unions generally did not regard them as anything more than window dressing.

29 Ontario, *Proceedings*, testimony of J. Aylesworth, 449; of D.W. Lang and K. Kilbourn, 450–90; of B. Laskin, 470. In the United States, litigation had been the employers' tactic to challenge the constitutionality of the Wagner Act, and when that failed, to undermine the legislation and the work of the National Labor Relations Board.

30 Ontario, *Proceedings*, testimony of F.A. Brewin, 9 March 1943, 527. 'At the present time in Ontario industrial workers are only organized in independent unions to the extent of about 25% The further extension of collective bargaining has been made impossible by the hostility of management and the complex of fear which has dominated many industrial workers.'

31 Ibid., testimony of J. Aylesworth, 47–9.

32 Ontario, *Proceedings*, 2 March 1943, 115. Finkelman said that the refusal of employers to sit down and bargain with their employees was a serious problem, which he had documented in his research and which, he thought, should be dealt with by legislation.

33 Submisson to the NWLB Enquiry by the Hamilton Labour Council, 1 June 1943, 672, vol. 34, J.L. Cohen Papers, NA. The notion that collective-bargaining legislation was part of a 'post-war settlement,' which was easily reached with business and government and which represented a sell-out by non-militant labour 'bosses,' has been repeatedly articulated by Marxist historians and social scientists. It is an ahistorical argument because there is much evidence of employer hostility to the new legislation, and of employee and union struggle to achieve it. For an influential example of the post-war settlement line of argument, see Leo Panitch and Donald Swartz, *The Assault on Trade Union Freedom* (Toronto: Garamond Press 1988). See Epilogue.

34 Bora Laskin, 'Collective Bargaining in Ontario: A New Legislative Approach,' *Canadian Bar Review* 21 (November 1943), 684; James C. Cameron and F.J.L. Young, *The Status of Trade Unions in Canada*, Department of Industrial Relations, Queen's University, (Kingston, Ont., 1960), 55.

35 Cameron and Young, *The Status of Trade Unions*, 63.

36 Willes, *The Ontario Labour Court*, 22.

37 *New Commonwealth*, 8 July 1943, 8.

38 Willes, *The Ontario Labour Court 1943–44*, 42, 73.

39 *Globe and Mail*, 25 May 1950.

40 'Summary of Activities of the Labour Court, June 14, 1943 to December 31, 1943,' RG7–60, Ontario Labour Court files, AO. By the end of 1943, the labour court had dealt with 86 cases and certified 64 bargaining agents, which represented 31, 000 employees. Cameron and Young, *The Status of Trade Unions*, 64.

41 *New Commonwealth*, 8 July 1943, 8.

42 These included Federal Union No. 22788 (AFL), the International Fur and Leather Workers Union, Mine Mill, the UAW, the UEW, the United Gas Coke and Chemical Workers of America, and the Windsor branch of the National Association of Technical Employees.

43 In fourteen cases where Cohen represented the applicant he won, and in three cases he lost. In eight cases in which he represented the intervenor he lost, and in one case he won.

44 RG 7–60, box 3, file 26, AO.

45 RG 27, series 60, OLRB 1935–69, labour court files 1943–44, boxes 1–12, AO. The foregoing analysis is based on a review of these files in the cases argued by J.L. Cohen.

46 David Michael Estok, 'All the Wrong People: The Trial and Career of Labour Lawyer J.L. Cohen,' Master of Journalism thesis, Carleton University, 1981, 180.

Chapter 6: National War Labour Board Service, 1943

1 L.S. MacDowell, *'Remember Kirkland Lake': The Gold Miners' Strike of 1941–42* (Toronto: University of Toronto Press 1983), chap. 10. In 1943 the level of strike activity was the highest since 1919; in 1943 the CCF became the Official Opposition in Ontario and was making gains in British Columbia, and in 1944 it formed the government in Saskatchewan.

2 H.D. Langer to J.L. Cohen, 13 Feb. 1943; Louis Coldoff to J.L. Cohen, 13 Feb. 1943; J.L. Cohen to Pat Conroy, 16 Feb. 1943, file 3052-1, vol. 34, J.L. Cohen Papers, NA.

3 Cohen to Judge McTague, 11 March 1943, file 3052-1, vol. 34, NA; L.S. Mac-Dowell, 'The Formation of the Canadian Industrial Relations System during World War Two,' *Labour/Le Travailleur*, 3 (1978), 192.

4 MacDowell, *'Remember Kirkland Lake,'* chap. 5.

5 Taylor Hollander, 'The Making of a Canadian Collective Bargaining Policy:

The Role of the National War Labour Board, 1943–44,' paper presented to the Organization of American Historians meeting, 25 April 1999, Toronto, 10.

6 *News*, 6 March 1943.

7 C.S. Jackson to J.L. Cohen, 17 Feb. 1943, file 3052-1, vol. 34, J.L. Cohen Papers, NA.

8 NWLB statement, n.d., file 3052-2, vol. 34, J.L. Cohen Papers, NA.

9 *Le Nouvelliste Trois-Rivières*, 25 Feb. 1943.

10 *L'Action catholique*, 15 Feb. 1943.

11 Herbert Quinn, *The Union Nationale: A Study in Quebec Nationalism* (Toronto: University of Toronto Press 1963), 32–3, 88.

12 Cohen to Judge McTague, 11 March 1943, file 3052-1, vol. 34, J.L. Cohen Papers, NA.

13 Hollander, 'The Making of a Canadian Collective Bargaining Policy,' 12.

14 *Globe and Mail*, editorial, 15 Feb. 1943; 17 Feb. 1943; *Financial Post*, 20 Feb. 1943.

15 Peter H. Irons, *The New Deal Lawyers* (Princeton, N.J.: Princeton University Press 1982), chap. 1.

16 Cohen to Roger Grant, *Canadian Tribune*, 16 Feb. 1943; J.L. Cohen to C.S. Jackson, 10 March 1943. He apologized for taking so long to answer his letter but had 'not a moment to deal with any but official communications,' and he could not become involved in the Alcan issue now because of his position; file LO8, vol. 3579 WPTB, Dept. of Finance Papers, NA.

17 Speech of J.L. Cohen to IBEW, Montreal, 4 April 1943, file 3052-3, vol. 34, J.L. Cohen Papers, NA.

18 There is a list of the major cases in which Cohen was involved; file 3052-4, vol. 34, J.L. Cohen Papers, NA.

19 The first wage order, P.C. 7440, was proclaimed in December 1940 and established a 'fair and reasonable' wage standard based on the wage level prevailing during the 1926–9, pre-Depression period. This was the guideline to be used by conciliation boards to resolve labour disputes. A uniform wartime bonus was paid separately from the basic wage rates and was meant to protect workers from increases in the cost of living. The next wage order (P.C. 8253 of October 1941) froze all wages and extended wage controls to virtually all employers and employees. P.C. 8253 established the National War Labour Board (NWLB), which was chaired by the dominion minister of labour and consisted of an equal number of employer and employee representatives. In addition, there were nine regional boards, chaired by the provincial labour ministers. Under the order, no employer could increase wages without permission of a wage board, and wages were set in relation to the prevailing rates for similar occupations 'in a locality which in the opinion

of the National Board is comparable.' The boards periodically adjusted the cost-of-living bonus, and in January 1942 P.C. 5963 made payment by all employers compulsory. Collective agreements had to conform to the order, and the wage boards could order the revision or suspension of any collective agreement that was inconsistent with the terms of the order.

20 L.S. MacDowell, 'The 1943 Steel Strike against Wartime Wage Controls,' *Labour/Le Travailleur* 10 (autumn 1982), 65–85.

21 Ibid., 78.

22 There were more minor issues, including confusion about the extent to which Trenton employees were covered by the agreement and whether the Algoma and Sydney plants should be designated national employers. The union argued that these issues were settled by the 'memorandum of understanding' and that all the board had to do was confirm them, while the companies argued that the union had to make a case.

23 Cohen to the prime minister, 31 March 1943, file 3052-1, vol. 34, J.L. Cohen Papers, NA.

24 The NWLB accepted that Trenton Works was part of the basic steel industry and subject to this decision but excluded employees at Eastern Car Company, so the union won only a part of this demand as well.

25 C.P. McTague to Humphrey Mitchell, 22 April 1943, file 3052-1, vol. 34, J.L. Cohen Papers, NA.

26 C.P. McTague to Prime Minister King, 22 April 1943, file 3052-1, vol. 34, J.L. Cohen Papers, NA. Previously, McTague had informally asked Mitchell about the alleged unwritten understanding to allay his forebodings, and the minister had denied any knowledge of it and insisted that Millard had simply drawn the wrong conclusions.

27 Ruth Pierson, 'They're Still Women After All': The Second World War and Canadian Womanhood (Toronto: McClelland and Stewart 1986).

28 Cohen to C.P. McTague, 1 June 1943, file 3052-1, vol. 34, J.L. Cohen Papers, NA.

29 Cohen to C.P. McTague, 19 March 1943, file 3052-1, vol. 34, J.L. Cohen Papers, NA. The order itself is in file 3052-2, vol. 34, J.L. Cohen Papers, NA.

30 Author's telephone conversation with E.B. Jolliffe, 26 May 1981; C.H. Millard to D. MacDonald, 12 Sept. 1942, CLC Papers, NA. Millard wrote that Cohen had 'definitely aligned himself with the left-wingers and I have taken the position that we can't afford to be identified with the solicitor of that group.'

31 Gerald Caplan, *The Dilemma of Canadian Socialism* (Toronto 1973), chap. 7.

32 Author's telephone conversation with E.B. Jolliffe, 26 May 1981.

33 The Lewis, Jolliffe and Osler firm was created in 1950. Labour leaders had proposed that David Lewis move to Toronto and practise labour law, even

though, as national secretary of the CCF for thirteen years, Lewis was a little rusty as a lawyer. Though John Osler was from an old Ontario family and was well-to-do, he was a social democrat by conviction. He and Lewis met in 1942 during the York South by-election which the CCF won, and Osler was the person who helped Lewis get used to his new role practising law. Jolliffe was still in the legislature, so at first he was not around very much, but the firm became, as Lewis wrote, 'one of the most active labour law firms in Canada.' David Lewis, *The Good Fight: Political Memoirs, 1909–1958* (Toronto: Macmillan 1981), 373. Andrew Brewin had a number of associations and broad political and legal interests but his later firm of Cameron Scott and Brewin did a considerable amount of labour law.

34 Cohen got even with Millard, though careful adjudication was his motive, not revenge. The NWLB's 1943 decision in the steel case was unanimous, and it made Millard unhappy. MacDowell, 'The 1943 Steel Strike,' 82. Brewin at this time was a member of the firm Mason, Cameron and Brewin; later, he would defend the civil liberties of Japanese in Canada. File: Legal proceedings 1945, vol. 1, Andrew Brewin Papers, NA. In 1944 the CCF government in Saskatchewan passed its Trade Union Act, drafted largely by Brewin and, according to David Lewis, 'by far the most advanced piece of labour legislation in the country.' Lewis, *The Good Fight*, 472.

35 Author's telephone conversation with E.B. Jolliffe, 26 May 1981.

36 The entire transcript of the NWLB's hearings is in Cohen's papers. NWLB, 'Labour Relations and Wage Conditions in Canada,' Transcript of Proceedings, vol. 34, J.L. Cohen Papers, NA.

37 Hollander, 'The Making of a Canadian Collective Bargaining Policy,' 4.

38 NWLB Minority Report, 8, RG7–12–0–849, AO.

39 Hollander, 'The Making of a Canadian Collective Bargaining Policy,' 15.

40 For further information on these production committees, see Peter S. McInnis, 'Teamwork for Harmony: Labour-Management Production Committees and the Postwar Settlement in Canada,' *Canadian Historical Review*, 77, 3 (September 1996), 317–52.

41 NWLB Minority Report, 76.

42 For information on how the no-strike policy issue exacerbated conflict between Communist and socialist trade unionists, see Norman Penner, *The Canadian Left: A Critical Analysis* (Scarborough, Ont.: Prentice-Hall 1977).

43 Hollander, 'The Making of a Canadian Collective Bargaining Policy,' 15.

44 Ibid., 12.

45 From 1941 to 1944, Leonard Marsh was research adviser for the dominion government's Advisory Committee on Post-War Reconstruction, which resulted in the publication of the *Report on Social Security for Canada*. Allan

Irving, 'Canadian Fabians: The Work and Thought of Harry Cassidy and Leonard Marsh, 1930–1945,' in Raymond B. Blake and Jeff Keshen, eds, *Social Welfare Policy in Canada* (Toronto: CoppClark 1995), 202.

46 When Mackenzie King introduced the family-allowances legislation in the House of Commons in June 1944, he justified the program on humanitarian and social grounds but also said that 'it was a great economic measure to stimulate the economy by increasing the purchasing power of the public.' Raymond B. Blake, 'Mackenzie King and the Genesis of Family Allowances in Canada, 1939–1944,' in Blake and Keshen, eds, *Social Welfare Policy in Canada*, 253.

47 Memo, n.d., file 3052-2, vol. 34, J.L. Cohen Papers, NA.

48 Cohen to C.P. McTague,18 Aug. 1943, file 3052-1, vol. 34, J.L. Cohen Papers; C.P. McTague to J.L. Cohen, 19 Aug. 1943, file 14, vol. 210, CLC Papers, NA.

49 Potential problems with openly biased appointees on tripartite boards have led to governments' creating some boards, such as the Canada Labour Board, that are not tripartite.

50 Cohen to C.P. McTague, 19 Aug. 1943, file 17, vol. 210, CLC Papers, NA.

51 A. McNamara to J.L. Cohen, 31 Aug. 1943, file 3052-1, vol. 34, J.L. Cohen Papers, NA.

52 'Diaries,' Transcript 192, 1 Sept. 1943, William Lyon Mackenzie King Papers, MG26 J13, NA, quoted in Hollander, 'The Making of a Canadian Collective Bargining Policy,' 17.

53 The Ontario election took place in early August 1943. J.W. Pickersgill, *The Mackenzie King Record, 1939–44*, vol. 1, (Toronto: University of Toronto Press 1960), 573.

54 After the board informed Millard that a follow-up case in the steel industry was delayed because of Cohen, Cohen told Millard that he would sit but the board then decided that a quorum would be the panel. Cohen to C.H. Millard, 4 Sept. 1943, file 3052-1, vol. 34, J.L. Cohen Papers, NA.

55 C.P. McTague to Prime Minister King, 9 Sept. 1943; P.C. 7143, 9 Sept. 1943, file 3052-1, vol. 34, J.L. Cohen Papers, NA.

56 Statement of J.L. Cohen, 9 Sept. 1943, file 3052-1, vol. 34, J.L. Cohen Papers, NA.

57 Pickersgill, *Record*, 574.

58 Press release of J.L. Cohen, 10 Sept. 1943, file 1052-1, vol. 34, J.L. Cohen Papers, NA. Years later, another radical lawyer, John Stanton, wrote that Cohen was discharged in 1944 'for having been too obviously pro-labour.' John Stanton, *Never Say Die: The Life and Times of John Stanton: A Pioneer Labour Lawyer* (Ottawa: Steel Rail Publishing, 1987), 75.

59 *Globe and Mail*, 10 Sept. 1943, in file 3052-10, vol. 34, J.L. Cohen Papers, NA.

60 Address, J.L. Cohen to TLC Convention, 1 Sept. 1943, 1, file 14, vol. 210, CLC Papers, NA.
61 Ibid., 4.
62 Eugene Forsey, *A Life on the Fringe: The Memoirs of Eugene Forsey* (Toronto: Oxford University Press 1990), 92.
63 Address, J.L. Cohen to TLC, 7.
64 Supplement to *Labour Gazette*, (February 1944), 2.
65 Speech, September 1943, file 3052-3, vol. 34, J.L. Cohen Papers, NA.
66 Hollander, 'The Making of a Canadian Collective Bargaining Policy,' 18.
67 Speech to Rotary Club, 3 Sept. 1943; speech to Business and Professional Men's Luncheon, 23 Dec. 1943, file 3052-3, vol. 34, J.L. Cohen Papers, NA.
68 David Lewis to J.L. Cohen, 23 Feb. 1944, file 3065, vol. 36, J.L. Cohen Papers, NA.
69 Hollander, 'The Making of a Canadian Collective Bargaining Policy,' 19.
70 Ibid., 1.
71 Such a provision became part of the Ontario legislation in 1970 and the federal legislation in 1972.
72 Peter G. Bruce, 'Political Parties and the Evolution of Labour Law in Canada and the United States, 'PhD thesis, Massachusetts Institute of Technology, 1988, chap. 6, 33; quoted in F. David Millar, 'Shapes of Power: The Ontario Labour Relations Board 1944–1950,' PhD thesis, York University, 1981, 226.
73 Press release, 21 Feb. 1944, file 3063, vol. 36; David Lewis to J.L. Cohen, 23 Feb. 1944; J.L. Cohen to David Lewis, 24 Feb. 1944, file 3065, vol. 36, J.L. Cohen Papers, NA.
74 Applications should be signed by only one party, which was the Ontario Labour Court procedure. Cohen to M.M. Maclean, 4 April 1944; A.MacNamara to J.L. Cohen, 20 March 1944, file 3065, vol. 36, J.L. Cohen Papers, NA.
75 Committee members included George Burt (UAW), George Harris (UEW), and C.H. Millard (USWA).
76 *CCL Convention Proceedings* (Toronto 1946), 21.
77 For a discussion of the differences between the Canadian and American systems on this point, see Daphne Gottlieb Taras, 'Why Nonunion Representation is Legal in Canada,' in B. Kaufman and D.G. Taras, eds, *Non-Union Employee Representation: History, Contemporary Practice and Policy* (Armonk, N.Y.: M.E. Sharpe 2000).
78 A union with 25 per cent of the cards signed should be able to apply for a vote before a certification hearing; 'majority' should mean a majority of workers in the bargaining unit, from which supervisors should be excluded. The committee favoured appeals from a provincial to the dominion board and a time limit of thirty days for employers to decide on an appeal.

79 The committee favoured the closed shop, equal status for strikes and lockouts in the regulations, language to protect unions more clearly from lawsuits, and no automatic contract renewals when certification was pending. It recommended that the notice of renewal of a contract be in the tenth month of the agreement, that there be provisions for wages in collective agreements, that the wartime wage-control policy be cancelled, and that boards hear unfair-labour-practice cases and establish enforcement penalties that would be implemented in the courts. It called for higher fines and clarification of the definitions of 'collective agreement' and 'employee' to exclude supervisors or managers, and it recommended that the right of association be protected by a provision similar to the Ontario Rights of Labour Act 1944, which would deal with the common law disability. Report of the Special Committee on P.C. 1003 and P.C. 9384 to the CCL Executive Council, file 3065, vol. 36, J.L. Cohen Papers, NA.

80 In 'P.C.1003 and an Effective Wartime Labour Policy' and 'P.C.1003 and Union Security,' Cohen wrote that it had gone 'some commendable distance in the direction of facilitating union recognition and collective bargaining.'

81 Two articles by J.L. Cohen, file 3065, vol. 36, J.L. Cohen Papers, NA.

82 Cohen to George Burt, 8 Aug. 1944, file 3065, vol. 36, J.L. Cohen Papers, NA.

83 Hollander, 'The Making of a Canadian Collective Bargaining Policy,' 2.

Chapter 7: Defending Wartime Internees, 1939–1943

1 Lister Sinclair, quoted at the introduction of a program by Doug Smith, 'The Defence of Canada: Civil Liberties during World War II,' CBC *Ideas*, Transcript 1991, in C.S. Jackson Papers, file 1, vol. 26, NA.

2 Daniel Robinson, 'Planning for the "Most Serious Contingency": Alien Internment, Arbitrary Detention, and the Canadian State 1938–9,' *Journal of Canadian Studies*, vol. 28, no. 2 (summer 1993), 8. Some of the precedents for massive and arbitrary exercise of power in the Second World War were established in Canada during the First World War. Desmond Morton, 'Sir William Otter and Internment Operations in Canada during the First World War,' *Canadian Historical Review*, 55, no. 1 (March 1974), 32.

3 Robinson 'Planning,' 14.

4 Ibid., 9. Reg Whitaker notes the discrepancy in the RCMP's lack of interest in right-wing groups and its vigilance in pursuing left-wing groups. Reg Whitaker 'Official Repression of Communism during World War II,' *Labour/Le Travail* 17 (spring 1986), 135–66.

5 Ibid., 15; Whitaker 'Official Repression.'

6 Robinson, 'Planning,' 11. There are several studies about the Second World War internment of the Japanese in Canada. See, for example, Ken Adachi, *The*

Enemy That Never Was: A History of Japanese Canadians (Toronto: McClelland and Stewart 1976); Ann Sunahara, *The Politics of Racism: The Uprooting of Japanese Canadians during the Second World War* (Toronto: James Lorimer 1981); J.L. Granatstein, Patricia Roy, Masako Iino, and Hiroko Takamura, *Mutual Hostages: Canadians and Japanese during the Second World War* (Toronto: University of Toronto Press 1990).

7 William Kaplan, *Everything That Floats: Pat Sullivan, Hal Banks and the Seamen's Unions of Canada* (Toronto: University of Toronto Press 1987), 33.

8 Ramsay Cook 'Canadian Freedom in Wartime,' in W.H. Heick and Roger Graham, eds, *His Own Man: Essays in Honour of A.R.M. Lower* (Montreal and Kingston: McGill-Queen's University Press: 1974), 38.

9 Robinson 'Planning' 6. By the end of the war, Canada had interned 2, 423 of its citizens or residents (not including the forced relocation of the entire Japanese population of British Columbia), of whom 847 were interned for being pro-Nazi, 632 pro-Italian, 782 pro-Japanese, 133 Communist, 27 National Unity, and two unclassified.Whitaker 'Official Repression' 146.

10 Mary Jane Lennon, *On the Homefront: A Scrapbook of Canadian World War II Memorabilia* (Erin, Ont.: 1981), 68–9. This book includes pictures of ads that warned Canadians not to aid the fifth column inadvertently.

11 Cohen represented several Italian anti-fascists who were arrested, including Attilio Bortolotti, who was charged under section 39 of the DOCR in October 1939, ordered deported in February 1940, but given permission to stay in Canada in April 1940. Another Italian, Agostino Confalonieri, whom Cohen represented, was also deported, but Cohen arranged that he could stay in Mexico since he could not return to Mussolini's Italy; files 2761 and 2761A, vol. 14, J.L. Cohen Papers, NA.

12 M. James Penton, *Jehovah's Witnesses in Canada* (Toronto: University of Toronto Press 1976), 127–9.

13 Reg Whitaker 'Official Repression' 144–5.

14 Howard Palmer 'Ethnic Relations in Wartime: Nationalism and European Minorities in Alberta during the Second World War' *Canadian Ethnic Studies*, 14, no. 3 (1982), 7.

15 *Debates*, House of Commons, 16 July 1940, 1646.

16 Memo on the Jehovah's Witnesses, 15 March 1941, RG 14, file 29, vol. 2481.

17 Pamphlet 'End of Nazism,' file 2800, vol. 19, J.L. Cohen Papers, NA; memo about the Jehovah's Witness's support of the Jews in Germany, RG14, file 29, vol. 2481.

18 Cohen to P.M. Anderson, Dept. of Justice, 3 July 1940; Anderson to Cohen, 4 July 1940; Cohen to Burgess, Parliamentary Committee, 7 July 1940; Cohen to E.J. McMurray, 7 July 1940, file 2800, vol. 19, J.L. Cohen Papers, NA.

19 Charles Morell was the retired secretary to the chief justice of Canada, Sir Lyman Duff. Penton, *Jehovah's Witnesses*, 137.

20 William Kaplan, *Another Man's Salvation: The Jehovah's Witnesses and Their Fight for Civil Rights* (Toronto: University of Toronto Press 1989), 60; memo by Charles Morrell on J.L. Cohen, 20 March 1943, Jehovah's Witness Papers, NA.

21 Sarnia *Canadian Observer*, 5 July 1940.

22 File 2803, vol. 20; file 2838, vol. 23, J.L. Cohen Papers, NA. There was a series of cases in 1940 in Goderich, Ottawa, Kingston, Sarnia, London, Guelph, Windsor, and Kirkland Lake.

23 These cases appear in files 2811, 2812, vol. 21, J.L. Cohen Papers, NA.

24 File 2931, vol. 32, J.L. Cohen Papers, NA.

25 File 2842, vol. 24, J.L. Cohen Papers, NA.

26 There was an American precedent for such actions. In 3 June 1940, the U.S. Supreme Court decided in *Minersville School District* v. *Gobitis* that public schools could require Witness children to salute the American flag and that if they refused they could be expelled. The decision sparked American attacks on Jehovah's Witnesses between 1940 and 1943. Penton, *Jehovah's Witnesses*, 130.

27 File 2803, vol. 20, J.L. Cohen Papers, NA.

28 File 2826A, vol. 22, J.L. Cohen Papers, NA.

29 Kaplan, *Another Man's Salvation*, 132.

30 File 2823, vol. 22, J.L. Cohen Papers, NA.

31 Cohen to Director of Internment, 12 June 1940; W.R. Jackett to J.L. Cohen, 22 June 1940; 5 July 1940, file 2796, vol. 19, J.L. Cohen Papers, NA.

32 Cohen to W.R.Jackett, 12 July 1940, file 2796, vol. 19, J.L. Cohen Papers, NA.

33 Mina Brodie to W.L.M. King, 5 Aug.1940, ibid.

34 Affidavit of R.M. Hearst, 5 Aug. 1940, ibid.

35 File 2796, vol. 19, J.L. Cohen Papers, NA.

36 G.H. Brodie to J.L. Cohen, 23 Oct. 1940, file 2799, vol. 19, J.L. Cohen Papers, NA.

37 File 2804, vol. 20; file 2813, vol. 21, J.L. Cohen Papers, NA.

38 Cohen to H. Covington, 31 Aug. 1940; H. Covington to J.L. Cohen, 3 Sept. 1940; C. MacDonald, counsel to the custodian to 'Sir,' 30 Aug. 1940, file 2799, vol. 19, J.L. Cohen Papers, NA. Cohen performed the same services for the ULFTA.

39 Kaplan, *Another Man's Salvation*, 108, 122.

40 R.B. Bennett outlawed the CPC in 1931; the Communists disbanded their revolutionary trade-union organization, the Workers' Unity League, in 1935, and its unions rejoined the TLC and ACCL as part of their 'common front' policy. Norman Penner, *The Canadian Left* (Scarborough, Ont.: Preintice Hall 1977), chap. 6.

41 Kaplan, *Everything That Floats*, 33.
42 List of labour people interned, RG 14, file 62, vol. 2483.
43 Michael Petroff 'A Conspiracy of Silence,' *Our Times* (May 1985), 33.
44 William Weintraub, *City Unique: Montreal Days and Nights in the 1940s and 50s* (Toronto: McClelland and Stewart 1996), 31.
45 Pat Sullivan, *Red Sails on the Great Lakes* (Toronto, 1955), 71–2.
46 Ibid., 73–6; memo by C.S. Jackson, n.d., file 27, vol. 1, C.S. Jackson Papers, NA.
47 Cohen to E. Lapointe, 25 June 1940; J.L. Cohen telegram to E. Lapointe, 26 June 1940, file 2801-2, vol. 19, J.L. Cohen Papers, NA.
48 E. de B. Panet, brigadier-general, director of internment operations, to J.L. Cohen, 28 June 1940, ibid.
49 Cohen to R.M. Anderson, n.d., Department of Justice, ibid.
50 Advisory Committee to P. Sullivan, 19 July 1940, ibid.
51 Cohen to Pat Sullivan, 30 July 1940, ibid.
52 Cohen to Charles Murray, 30 June 1941, file 2825, vol. 22, J.L. Cohen Papers, NA.
53 *Debates*, House of Commons, 27 Feb.1941, 1073.
54 D. Ferguson, vice-president, CSU, to J.W. Buckley, secretary, Trades and Labour Council, 28 June 1940, file 2801-2, vol. 19, J.L. Cohen Papers, NA.
55 *Debates*, House of Commons, 4 May 1942, 2095.
56 T. Moore to W.R. Eggleton, August 1940, file 2917S, vol. 31, J.L. Cohen Papers, NA.
57 Nigel Morgan to W.R.Eggleton, 14 Aug. 1940, file 2917S, vol. 31, J.L. Cohen Papers, NA.
58 C.S. Jackson memo, n.d., file 27, vol. 1, C.S. Jackson Papers, NA.
59 Norman Dowd to J.L. Cohen, 23 Sept. 1941; J.L. Cohen to Norman Dowd, 29 Sept. 1941, file 2872A, vol. 26, J.L. Cohen Papers, NA.
60 *Debates*, House of Commons, 27 Feb. 1941, 1072.
61 'Substitute for resolutions, nos.1 to 25 inclusive, and Executive Board Report Dealing with Defence of Canada Regulations,' file 2872A, vol. 26, J.L. Cohen Papers, NA.
62 *Debates*, House of Commons, 5 June 1940, 533. The banned organizations included the CPC, the Young Communist League, the League for Peace and Democracy, ULFTA, the Finnish Organization of Canada, the Russian Workers and Farmers Club, the Croatian Cultural Association, the Hungarian Workers Club, the Polish Peoples Association, and the Canadian Ukrainian Youth Federation.
63 Kaplan, *Another Man's Salvation*, 84.
64 Ibid., 82. Cohen apparently took a good part of twenty days to prepare his

brief which was submitted to the committee in July 1940. File 2803, vol. 20, J.L. Cohen Papers, NA.

65 RG14, file 1, vol. 2481.

66 Kaplan, *Another Man's Salvation*, 82.

67 *Saturday Night*, 13 July 1940.

68 Tom Moore to J.L. Cohen, 17 July 1940, file 2803, vol. 20, J.L. Cohen Papers, NA.

69 Reg Whitaker 'Official Repression,' 161.

70 RG14, file 85, vol. 2483. They were sections 15, 39, 39a, and 62.

71 RG14, file 3, vol. 2481.

72 Cohen to Tom Moore, 7 Aug. 1940; P. Sullivan to J.L. Cohen, 23 Aug. 1940; J.L. Cohen to Tom Moore, 28 Aug. 1940, file 2803, vol. 20, J.L. Cohen Papers, NA.

73 Cohen to W.R. Jackett, 30 Aug. 1940; 6 Sept. 1940; J.L. Cohen to Panet, 13 Sept. 1940; W.R. Jackett to J.L. Cohen, 4 Sept. 1940; 5 Sept. 1940; Advisory Committee to J.L. Cohen, 9 Sept. 1940, ibid.

74 J.L. Cohen's speech to the TLC Convention, September 1940; Tom Moore to J.L. Cohen, 9 Oct. 1940, ibid.

75 The result was a document, 'Rules Made by the Minister of Justice under the Regulation 22 as to the Manner in which Objections to Orders under Regulation 21 May Be Made,' file 2811, vol. 21, J.L. Cohen Papers, NA. The House of Commons did not debate the recommendation, but cabinet amended the regulations at the end of August.

76 'Regulation 21: An Address by J.L. Cohen K.C.,' delivered to the Civil Liberties Association of Toronto, at Emmanuel College, University of Toronto, 1 Nov. 1940, file 2807, vol. 20, J.L. Cohen Papers, NA. There is also a copy of this speech in the CPC Papers, NA.

77 Civil Liberties Association to J.L Cohen, 5 Oct. 1940; J.L. Cohen to Tom Moore, 12 Oct. 1940; M.J. Coldwell to J.L. Cohen, 9 Nov. 1940; J.L. Cohen to M.J. Coldwell, 11 Nov. 1940, file 2807, vol. 20, J.L. Cohen Papers, NA.

78 *Debates*, House of Commons, 4 March 1941, 1198.

79 J.L. Cohen 'Is Canada Setting up a Gestapo?' *Saturday Night*, 23 Nov. 1940.

80 Cohen to Charles Murray, 30 June 1941, file 2825, vol. 22, J.L. Cohen Papers, NA.

81 William Kaplan, 'Communism, Corruption and Reform: A History of Maritime Unions in Canada 1935–67,' MA thesis, University of Toronto, 1985, 69.

82 File 33, vol. 1, C.S. Jackson Papers, NA. The Toronto Shop Stewards Council of the UEW endorsed the conference unanimously in February 1941 and planned to send delegates.

83 Clifford Sifton had been a senior cabinet minister in Wilfrid Laurier's

government; Andrew Brewin was the young counsel for the Civil Liberties Association and later an NDP MP; Leslie Blackwell was the attorney general of Ontario; and John Osler was a young progressive lawyer from an old, respected Canadian family. RG14, file 86, vol. 2483.

84 RG14, file 4, vol. 2481. The 'wives of interned labour leaders,' representing the families of over one hundred interned men, presented a brief to the committee, with J. Bourget, Kate Magnusson, and Norman Penner as their spokespersons.

85 It appears from the early records of the committee that only two women were interned and that the committee discussed the treatment of female internees once. The number later increased to four.

86 RG14, file 6, vol. 2481.

87 RG14, file 62, vol. 2483. It contains an undated list of one hundred and one interned and imprisoned 'labour people' and five others whose trials were pending. There were prominent radicals like Fred Collins and Tom McEwen, three elected municipal officials including Alderman Jacob Penner from Winnipeg, and four women among them.

88 Ibid.

89 Many of these persons were Jewish refugees from Germany and Austria and young people whose relatives had been consigned to European concentration camps. Six hundred of four thousand in Canada had returned to Britain, but three hundred more would arrive in Canada later. These people were a totally different category of internee; they were detained for their own protection and were in Canada because Britain had no room for them. For a memoir on such persons, see Henry Kreisel, *Another Country*, Shirley Neuman, ed. (Edmonton: NeWest Press 1985).

90 *Debates*, House of Commons, 9 June 1941, 3657.

91 Ferguson to Cohen, 18 June 1941; Cohen to Sullivan, 17 June 1941, file 2801-2, vol. 19, J.L. Cohen Papers, NA.

92 Sullivan, *Red Sails*, chap. 6.

93 Cohen to E. Lapointe, 30 June 1941, file 2801-2, vol. 19, J.L. Cohen Papers, NA.

94 Sullivan, *Red Sails*, 79.

95 RG14, file 63, vol. 2483. It contains a list of the names of and dates of release of twenty fascist agents. Francheshini was apparently hospitalized in a military hospital for ten days and was then returned to the camp hospital, where he told Pat Sullivan that he had made arrangements for his and his brother's early release. His brother, Leonard, was released a month after his arrest, and Francheshini was soon released 'on compassionate grounds.' The memo states 'Both these individuals were heard on more than one occasion, making

pro-nazi statements, and attended all banquets, socials etc at which both were quite prominent and always gave the fascist salute.'

96 Ibid.; petition to E. Lapointe; Ferguson to unions, 2 July 1941, file 2801-2, vol. 19, J.L. Cohen Papers, NA.

97 P.M. Anderson to J.L. Cohen, 17 July 1941, file 2802, vol. 20, J.L. Cohen Papers, NA.

98 *Debates*, House of Commons, 25 Feb. 1942, 813. Justice Taschereau later presided over the secret sessions of the Royal Commission on Espionage in 1946. Reg Whitaker 'Official Repression,' 148.

99 Cohen to Judge D.J. O'Connell, 24 July 1941, ibid.

100 A copy of the amendment in Cohen's papers is dated 12 July 1941 and reads 'It shall be the duty of the chairman to inform the objector within a reasonable time before the hearing of the grounds on which the order has been made against him, and, in order to enable him to present his case, to furnish him with as full particulars of the reasons for such order as in the opinion of the chairman the circumstances permit, and such particulars shall be further supplemented by the committee at the hearing by giving the objector all such further particulars as it shall deem necessary and advisable.' File 2825, vol. 22, J.L. Cohen Papers, NA.

101 Cohen to E. Lapointe, 9 Aug. 1941, file 2801-2, vol. 19, J.L. Cohen Papers, NA.

102 Ibid.

103 Memo by C.S. Jackson, n.d., file 27, vol. 1, C.S. Jackson Papers, NA.

104 Sullivan, *Red Sails*, 80.

105 Cohen to Sullivan, 14 Aug. 1941; Lapointe to Cohen, 16 Aug. 1941; Cohen to Capt. H.M. Swaybey, director of internment, 26 Aug. 1941, file 2801-2, vol. 19, J.L. Cohen Papers, NA; Sullivan, *Red Sails*, 80, 83.

106 Memo by C.S. Jackson, n.d., file 27, vol. 1, C.S. Jackson Papers, NA.

107 Transcript of hearing, 5 Sept. 1941, 95, file 2872A, vol. 26, J.L. Cohen Papers, NA.

108 Cohen's annotated bill 're Jackson internment,' ibid.

109 Cohen to UEW international office, 20 Oct. 1941, ibid.

110 Editorial, Toronto *Star*, n.d. in file 27, vol. 1, C.S. Jackson Papers, NA.

111 UEW Convention Proceedings, 1–5 Sept. 1941, file 27, vol. 1, C.S.Jackson Papers, NA. The American government was also called on to assist the Jehovah's Witnesses in Canada.

112 Transcript of hearing, 11 Sept. 1941, 96, file 2872A, vol. 26, J.L. Cohen Papers, NA.

113 Cohen to UEW international office, 29 Oct. 1941; transcript of hearing, 5 Sept. 1941, 95–100, ibid.

114   F.P. Varcoe, deputy minister of justice, memorandum for the acting minister of justice, 19 Nov. 1941, Privy Council Office, RG2, Series 18, file D-15, vol. 2; copy in file 27, vol. 1, C.S. Jackson Papers, NA.
115   Jackson's submission to the advisory committee, n.d., 7, file 2872A, vol. 26, J.L. Cohen Papers, NA.
116   Toronto *Star*, 13 Sept. 1941.
117   Cohen to UEW international office, 12 Nov. 1941, file 2872A, vol. 26, J.L. Cohen Papers, NA.
118   Toronto *Star*, 20 Dec. 1941 'Jackson Freed, Keen to Help War Effort.'
119   *Telegram*, file 2885, vol. 27, J.L. Cohen Papers, NA.
120   Sullivan, *Red Sails*, 38; Kaplan, *Everything That Floats*, 18.
121   Sullivan, *Red Sails*, 16–19.
122   For a description of the group of Communists in Montreal in the 1930s, see Merrily Weisbord, *The Strangest Dream: Canadian Communists, the Spy Trials and the Cold War* (Montreal: Vehicule Press 1994), chaps. 1–4.
123   Transcript of evidence, file 2801-7, vol. 19, J.L. Cohen Papers, NA. A secret memo in the Department of Justice files on 'J.A. (Pat) Sullivan' outlines his CPC activities and their relationship with his CSU work. It is critical of the union work and portrays Sullivan as manipulated by the CPC and as diverting union funds to Communist political activities. RG14, file 25, vol. 2481, NA.
124   Memorandum for the acting minister of justice, Re. Clarence Shirley Jackson, 19 Nov. 1941, Privy Council Office, RG2, Series 18, file D-15, vol. 2; copy in file 27, vol. 1, C.S. Jackson Papers, NA.
125   Transcript of evidence, 63, file 2801-7, vol. 19, J.L. Cohen Papers, NA.
126   Ibid., 20, 21, 53. Cohen said, 'If he is going to be asked further as he has been all day and with all kinds of sharp innuendos as to trade union activities, we should be informed as to what is alleged against him in respect to these matters.'
127   CSU internees to J.L. Cohen, 12 Dec. 1941, file 2801-2, vol. 19, J.L. Cohen Papers, NA.
128   Cohen to J.G. McManus, 20 Dec. 1941; McManus to Cohen, 22 Dec. 1941, file 2885, vol. 27, J.L. Cohen Papers, NA.
129   *Debates*, House of Commons, 25 Feb. 1942, 813.
130   Taschereau to Cohen, 4 Feb. 1942; Cohen to advisory committee, 9 Feb. 1942; Cohen to Tom Moore, 27 Feb. 1942, file 2801-2, vol. 19, J.L. Cohen Papers, NA.
131   Deputy minister to Cohen, 18 March 1942; Sullivan to Cohen, 25 March 1942; 28 March 1942; Cohen to CSU, 28 March 1942; Chapman to Cohen, 9 July 1942; 14 July 1942, file 2801-2, vol. 19, J.L. Cohen Papers, NA.

132 *Debates*, House of Commons, 4 May 1942, 2096–7.

133 RG14, file 11, vol. 2481.

134 Smith to Michaud, 23 Jan. 1942, file 2801-2, vol. 19, J.L. Cohen Papers, NA.

135 Kaplan, *Everything That Floats*, 35.

136 Ibid., 38.

137 The delegation included H.S. Menard, Local 200 UAW/CIO; H. Pearce, District 5 UEW; M.G. Hay, Brotherhood of Railway Carmen, Lodge 488; J.M. Freemen, FCSO; F.A. Sayles, United Church of Canada; Mary Birchard, Toronto Board of Education; and A.A. MacLeod, editor of the *Canadian Tribune*. RG14, file 87, vol. 2483.

138 RG14, file 97, evidence, 2, vol. 2484.

139 The belief by non-Communists that the Communists' public stance did not necessarily represent their real position dated back to the beginning of the movement in Canada, when there was briefly an underground party and a public party. See Ian Angus, *Canadian Bolsheviks: The Early Years of the CPC* (Montreal: Vanguard 1981), chap. 5. When the party was banned in the 1930s, it did have front organizations such as the CLDL and the WUL and later in the 1940s would set up a new party, the LPP.

140 Cohen discussed the Communists' anti-fascist, anti-Nazi, pro-collective security position from 1935 to 1938. Just as Cohen accepted the party line about Stalin's enemies at home, he held a rosy view of the Soviet Union's motives. He argued that the Soviet Union signed a non-aggression pact with Germany for defensive reasons so that the war would be against fascist states, not against the Soviet Union, and he blamed this tactic on the appeasement policies of the West. Stalin, he said, did not want a war in central Europe without allies. 'At home he was just completing the final liquidation of the military opposition and had no wish to plunge the Red Army into hostilities against the Reichswehn.' Since Prague was occupied, Stalin was just completing his annihilation of the last of the old opposition groupings, for the Bukharin-Rykov trial was in March 1938. The Soviet Union was unready to fight and feared attack, so it made a pact. Cohen argued that that country's march into Poland was not for its own ends but for protection in the event of a war with Germany.

141 RG14, file 87, vol. 2483; Freed to Cohen, 8 July 1942, file 2917, vol. 30, J.L. Cohen Papers, NA.

142 Brief, file 2772, vol. 14, J.L. Cohen Papers, NA. That year the delegation consisted of Brewin, Osler, Sandwell, R.E.G. Davies, Joe Noseworthy, and Arthur Roebuck, former attorney general in Mitchell Hepburn's government.

143 Andrew Brewin, in an undated book review, took a similar position

towards the Communists in Canada, which combined opposition to them politically with support for their civil liberties. He wrote, 'Here too, after a few weeks of indecision at the beginning of the war, the local party swung into line. Since then the communists of Canada have been faithful to the policy of revolutionary defeatism.' When the CPC had been declared illegal and Communists interned, Communists 'have been prevented from cutting their own throats and from exposing their defeatist, if not treasonable out-look to a public far too sensible to accept their doctrine of revolutionary defeatism. Instead they have been enabled to achieve something of a silent martyrdom and no doubt will be in a strong position to exploit economic discontent and war weariness when they emerge from internment camps at the end of the war.' He concluded, 'Communists should be accorded the rights of fair trial and the protection of democratic processes. To deny them their rights is to give them ammunition for time to come and to strengthen the conviction upon which their whole philosophy is based. To refuse them such trials is to admit weakness and inability to cope with their ideas, which is entirely unnecessary. It is based upon a fatal mistrust of the people of Canada, who are quite as hostile to Nazism as are Canadian leaders.' File 17, vol. 7, Andrew Brewin Papers, NA.

144 *Debates*, House of Commons, 15 May 1944; file 2917, vol. 30, J.L. Cohen Papers, NA. Among Cohen's thirty other clients were Stewart Smith, Sam Carr, Stanley Ryerson, Leslie Morris, Fred Rose, A.T. Hill, William Kashtan and Oscar Kane, all well-known figures on the Communist left in the 1930s and 1940s. After his release, Buck thanked Cohen for his splendid job.

145 'A Hearing for Communists,' *Globe and Mail*, 28 Sept. 1942.

146 RG14, file 93, vol. 2483.

147 File 2917 A-10, vol. 31, J.L. Cohen Papers, NA.

148 Reg Whitaker 'Official Repression,' 150. He attributes the continued official ban on the CPC to pressure from the Catholic Church, the influence of Quebec, and the position of the RCMP on the issue.

149 The Ukrainian-Canadian Committee emerged apparently from prolonged negotiations in 1940 between the Department of National War Service, working through two academics – George Simpson at the University of Saskatchewan and Watson Kirkconnell at McMaster University – and Ukrainian groups. Howard Palmer 'Ethnic Relations,' 18.

150 Ibid., 17.

151 Reg Whitaker 'Official Repression,' 158. The forty ULFTA leaders interned included M. Shatulski, editor, and John Navis (Navizivski) manager, of the *People's Gazette*; Michael Saviak, editor of *Farmer's Life*; Michael Kostiniuk, president, John Dubno, vice-chair, and Peter Prokopchik, recording secre-

tary, of ULFTA; and William Kolisnik, former Winnipeg alderman. John
Boychuk, secretary-treasurer of ULFTA, was arrested somewhat later.
'Canadian-Ukrainians in Canada,' 28, file 2893, vol. 27, J.L. Cohen Papers,
NA. An affidavit by Ford worker Mike Andrichuk, dated 12 May 1943,
recounted how he was employed as a janitor of the ULFTA hall in Edmonton between 1938 and 1941. That hall was sold by the Custodian of Enemy
Property to the Ukrainian National Federation in April 1941. The custodian's office told Andrichuk to burn five hundred books of the existing
library of one thousand and to help load the others in a truck going to the
garbage disposal plant in Edmonton. Many of the books were in the Ukrainian and Russian languages; the collection had taken fifteen years to collect
and was used by between five hundred and seven hundred people a year.
The custodian also auctioned off some furniture and office equipment to
the public. Affidavit, file 2893, vol. 27, J.L. Cohen Papers, NA. In August
1942 Cohen told his client that he had received assurances from Ottawa
that action would be witheld on most of the Oshawa property but that possibly 236 Bloor Street East in Oshawa might be offered for sale to the Polish
Alliance Friendly Society by the real-estate department of the Canadian
Bank of Commerce. File 2917, vol. 31, J.L. Cohen Papers, NA.
152 J. Boychuk and M. Kostaniuk, brief to Special Parliamentary Committee,
file 2917, vol. 31, J.L. Cohen Papers, NA.
153 Reg Whitaker, 'Official Repression,' 157.
154 Correspondence, file 2893, vol. 27, J.L. Cohen Papers, NA.
155 Brief, file 2893, vol. 27, J.L. Cohen Papers, NA.
156 Cohen's depiction of ULFTA as independent of the CPC was probably
overstated, but it was true that ULFTA had operated in an autonomous
fashion not only in its community functions but even in political debates
within the party. See Angus, *Canadian Bolsheviks*, chap. 16.
157 *Saturday Night*, 17 Oct. 1942.
158 RG14, file 93, vol. 2483.
159 RG14, file 27, vol. 2481. The Civil Liberties Association of Toronto set up a
Committee on Ukrainian Property chaired by Sir Ellsworth Flavelle. The
members of its council at that time included lawyers Andrew Brewin,
J.L. Cohen, David Goldstick, and John Osler. Other members included
Flavelle Barrett, Barbara Cadbury, Morley Callaghan, Barker Fairley,
George Grube, C.S. Jackson, E.B. Jolliffe, Agnes Macphail, C.H. Millard,
the Rev. J.R. Mutchmor, J.W. Noseworthy, MP, and Drummond Wren – a
remarkable group of distinguished people representing all variants of progressive forces within the community at that time.
160 *Debates*, House of Commons, 18 Feb. 1944, 634.

161 Since the ban in June 1940, the custodian had seized 108 properties, returned 92 halls, with some taxes owing and with equipment either deteriorating or missing, and sold 16. The value of the 16 properties was estimated at $269,270.82, for which the custodian's office offered $38,176.33. 'An Appeal for Justice' file 3148, vol. 44, J.L. Cohen Papers, NA.
162 Reg Whitaker 'Official Repression,' 159.
163 PCO, vol. 43, file U–15–2 (1943–5); WLMK/PMO, vol. 380, file W–321–11943–5; Cohen memorandum, 1945, 5 Jan. quoted in Reg Whitaker 'Official Repression,' 159.
164 Whitaker 'Official Repression,' 146.

Chapter 8: Politics and Espionage, 1944–1946

1 *New Commonwealth*, 13 July 1944.
2 Windsor *Star*, 27 June, 10 July 1944.
3 *Canadian Tribune*, 15 July 1944.
4 Windsor *Star*, 14 July 1944.
5 National council and executive minutes, 1940–6, vol. 3, CCF Papers, NA. For background on these conflicts, see Gad Horowitz, *Canadian Labour in Politics* (Toronto: University of Toronto Press 1968), and Norman Penner, *The Canadian Left: A Critical Analysis* (Scarborough, Ont.: Prentice Hall 1977).
6 For more on this point, see L.S. MacDowell, 'The Career of Canadian Trade Union Leader C.H. Millard 1936–46,' *Rélations industrielles/Industrial Relations* 43, no. 3 (1988).
7 All these anxieties were expressed by Fred Burr to Morden, 9 Aug. 1944, file 1, vol. 50, J.L. Cohen Papers, NA.
8 Windsor *Star*, 10 July 1944.
9 Ontario Council and Executive Minutes, 1940–4, vol. 2, CCF Papers, NA.
10 Windsor *Star*, 14 July 1944.
11 Ibid., 14 July, 15 July 1944.
12 Ibid., 15 July 1944.
13 Fred Burr to J.L. Cohen, 29 July 1944, scrapbook on Cohen's candidacy, vol. 53, J.L. Cohen Papers, NA.
14 George Grube to Fred Burr, Herb Henderson, and E.L. Waterman, n.d., ibid.. Between elections the Ontario party organization was predominant and therefore cooperated with the national party organization in preparation for dominion elections.
15 George Grube to J.L. Cohen, 15 Aug. 1944, ibid.
16 David Lewis to J.L. Cohen, 12 June 1944, file 1, vol. 50, J.L. Cohen Papers, NA.

17 Windsor *Star*, 29 July 1944.

18 *Ford Facts*, 20 July 1944.

19 Ibid.

20 Windsor *Star*, 26 July 1944.

21 Ibid., 10 Aug. 1944.

22 Toronto *Star*, 1 July 1944.

23 Windsor *Star*, 18 July 1944. Fred Rose had been elected as an LPP candidate in August 1943 in a dominion by-election in Montreal-Cartier riding, defeating CCF National Secretary David Lewis.

24 Ibid., 24 Aug. 1944.

25 Fred Burr to Morden, 9 Aug. 1944, file 1, vol. 50, J.L. Cohen Papers, NA.

26 Windsor *Star*, 3 Oct. 1944.

27 Paul Martin, *A Very Public Life*, vol. 1 (Ottawa: Deneau 1983), 367.

28 Windsor *Star*, 18 July 1944. This speech or one similar to it was reported to the Ontario CCF executive committee on 3 October 1944; vol. 2, CCF Papers, NA. Park was on the Ontario CCF-Trade Union Committee, the CCL's PAC, and the Toronto Labour Council.

29 Paul Martin, *Public Life*, 336, 366.

30 Cohen to George Burt, 6 Oct. 1944, file 1, vol. 50, J.L. Cohen Papers, NA; Windsor *Star*, 7 Oct. 1944.

31 Windsor *Star*, 9 Oct. 1944; 7 Dec. 1944.

32 Paul Martin, *Public Life*, 375–6.

33 Cohen to George Burt, 6 Oct. 1944, file 1, vol. 50, J.L. Cohen Papers, NA.

34 Marilyn F. Nefsky, 'The Shadow of Evil: Nazism and Canadian Protestantism' in Alan Davies ed., *Antisemitism in Canada: History and Interpretation* (Waterloo, Ont.: Wilfrid Laurier University Press 1992), 203. Nefsky discusses the extent to which the Protestant churches knew about Nazi persecution of the Jews. Clearly, they were aware of it, but as the war continued there were fewer reports on the subject, so that the discoveries of death camps by Allied troops at the end of the war were a shock.

35 'Statement by Cohen to Royal Commission,' *Gazette*, 27 Jan. 1945, file 3120, vol. 40, J.L. Cohen Papers, NA.

36 Cohen to Mr Justice Hogg, 17 Feb. 1945, file 3070, vol. 37, J.L. Cohen Papers, NA.

37 Cohen to C. Wade, 27 Feb. 1945; Prof. Douglas to J.L. Cohen, 16 Feb. 1945, file 3120, vol. 40, J.L. Cohen Papers, NA.

38 Dymond to J.L. Cohen, 22 July 1945, file 3120, vol. 40, J.L. Cohen Papers, NA.

39 Files 3141 and 3143, vol. 44, J.L. Cohen Papers, NA.

40 David Lewis, *The Good Fight: Political Memoirs 1909–1958* (Toronto: Macmillan 1981), 266–7. Another account of the LeBel Commission is in Gerald

Caplan, 'The "Gestapo Affair" 1943–45,' *Canadian Journal of Economics and Political Science*, (September 1964).

41 The commissioner found: 1. that Osborne-Dempster observed and prepared reports on CCF and labour people; 2. that Osborne-Dempster had made some of these reports available to M.A. Sanderson; 3. that Sanderson paid Dempster for the material; 4. that Sanderson used the material for anti-CCF advertisements; 5. that the special branch was closed in the spring of 1943 but reopened in November 1943, three months after Drew took office; 6. that from August 1943 to May 1945, the period from Drew's taking office to Jolliffe's public charges, Dempster operated without supervision; 7. that Dempster used the code name D.208; 8. that he had a private unlisted phone number; 9. that six or eight copies of each report were typed by Constable Rowe; 10. that Dempster told Rowe to give reports to OPP Commisioner Stringer and that copies would go to the premier, the cabinet, and Gladstone Murray; 11. that forty-one reports signed D.208 went directly from Stringer to Attorney General Blackwell; 12. that Dempster and Sanderson were in contact frequently with Gladstone Murray. Rowe was the person who risked his job to tell Jolliffe about this arrangement. Ibid., 271–2.

42 Ibid., 286.

43 LeBel Royal Commission, Exhibits, vol. 43, J.L. Cohen Papers, NA.

44 David Michael Estok, 'All the Wrong People: The Trial and Career of Labour Lawyer, J.L. Cohen,' Master of Journalism thesis, Carleton University, 1981, 119.

45 LeBel Commission proceedings, 5–7 and 9–10 July 1945, vol. 3, 2248, vol. 44, J.L. Cohen Papers, NA.

46 Lewis, *The Good Fight*, 286.

47 LeBel Commission proceedings, 5–7 July and 9–10 July 1945, vol. 3, 2248, vol. 44, J.L. Cohen Papers, NA.

48 LeBel Commission, Arguments of Counsel, vol. 4, 3588–3627, vol. 44, J.L. Cohen Papers, NA.

49 Ibid., 3645–81.

50 Ibid., 3645. In May 1946 Cohen was collecting outstanding bills because he needed the money and wrote an angry letter to George Burt who had questioned the amount of his bill. Cohen pointed out that his fee was one thousand dollars, he had had disbursements of $749.37, and he had worked night and day on the proceedings for three weeks and did not feel that his fee was excessive. The work had been done a full year before, and the bill had been sent out seven months earlier. Cohen to G. Burt, 23 May 1946, file 2, vol. 50, J.L. Cohen Papers, NA.

51 Gerald Tulchinsky, *Branching Out: The Transformation of the Jewish Community* (Toronto: Stoddart 1998), chap.10.

52 Press release, n.d., file 6, vol. 50, J.L. Cohen Papers, NA; Robert Bothwell and J.L. Granatstein, eds., *The Gouzenko Transcripts* (Ottawa: Deneau, n.d.), 338–40.

53 Reg Whitaker and Gary Marcuse, *Cold War Canada: The Making of the National Insecurity State, 1945–57* (Toronto: University of Toronto Press 1994), 30, 33, 35, 40, 43, 50.

54 Both men had been clients of Cohen's. He defended Rose during the free-speech cases in the late 1920s and early 1930s, and during the war he handled a naturalization case for Carr which was not successful.

55 Ibid., 64.

56 Cohen, 'World Peace and the Canada "Spy" Case,' file 1, vol. 49, J.L. Cohen Papers, NA.

57 Bothwell and Granatstein, eds, *The Gouzenko Transcrips*, 256, 260.

58 File: Kellock-Taschereau Royal Commission Report and Misc. Documents 1946, vol. 42, J.L. Cohen Papers, NA.As a result of the commission's findings, there were thirteen detainees and nine others it considered guilty of spying. The courts' judges and juries gave different verdicts. Of the thirteen detainees, seven were convicted; of the nine others, three were convicted and two were never charged. Whitaker and Marcuse, *Cold War Canada*, 71, 432n36.

59 Correspondence, file 3155, vol. 45, J.L. Cohen Papers, NA; Bothwell and Granatstein, eds., *The Gouzenko Transcripts*, 279.

60 Gordon Lunan, *The Making of a Spy: A Political Odyssey* (Montreal: R. Davies 1995), 211.

61 H.L. Cartwright to Cohen, 4 Nov. 1946; Cohen to John Cartwright, 7 Nov. 1946; John Cartwright to Cohen, 8 Nov. 1946, file 3156, vol. 45, J.L. Cohen Papers, NA.

62 Rex vs. David Gordon Lunan, file 3156, vol. 45, J.L. Cohen Papers, NA; Whitaker and Marcuse, *Cold War Canada*, 103–4, 432n36.

63 Toronto *Star*, 14 Nov. 1946.

64 Document 17D, for example, was an organizational letter about the research group from 'Back,' in which he referred to the three scientists as 'Bacon, Bagley and Badeau.' He approached them cautiously, reported that they 'feel the need for maintaining a very high degree of security,' and discussed the difficulties of getting together for meetings. He then conveyed some of the information that they were providing, noting, that the most secret work was on nuclear physics and that the government's purchase of a radium-producing plant was connected with this research. One member did not think that the information should be secret and could be as easily obtained through official channels, and one person was not enthusiastic

about being involved, but with Lunan's coaxing he warmed up to the idea. Lunan also received biographical notes on the men and photographs, which he passed along. He commented on the political naivete of one group member, but his impression actually applied to at least two of the men and possibly all three. Some of the exhibits and the photographs are in file 3156, vol. 45, J.L. Cohen Papers, NA.

65 Lunan, *The Making of a Spy*, 211–13.

66 Correspondence between Cohen and D.J. Keele, December 1946, file 3156, vol. 45, J.L. Cohen Papers, NA.

Chapter 9: On Trial, 1946–1947

1 David Michael Estok, 'All the Wrong People: The Trial and Career of Labour Lawyer, J.L. Cohen,' Master of Journalism thesis, Carleton University, 1981, 49. I would like to thank Mary Jane Mossman, professor of law, Osgoode Hall Law School, for reading and commenting on an earlier version of this and the succeeding two chapters.

2 Ibid., 184.

3 There is a distinct difference in this respect between Cohen's papers and those of Andrew Brewin, David Lewis, Ivan Rand, and Eugene Forsey (who was not a lawyer but was engaged by legal matters).

4 Estok, 'All the Wrong People,' 90.

5 Cohen to I. Freiman, 1 Nov. 1941, file 2787, vol. 18, J.L. Cohen Papers, NA.

6 Estok, 'All the Wrong People,' 49, 123.

7 Ibid., 10.

8 Ibid., 11.

9 The issue of wage levels was front-page news in the United States in 1945. Reid Robinson to J.L. Cohen, November 1945, file 3080, vol. 37, J.L. Cohen Papers, NA.

10 Estok, 'All the Wrong People,' 12.

11 Ibid..

12 Handwritten notes, file 2, vol. 49, J.L. Cohen Papers, NA.

13 Estok, 'All the Wrong People' 1.

14 Trial transcript, J.L. Cohen file, Law Society of Upper Canada, 13, 15.

15 Estok, 'All the Wrong People,' 21.

16 Elizabeth Guenard to Sgt. Braney, 12 Feb. 1946, file 3, vol. 50, J.L. Cohen Papers, NA.

17 Windsor *Star*, 7 Jan. 1946.

18 Institute of Living to Mrs Cohen, 12 Jan. 1946, file – Mrs. Dorothy Cohen, Misc. Personal Correspondence, n.d., 1938–51, vol. 50, J.L. Cohen Papers,

NA. Dorothy had sent a cheque for $105 and asked for a lowering of fees for the balance.

19 Estok, 'All the Wrong People,' 129; Sam Gotfrid to J.L. Cohen, file 3, vol. 50, J.L. Cohen Papers, NA.

20 Unsigned statement, 12 Feb. 1946, file 3, vol. 50, J.L. Cohen Papers, NA.

21 Estok, 'All the Wrong People,' 127; Snyder was treated for insomnia and overwork and was prescribed assorted medication such as nembutal, triple bromides, and chloral hydrate. Dr J.F. Cantelon to Mitchell Hepburn, Private Correspondence, AO.

22 Estok, 'All the Wrong People,' 130; Jane to Jack, 12 March 1946, file 3, vol. 50, J.L. Cohen Papers, NA.

23 Under the Criminal Code, the attorney general or designate can investigate a charge under a preferred indictment. By this process, the accused is denied a preliminary hearing and the charge is reviewed by the grand jury. The crown attorney must satisfy the grand jury that there are 'reasonable grounds' to continue the case, but the accused is not permitted to offer a defence.

24 Estok, 'All the Wrong People,' 131. The procedure of a preferred indictment followed by the attorney-general is *very* unusual. It is used if there is concern that were there a preliminary hearing the accused might be acquitted, or where it is decided that in the public interest there should be no delay. In Cohen's case it is possible that both motives were factors.

25 Joseph Sedgwick began to practise law in Toronto in the 1920s and worked for the Ontario Attorney General's Department for eight years, from 1929 to 1937. He assisted in the prosecutions of CPC leader Tim Buck and of David Meisner, charged with kidnapping John Labatt. In 1935 he and David Croll drafted the Dionne Quintuplets Protection Act. Mitchell Hepburn fired him at the same time as he got rid of Croll. Sedgwick defended Charlotte Whitton on a libel charge, prairie lawyer Morris Shumiatcher, and British Columbia businessman Ralph Farris, and he sued Prime Minister Pierre Trudeau on behalf of Steve Roman, president of Denison Mines. Jack Batten writes that 'when Canadians with recognizable names and significant connections got into trouble, Sedgwick was summoned to the scene.' J.L. Cohen was not one of them. Jack Batten, *Lawyers* (Markham, Ont.: Penguin Books 1985), 232–3.

26 Ibid., 158.

27 Memorandum, 10 June 1947, vol. 50, J.L. Cohen Papers, NA; Estok, 'All the Wrong People,' 132. Joseph Sedgewick wanted nothing to do with the matter at any stage. He wrote to the secretary of the Law Society regarding the Discipline Committee hearing, 'I have already expressed my view that I should not sit on this matter and as I am still of that opinion I will not be present at

the meeting.' Jospeh Sedgwick to secretary, 10 March 1947, J.L. Cohen file, Law Society of Upper Canada.

28 Estok, 'All the Wrong People,' 133.

29 E.D. Wilkins to J.J. Robinette, 14 June 1946, file 3, vol. 50; affadavits of Samuel Gotfrid (two drafts) and of J.L. Cohen, file 7, vol. 50; Statement of Yvette Vallee, file 5, vol. 50, J.L. Cohen Papers, NA. Yvette's last name is spelled three different ways, this way on her statement but most often 'Vallie' is in the correspondence. On 10 January 1947 she swore a second statement which reversed the first and said that Cohen behaved decently and that in the cab he was cold and sick. J.J. Robinette to E.D. Wilkins, 21 May 1946; E.D. Wilkins to J.J. Robinette, 28 May 1946; E.D. Wilkins to J.J. Robinette, 14 June 1946, file 3, vol. 50, J.L. Cohen Papers, NA; Estok, 'All the Wrong People,' 134.

30 Cohen to E. Pearlman, 23 Oct. 1946, file 3, vol. 50, J.L. Cohen Papers, NA. This letter indicates that Cohen knew quite a bit about the woman, including the fact that she was separated from her husband and how much support money she received each month.

31 Statements of J.A. Letourneau and Yvette Vallie, 22 Dec. 1945; statement of Yvette Vallie, 10 Jan. 1947, file 5, vol. 50, J.L. Cohen Papers, NA.

32 Estok, 'All the Wrong People,' 136; E.C. Facer to J.J. Robinette, 3 Aug. 1946; J.J. Robinette to E.D. Wilkins, 1 Oct. 1946, file 3, vol. 50, J.L. Cohen Papers, NA.

33 J.B. Robinson to J.J. Robinette, 3 Oct. 1946, file 3, vol. 50, J.L. Cohen Papers, NA.

34 E.C. Facer to J.J. Robinette, 15 Nov. 1946, file 3, vol. 50, J.L. Cohen Papers, NA.

35 Estok, 'All the Wrong People,' 139.

36 Affadavit of Jacob Markovitz, file 7, vol. 50, J.L. Cohen Papers, NA.

37 Estok, 'All the Wrong People,' 140. In RG 4–32, the Office of the Deputy Attorney-General, AO, there once existed a file 340: Re: Rex vs J.L. Cohen–Assault, Haileybury Assizes. I was hoping to find correspondence here that would indicate the extent of departmental involvement in the case and the identity of the complainant. Unfortunately, the file was destroyed, so some aspects of the case will never be known. Apparently, the series was heavily culled immediately prior to its transfer to the Archives of Ontario in 1964. My research assistant, Amy Sproule-Jones, investigated the situation for me and wrote in her report to me. 'The man who did the culling was an A.W. Nichol who had run the Central Registry Unit until 1939 when he was promoted to Executive Officer of the Office of the Attorney General. Nichol was told to use his own best judgment about what to transfer to the Archives and

what to throw out. Nichol's selection criteria reflects the historiographical interests of the day. He appears to have kept virtually all the files on famous murder cases, constitutional issues, federal-provincial relations and communism; he seems to have retained a selection of files on prohibition, industrial regulation and the *Lord's Day Act*; and he appears to have destroyed most of the files about minor criminal offences, women's issues and native land claims. For the period 1871 to 1947 Nichol seems to have selected less than 10% of the files for transfer to the Archives and then destroyed the rest. Files for the period 1948 to 1964 were transferred to the Archives at a later date and have been preserved in their entirety.'

38 Notes, file 6, vol. 50, J.L. Cohen Papers, NA.
39 Trial transcript, 2, J.L. Cohen file, Law Society of Upper Canada.
40 Transcript, 8; handwritten notes, 1, 3; file 6, vol. 50, J.L. Cohen Papers, NA.
41 Transcript, 18–19.
42 In addition to the transcript of the trial, this incident is related in a statement by Dora McLean, 21 December 1945, file 5, vol. 50, J.L. Cohen Papers, NA.
43 Transcript, 21.
44 Ibid., 25.
45 Ibid., 26–7.
46 Police statement, 29 Dec. 1945, file 7, vol. 50, J.L. Cohen Papers, NA.
47 Transcript, 33.
48 Ibid., 35.
49 Ibid., 45.
50 Ibid., 48.
51 This statement was made in cross-examination. Ibid., 65.
52 Ibid., 59.
53 Ibid., 61.
54 Ibid., 64.
55 Ibid., 70.
56 Newspaper clipping, n.d., file 6, vol. 50, J.L. Cohen Papers, NA.
57 Transcript, 78.
58 Apparently, the prosecution had found another woman in town who claimed that Cohen had assaulted her at an earlier time. The prosecution had no proof, and there are indications that the woman was willing to testify for money. There is evidence that Cohen did know the woman named in the second charge. J.L. Cohen to E. Pearlman, 23 Oct. 1946, file 3, vol. 50, J.L. Cohen Papers, NA. The trial was reported in all the major Toronto papers.
59 File 6, vol. 50, J.L. Cohen Papers, NA.
60 Estok, 'All the Wrong People,' 152–3.
61 File 6 – Rex v. J.L. Cohen: Newspaper Clippings and Misc. 1947, vol. 50, J.L.

Cohen Papers, NA. The file contains handwritten notes in which Cohen set out irregularities in the evidence, noted that he had people checking, and made points that would be made to the appeal court.

62 Estok, 'All the Wrong People,' 154.

63 Notice of Appeal, 13 Dec. 1946, by John J. Robinette, file 7, vol. 50, J.L. Cohen Papers, NA; Robinette's *Memorandum-Rex v. Cohen*, J.L. Cohen file, Law Society of Upper Canada.

64 Correspondence, files 4 and 5, vol. 50, J.L. Cohen Papers, NA.

65 Affidavit of J.J. Robinette, file 7, vol. 50, J.L. Cohen Papers, NA.

66 Affidavits of James Campbell and Kenneth Windover, file 7, vol. 50, J.L. Cohen Papers, NA.

67 Reasons for judgment, Judge J.A.S. Plouffe, 28 Jan. 1947, file 7, vol. 50, J.L. Cohen Papers, NA.

68 *Toronto Telegram*, 18 Feb. 1947; *Rex v. Cohen*, judgment of C.J.O. Robertson, J.L. Cohen file, Law Society of Upper Canada.

69 Estok, 'All the Wrong People,' 177–8. Guenard's reference to not being paid for her statement is interesting. The theme of money surfaced several times and indicated both how vulnerable Cohen was and how mercenary and possibly corruptible the people around him were. Cohen thought that some witnesses, such as Vallie and Jelly, were being put up to their statements; the taxi driver who had told Cohen that he would drive him to Toronto for $75 eventually was paid $100 plus a $5 tip by Cohen's sister, and Vallie received the $20 as promised for payment of her babysitter. Apparently, Mrs Cohen in June 1947 had an interview with Dora McLean, who said that she would sign a statement if the Cohens paid her, as, she implied, they had done with other witnesses. Mrs Cohen became indignant and had nothing more to do with her. Guenard was honest; she not only was not paid for her role in the trial but she returned the $25 that Mitchell had lent her shortly after the incident. Correspondence, file 5, vol. 50, J.L. Cohen Papers, NA.

70 Estok, 'All the Wrong People,' 158.

71 Ibid., 159.

72 Handwritten note, file 6, vol. 50, J.L. Cohen Papers, NA.

73 Cohen to W. Earle Smith, Secretary, 10 May 1947, 2, J.L. Cohen file, Law Society of Upper Canada.

74 Estok, 'All the Wrong People,' 160; J.L. Cohen to J.J. Robinette, 10 March 1947, file 8, vol. 50, J.L. Cohen Papers, NA.

75 Estok, 'All the Wrong People,' 162.

76 Ibid., 161; Pat Conroy to Dorothy Cohen, 1 April 1947, file 8, vol. 50, J.L. Cohen Papers, NA.

Chapter 10: Disbarment, 1947

1 Secretary to warden, Ontario Reformatory, Guelph, 26 Feb. 1947, J.L. Cohen file, Law Society of Upper Canada; the letter served notice of a complaint to Cohen. Discipline Committee Report to the Benchers of the Law Society of Upper Canada, 26 April 1947, file 8, vol. 50, J.L. Cohen Papers, NA.
2 Christopher Moore, *The Law Society of Upper Canada and Ontario's Lawyers, 1797–1997* (Toronto: Osgoode Society and University of Toronto Press 1997), 203, 238.
3 David Michael Estok, 'All the Wrong People: The Trial and Career of Labour Lawyer, J.L. Cohen,' Master of Journalism thesis, Carleton University, 1981, 163.
4 Secretary to W.C. Common, Attorney General's Department, 28 Feb. 1947; W.C. Common to Secretary, 1 March 1947; secretary to A.A. MacDonald, 8 March 1947, J.L. Cohen file, Law Society of Upper Canada.
5 Carson to secretary, 13 March 1947, J.L. Cohen file, Law Society of Upper Canada.
6 Cohen to J.J. Robinette, 24 March 1947, file 8, vol. 50, J.L. Cohen Papers, NA.
7 Decision in the matter of the Law Society Act and J.L. Cohen, 7 April 1936, J.L. Cohen file, Law Society of Upper Canada.
8 This separation in Cohen's life between the public and private person made me decide to write the biography in a way that dealt with his career and professional life as he lived it, with victories and defeats on the public stage, and then to reveal details of his private life only when he did, as a result of his affair with Guenard, his trial, and disbarment. Many men of Cohen's generation separated their professional and emotional lives almost completely, as they shouldered the responsibilities and enjoyed the privileges of what it was to be a man at this time, so Cohen was not exceptional in this behaviour, only perhaps a little extreme, reaching great heights in the world and great depths at home.
9 Transcript of the Discipline Committee hearing, 15 March 1947, 8, file 9, vol. 50, J.L. Cohen Papers, NA. On Cohen's own copy, he scribbled a handwritten note to MacDonald: 'This report, pretending to be a textual record of what was said, is the most ridiculous thing I have read. I have tried to correct it here and there but it is a hopeless task. Surely, if nothing else, Convocation is entitled to hear the story from my lips, before they judge me, and not from this garbled text.' In the parts of the text that Cohen has corrected, the changes include minor details only. The transcript is also supplemented by letters, including Cohen's lengthy correspondence at this stage with the com-

mittee, which is in the Law Society files. Thus, the transcript retains value as
a source, if used carefully. Cohen's chronology is not precisely accurate and
he may have overstated his inactivity, but the nature of his condition, as he
describes it, is interesting.

10 Misc. notes, file 2, vol. 49, J.L. Cohen Papers, NA. See especially his extensive
notes, made in 1938 on *A Man against Himself*, by Karl A. Menninger.

11 At this time, he would have been working in the Labour Court's successor,
the Ontario Regional War Labour Board and then the Ontario Labour Relations Board.

12 Dr Wintrob to Dorothy Cohen, 19 Jan. 1946, file: Mrs. Dorothy Cohen – Misc.
Personal Correspondence, n.d., 1938–51, vol. 50, J.L. Cohen Papers, NA.

13 I appreciate information received from Professors William Magee and
Michael Bliss on this point.

14 For information on this point, I am grateful to professors Michael Bliss of the
Department of History and William Magee of the Department of Sociology,
both at the University of Toronto, and to Rick MacDowell, an arbitrator who
has dealt with cases on the effects of addiction on employees in the workplace.

15 Testimony of J.L. Cohen, transcript of the Discipline Committee hearing,
15 March 1947, 6, 7, 8, 9, 10, 13, 14, 23, 26, 35, 36, J.L. Cohen file, Law Society
of Upper Canada.

16 Estok, 'All the Wrong People,' 164.

17 Cohen to J.J. Robinette, 29 March 1947, file 8, vol. 50, J.L. Cohen Papers, NA.

18 Thanks to Professor William Magee, Department of Sociology, University of
Toronto, a specialist on the cause of phobias.

19 Transcript of the Discipline Committee hearing, 15 March 1947, 51, 52, 55,
J.L. Cohen file, Law Society of Upper Canada.

20 Ibid., 42.

21 Ibid., 43, 47.

22 Ibid., 45.

23 Ibid., 39.

24 Ibid., 40.

25 Ibid., 60.

26 Ibid., 62.

27 Ibid., 63.

28 Ibid., 64. Some of the rumours were mentioned in a conversation between
the author and Toby Levinson Cole, April 1997.

29 Ibid., 66.

30 Affidavit, 10 Feb. 1947; A.A. MacDonald to J.J. Robinette, 18 March 1947,
file 8, vol. 50, J.L. Cohen Papers, NA; A.A. MacDonald to secretary, Law
Society, 20 March 1947, J.L. Cohen file, Law Society of Upper Canada.

31 Letter from R.H. Carlin, 25 March 1947, in transcript of the Discipline Committee meeting, 4, J.L. Cohen file, Law Society of Upper Canada.

32 Secretary to Carson, 24 March 1947; Secretary to W.J. Beaton, 25 March 1947; minutes of Discipline Committee meeting, 29 March 1947, J.L. Cohen file, Law Society of Upper Canada; A.A. MacDonald to J.L. Cohen, 5 April 1947, file 8, vol. 50, J.L. Cohen Papers, NA.

33 A. MacDonald to J.L. Cohen, 24 March 1947, file 8, vol. 50, J.L. Cohen Papers, NA.

34 'Memo of Law – W.J. Beaton,' *Re: The Law Society of Upper Canada and J.L. Cohen*, J.L. Cohen file, Law Society of Upper Canada.

35 Secretary to Pickup, 21 April 1947; 28 April 1947; Secretary to J.L. Cohen, 30 April 1947, J.L. Cohen file, Law Society of Upper Canada.

36 Report of the Discipline Committee, 26 April 1947, file 8, vol. 50, J.L. Cohen Papers, NA.

37 Memo on the *Weare* case for the Discipline Committee, J.L. Cohen file, Law Society of Upper Canada.

38 Ibid., 13.

39 A.A. MacDonald to J.L. Cohen, 2 May 1947, file 8, vol. 50, J.L. Cohen Papers, NA.

40 Secretary to Carson, 8 April 1947, J.L. Cohen file, Law Society of Upper Canada.

41 'Extract from Minutes of Convocation: 19th March 1946.' The motion read: 'That in the opinion of Convocation it would be injurious to the work of Convocation and its Discipline Committee in investigating charges of professional misconduct or of conduct unbecoming a barrister, solicitor or student-at-law, if evidence or proceedings before Convocation or the Discipline Committee were made use of in civil or criminal proceedings. The Secretary is therefore directed to refuse to furnish copies of evidence taken before Convocation or the Committee to persons desiring the same for use other than by Convocation or the Committee.' J.L. Cohen file, Law Society of Upper Canada.

42 Cohen to J.J. Robinette, 8 May 1947, file 8, vol. 50, J.L. Cohen Papers, NA.

43 A.A. MacDonald to W. Earl Smith, secretary, 14 May 1947, J.L. Cohen file, Law Society of Upper Canada.

44 Cohen to W. Earl Smith, secretary, 10 May 1947, 3, 4, 7, 8, 17, 18, 21, 24, 26, 27, 28, J.L. Cohen file, Law Society of Upper Canada.

45 Moore, *The Law Society*, 248.

46 C.F.H. Carson memo re: J.L. Cohen, 10 May 1947; secretary to MacDonald, 21 May 1947, J.L. Cohen file, Law Society of Upper Canada.

47 Markowitz to Smith, 29 May 1947, file 8, vol. 50, J.L. Cohen Papers,

NA. Cohen thought that Markowitz's evidence at the hearing was wrong and harmful, but he decided that the doctor's letter about his present condition did not contradict his testimony concerning his past condition and therefore could be used, particularly since the Benchers apparently regarded the doctor as a sound witness. Cohen always paid attention to detail. Cohen to MacDonald, 18 June 1947, file 8, vol. 50, J.L. Cohen Papers, NA.

48 LeBlond to MacDonald, 14 June 1947, file 8, vol. 50, J.L. Cohen Papers, NA.

49 Cohen to MacDonald, 18 June 1947, file 8, vol. 50, J.L. Cohen Papers, NA.

50 She was not called into the meeting, Cohen to MacDonald, 18 June 1947, file 8, vol. 50, J.L. Cohen Papers, NA.

51 Toronto *Telegram*, 20 June 1947.

52 Between January 1916 and January 1943, 117 lawyers, of whom 13 were KCs, were disbarred. 'Solicitors struck Off the Rolls since January 1st 1916.' On a list of disbarments between 1920 and 1950, there were 138 lawyers. Of sixteen KCs disbarred, only one, J.L. Cohen, was reinstated, though three solicitors after being reinstated went on to become KCs. 'List of Solicitors who were K.C.s at the time of their disbarrment,' 4 July 1951, Records of the Law Society of Upper Canada, Osgoode Hall. In 1918, the year that Cohen was called to the bar, there were 4,595 lawyers in Ontario, and in 1947, the year that Cohen was disbarred, there were 102 students-at-law called to the bar and 7, 722 lawyers practising. 'Statistical Analysis of Records of Calls to the Bar in Upper Canada and Ontario 1797–1969,' compiled by Nora Jaffary, Law Society of Upper Canada Archives, December 1992.

53 S. Arthurs, 'Discipline in the Legal Profession in Ontario,' *Osgoode Hall Law Journal* 7, no. 3. (March 1970), 235–69.

54 There was concern within the profession that increased commercialization and decreased independence of practitioners caused professional standards to decline because many lawyers became as interested in money as in justice, but Cohen did not reflect that trend. James A. Smith, '"Artificial conscience": Professional Elites and Professional Discipline from 1920 to 1950,' *Osgoode Hall Law Journal* 32, no. 1 (1994), 80, 82.

55 Estok, 'All the Wrong People,' 181. Estok interviewed Croll for his thesis, which was examined in 1981.

Chapter 11: The Struggle for Reinstatement, 1947–1950

1 Memo on the *Weare* case for the Discipline Committee, J.L. Cohen file, Law Society of Upper Canada. In the nineteenth century, the courts dominated the disciplinary review of lawyers, but in the 1870s the Law Society expanded its independent disciplinary role, and in 1877 it established the

Discipline Committee and developed thorough procedures. J.A. Smith, '"Artificial Conscience": Professional Elites and Professional Discipline from 1920 to 1950,' *Osgoode Hall Law Journal*, vol. 32, no. 1 (1994), 77.

2 A. MacDonald to J.L. Cohen, 14 Oct. 1947, file 8, vol. 50, J.L. Cohen Papers, NA.

3 G.N. Gordon to J.L. Cohen, 28 June 1947, file 8, vol. 50, J.L. Cohen Papers, NA.

4 Mrs. Frank Gysalinek to Dorothy Cohen, 26 Jan. 1948; Sarita Beals to Donia, 27 Jan. 1948; 18 Feb. 1948, File: Mrs. Dorothy Cohen – Misc. Personal Correspondence, n.d., 1938–51, vol. 50, J.L. Cohen Papers, NA.

5 Robert Knight to Mrs Cohen, 4 Feb. 1948, ibid.

6 Birdie Spivak to Dorothy, 18 Feb. 1948; Ethel to 'Dearest Dorothy,' 17 March 1948, ibid.

7 Report of the Discipline Committee to Convocation, *re Restoration to the Rolls*, 19 Oct. 1938, J.L. Cohen file, Law Society of Upper Canada.

8 Cohen to MacDonald, 10 Jan. 1948; Cohen to MacDonald, 6 Dec. 1948; Cohen to MacDonald, 7 Dec. 1948; MacDonald to Cohen, 20 Dec. 1948, file 8, vol. 50, J.L. Cohen Papers, NA.

9 MacDonald to J.L. Cohen, 31 May 1949, file 8, vol. 50, J.L. Cohen Papers, NA; MacDonald to Sir, June 1949, J.L. Cohen file, Law Society of Upper Canada.

10 Cohen to MacDonald, 6 Dec. 1948, 30 May 1949; MacDonald to Cohen, 21 Feb. 1949; 18 March 1949, file 8, vol. 50, J.L. Cohen Papers, NA. In January 1949 MacDonald wrote to Cohen that the benchers had recently passed a new rule, after considerable contemplation and not in response to Cohen's case, which required publication in advance of future applications for reinstatement. They would have to follow this role in Cohen's case.

11 Cohen rephrased the petition, which originally read 'so he can be trusted with professional responsibilities,' to 'and that he can be relied upon to discharge the responsibilities and proprieties of the profession,' presumably to make it easier for his peers to agree to it. Cohen to MacDonald, 25 June 1949, ibid.

12 Cohen to MacDonald, 22 Oct. 1949, ibid.

13 They were Beaton, Blackwell, Common, Davis, Mason, McKay, McLaughlin, Rigney, Sedgwick, Seymour, and Wilson. Report of the Discipline Committee to the Benchers of the Law Society of Upper Canada in Convocation Assembly, 18 Nov. 1949, J.L. Cohen file, Law Society of Upper Canada.

14 'The Petition of Jacob Lawrence Cohen,' 27 June 1949, J.L. Cohen file, Law Society of Upper Canada.

15 A. MacDonald to Judge J.C. Reynolds, 25 Oct. 1949, file 8, vol. 50, J.L. Cohen Papers, NA. He wanted Reynolds to be a witness. For whatever reason, Reynolds was not at the hearing but did send a positive letter.

16 Markowitz to MacDonald, 20 June 1949; Wintrob to MacDonald, 21 June 1949; Blake to MacDonald, 22 June 1949; Armour to MacDonald, 17 June 1949, in J.L. Cohen file, Law Society of Upper Canada.

17 Testimony of Armour and Cohen, Discipline Committee hearing, 18 Nov. 1949, 35–47, J.L. Cohen file, Law Society of Upper Canada.

18 Cohen to MacDonald, 2 Aug. 1949; Allan Bell to MacDonald, 12 Aug. 1949, file 8, vol. 50, J.L. Cohen Papers, NA.

19 Waldon Lawr to MacDonald, 9 June 1949; Norman Matthews to MacDonald, 14 June 1949; Judge Egerton Lovering to MacDonald, 15 June 1949; G. Marshall Ferguson to MacDonald, 23 June 1949; Judge D.J. Cowan to MacDonald, 17 June 1949; G.E. Collins to MacDonald, 16 June 1949, ibid.

20 T.W. Learie to secretary, Law Society, 10 Nov. 1949, J.L. Cohen file, Law Society of Upper Canada.

21 *Globe and Mail*, 23 Jan. 1950; 24 Jan. 1950.The ruling backdated his reinstatement to 1 January 1950. The Law Society refused Cohen's request for the Discipline Committee's report on reinstatement, in accordance with their usual policy. Secretary to MacDonald, 7 Feb. 1950, J.L. Cohen file, Law Society of Upper Canada.

22 H. Ladd to Cohen, 27 Jan. 1950; Judge Reynolds to Cohen, 24 Jan. 1950, file 8, vol. 50, J.L. Cohen Papers, NA.

23 J. Fizel to Cohen, 24 Jan. 1950, ibid.

24 L. Jessel to J.L. Cohen, 22 March 1947, file 2, vol. 50, J.L. Cohen Papers, NA.

25 Handwritten notes, files 1 and 2, vol. 49, J.L. Cohen Papers, NA.

26 Several letters between Eugene Forsey and J.L. Cohen appear in file 2, vol. 50, J.L. Cohen Papers, NA.

27 Selected correspondence, file 2, vol. 50, J.L. Cohen Papers, NA.

28 David Michael Estok, 'All the Wrong People: The Trial and Career of Labour Lawyer, J.L. Cohen,' Master of Journalism thesis, Carleton University, 1981, 171.

29 Ibid., 172.

30 Ibid., 181.

31 Cohen to Dana Porter, 3 Feb. 1950; 10 April 1950, file 8, vol. 50, J.L. Cohen Papers, NA.

32 Toronto *Telegram*, 5 May 1950.

33 George Burt recalled that the last time he saw Cohen was at the Norton Palmer Hotel in Windsor. He went to visit him and Cohen was sick in bed and 'in a fog' and returned home the next day. Estok, 'All the Wrong People,' 182.

34 J.L. Cohen's will, filed 17 July 1950, AO. Cohen left an estate of $3198.95. His wife apparently owned their home at 1 Connable Drive. He had no life insurance, or if he had and committed suicide, his heirs, Dorothy and Phyllis,

received no money. The legal bills in the last five years of his life and his inability to practise had been a financial disaster. In these circumstances, the lack of work after his reinstatement must have been an additional pressure.

35 The coroner's report has not been located. Normally such a report would not mention suicide, but there were rumours at the time that this was the case. Suicide is also the most logical explanation given the downward spiral Cohen was on, evidence of his resumption of drug taking, earlier hints that he did not think he would live long, his sense of his own self-destructive tendencies, and his interest in and reading on the subject of suicide from as early as 1938.

Epilogue

1 *Globe and Mail*, 25 May 1950.

2 Letters of condolence 1950, file 2, vol. 51, J.L. Cohen Papers, NA.

3 Cohen's funeral did not take place in a synagogue, which suggests that, to the end of his life, he was not religious even though he remained culturally a Jew. This was not unusual for Jewish radicals, particularly Marxists; Joe Salsberg and David Lewis are other examples of secular Jews on the left. At the time of his death Cohen had friends and associates who had no religion or who were from many different religious backgrounds.

4 In the 1962 national election, Phyllis Clarke ran as the Communist Party candidate against Liberal Party candidate Walter Gordon, who won in Toronto's riding of Davenport against John Morton for the Conservatives and Bill Sefton for the CCF. Sefton was my uncle and I worked in his campaign (my first) and was the youngest scrutineer in Toronto in that election. I remember seeing Phyllis from a distance at that time, and I later met her when I requested permission to work with the Cohen Papers.

5 Leo Panitch and Donald Swartz, *The Assault on Trade Union Freedom* (Toronto: Garamond Press 1988); idem., 'The Economic Crisis and the Transformation of Industrial Relations in Canada,' *Canadian Association of University Teachers Bulletin*, vol. 30, no. 7 (December 1983). Certification procedures weakened 'the apparent importance of militant organization and directed the efforts of union leaders away from mobilizing and organizing towards the judicial arena of the labour boards.' Aaron James McCorie, 'P.C. 1003: Labour, Capital and the State.' 'The Canadian working class, and organized labour was to be defined and bound by law in a manner which controlled them while limiting their possibilities and ensured their incorporation into capitalist society.' P.C. 1003 conference paper, University of Manitoba, 1994, 28; Kirby Abbott, 'The Coal Miners and the Law in Nova Scotia: From the 1864 Combination of

Workmen Act to the 1947 Trade Union Act,' in Michael Earle, ed., *Workers and the State* (Fredericton: *Acadiensis* 1989), 25: 'Existing labour law is basically a mechanism of domination that hinders workers' aspirations for a democratic workplace.' For an brief analysis of this 'new left' critique of the North American labour relations systems, see Paul Weiler, *Governing the Workplace: The Future of Labor and Employment Law* (Cambridge, Mass.: Harvard University Press 1990), viii, 2, 30.

6 David Kettler, James Struthers and Christopher Huxley, 'Unionization and Labour Regimes in Canada and the United States: Considerations for Comparative Research,' *Labour/Le Travail* 25 (spring 1990), 176. This article is an interesting summary of writing on the Canadian and American industrial-relations 'regimes'; it reviews political theories of the state and legal theory related to labour-relations issues, as well as the unitary, pluralist, and Marxist approaches to industrial relations. It concludes that, to investigate further the divergent trends regarding union density in the Canadian and American systems, a different, more political and historical analysis is required. For a discussion of state-formation theory as it evolved in the 1970s and 1980s, see Louis A. Knafla and Susan W.S. Binnie, eds., *Law Society and the State: Essays in Modern Legal History* (Toronto: University of Toronto Press 1995), Introduction, 7. They write that many legal historians saw the rise of institutions of law and order as an expression of the state's desire for social control over sources of disorder, dissent, and revolt. 'For Marxist and some neo-Marxist analysts of the law, these forms of state control were predicated on certain requirements of capitalism. For example, analyses of the "disciplining" of labour forces allowed law to be seen as directly "instrumental" in relation to the purposes of the capitalist state.'

7 Christopher Schenk, 'Fifty Years after P.C. 1003: The Need for New Directions,' 3, paper, P.C. 1003 Conference, University of Manitoba, 1994.

8 Ibid., 4.

9 Such Marxist arguments are not original. Richard Hyman, *Marxism and the Sociology of Trade Unionism* (London: Pluto Press 1971), 11–14, 18, 20, 23, 36. Hyman reviews the ambivalent attitude to unions held by Marx, Lenin, Trotsky, and more recent Marxist theorists. Marxists have argued that unions represent a minority of the working class and have corrupt leaders who undermine revolutionary activity by their 'embourgeoisement' of the working class and by integrating workers into the capitalist system. Once organization is established, they argue that management and labour seek a more amicable relationship and policies of moderation and responsibility. They assume a labour bureaucracy divorced from rank-and-file control, with the leaders exercising oligarchic control over their members and using their

authority to assist capital in controlling workers. They invariably attribute a passive role to the rank-and-file unionist. The Marxist view of unions has been consistent and theoretical but also static, and it ignores the surprises of history. Like the 'end of ideology' theorists of the 1950s who thought the need for unions would disappear, the Marxists believe that organizations 'established by workers in one historical period in opposition to the controlling structures of capitalism, may come to constitute an element in a new framework of control over workers in a later period.' Historically however, the quiet 1950s were followed by the turbulent 1960s, and as Dahrendorf notes, 'experience shows that in the history of specific conflicts more and less violent, more and less intense periods follow each other in unpredictable rhythms.' *Class and Conflict*, 278–9, quoted in Hyman, 36n.123.

10 Marxists invariably see the purges of Communist-led unions as weakening and deradicalizing the labour movement, whereas many trade unionists saw themselves as expelling a disruptive, undemocratic element within it which divided labour and undermined worker solidarity. Desmond Morton, lecture to Niagara Institute, 3 June 1982, 'Unions in Canada: The Nature of the Beast,' 3, Centre for Industrial Relations library, University of Toronto. During the 1950s, in the context of the Cold War but also as a result of internal union conflicts that had originated in the war years, there was a decline in Communist-led unions except insofar as they adopted business-union approaches. The UEW, for example, retained its Communist leadership after it was expelled from the CCL, but its members remained loyal because the union was well run and their needs were well serviced. Doug Smith, *Cold Warrior: C.S. Jackson and the United Electrical Workers* (St John's: Canadian Committee of Labour History 1997), chaps. 11, 12.

11 See, for example, Bryan Palmer, 'Where the Working Class Is Going,' *Canadian Dimension*, vol. 18, no. 5 (October–November 1984). A particularly virulent version of the 'post-war settlement' theme and the attack on 'labour bosses' appears in Bryan D. Palmer, 'The Rise and Fall of British Columbia's Solidarity,' in Palmer, ed., *The Character of Class Struggle* (Toronto: McClelland and Stewart 1986), 176–200.

12 Trade unionist Larry Sefton often referred to the 'pressure of the membership' as one element that guaranteed internal union democracy; the threat of decertification is another.

13 Larry Haiven, 'P.C. 1003 and the (Non)Right to Strike: A Sorry Legacy,' P.C. 1003 Conference paper, University of Manitoba, 1994, 14.

14 L.S. MacDowell, 'Ruminations on the Post-War Settlement,' paper presented at the 'What We Fought For': Ontario Workers' Struggles, 1935–55 conference, Hamilton, 28–9 May 1996.

15 David Michael Estok, 'All the Wrong People: The Trial and Career of Labour Lawyer J.L. Cohen,' Master of Journalism thesis, Carleton University, 1981, 85.
16 E.E. Sparrow to Arthur MacDonald, 14 June 1949, J.L. Cohen file, Law Society of Upper Canada.
17 Esther Cohen, *Esther's Story: The Reminiscences of Esther Kreengle-Bach Cohen* (Toronto: Acadian Press 1953), 96.

Glossary

appropriate bargaining unit: unit of employees determined by a labour board as appropriate for collective-bargaining purposes

arbitration: adjudication of a dispute by an impartial third party, normally but not always chosen by the parties themselves

arbitration, compulsory: arbitration required by law; ordinarily used with reference to interest (i.e., third party) arbitration

arbitration, grievance, or rights: arbitration of a dispute concerning the interpretation, application, or alleged violation of a collective agreement; the standard mechanism for solving disputes during the term of a collective agreement

arbitration, interest: arbitration to establish the terms of a collective argreement where the parties are unable to do so by negotiation; occurs primarily under statutes which remove the right to strike and make arbitration compulsory; parties can resolve an impasse by voluntarily submitting their differences to arbitration

certification: process by which a labour board, ordinarily on the basis of majority support, grants exclusive bargaining rights to a trade union for a bargaining unit of employees; majority support may be demonstrated, depending on the circumstances, by the filing of membership evidence or by a secret-ballot representation vote

check-off: arrangement whereby employer deducts union dues and assessments from employees' pay and remits same directly to the trade union representing the employees; check-off is voluntary where an authorization from the employee is necessary, and automatic or compulsory where it is required by statute or collective agreement

closed shop: union-security provision whereby employer is required to hire and employ only union members

collective agreement: signed agreement in writing between an employer or employers' organization and a trade union or council of unions respecting terms and conditions of employment; legally enforceable, in almost all Canadian jurisdictions, through arbitration procedures; ordinarily deemed by statute to contain certain provisions, such as a minimum term of one year, and a requirement that all disputes arising under the agreement be resolved without a strike or lockout

conciliation: process of non-binding, third-party intervention designed to assist the parties in the resolution of differences in negotiations, so that they can arrive at a collective agreement; the process is generally a prerequisite to a legal strike or lockout

exclusive bargaining agent: trade union certified by a labour board recognized by the employer as the sole representative of all employees in a bargaining unit and as a result entitled to bargain on their behalf regarding terms and conditions of employment

grievance procedure: steps spelled out in a collective agreement for the handling of grievances; usually involves several steps beginning at the shop-floor level and, if unsettled, culminates in arbitration

hostile witness: witness who displays hostility towards a party examining her/him and who may therefore be cross-examined

just cause: sufficient or proper reason for discipline or discharge

privative clause: legislative provision enacted in some Canadian jurisdictions that limits or negates the power of the courts to review a decision of an arbitrator or other administrative tribunal; ordinarily, the effect of such a provision is to exclude judicial intervention unless there has been jurisdictional error or a denial of a fair hearing by the arbitrator or tribunal involved

unfair labour practice: activities of an employer or union that interfere with the right of employees to join a trade union or engage in its lawful activities, or that otherwise involve prohibited conduct under labour-relations legislation

union shop: union-security provision under which the employer may hire workers who are not union members but which requires all employees to join the union upon being hired and remain union members as a condition of employment

Source: Jeffrey Sack and Ethan Poskanzer, *Labour Law Terms: A Dictionary of Canadian Labour Law* (Toronto: Lancaster House 1984).

Bibliography

PRIMARY SOURCES

Manuscript Collections

Andrew Brewin Papers, National Archives of Canada (NA), Ottawa
Attorney-General Papers, Public Archives of Ontario (AO), Toronto
Canada Law List, 1920–35
Canadian Labour Congress Papers, NA
CCF Papers (federal), NA
CCF Papers (Ontario), Queen's University, Kingston
J.L. Cohen Papers, NA
Communist Party of Canada Papers, NA
Department of Justice Papers, NA
Department of Labour Papers, NA
Department of Labour Papers, AO
Eugene Forsey Papers, NA
C.S. Jackson Papers, NA
William Lyon Mackenzie King Papers, NA
David Lewis Papers, NA
Ivan Rand Papers, NA
United Steelworkers of America Papers, NA
University of Toronto calendars and president's reports, 1930–45, University of
    Toronto Archives

J.L.Cohen file and study on disbarment, Law Society of Upper Canada, Osgoode
    Hall, Toronto

Government Documents

Debates, House of Commons
Debates, Legislative Assembly of Ontario
Labour Organizations in Canada, Department of Labour, Ottawa
Mathers Commission, Ontario evidence, 1919
Memorandum on the Industrial Standards Act of Ontario 1935–6, prepared for
    the Royal Commission on Labour Relations in the Construction Industry,
    September 1961
Ontario, Proceedings of Select Committee re Bargaining Between Employers
    and Employees, 1943, Legislative Library, Toronto
Strikes and Lockouts in Canada, Department of Labour, Ottawa

Newspapers and Periodicals

L'Action Catholique
Canadian Forum
Canadian Labour
Canadian Tribune
Canadian Unionist
CCL Convention Proceedings
Financial Post
Ford Facts
Gazette (Montreal)
Globe
Globe and Mail
Hamilton Spectator
Industrial Canada
Kitchener Daily Record
Labour
Labour Gazette
New Commonwealth
New Outlook
The News (Toronto)
Le Nouvelliste Trois-Rivières
Sarnia Canadian Observer
Saturday Night

Standard Freeholder, Cornwall
Steel Labor
Sudbury Star
TLC Journal
Toronto Star
Toronto Telegram
Windsor Daily Star
The Worker

Memoirs

Forsey, Eugene. *A Life on the Fringe: The Memoirs of Eugene Forsey.* Toronto:
   University of Toronto Press 1990
Lewis, David. *The Good Fight: Political Memoirs, 1909–58.* Toronto: Macmillan 1981
Lunan, Gordon. *The Making of a Spy: A Political Odyssey.* Montreal: R. Davies
   Publishing 1995
Martin, Paul. *A Very Public Life.* Vol. 1. Ottawa: Deneau 1983
Sullivan, Pat. *Red Sails on the Great Lakes.* Toronto: Macmillan 1955

Oral History

Conversation with Toby Levinson Cole. 20 April 1997
Interview by author with Bob Carlin. Gowganda, August 1973
Interview by author with J.B. Salsberg. Summer 1980

SECONDARY SOURCES

Contemporary Sources

Cassidy, H.M. *Unemployment Relief in Ontario, 1929–32.* Toronto: J. Dent 1932
Cohen, Esther. *Esther's Story: The Reminiscences of Esther Kreengle-Bach Cohen.*
   Toronto: Arcadian Press 1953
– 'The Story of the Years Following the Death of Philip ...' Unpublished manu-
   script, n.d.
Cohen, J.L. *Mothers' Allowance Legislation in Canada.* Toronto: Macmillan 1927
– *The Canadian Unemployment Insurance Act.* Toronto: T. Nelson 1935
– *Collective Bargaining in Canada.* Toronto: Steelworkers' Organizing Committee
   1941
–, ed. *Labour's Case in Parliament: Mr. Woodsworth's Speeches.* Toronto: Canadian
   Brotherhood of Railway Employees 1929

Cox, Carolyn. 'J.L. Cohen Has a Philosophy.' *Saturday Night*, 26 June 1943
Laskin, Bora. 'Collective Bargaining in Ontario: A New Legislative Approach.'
   Canadian Bar Review 21 (November 1943)
Logan, H.A. *Trade Unions in Canada*. Toronto: Macmillan 1948
Seidman, Joel. *The Needle Trades*. New York: Farrar and Rinehart 1942

Canadian History

Abbott, Kirby. 'The Coal Miners and the Law in Nova Scotia: From the 1864
   Combination of Workmen Act to the 1947 Trade Union Act.' In Michael Earle,
   ed., *Workers and the State in Twentieth Century Nova Scotia*. Fredericton: Acadi-
   ensis Press 1989
Abella, Irving. 'Anti-Semitism in the Interwar Years.' In Moses Rischin, ed., *The
   Jews of North America*. Detroit: Wayne State University Press 1987
– , ed. *On Strike: Six Key Labour Struggles in Canada, 1919–1949*. Toronto: James
   Lewis and Samuel 1974
Irving Abella, and Harold Troper. *None Is Too Many: Canada and the Jews of
   Europe, 1933–38*. Toronto: Lester and Orpen Dennys 1982
Abella, Irving, and David Millar, eds. *The Canadian Worker in the Twentieth
   Century*. Toronto: Oxford 1978
Adachi, Ken. *The Enemy That Never Was: A History of Japanese Canadians*. Toronto:
   McClelland and Stewart 1976
Angus, Ian. *Canadian Bolsheviks: The Early Years of the CPC*. Montreal: Vanguard
   1981
Arthurs, S. 'Discipline in the Legal Profession in Ontario.' *Osgoode Hall Law
   Journal* 7, no. 3 (March 1970)
Avakumovic, Ivan. *The Communist Party of Canada*. Toronto: McClelland and
   Stewart 1975
Baruth-Walsh, Mary E., and G. Mark Walsh. *99 Days on the Line*. Winnipeg:
   Penumbra Press 1995
Batten, Jack. *Lawyers*. Markham, Ont.: Penguin 1985
Bercuson, D.J. *True Patriot: The Life of Brooke Claxton, 1898–1966*. Toronto: Univer-
   sity of Toronto Press 1994
Betcherman, Lita-Rose. *The Little Band*. Ottawa: Deneau 1982
Bickenbach, Jerome E. 'Lawyers, Law Professors and Racism in Ontario.' *Queen's
   Quarterly* 96, no. 3 (autumn 1989)
Bishop, Mary. 'Vivian Dowding: Birth Control Activist.' In Veronica Strong-
   Boag and Anita Clair Fellman, eds., *Rethinking Canada*. Toronto: Copp Clark
   1986
Blake, Raymond B. 'Mackenzie King and the Genesis of Family Allowances in

Canada, 1939–44.' In Raymond B. Blake and Jeff Keshen, eds., *Social Welfare Policy in Canada*. Toronto: Copp Clark 1995

Bothwell, Robert, and J.L. Granatstein, eds. *The Gouzenko Transcripts*. Ottawa: Deneau, n.d.

Caplan, Gerald. 'The "Gestapo Affair," 1943–45.' *Canadian Journal of Economics and Political Science* 30 (September 1964)

– *The Dilemma of Canadian Socialism: The CCF in Ontario*. Toronto: McClelland and Stewart 1973

Cook, Ramsay. 'Canadian Freedom in Wartime.' In W.H. Heick and Roger Graham, eds., *His Own Man: Essays in Honour of A.R.M. Lower*. Montreal: McGill-Queen's University Press 1974

Donegan, Rosemary. *Spadina Avenue*. Toronto: Douglas and McIntyre 1985

Finkel, Alvin. 'The Cold War, Alberta Labour and the Social Credit Regime.' In L.S. MacDowell and Ian Radforth, eds., *Canadian Working Class History: Selected Readings*. Toronto: Canadian Scholars' Press 1992

Frager, Ruth. 'Class and Ethnic Barriers to Feminist Perspectives in Toronto's Jewish Labour Movement 1919–39.' *Studies in Political Economy* 30 (autumn 1989)

– *Sweatshop Strife: Class, Ethnicity, and Gender in the Jewish Labour Movement of Toronto, 1900–1939*. Toronto: University of Toronto Press 1992

Granatstein, J.L., P. Roy, M. Ino, H. Takamura. *Mutual Hostages: Canadians and Japanese during the Second World War*. Toronto: University of Toronto Press 1990

Horowitz, Gad. *Canadian Labour in Politics*. Toronto: University of Toronto Press 1968

Howard, Victor. *'We Were the Salt of the Earth!' A Narrative on the On-to-Ottawa Trek and the Regina Riot*. Regina: Canadian Plains Research Center 1985

Irving, Allan. 'Canadian Fabians: The Work and Thought of Harry Cassidy and Leonard Marsh, 1930–45.' In Raymond B. Blake and Jeff Keshen, eds., *Social Welfare Policy in Canada*. Toronto: Copp Clark 1995

James, R. Warren. *The People's Senator: The Life and Times of David A. Croll*. Vancouver: Douglas and MacIntyre 1990

Kaplan, William. *Everything That Floats: Pat Sullivan, Hal Banks, and the Seamen's Unions of Canada*. Toronto: University of Toronto Press 1977

– *Another Man's Salvation: Jehovah's Witnesses and Their Fight for Civil Rights*. Toronto: University of Toronto Press 1989

Kealey G.S., and Reg Whitaker. *RCMP Security Bulletins: The Early Years, 1919–1939*. St John's: Committee on Canadian Labour History 1994

Knafla, Louis A., and Susan W.S. Binnie, eds. *Law, Society and the State: Essays in Modern Legal History*. Toronto: University of Toronto Press 1995

Kreisel, Henry. *Another Country.* Edited by Shirley Neuman. Edmonton: NeWest Press 1985

Kyer, C. Ian, and Jerome E. Bickenbach. *The Fiercest Debate: Cecil A. Wright, the Benchers, and Legal Education in Ontario, 1923–1957.* Toronto: Osgoode Society and University of Toronto Press 1987

Leach, James D. 'The Workers' Unity League and the Stratford Furniture Workers: The Anatomy of a Strike.' *Ontario History* 60 (June 1968)

Lennon, Mary Jane. *On the Homefront: A Scrapbook of Canadian World War II Memorabilia.* Erin, Ont.: Boston Mills Press 1981

Liversedge, Ronald. *Recollections of the On-to-Ottawa Trek.* Edited by Victor Hoar. Toronto: McClelland and Stewart 1973

MacDowell, L.S. 'The 1943 Steel Strike against Wage Controls.' *Labour/Le Travail* 10 (1982)

– 'Remember Kirkland Lake': The Gold Miners' Strike, 1941–1942.* Toronto: University of Toronto Press 1983

– 'The Career of Canadian Trade Union Leader: C.H. Millard, 1936–46.' *Relations industrielles/Industrial Relations* 43, no. 3 (1988)

MacDowell, Laurel S., and Ian Radforth, eds. *Canadian Working Class History: Selected Readings.* Toronto: Canadian Scholars' Press 1992

McCallum, Margaret. 'Keeping Women in Their Place: The Minimum Wage in Canada, 1910–25.' *Labour/Le Travail* 17 (spring 1986)

Moore, Christopher. *The Law Society of Upper Canada and Ontario Lawyers, 1797–1997.* Toronto: Osgoode Society and University of Toronto Press 1997

Morgan, Cecilia. '"An Embarrassingly and Severely Masculine Atmosphere": Women, Gender and the Legal Profession at Osgoode Hall, 1920s–1960s.' *Canadian Journal of Law and Society* 11, no. 2 (fall 1996)

Morton, Desmond. 'Sir William Otter and Internment Operations in Canada during the First World War.' *Canadian Historical Review* 55, no. 1 (March 1974)

Morton, Desmond. 'Aid to Civil Power: The Stratford Strike of 1933.' In Irving Abella, ed., *On Strike.* Toronto: James Lewis and Samuel 1974

Moulton, David. 'Ford Windsor 1945.' In Irving Abella, ed., *On Strike.* Toronto: James Lewis and Samuel 1974

Nefsky, Marilyn F. 'The Shadow of Evil: Nazism and Canadian Protestantism.' In Alan Davies, ed., *Antisemitism in Canada: History and Interpretation.* Waterloo: Wilfrid Laurier University Press 1992

Palmer, Bryan. 'Where the Working Class Is Going.' *Canadian Dimension* 18, no. 5 (October–November 1984)

– , ed. *The Character of Class Struggle: Essays in Canadian Working Class History, 1850–1985.* Toronto: McClelland and Stewart 1986

Palmer, Howard. 'Ethnic Relations in Wartime: Nationalism and European

Minorities in Alberta during the Second World War.' *Canadian Ethnic Studies* 14, no. 3 (1982)

Paris, Erna. *Jews.* Toronto: Macmillan 1980

Penner, Norman. *The Canadian Left: A Critical Analysis.* Scarborough, Ont.: Prentice-Hall 1977

Penton, M. James. *Jehovah's Witnesses in Canada.* Toronto: University of Toronto Press 1976

Petroff, Michael. 'A Conspiracy of Silence.' *Our Times,* May 1985

Pickersgill, J.W., ed. *The Mackenzie King Record, 1939–1944.* Vol. 1. Toronto: University of Toronto Press 1960

Pierson, Ruth. *'They're Still Women After All': The Second World War and Canadian Womanhood.* Toronto: McClelland and Stewart 1986

– 'Gender and Unemployment Insurance Debates in Canada, 1934–40.' *Labour/ Le Travail* 25 (1990)

Quinn, Herbert. *The Union Nationale: A Study of Quebec Nationalism.* Toronto: University of Toronto Press 1963

Radforth, Ian. *Bushworkers and Bosses: Logging in Northern Ontario, 1900–1980.* Toronto: University of Toronto Press 1987

Repo, Satu. 'Rosvall and Voutilainen: Two Union Men Who Never Died.' *Labour/ Le Travail* 8–9 (1981–2)

Robinson, Daniel. 'Planning for the "Most Serious Contingency": Alien Internment, Arbitrary Detention and the Canadian State 1938–39.' *Journal of Canadian Studies* 28, no. 2 (summer 1993)

Saywell, John T. *'Just Call Me Mitch': The Life of Mitchell F. Hepburn.* Toronto: University of Toronto Press 1991

Schultz, Patricia. *The Toronto East York Workers Association.* Toronto: New Hogtown Press 1975

Smith, Doug. *Cold Warrior: C.S. Jackson and the United Electrical Workers.* St John's: Committee of Canadian Labour History 1997

Speisman, Stephen A. *The Jews of Toronto: A History to 1937.* Toronto: McClelland and Stewart 1979

– 'Antisemitism in Ontario: The Twentieth Century.' In Alan Davies, ed., *Antisemitism in Canada: History and Interpretation.* Waterloo: Wilfrid Laurier University Press 1992

Stanton, John. *Never Say Die: The Life and Times of John Stanton, a Pioneer Labour Lawyer.* Ottawa: Steel Rail Publishing 1987

Steedman, Mercedes. 'Skill and Gender in the Canadian Clothing Industry, 1890–1940.' In C. Heron and R. Storey, eds., *On the Job.* Montreal: McGill-Queen's University Press 1985

– *Angels of the Workplace: Women and the Construction of Gender Relations in the Canadian Clothing Industry, 1890–1940*. Toronto: Oxford University Press 1997

Strong-Boag, Veronica. 'Wages for Housework: Mothers' Allowances and the Beginnings of Social Security in Canada.' *Journal of Canadian Studies* 14, no. 1 (spring 1979)

Struthers, James. *'No Fault of Their Own': Unemployment and the Canadian Welfare State, 1914–1941*. Toronto: University of Toronto Press 1983.

Sunahara, Ann. *The Politics of Racism: The Uprooting of Japanese Canadians during the Second World War*. Toronto: James Lorimer 1981

Tucker, Eric. 'The Law of Employers' Liability in Ontario 1861–1900: The Search for a Theory.' *Osgoode Hall Law Journal* 22, no. 2 (1984)

Tulchinsky, Gerald. *Taking Root: The Origins of the Canadian Jewish Community*. Toronto: Lester Publishing 1992.

– *Branching Out: The Transformation of the Jewish Community*. Toronto: Stoddart 1998.

Weisbord, Merrily. *The Strangest Dream: Canadian Communists, the Spy Trials and the Cold War*. Montreal: Vehicule Press 1994

Weintraub, William. *City Unique: Montreal Days and Nights in the 1940s and 1950s*. Toronto: McClelland and Stewart 1996

Whitaker, Reg. 'Official Repression of Communism during World War II.' *Labour/Le Travail* 17 (spring 1986)

Whitaker, Reg, and Gary Marcuse. *Cold War Canada: The Making of the National Insecurity State, 1945–1957*. Toronto: University of Toronto Press 1994

Industrial Relations

Bain, G., and R. Price. *Profiles of Union Growth*. London: Oxford University Press 1980

Bruce, Peter G. 'Political Parties and Labor Legislation in Canada and the United States.' *Industrial Relations* 28, no. 2 (spring 1989)

Cameron, James C., and F.J.L. Young. *The Status of Trade Unions in Canada*. Kingston, Ont.: Department of Industrial Relations, Queen's University 1960

Diamond, Stephen F. 'Labor Rights in the Global Economy: A Case Study of the North American Free Trade Agreement.' In Lance A. Compa and Stephen F. Diamond, *Human Rights, Labor Rights and International Trade*. Philadelphia: University of Pennsylvania Press 1996

Finkin, Matthew, ed. *The Legal Future of Employee Representation*, Ithaca, N.Y.: ILR Press 1994.

Gould, William B., IV. *Agenda for Reform: The Future of Employment Relations and the Law*. Cambridge, Mass.: MIT Press 1993

Grant, Hugh. 'Solving the Labour Problem at Imperial Oil: Welfare Capitalism in the Canadian Petroleum Industry, 1919–1929.' *Labour/Le Travail* 41 (spring 1998)

Gross, James A. *Broken Promise: The Subversion of U.S. Labor Relations Policy, 1947–1994*. Philadelphia: Temple University Press 1995

Gunderson, Morley, and Douglas Hyatt. 'Canadian Public Sector Employment Relations in Transition.' In Dale Belman, M. Gunderson, and D. Hyatt, eds., *Industrial Relations Research Association Series*. Madison: University of Wisconsin – Madison 1996.

Hyman, Richard. *Marxism and the Sociology of Trade Unionism*. London: Pluto Press 1971

Jamieson, S.M. *Times of Trouble: Labour Unrest and Industrial Conflict in Canada, 1900–1966*. Ottawa: Task Force on Labour Relations 1968

Kettler, David, James Struthers, and Christopher Huxley. 'Unionization and Labour Regimes in Canada and the United States: Considerations for Comparative Research.' *Labour/Le Travail* 25 (spring 1990)

Lipset, S.M. *Unions in Transition*. San Francisco: ICS Press 1986

MacDowell, L.S. 'The Formation of the Industrial Relations System in Canada during World War Two.' *Labour/Le Travail* 3 (1978)

– 'Company Unionism in Canada 1915–1948.' In Bruce Kaufman and Daphne Taras, eds., *Non-Union Employee Representation: History, Contemporary Practice and Policy*. Armonk N.Y.: M.E. Sharpe 2000

Panitch Leo, and Donald Schwarz. 'The Economic Crisis and the Transformation of Industrial Relations in Canada.' Canadian Association of University Teachers' *Bulletin* 30, no.7 (December 1983)

– *The Assault on Trade Union Freedom*. Toronto: Garamond Press 1988

Rose, Joseph, and Gary Chaison. 'Linking Union Density and Union Effectiveness: The North American Experience.' *Industrial Relations* 35, no. 1 (January 1996)

Saporta, Ishak, and Bryan Lincoln. 'Managers and Workers' Attitudes towards Union in the U.S. and Canada.' *Relations industrielles/Industrial Relations* 50, no. 3 (1995)

Smith, James A. '"Artificial Conscience': Professional Elites and Professional Discipline, 1920–50." *Osgoode Hall Law Journal* 32, no. 1 (1994)

Troy, Leo. 'Is the U.S. Unique in the Decline of Private Sector Unionism?' *Journal of Labor Research* 11, no. 2 (spring 1990)

Weiler, Paul. *Governing the Workplace: The Future of Labor and Employment Law*. Cambridge, Mass.: Harvard University Press, 1990.

Willes, John. *The Ontario Labour Court, 1943–1944*. Kingston, Ont.: Industrial Relations Centre, Queen's University 1979

American Studies

Bernstein, Irving. *The Turbulent Years: A History of the American Worker, 1933–1941*. Boston: Houghton Mifflin 1971

Carnes, Mark, and Clyde Grifen, eds. *Meanings for Manhood: Constructions of Masculinity in Victorian America*. Chicago: University of Chicago Press 1990

Connell, R.W. *Masculinities*. Cambridge, Mass.: Polity Press 1995

Grossberg, Michael. 'Institutionalizing Masculinity: The Law as a Masculine Profession.' In Mark Carnes and Clyde Grifen, eds., *Meanings for Manhood: Constructions of Masculinity in Victorian America*. Chicago: University of Chicago Press 1990

Hall, Catherine. *White, Male and Middle Class: Explorations in Feminism and History*. New York: Routledge 1996

Irons, Peter. *The New Deal Lawyers*. Princeton, N.J.: Princeton University Press 1982

Kimmel, Michael S. *Manhood in America: A Cultural History*. New York: Free Press 1996

Kimmel, Michael S. 'Judaism, Masculinity and Feminism.' In Michael S. Kimmel and Michael A. Messner, eds., *Men's Lives*. Needham Heights, Mass.: Allyn and Bacon 1995

Theses and Unpublished Articles

Bruce, Peter G. 'Political Parties and the Evolution of Labour Law in Canada and the United States.' PhD thesis, Massachusetts Institute of Technology 1988

Coates, Daniel. 'Organized Labor and Politics in Canada: The Development of a National Labor Code.' PhD thesis, Cornell University 1973

Estok, David Michael. '"All the Wrong People": The Trial and Career of J.L. Cohen.' Master of journalism thesis, Carleton University 1981

Haiven, Larry. 'P.C.1003 and the (Non) Right to Strike: A Sorry Legacy.' Paper presented to the P.C.1003 Conference, University of Manitoba 1994

Hollander, Taylor. 'The Making of a Canadian Collective Bargaining Policy: The Role of the National War Labour Board, 1943–44.' Paper presented to the Organization of American Historians meeting, Toronto, April 1999.

Kaplan, William. 'Communism, Corruption and Reform: A History of Maritime Unions in Canada, 1935–67.' MA thesis, University of Toronto 1985

MacDowell, L.S. 'Ruminations on the Post-War Settlement.' Paper presented at the 'What We Fought For': Ontario Workers' Struggles, 1935–55, Conference, Hamilton 1996

McCorie, Aaron James. 'P.C.1003: Labour, Capital and the State.' Paper presented to the P.C. 1003 Conference, Winnipeg, University of Manitoba 1994

Millar, David F. 'Shapes of Power: The Ontario Labour Relations Board 1944–50.' PhD thesis, York University 1981

Schenk, Christopher. 'Fifty Years after P.C. 1003: The Need for New Directions.' Paper presented at P.C.1003 Conference, Winnipeg, University of Manitoba 1994

Storey, R.H. 'Workers, Unions and Steel: The Shaping of the Hamilton Working Class 1935–48.' PhD thesis, University of Toronto 1981

Workman, Andrew A. 'Creating the National War Labor Board: Franklin Roosevelt and the Politics of State Building in the Early 1940s.' Paper presented to the Organization of American Historians meeting, Toronto 1999

Picture Credits

Law Society of Upper Canada, Osgoode Hall Archives: graduation photo, P416; application notice, *Ontario Weekly Notes*

Robert S. Kenny Collection, Thomas Fisher Rare Book Library, University of Toronto: map of Queen's Park; leading Communists: Buck, Freed, Buller, Smith; Rosvall's body is found; Phyllis Clarke

John Scott Cohen: Esther Cohen, circa 1940s; Abraham Isaac Cohen

Lynn Francis: Jane Cowan de Munnik

National Archives of Canada: Textile Workers Union leaflet, file 2629, vol. 9, J.L. Cohen Papers; National War Labour Board, PA-112763

City of Toronto Archives, *Globe and Mail* Collection, Toronto, Ontario: J.L. Cohen in the midst of negotiations, 19 April 1937; Cohen with Hepburn and Millard, 23 April 1937; Cohen representing auto workers

Mike Solski and John Smaller, *Mine Mill* (Toronto: Steel Rail Publishers 1984): Cohen on conciliation board

Toronto Daily Star, Toronto, Ontario: Buck and thirteen others surrender, 25 September 1942

Ford Facts, Windsor, Ontario: Cohen to run in Essex West, 20 July 1944

Index

1981 David H. Flaherty, ed., *Essays in the History of Canadian Law: Volume I*

1982 Marion MacRae and Anthony Adamson, *Cornerstones of Order: Courthouses and Town Halls of Ontario, 1784–1914*

1983 David H. Flaherty, ed., *Essays in the History of Canadian Law: Volume II*

1984 Patrick Brode, *Sir John Beverley Robinson: Bone and Sinew of the Compact*
David Williams, *Duff: A Life in the Law*

1985 James Snell and Frederick Vaughan, *The Supreme Court of Canada: History of the Institution*

1986 Paul Romney, *Mr Attorney: The Attorney General for Ontario in Court, Cabinet, and Legislature, 1791–1899*
Martin Friedland, *The Case of Valentine Shortis: A True Story of Crime and Politics in Canada*

1987 C. Ian Kyer and Jerome Bickenbach, *The Fiercest Debate: Cecil A. Wright, the Benchers, and Legal Education in Ontario, 1923–1957*

1988 Robert Sharpe, *The Last Day, the Last Hour: The Currie Libel Trial*
John D. Arnup, *Middleton: The Beloved Judge*

1989 Desmond Brown, *The Genesis of the Canadian Criminal Code of 1892*
Patrick Brode, *The Odyssey of John Anderson*

1990 Philip Girard and Jim Phillips, eds., *Essays in the History of Canadian Law: Volume III – Nova Scotia*
Carol Wilton, ed., *Essays in the History of Canadian Law: Volume IV – Beyond the Law: Lawyers and Business in Canada, 1830–1930*

1991 Constance Backhouse, *Petticoats and Prejudice: Women and Law in Nineteenth-Century Canada*

1992 Brendan O'Brien, *Speedy Justice: The Tragic Last Voyage of His Majesty's Vessel* Speedy
Robert Fraser, ed., *Provincial Justice: Upper Canadian Legal Portraits from the Dictionary of Canadian Biography*

1993 Greg Marquis, *Policing Canada's Century: A History of the Canadian Association of Chiefs of Police*
F. Murray Greenwood, *Legacies of Fear: Law and Politics in Quebec in the Era of the French Revolution*

1994 Patrick Boyer, *A Passion for Justice: The Legacy of James Chalmers McRuer*
Charles Pullen, *The Life and Times of Arthur Maloney: The Last of the Tribunes*
Jim Phillips, Tina Loo, and Susan Lewthwaite, eds., *Essays in the History of Canadian Law: Volume V – Crime and Criminal Justice*
Brian Young, *The Politics of Codification: The Lower Canadian Civil Code of 1866*

1995   David Williams, *Just Lawyers: Seven Portraits*
        Hamar Foster and John McLaren, eds., *Essays in the History of Canadian Law: Volume VI – British Columbia and the Yukon*
        W.H. Morrow, ed., *Northern Justice: The Memoirs of Mr Justice William G. Morrow*
        Beverley Boissery, *A Deep Sense of Wrong: The Treason Trials and Transportation to New South Wales of Lower Canadian Rebels after the 1838 Rebellion*
1996   Carol Wilton, ed., *Essays in the History of Canadian Law: Volume VII – Inside the Law: Canadian Law Firms in Historical Perspective*
        William Kaplan, *Bad Judgment: The Case of Mr Justice Leo A. Landreville*
        F. Murray Greenwood and Barry Wright, eds., *Canadian State Trials: Volume I – Law, Politics, and Security Measures, 1608–1837*
1997   James W. St.G. Walker, *'Race,' Rights, and the Law in the Supreme Court of Canada: Historical Case Studies*
        Lori Chambers, *Married Women and Property Law in Victorian Ontario*
        Patrick Brode, *Casual Slaughters and Accidental Judgments: Canadian War Crimes and Prosecutions, 1944–1948*
        Ian Bushnell, *A History of the Federal Court of Canada, 1875–1992*
1998   Sidney Harring, *White Man's Law: Native People in Nineteenth-Century Canadian Jurisprudence*
        Peter Oliver, *'Terror to Evil-Doers': Prisons and Punishments in Nineteenth-Century Ontario*
1999   Constance Backhouse, *Colour-Coded: A Legal History of Racism in Canada, 1900–1950*
        G. Blaine Baker and Jim Phillips, eds., *Essays in the History of Canadian Law: Volume VIII – In Honour of R.C.B. Risk*
        Richard W. Pound, *Chief Justice W.R. Jackett: By the Law of the Land*
        David Vanek, *Fulfilment: Memoirs of a Criminal Court Judge*
2000   Barry Cahill, *The Thousandth Man: A Biography of James McGregor Stewart*
        A.B. McKillop, *The Spinster and the Prophet: Florence Deeks, H.G. Wells, and the Mystery of the Purloined Past*
        Beverley Boissery and F. Murray Greenwood, *Uncertain Justice: Canadian Women and Capital Punishment, 1754–1953*
        Bruce Ziff, *Unforeseen Legacies: Reuben Wells Leonard and the Leonard Foundation Trust*
2001   Ellen Anderson, *Judging Bertha Wilson: Law as Large as Life*
        Judy Fudge and Eric Tucker, *Labour before the Law: The Regulation of Workers' Collective Action in Canada, 1900–1948*
        Laurel Sefton MacDowell, *Renegade Lawyer: The Life of J.L. Cohen*

. how effective as psycho-history?

· incongruity in Cohen: believes in law as a
means to effect social change & believes
legal system favors the wealthy

· 123 → on the law & Cohen's view

203 → the crux of Cohen's story.